IMAGE COMICS PRESENTS

CHRISTIAN GOSSETT'S

THE RED STAR

THE BATTLE OF KAR DATHRA'S GATE

TABLE OF CONTENTS

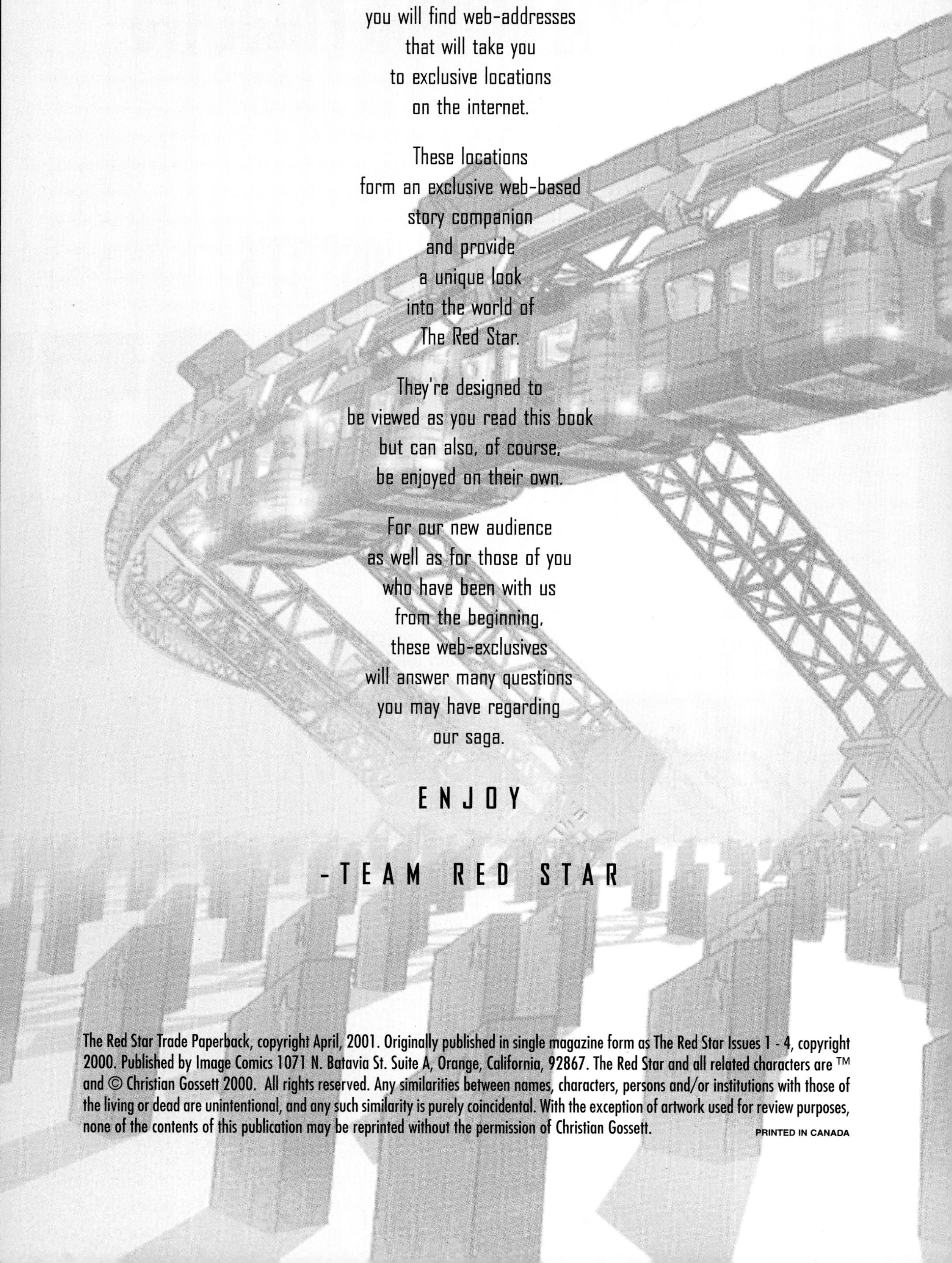

W E L C O M E

Throughout this book
you will find web-addresses
that will take you
to exclusive locations
on the internet.

These locations
form an exclusive web-based
story companion
and provide
a unique look
into the world of
The Red Star.

They're designed to
be viewed as you read this book
but can also, of course,
be enjoyed on their own.

For our new audience
as well as for those of you
who have been with us
from the beginning,
these web-exclusives
will answer many questions
you may have regarding
our saga.

E N J O Y

- T E A M R E D S T A R

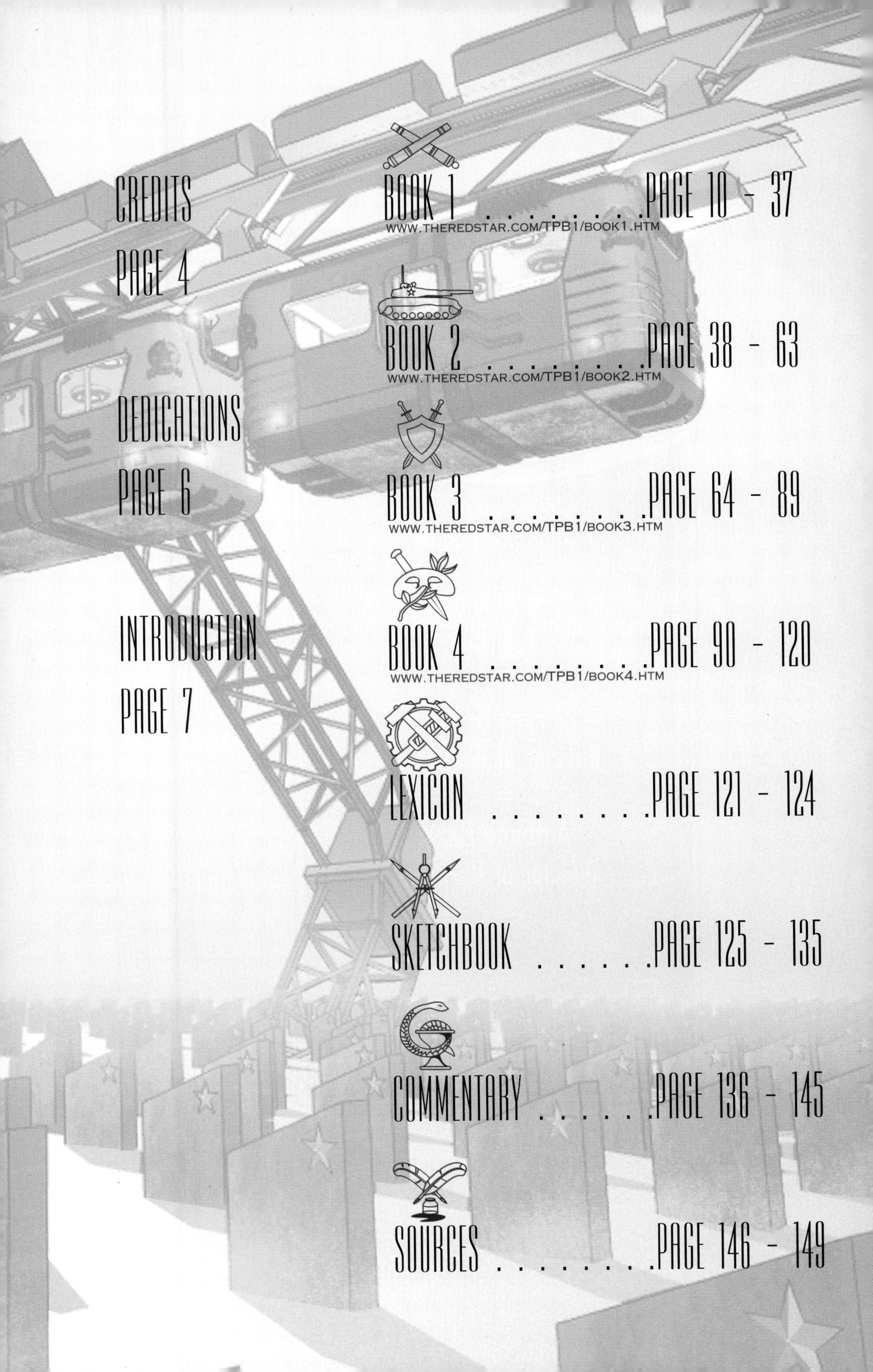

Jim Valentino
Publisher

Brent Braun
Director of Production

Anthony Bozzi
Director of Marketing

image

TEAM RED STAR

Christian Gossett :
Creator - Penciller - Writer
Bradley Kayl : Co-Writer
A.D. Coulter : 3D Artist
Snakebite : Colorist - Composites
Jon Moberly : 3D Models
Johanna Olson, MD : Ministry of Business Affairs
Nathaniel Downes : Ministry of Finance
Richard Starkings : Letterer
JG Roshell : Font Designer
Saida Temofonte : Letterer
Creative Visions : TPB Design

STATION

STAT

N II

STA

STATION

STAT

HUB STATION 05

STATION 2

STATION 18

ACKNOWLEDGEMENTS

CHRISTIAN GOSSETT

The first thing I wrote in my first Red Star sketchbook was in April of 1994. It read "For Adam" referring to my younger brother, my favorite person in the world, whose inherent nobility of character inspires so much of this work.

Since then, I have been joined by many new brothers and sisters who have helped me in forging this work into a reality. To all of them, in sincere humility, (for they've all known me at my worst) I give my most heartfelt thanks.

Finally, but most importantly, to my mother and father, who raised my brother and I to observe the mundane without fear, and to believe in the miraculous without naivete.

BRAD KAYL

I would like to dedicate this book to my mother, Tina Kayl, without whom I would not have had the courage to write, the fortitude to persevere, or the vision to make either of those worthwhile endeavors. I would also like to dedicate this book to anyone who has ever held a pen, and written.

ALLEN COULTER

Elfie and Sean - for being so damned hard to impress.

SNAKEBITE

Dedicated to the lil' kid in all of us. Dedicated to the ones who believe when most don't. Dedicated to my Ma and Pop. Dedicated to ones who got my back, most importantly my love, Lisa, who lives with my crazy schedule. All Praises to the Unmoved Mover!

JO OLSON, MD

For my mom, who imparted organizational skills to me via her DNA, and for my dad, who imparted an interest in graphic storytelling to me via his DNA. Thanks to my partners on Team Red Star, who worked tirelessly to put out a trade that would go down in history.

NATHANIEL DOWNES

First, to my parents, a heartfelt thanks! You both inspire me to be better than I am... Dunno if there are rules against thanking partners, but mine were friends LONG before we ever dreamed of working together. Most people never meet the equal of any one of them, yet I've been fortunate enough to know all three and will always be better for it. Group hug!

INTRODUCTION
BY BRIAN MICHAEL BENDIS

Back in '94 when I first created The Red Star...No, no, no I'm just kidding, of course, I didn't create The Red Star, but I always wanted to start an intro like that.

I did create Kabuki, but that's a whole 'nother story.

I had nothing to do with The Red Star, but the fates of comic book timing have infused the success stories of my comic 'Powers' with this book, The Red Star. We both debuted at the same time with the same publisher and we both had much more success than anyone expected. So all year long, anytime anyone referred to Image, they would use the words The Red Star and Powers in the same sentence.

Now here's a little secret for the kids looking in; anytime you see two unrelated books being lumped together like that, it is usually insanely annoying to the creators of either work. The creators of the individual titles want to stand on their own. They don't want to be lumped in with all the other crap that floats out there in comic land.

And so was my first reaction to The Red Star. I heard The Red Star and Powers in my sleep. I was like Jan Brady: Red Star, Red Star, Red Star!!

But then I started getting my free copies. 'My image comps.' The real reason I got into the biz. Free comics. And I sat my ass down in my porcelain reading room and I said: "Ok, lets take a look at this god damn Red Star." And I quickly understood that if anybody should be annoyed about our two books being lumped together- it's TEAM RED STAR!

What a ballsy book!

A story line and genre that defies all mainstream convention. A Russian war epic?! And it's a hit mainstream book! That's fantastic. Think about that. It sells superhero numbers. What are the odds of that?

And I think it's an epic so big it had to be a comic. It's too big for a Hollywood movie. In fact, I defy Hollywood to try and make it.

This is also a totally original use of computer generated art. The first computer generated comic that made me feel something. Before Red Star I always looked at computer comics as admirable attempts at furthering the art form. Not this book- this book will grab you.

The pages somehow seem too small for the book. As if the book were desperately trying to enlarge itself right in front of you. (And judging from the size of this collection, it seems I was right.)

Man this book really does excite me. If I weren't getting it for free, I would buy it. But, I do get it for free. (man, I love rubbing that in.)

In fact, before I leave to enjoy it I will confess a little something. I ripped off the Red Star two-page logo design that defines Red Star so well in the opening to the Powers graphic novel. That's right. A blatant rip off. My highest compliment.

I've read Red Star twice so far, and I enjoyed it even more the second time. When you're done reading it, don't put it away. Leave it out until you're ready to read it again. And in the meantime leave it out where your friends and loved ones can see it. Because like Maus, Stray Toasters, and Cages before it, this is the kind of graphic novel you can actually impress your friends with.

Ok, enough of me. Time for you to get into it. But stand back, this book gets huge!

BENDIS!
CLEVELAND   2/01

BRIAN MICHAEL BENDIS IS THE EISNER AWARD WINNING AUTHOR OF MANY COMIC SERIES INCLUDING POWERS, TORSO, JINX, GOLDFISH, AND ULTIMATE SPIDERMAN.

What you are about to read is the beginning of an allegory, the prologue to a fairy-tale, inspired by the history of Russia. It was inspired by the writings and works of the most vital group of artists in the twentieth century, those of the Soviet Avant-Garde. These courageous souls worked in an all too brief period that emerged in the early 1900's, proudly declaring that their goal was nothing less than to transform the world into a Utopia of their own design. By 1932, their dreams were shattered under the terrible will of Joseph Stalin's regime.

It would be impossible to describe the incredible depth of their influence upon our world today, even though reality proved unable to support a more complete form of their vision.

It would be unjust to list only a few of the names of their most famous members, for as any of them would surely say, there can be no fame other than that which is constructed by the effort of countless anonymous participants. Since it is impossible to mention each individual, I will honor them here as they might have wished; in nameless unity.

It would be a very different world today, and a very different Russia, if the future they had envisioned, a future of equality and peace and world brotherhood; had not been crushed by the power hunger of Lenin, the brutality of Stalin, or the greed of industrialists the world over.

This fantasy is a tribute to a world that might have been.

CHRISTIAN GOSSETT

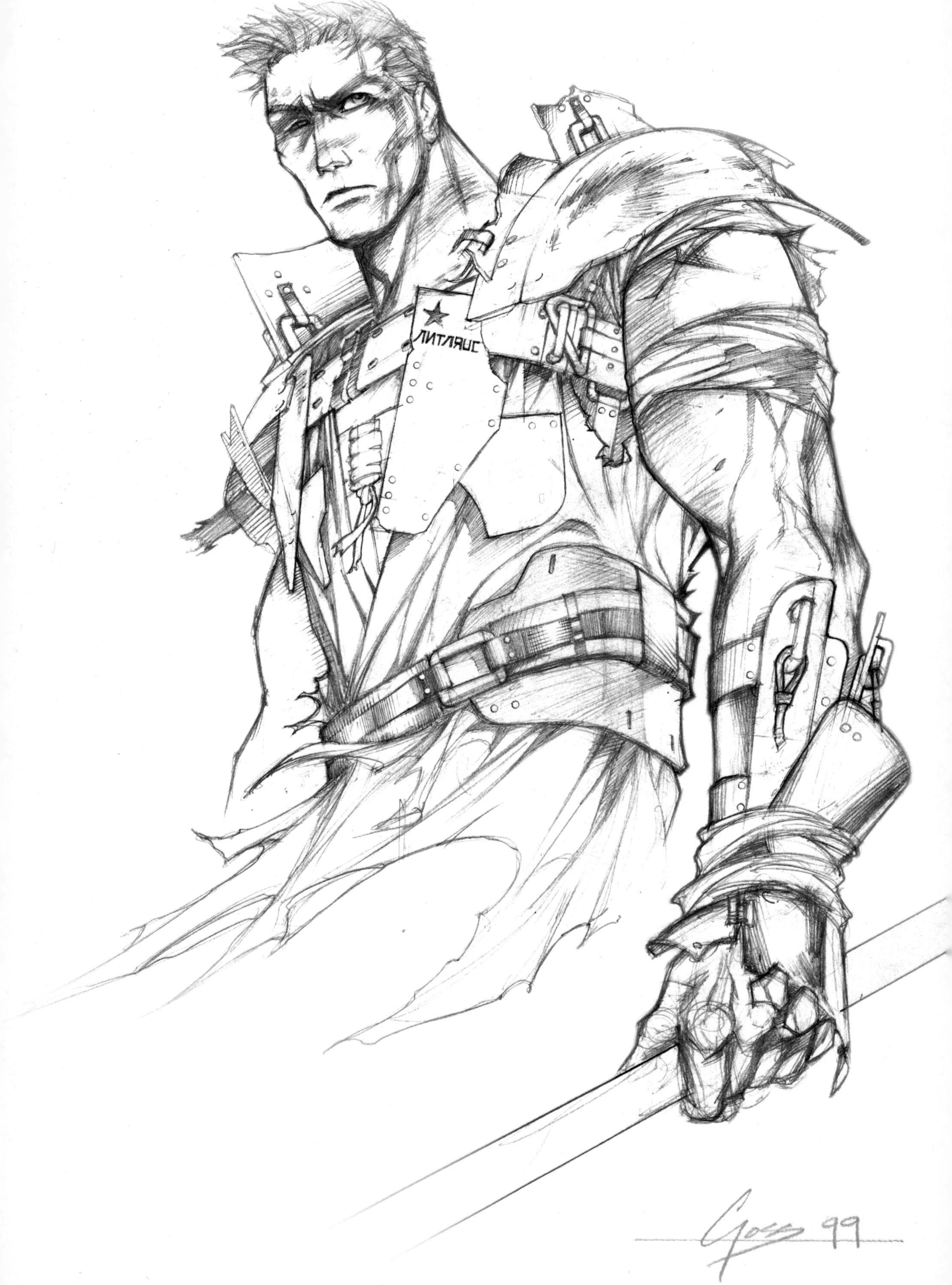
Goss 99

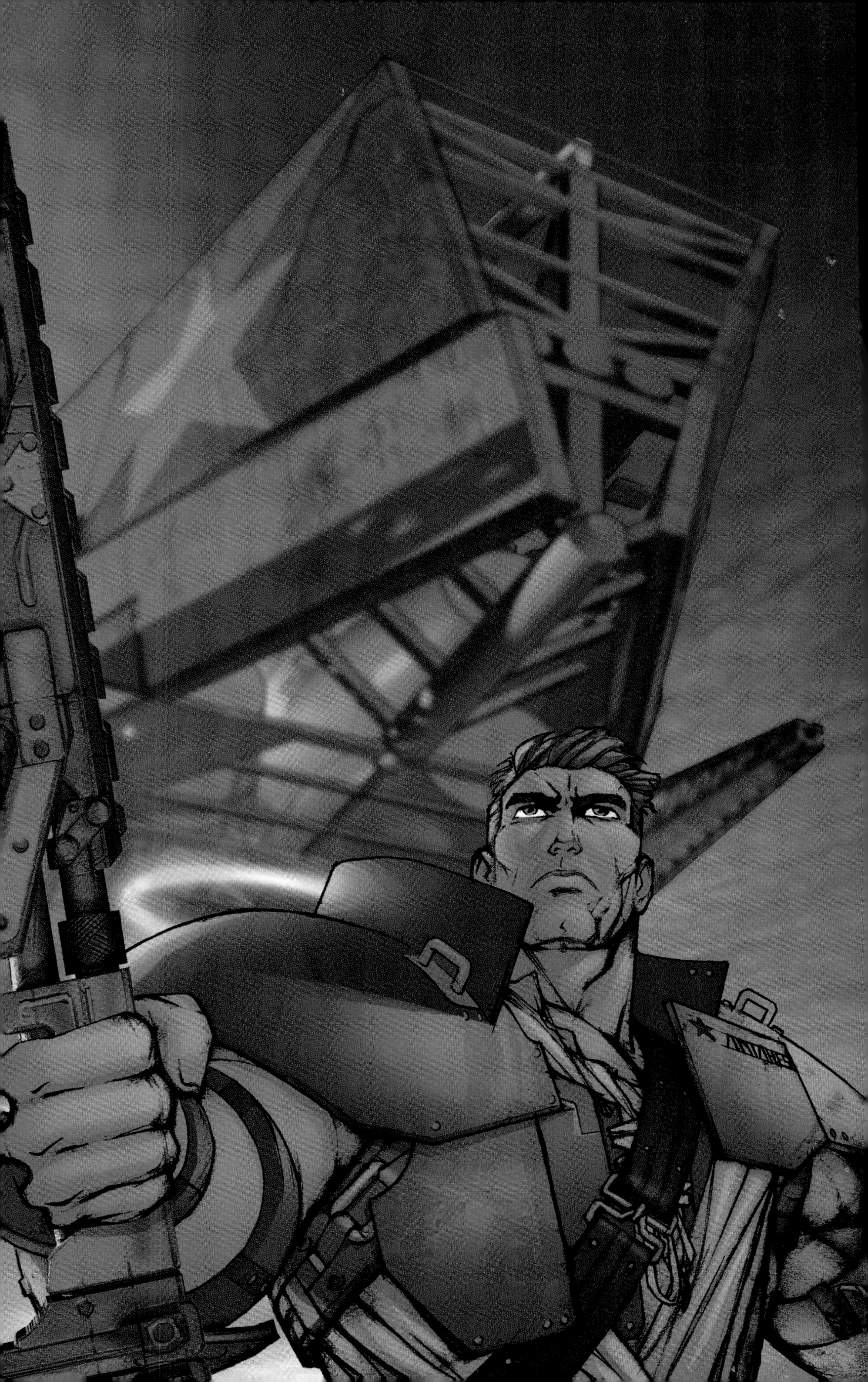

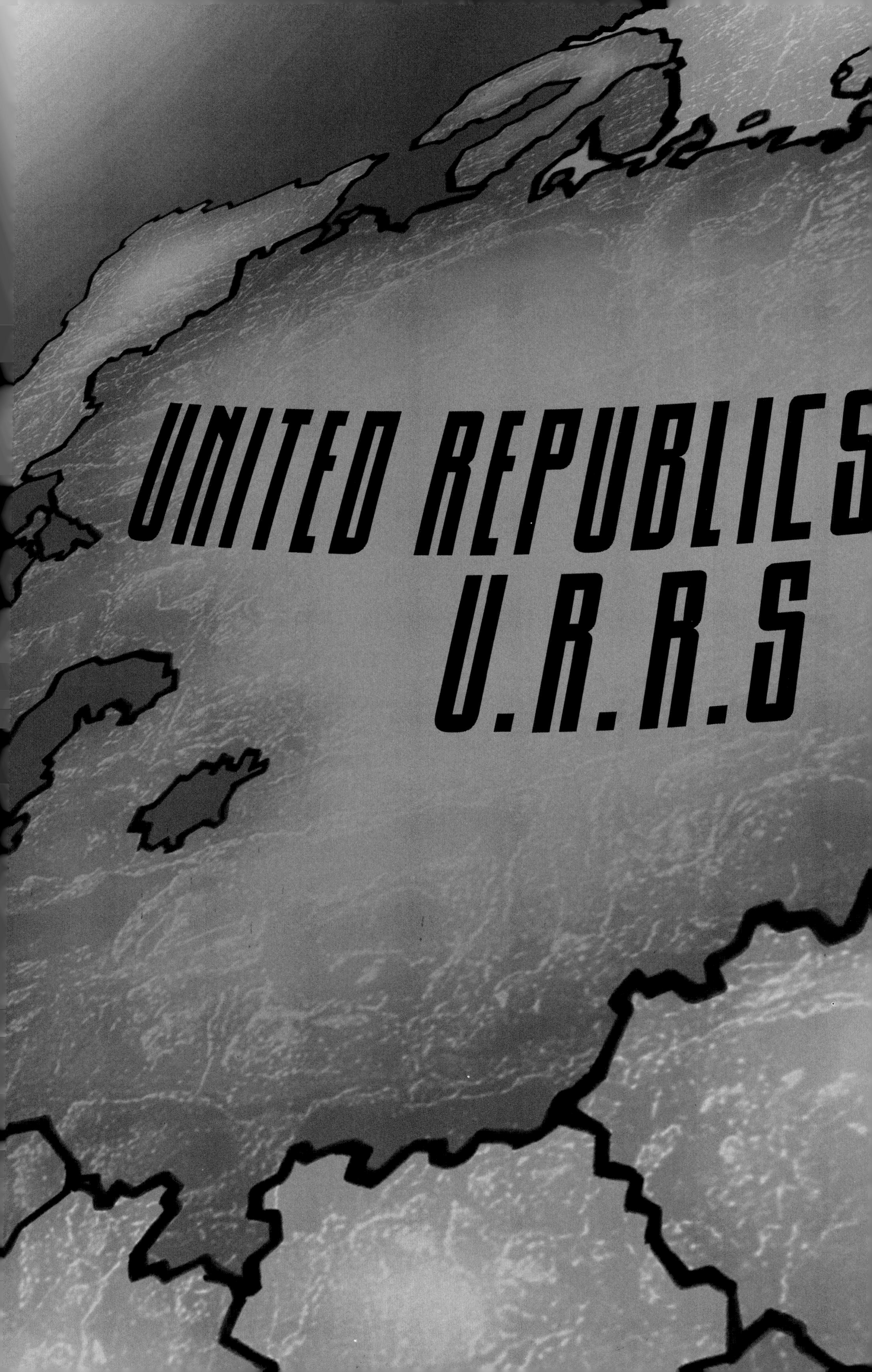
UNITED REPUBLICS
U.R.R.S

OF THE RED STAR

Beloved Marcus,

Today is the ninth anniversary of our nation's defeat at Kar Dathra's Gate. The day that would prove an omen of catastrophe. How could we have known then, as we marched onto the battlefield, the pride of the Red Fleet, that losing the war of Al'istaan would mean the end of our country itself?

Such fools we were, to believe ourselves invincible. To allow military parades and patriotic slogans to convince us that triumph was guaranteed. Victory our destiny. Destiny does not speak in slogans, but in cruelties. The United Republics of the Red Star are no more. Lost forever. All of our sacrifices powerless to stop their collapse.

Still, I shed no tears for their passing. What was taken from me at Kar Dathra's Gate was far more precious than the ambitions of any government. I would watch the decay of a Thousand Empires for one moment spent in the warmth of your arms; one more taste of your kiss. Our people lost a war. I lost you. My Marcus. My Love.

I no longer fight against the memories of you. They have become my treasures. In this shattered place that was our homeland, all we have left are Ghosts.

for Eternity,

Maya

AL'ISTAAN

★ KAR DATHRA'S GATE

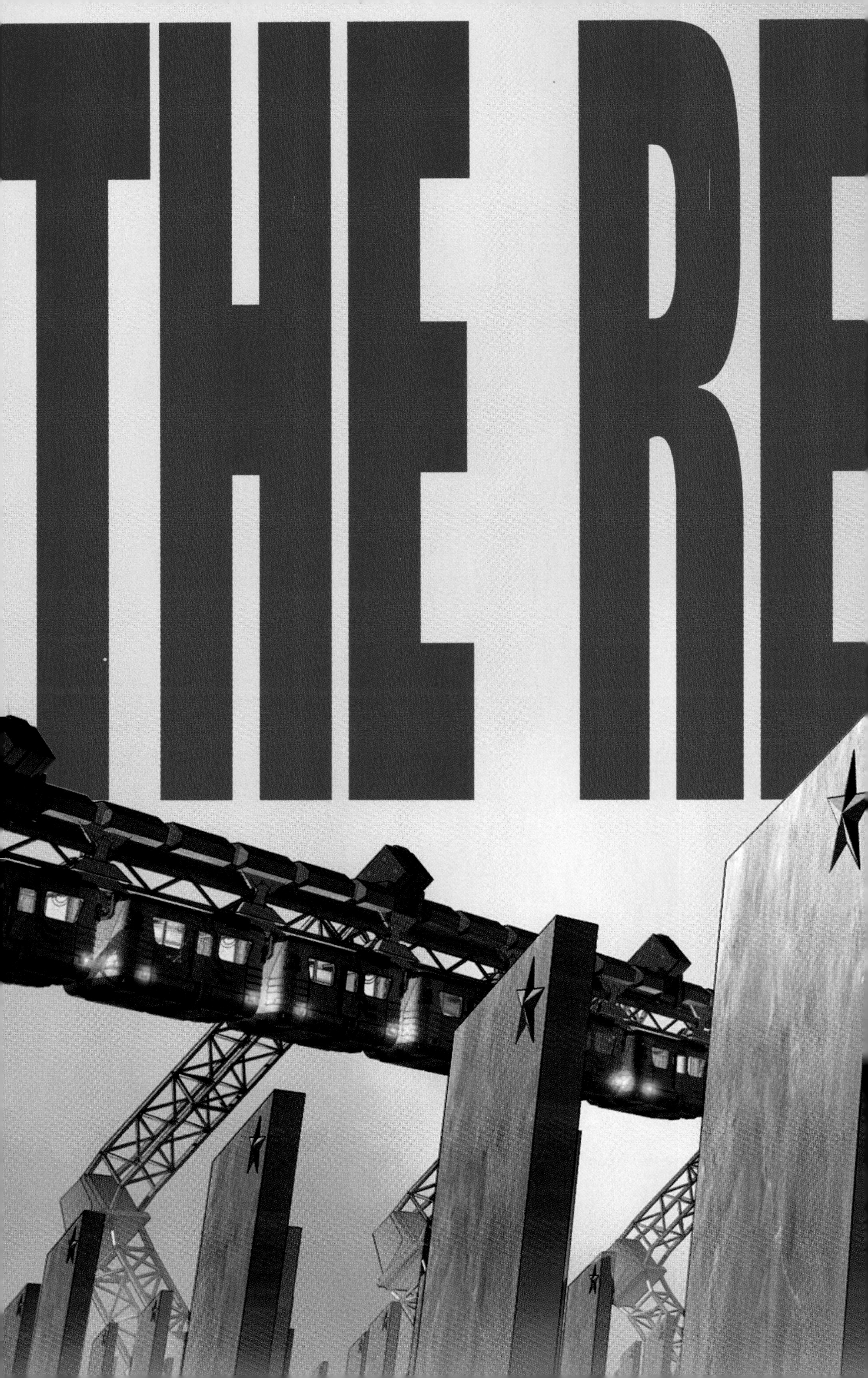
THE RE

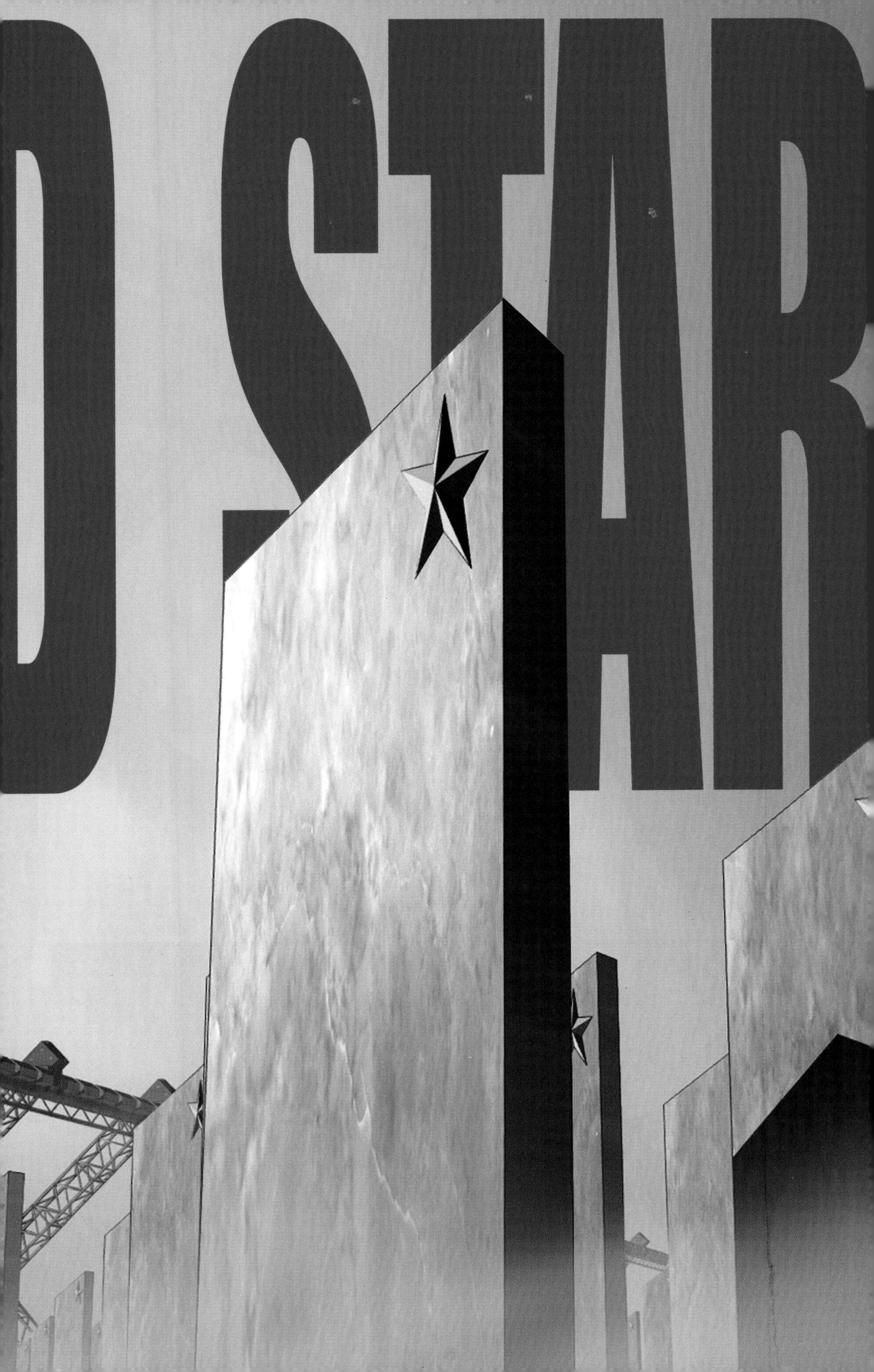
D STAR

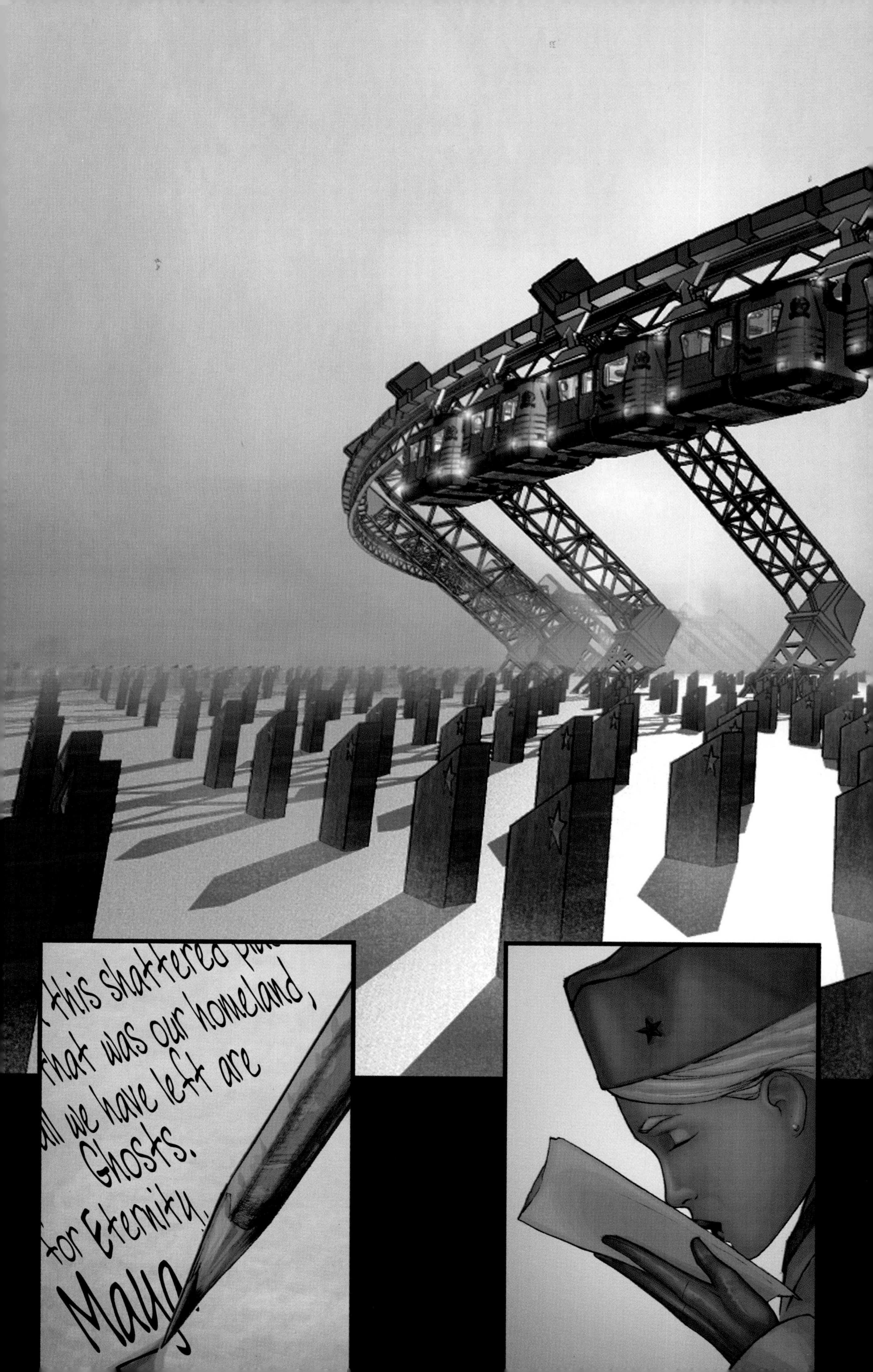
this shattered
that was our homeland,
all we have left are
Ghosts.
for Eternity.

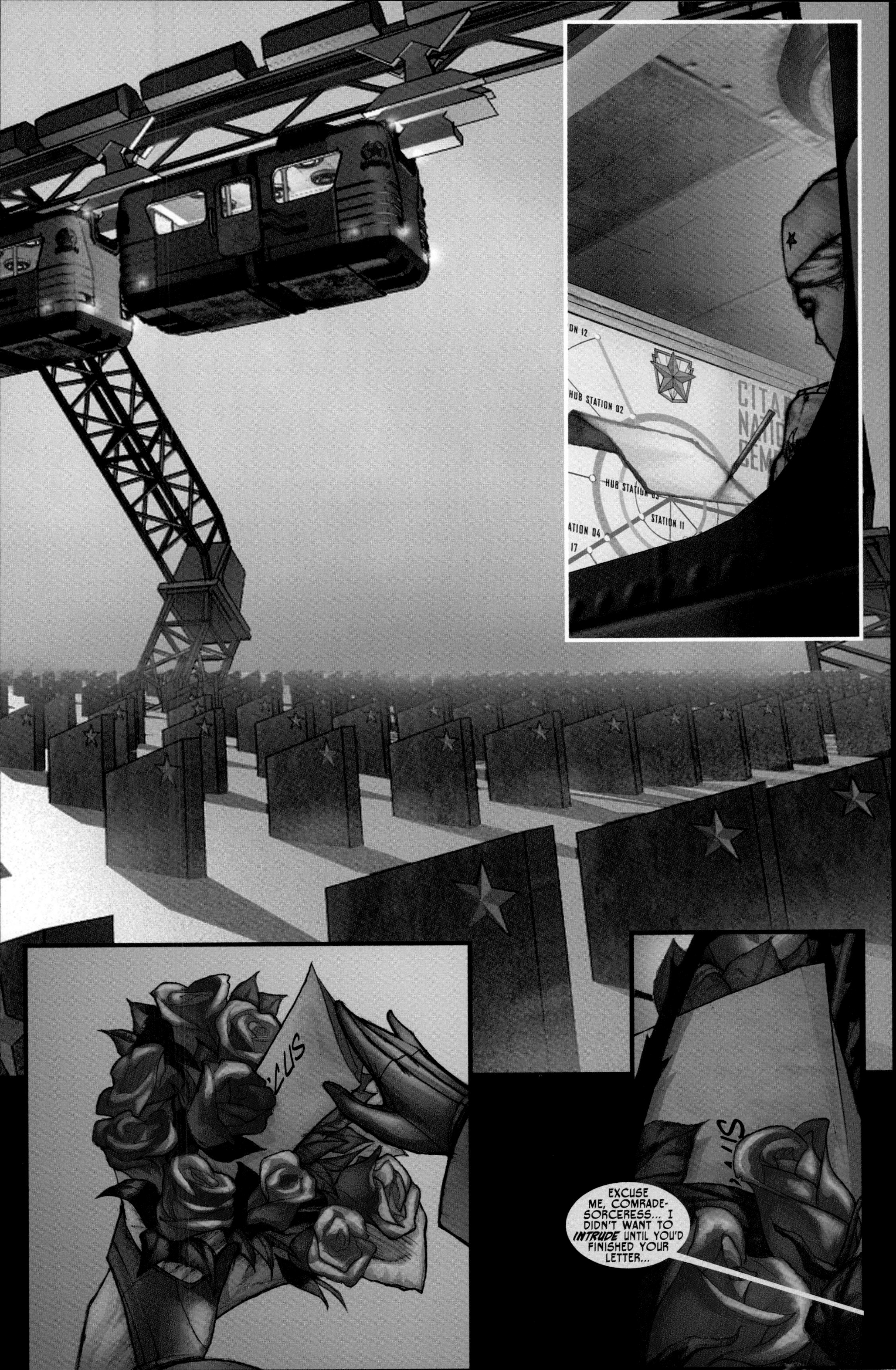
HUB STATION 02
STATION 11
EXCUSE ME, COMRADE-SORCERESS... I DIDN'T WANT TO INTRUDE UNTIL YOU'D FINISHED YOUR LETTER...

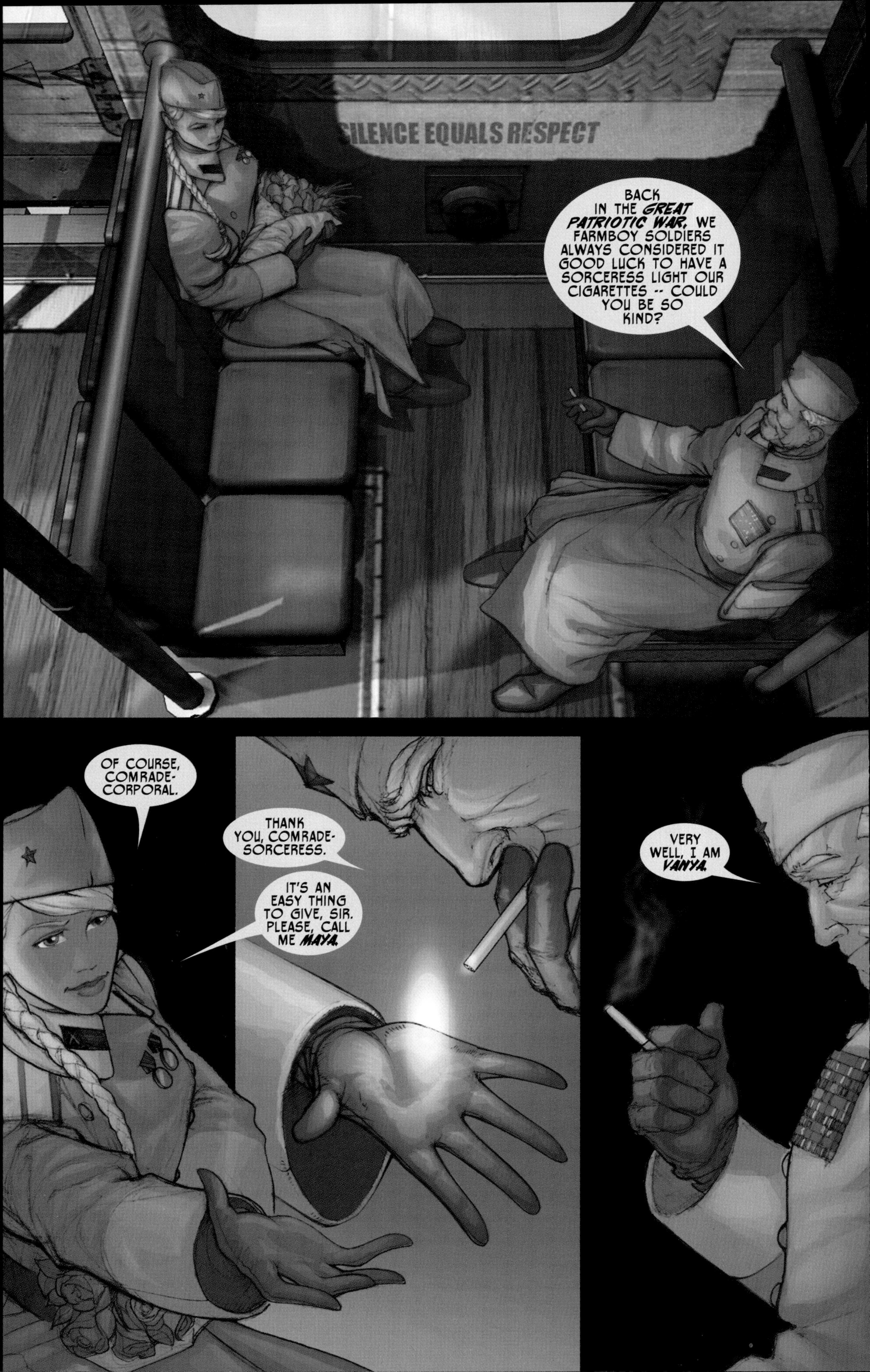
SILENCE EQUALS RESPECT
BACK IN THE GREAT PATRIOTIC WAR, WE FARMBOY SOLDIERS ALWAYS CONSIDERED IT GOOD LUCK TO HAVE A SORCERESS LIGHT OUR CIGARETTES -- COULD YOU BE SO KIND?
OF COURSE, COMRADE-CORPORAL.
THANK YOU, COMRADE-SORCERESS.
IT'S AN EASY THING TO GIVE, SIR. PLEASE, CALL ME MAYA.
VERY WELL, I AM VANYA.

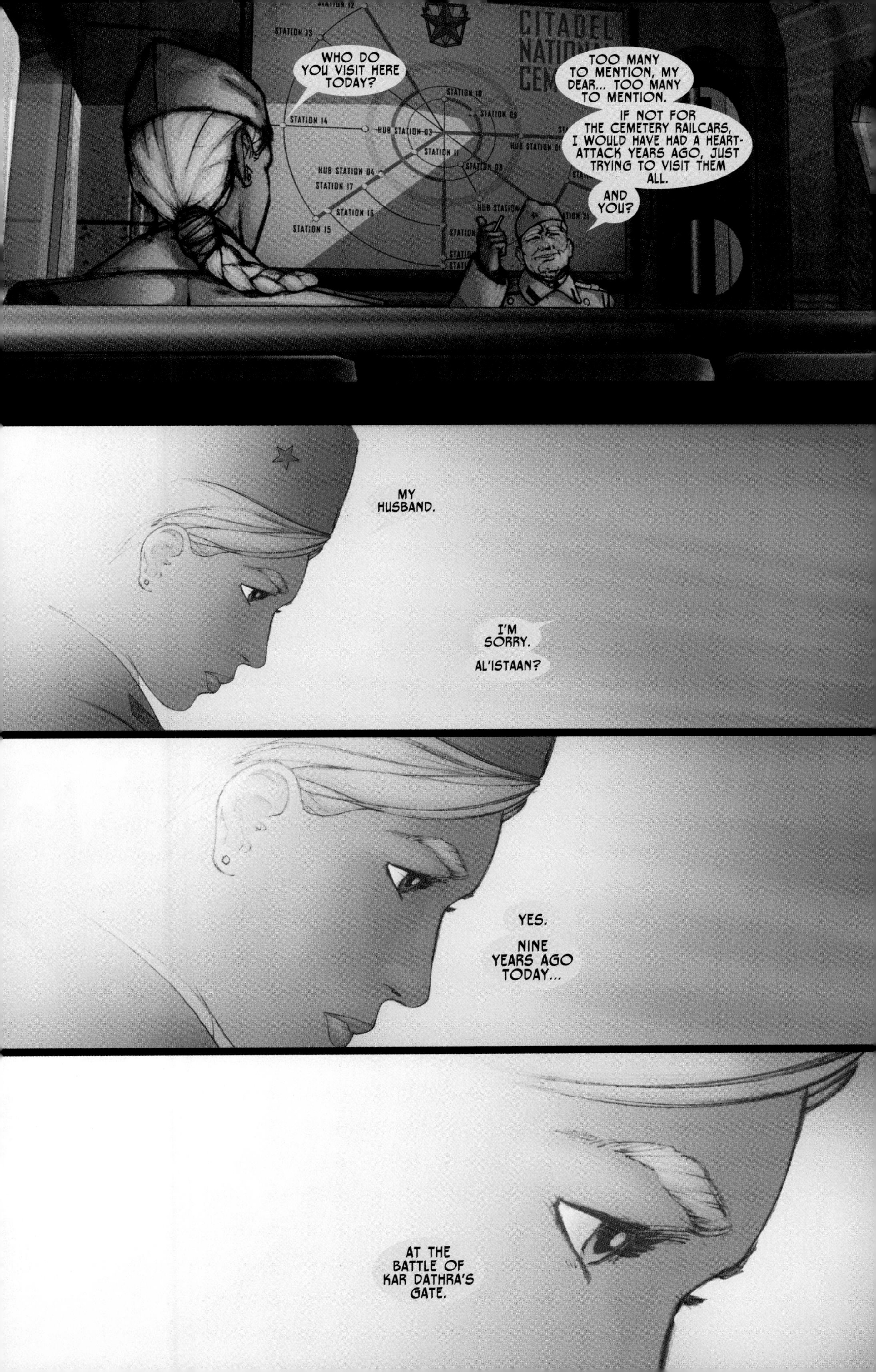
STATION 12
STATION 13
CITADEL NATIONAL CEM
STATION 14
HUB STATION 03
STATION 10
STATION 09
STATION 11
HUB STATION 04
STATION 08
STATION 17
STATION 16
STATION 15
STATION 21
WHO DO YOU VISIT HERE TODAY?
TOO MANY TO MENTION, MY DEAR... TOO MANY TO MENTION.
IF NOT FOR THE CEMETERY RAILCARS, I WOULD HAVE HAD A HEART-ATTACK YEARS AGO, JUST TRYING TO VISIT THEM ALL.
AND YOU?
MY HUSBAND.
I'M SORRY.
AL'ISTAAN?
YES.
NINE YEARS AGO TODAY...
AT THE BATTLE OF KAR DATHRA'S GATE.

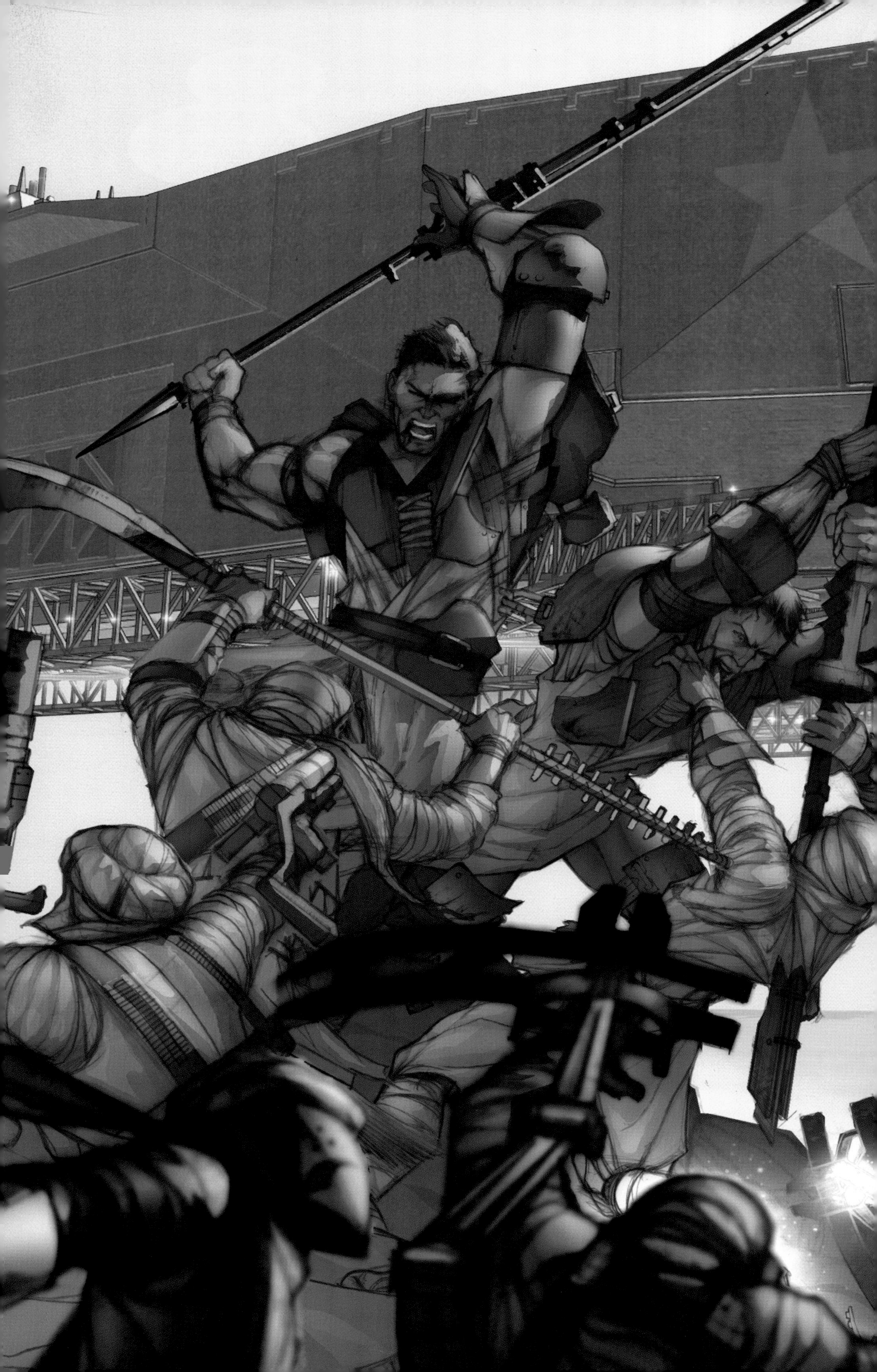

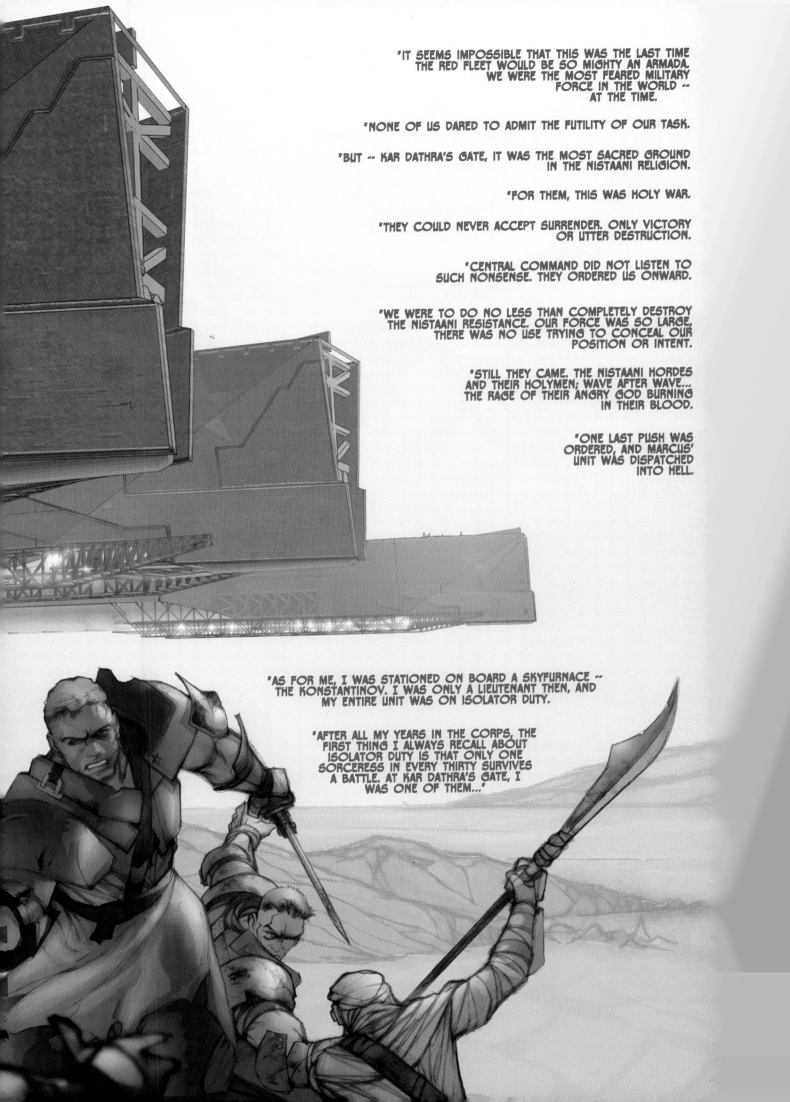

'IT SEEMS IMPOSSIBLE THAT THIS WAS THE LAST TIME THE RED FLEET WOULD BE SO MIGHTY AN ARMADA. WE WERE THE MOST FEARED MILITARY FORCE IN THE WORLD -- AT THE TIME.

'NONE OF US DARED TO ADMIT THE FUTILITY OF OUR TASK.

'BUT -- KAR DATHRA'S GATE, IT WAS THE MOST SACRED GROUND IN THE NISTAANI RELIGION.

'FOR THEM, THIS WAS HOLY WAR.

'THEY COULD NEVER ACCEPT SURRENDER. ONLY VICTORY OR UTTER DESTRUCTION.

'CENTRAL COMMAND DID NOT LISTEN TO SUCH NONSENSE. THEY ORDERED US ONWARD.

'WE WERE TO DO NO LESS THAN COMPLETELY DESTROY THE NISTAANI RESISTANCE. OUR FORCE WAS SO LARGE, THERE WAS NO USE TRYING TO CONCEAL OUR POSITION OR INTENT.

'STILL THEY CAME. THE NISTAANI HORDES AND THEIR HOLYMEN; WAVE AFTER WAVE... THE RAGE OF THEIR ANGRY GOD BURNING IN THEIR BLOOD.

'ONE LAST PUSH WAS ORDERED, AND MARCUS' UNIT WAS DISPATCHED INTO HELL.

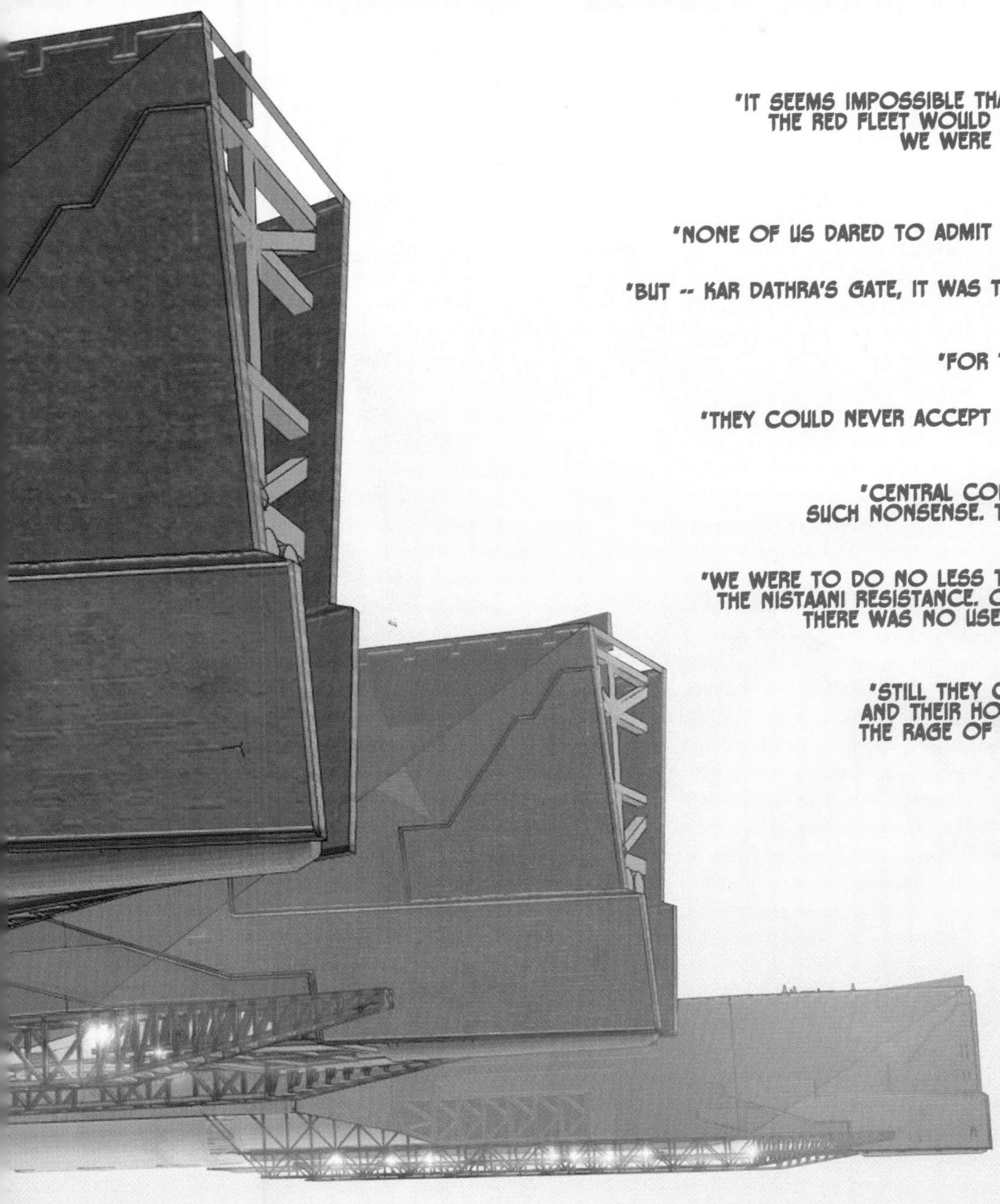

'AS FOR ME, I WAS STATIONED ON BOARD A SKYFURNACE -- THE KONSTANTINOV. I WAS ONLY A LIEUTENANT THEN, AND MY ENTIRE UNIT WAS ON ISOLATOR DUTY.

'AFTER ALL MY YEARS IN THE CORPS, THE FIRST THING I ALWAYS RECALL ABOUT ISOLATOR DUTY IS THAT ONLY ONE SORCERESS IN EVERY THIRTY SURVIVES A BATTLE. AT KAR DATHRA'S GATE, I WAS ONE OF THEM...'

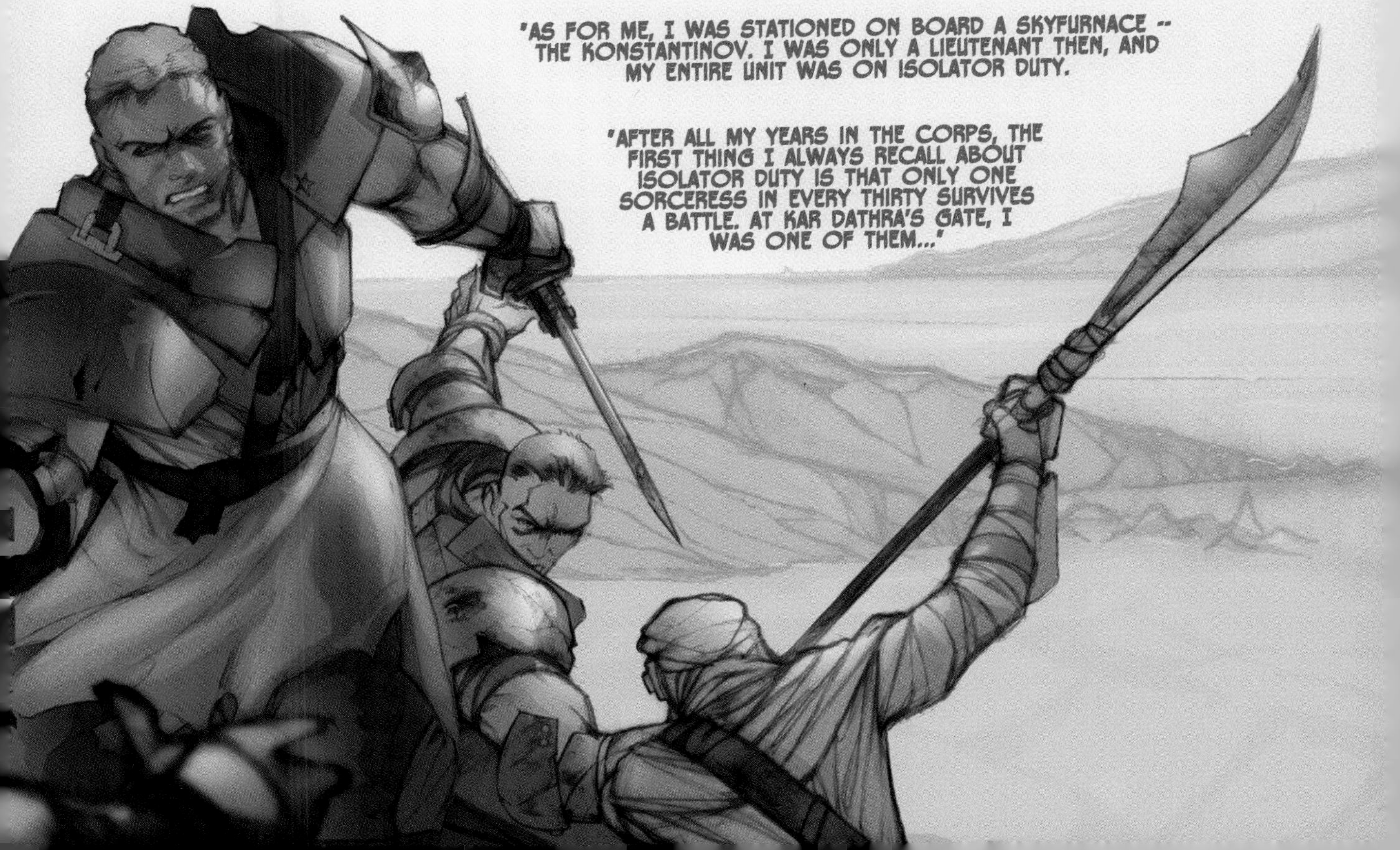

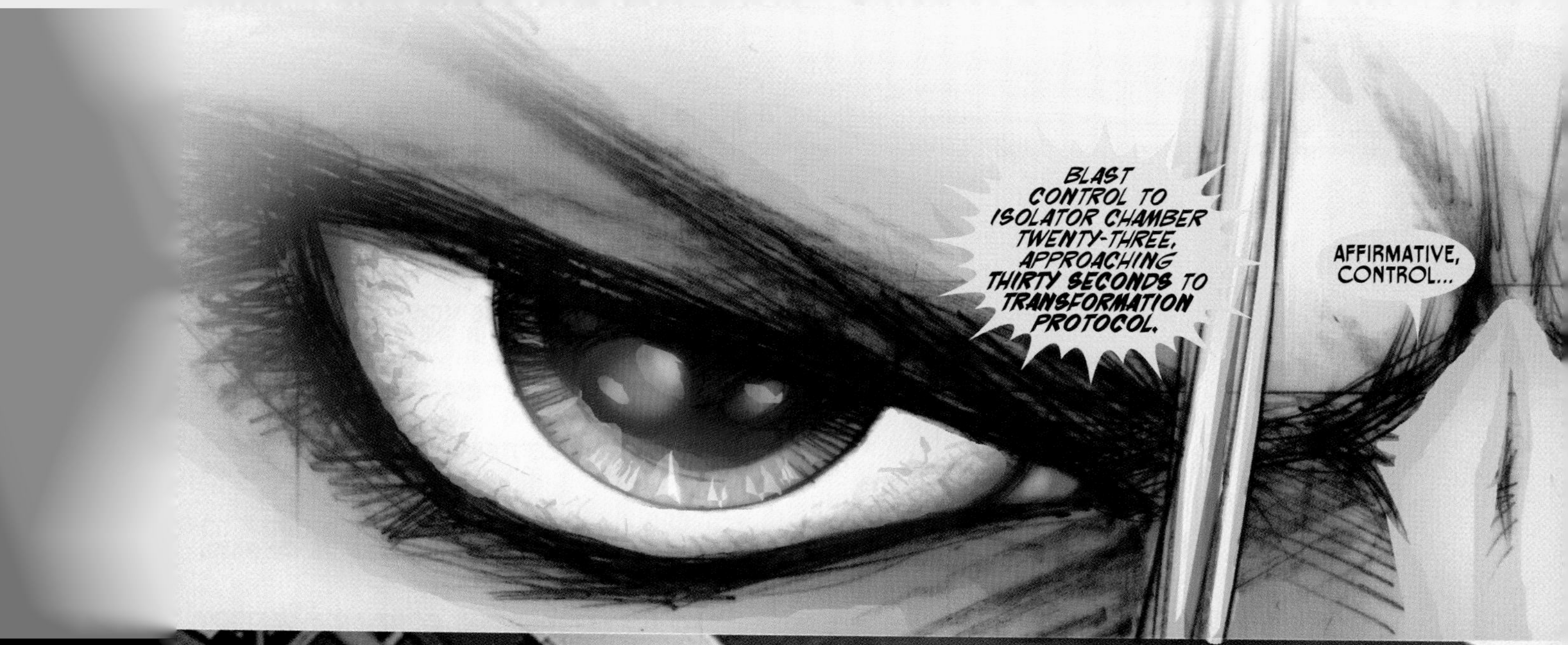
BLAST CONTROL TO ISOLATOR CHAMBER TWENTY-THREE. APPROACHING THIRTY SECONDS TO TRANSFORMATION PROTOCOL.
AFFIRMATIVE, CONTROL...

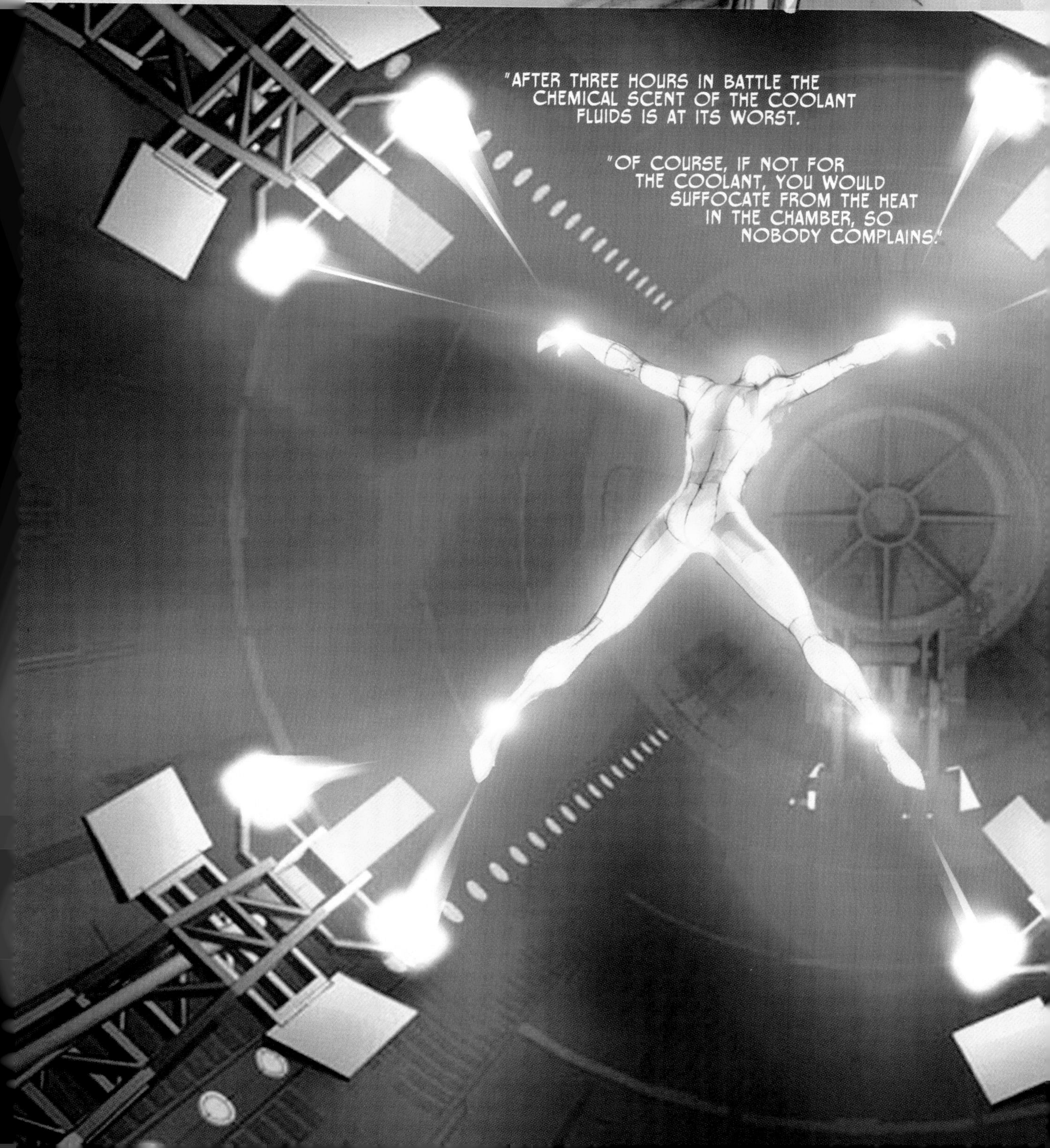
"AFTER THREE HOURS IN BATTLE THE CHEMICAL SCENT OF THE COOLANT FLUIDS IS AT ITS WORST.
"OF COURSE, IF NOT FOR THE COOLANT, YOU WOULD SUFFOCATE FROM THE HEAT IN THE CHAMBER, SO NOBODY COMPLAINS."

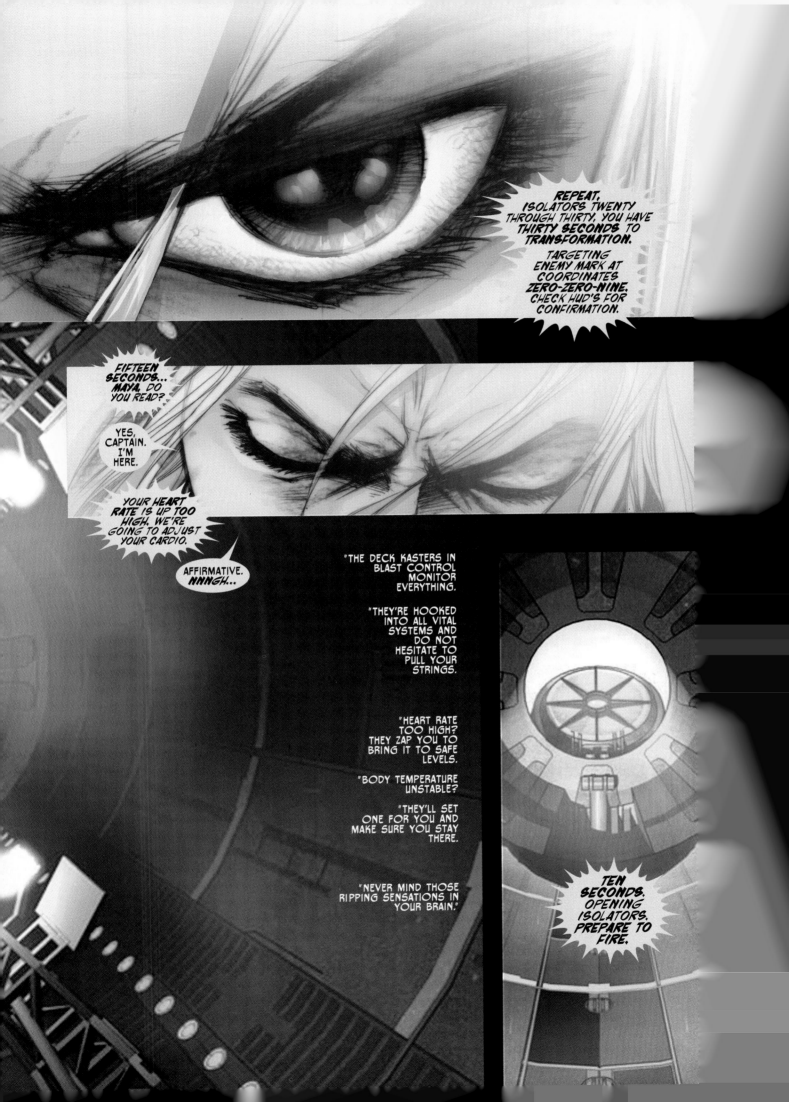

REPEAT, ISOLATORS TWENTY THROUGH THIRTY, YOU HAVE **THIRTY SECONDS** TO **TRANSFORMATION.**

TARGETING ENEMY MARK AT COORDINATES ZERO-ZERO-NINE. CHECK HUD'S FOR CONFIRMATION.

FIFTEEN SECONDS... MAYA, DO YOU READ?

YES, CAPTAIN. I'M HERE.

YOUR HEART RATE IS UP TOO HIGH. WE'RE GOING TO ADJUST YOUR CARDIO.

AFFIRMATIVE. NNNGH...

"THE DECK KASTERS IN BLAST CONTROL MONITOR EVERYTHING.

"THEY'RE HOOKED INTO ALL VITAL SYSTEMS AND DO NOT HESITATE TO PULL YOUR STRINGS.

"HEART RATE TOO HIGH? THEY ZAP YOU TO BRING IT TO SAFE LEVELS.

"BODY TEMPERATURE UNSTABLE?

"THEY'LL SET ONE FOR YOU AND MAKE SURE YOU STAY THERE.

"NEVER MIND THOSE RIPPING SENSATIONS IN YOUR BRAIN."

TEN SECONDS. OPENING ISOLATORS. PREPARE TO FIRE.

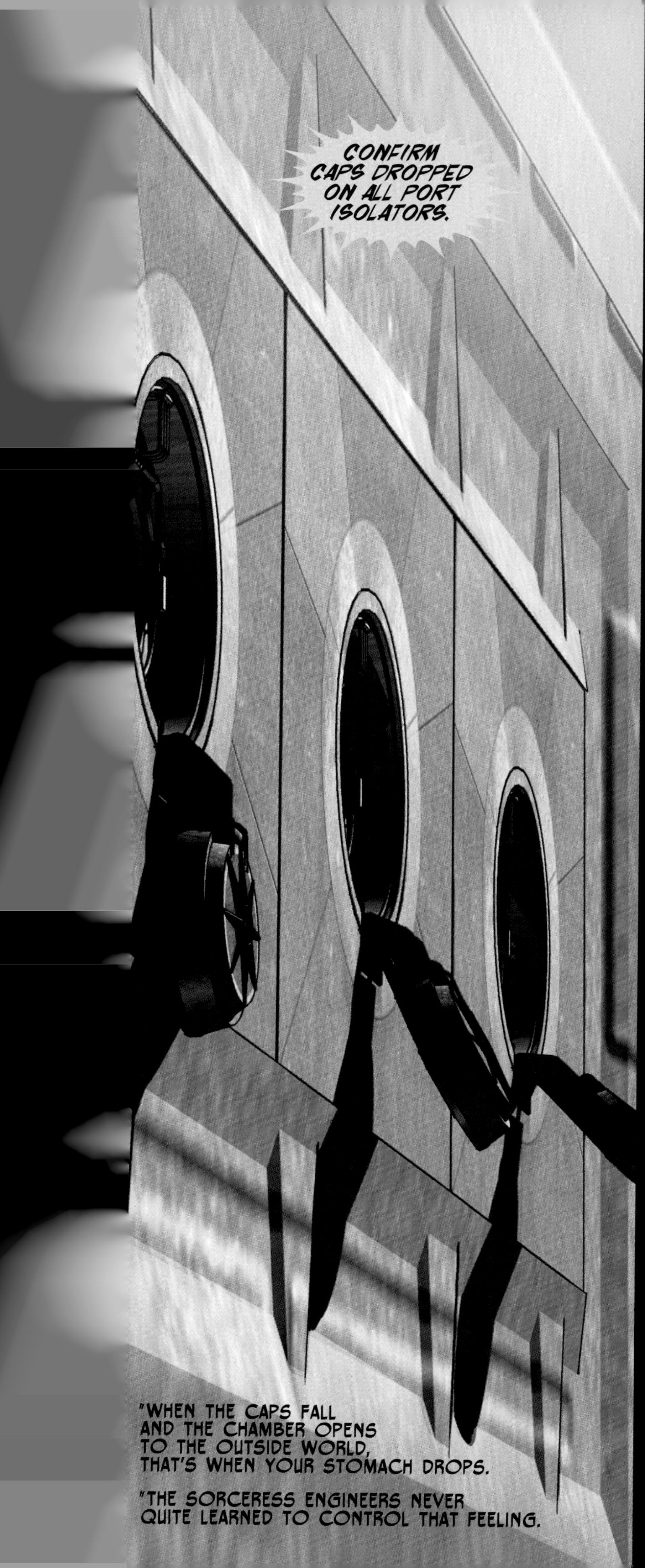
CONFIRM CAPS DROPPED ON ALL PORT ISOLATORS.
"WHEN THE CAPS FALL AND THE CHAMBER OPENS TO THE OUTSIDE WORLD, THAT'S WHEN YOUR STOMACH DROPS.
"THE SORCERESS ENGINEERS NEVER QUITE LEARNED TO CONTROL THAT FEELING.
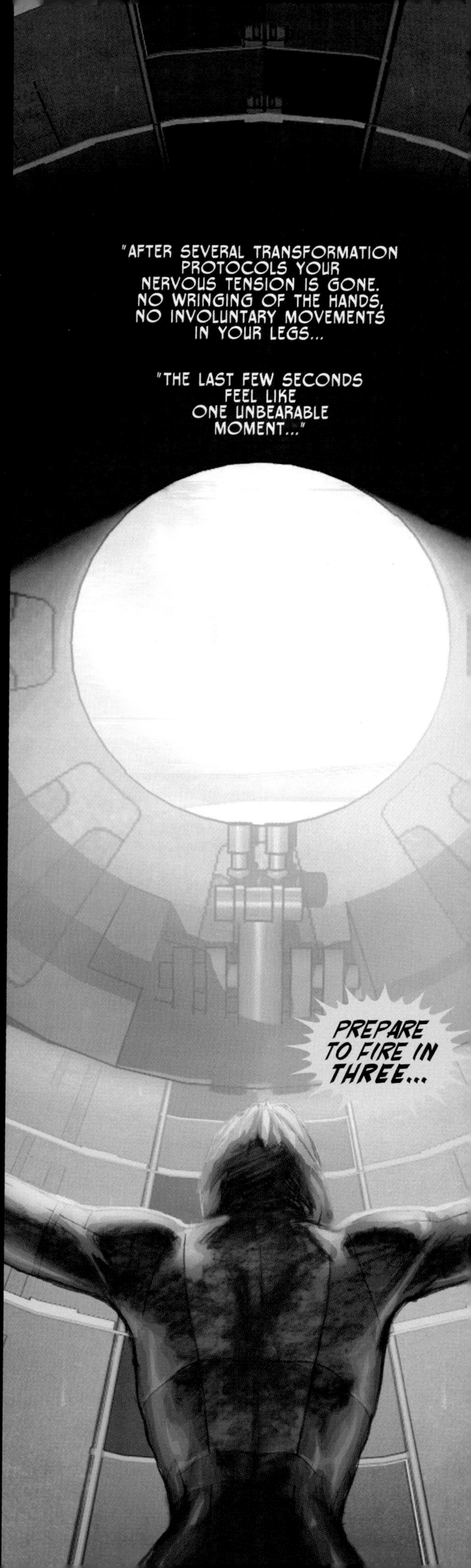
"AFTER SEVERAL TRANSFORMATION PROTOCOLS YOUR NERVOUS TENSION IS GONE. NO WRINGING OF THE HANDS, NO INVOLUNTARY MOVEMENTS IN YOUR LEGS...
"THE LAST FEW SECONDS FEEL LIKE ONE UNBEARABLE MOMENT..."
PREPARE TO FIRE IN THREE...

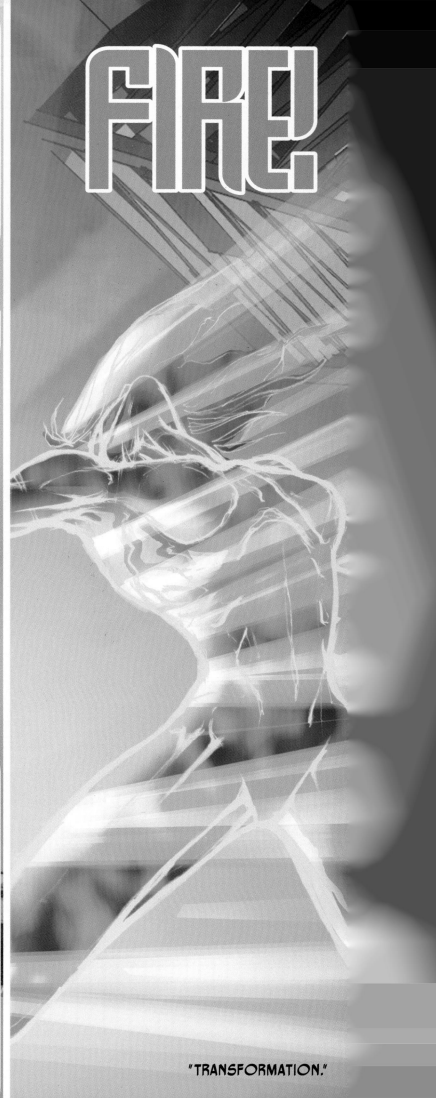

FIRE!

"YOUR BODY IS DEAD WEIGHT, BUT YOUR MIND SCREAMS AT YOU...

"WILL I KAST THE PROTOCOL CORRECTLY?

"WILL THE ISOLATOR CHAMBER FUNCTION PROPERLY UPON MY RETURN?

"WILL THE COOLANT SPRAY, OR WILL I SUFFOCATE IN THE DARKNESS?

"THEN, THANKFULLY THE MIND IS SILENCED."

"TRANSFORMATION."

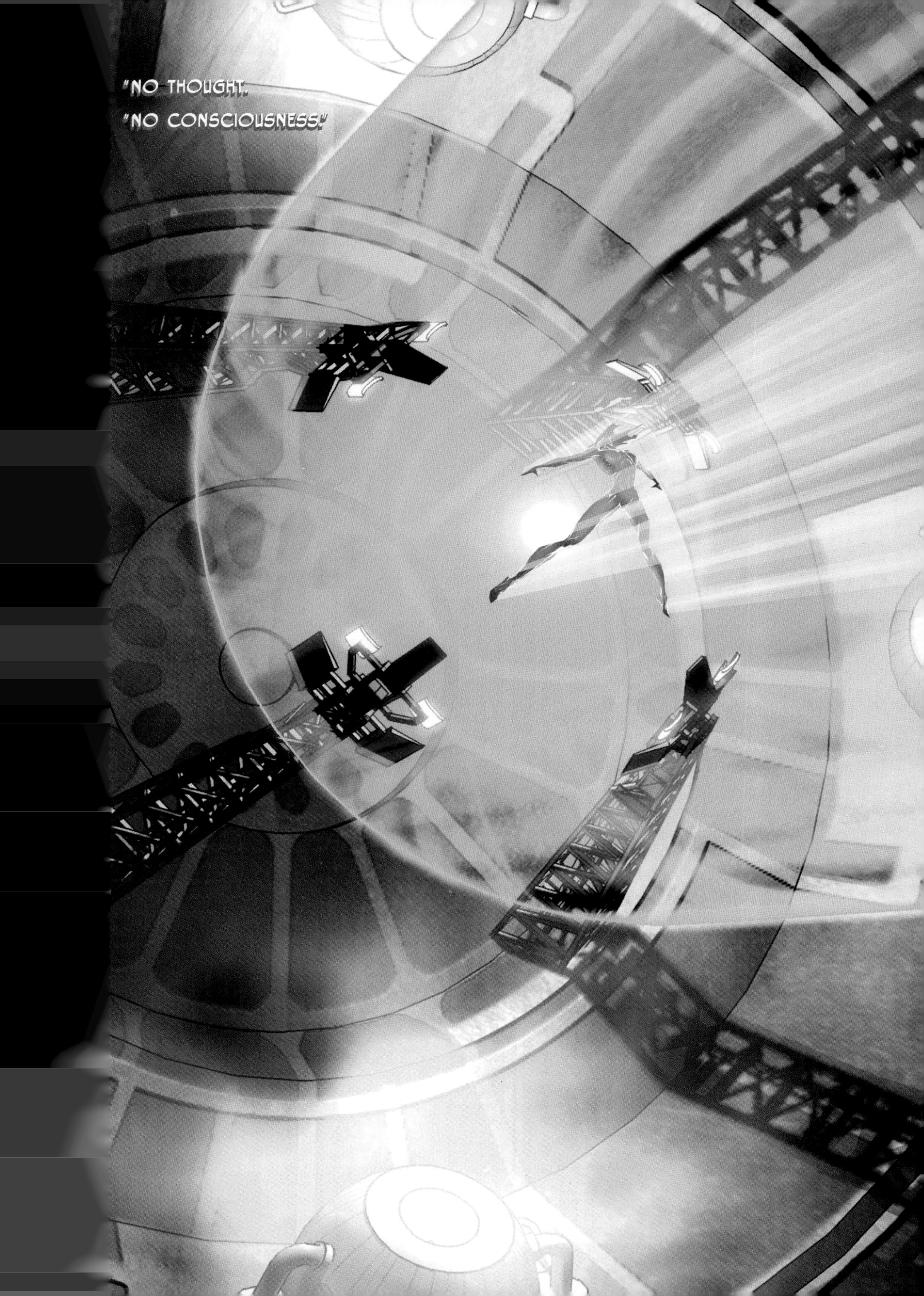
"NO THOUGHT.
"NO CONSCIOUSNESS."

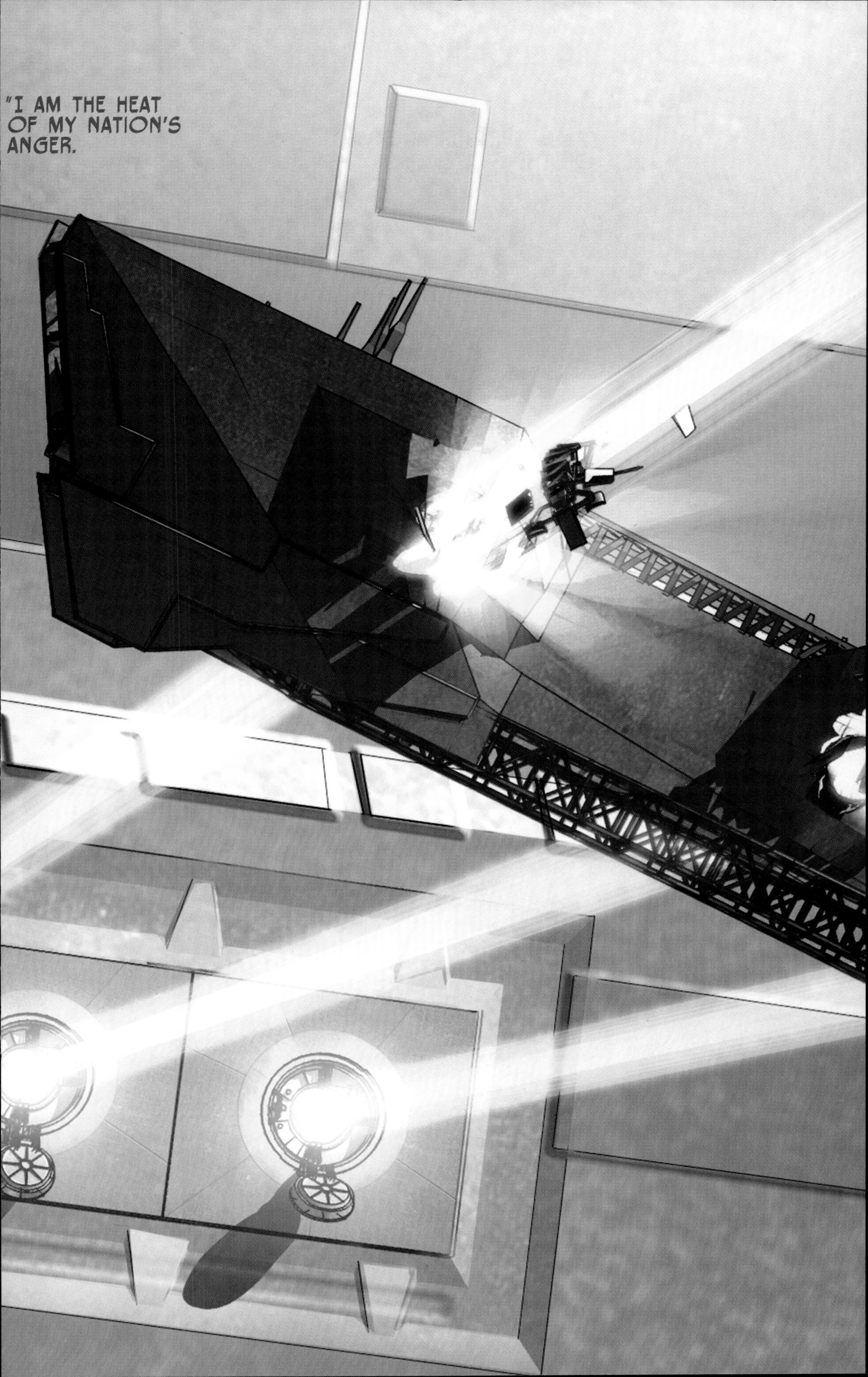
"I AM THE HEAT
OF MY NATION'S
ANGER.

BK1

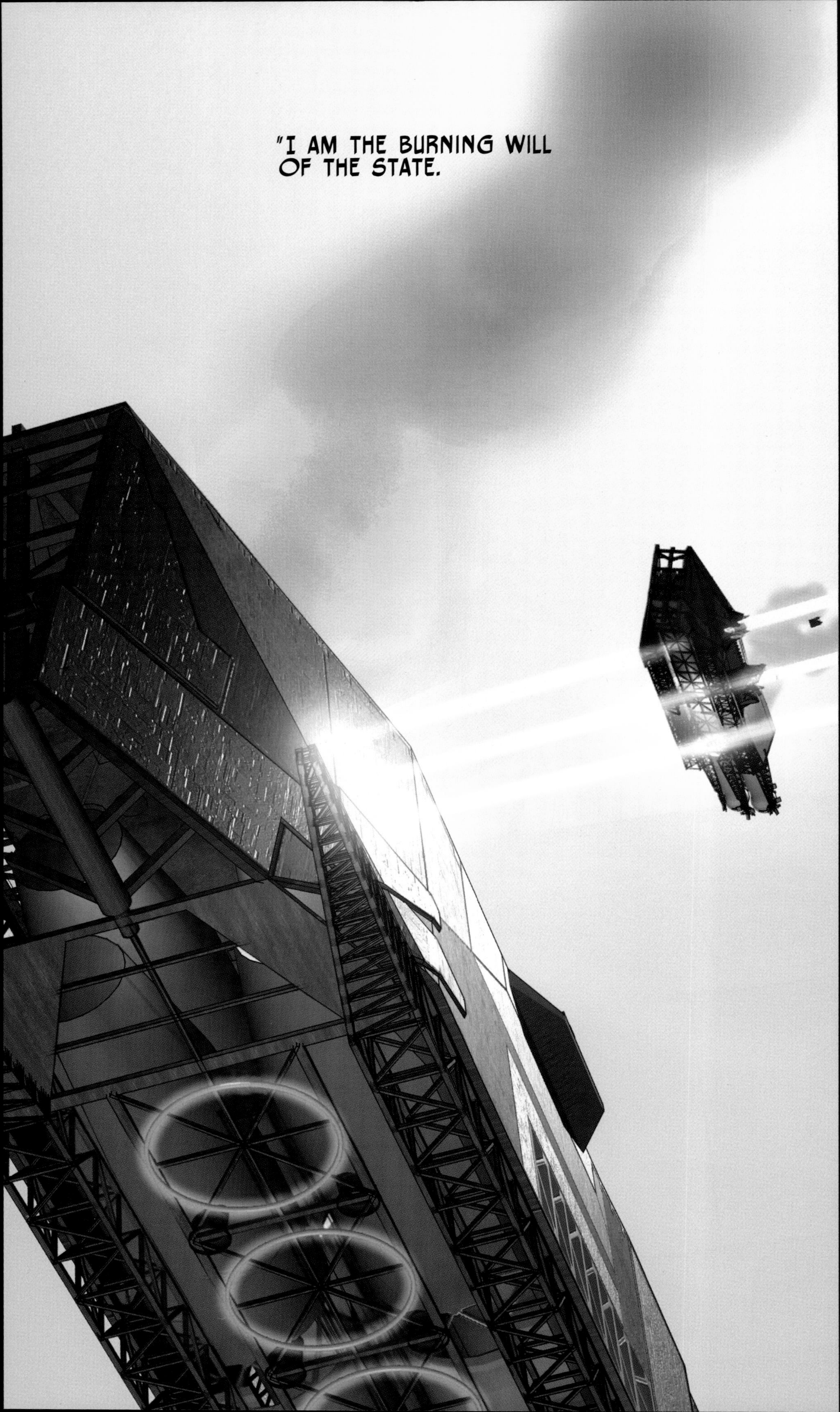
"I AM THE BURNING WILL OF THE STATE.

"AN INFERNO, CLEARING THE PATH OF THOSE WHO RESIST.

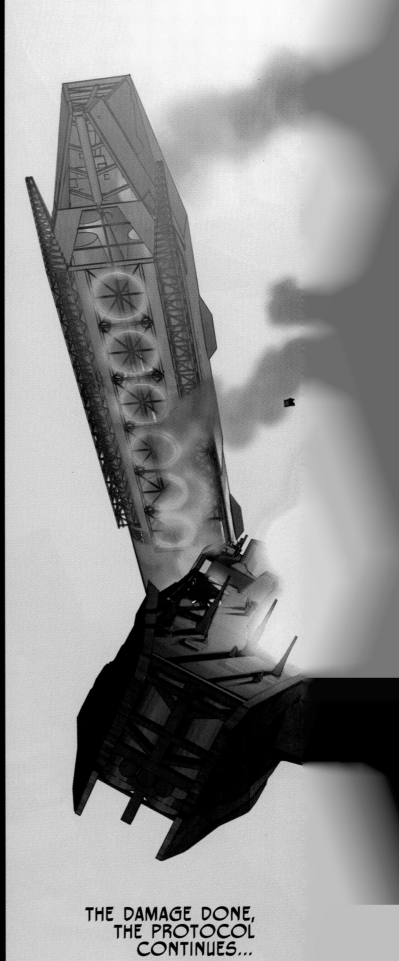

THE DAMAGE DONE, THE PROTOCOL CONTINUES...

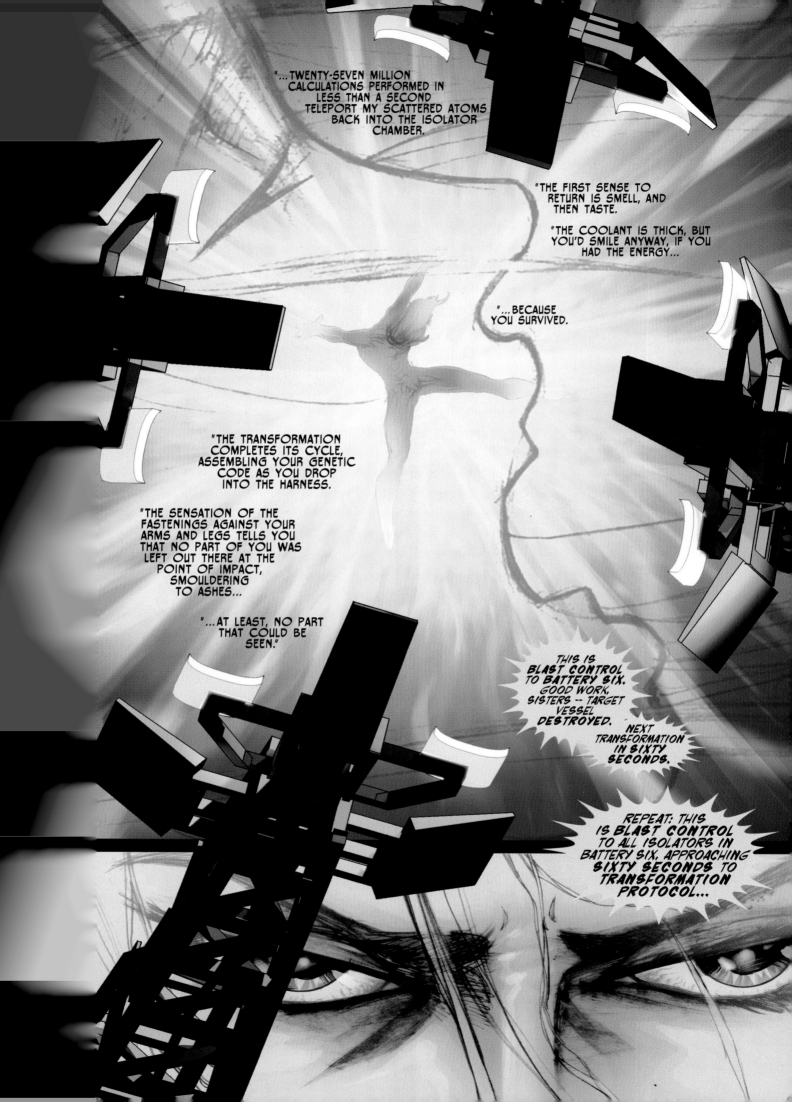

"...TWENTY-SEVEN MILLION CALCULATIONS PERFORMED IN LESS THAN A SECOND TELEPORT MY SCATTERED ATOMS BACK INTO THE ISOLATOR CHAMBER.

"THE FIRST SENSE TO RETURN IS SMELL, AND THEN TASTE.

"THE COOLANT IS THICK, BUT YOU'D SMILE ANYWAY, IF YOU HAD THE ENERGY...

"...BECAUSE YOU SURVIVED.

"THE TRANSFORMATION COMPLETES ITS CYCLE, ASSEMBLING YOUR GENETIC CODE AS YOU DROP INTO THE HARNESS.

"THE SENSATION OF THE FASTENINGS AGAINST YOUR ARMS AND LEGS TELLS YOU THAT NO PART OF YOU WAS LEFT OUT THERE AT THE POINT OF IMPACT, SMOULDERING TO ASHES...

"...AT LEAST, NO PART THAT COULD BE SEEN."

THIS IS BLAST CONTROL TO BATTERY SIX. GOOD WORK, SISTERS -- TARGET VESSEL DESTROYED.

NEXT TRANSFORMATION IN SIXTY SECONDS.

REPEAT: THIS IS BLAST CONTROL TO ALL ISOLATORS IN BATTERY SIX. APPROACHING SIXTY SECONDS TO TRANSFORMATION PROTOCOL...

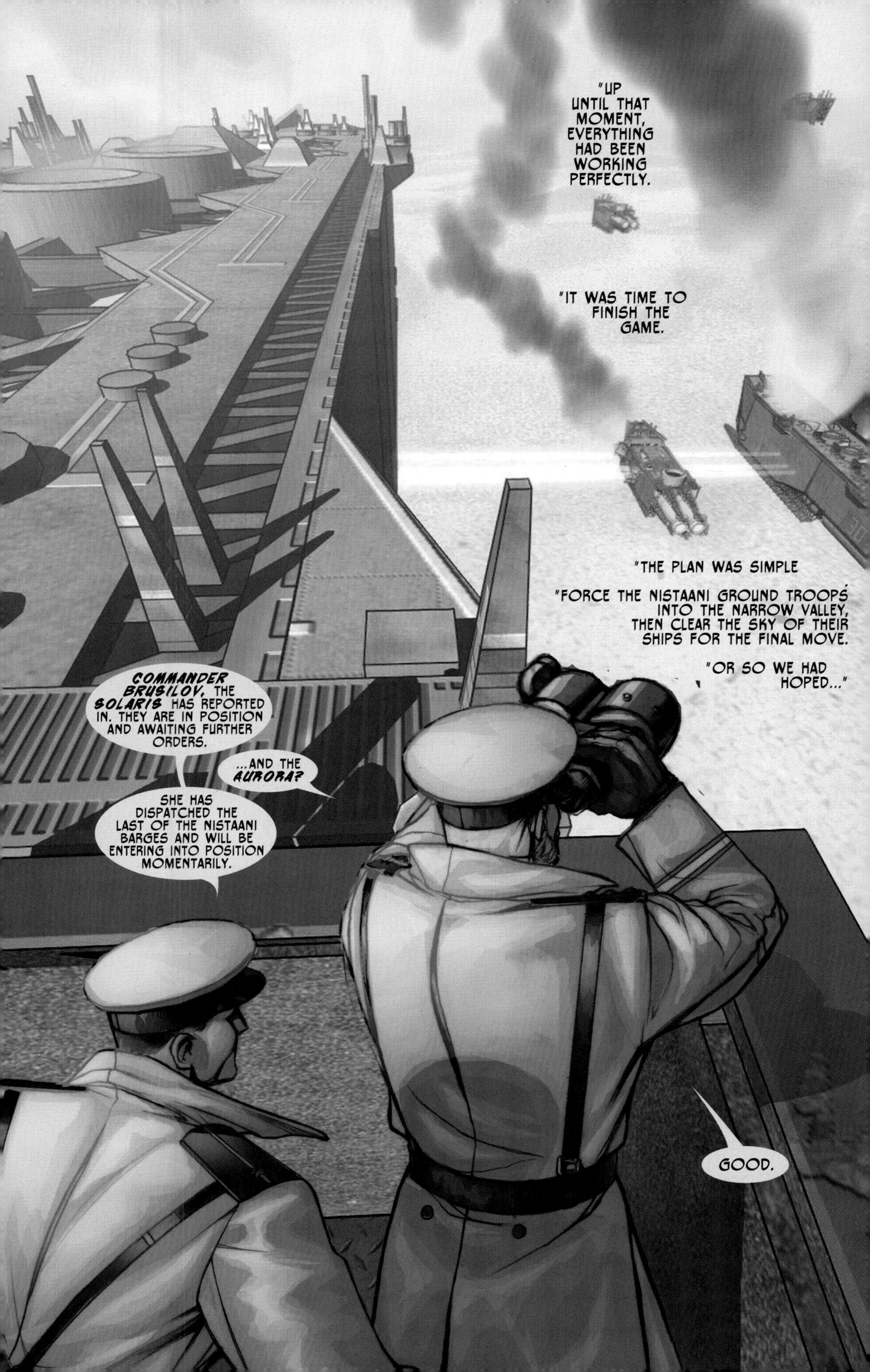
"UP UNTIL THAT MOMENT, EVERYTHING HAD BEEN WORKING PERFECTLY.
"IT WAS TIME TO FINISH THE GAME.
"THE PLAN WAS SIMPLE
"FORCE THE NISTAANI GROUND TROOPS INTO THE NARROW VALLEY, THEN CLEAR THE SKY OF THEIR SHIPS FOR THE FINAL MOVE.
"OR SO WE HAD HOPED..."
COMMANDER BRUSILOV, THE SOLARIS HAS REPORTED IN. THEY ARE IN POSITION AND AWAITING FURTHER ORDERS.
...AND THE AURORA?
SHE HAS DISPATCHED THE LAST OF THE NISTAANI BARGES AND WILL BE ENTERING INTO POSITION MOMENTARILY.
GOOD.

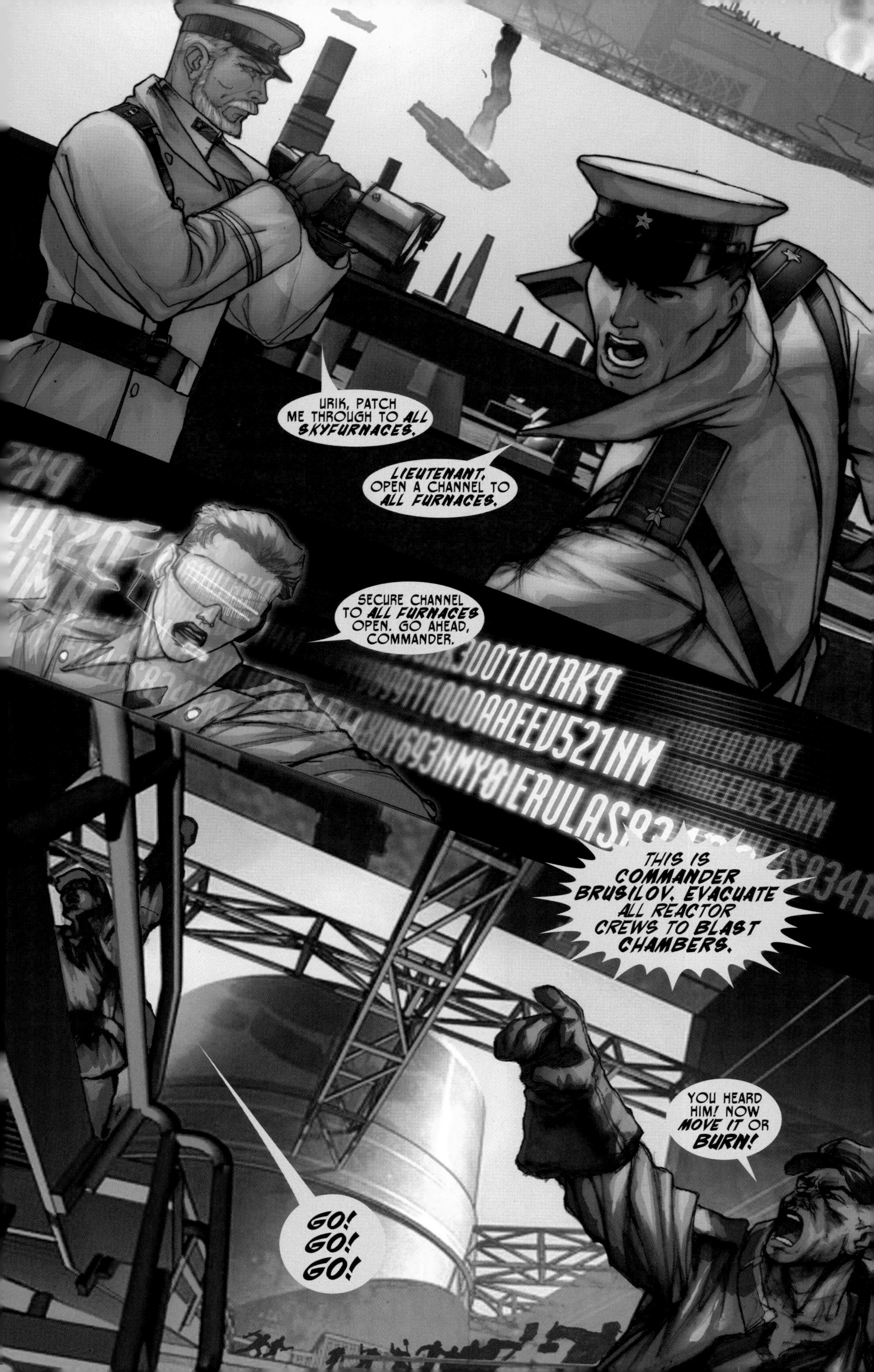
URIK, PATCH ME THROUGH TO ALL SKYFURNACES.
LIEUTENANT, OPEN A CHANNEL TO ALL FURNACES.
SECURE CHANNEL TO ALL FURNACES OPEN. GO AHEAD, COMMANDER.
THIS IS COMMANDER BRUSILOV. EVACUATE ALL REACTOR CREWS TO BLAST CHAMBERS.
YOU HEARD HIM! NOW MOVE IT OR BURN!
GO! GO! GO!

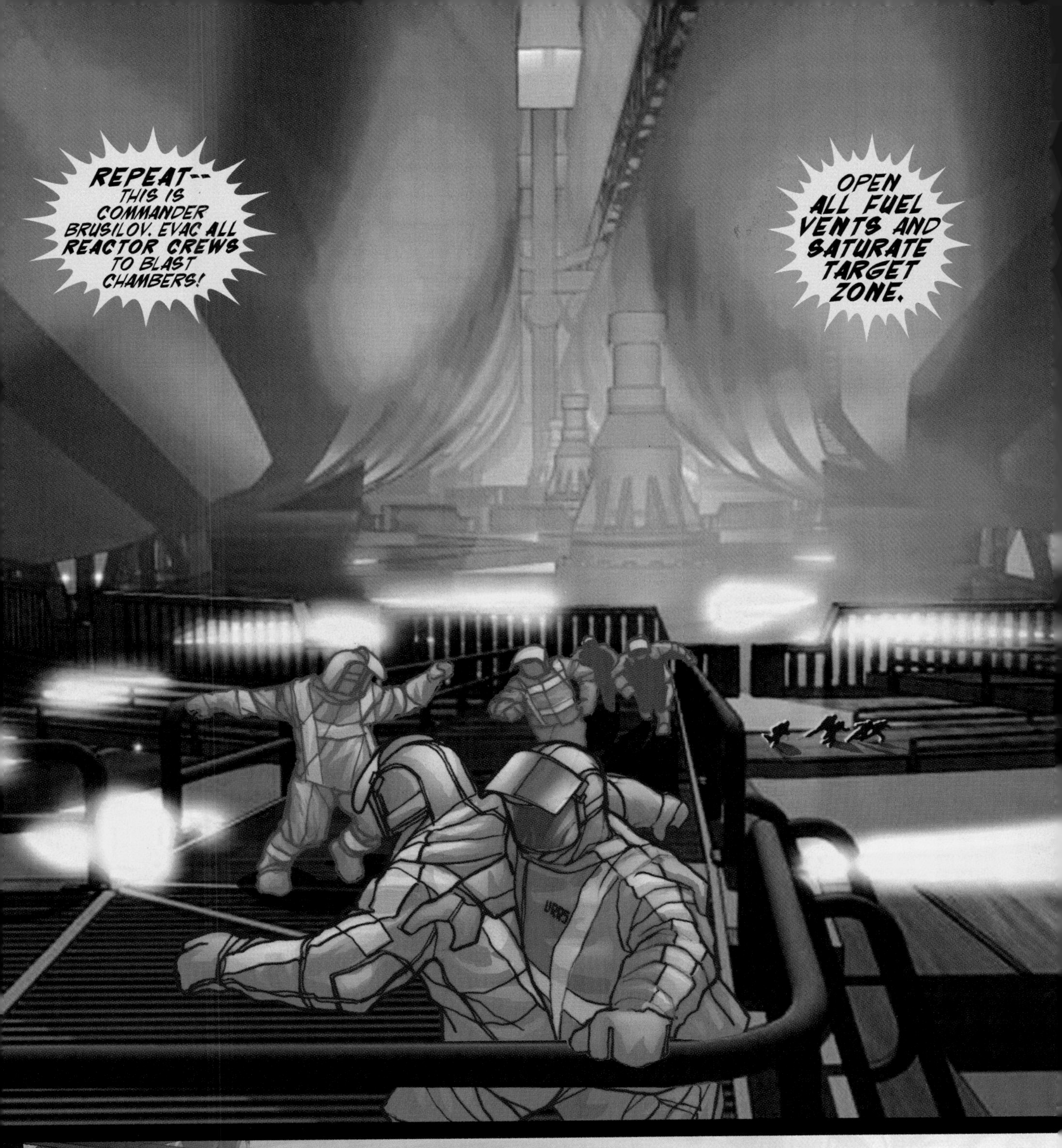
REPEAT-- THIS IS COMMANDER BRUSILOV. EVAC ALL REACTOR CREWS TO BLAST CHAMBERS!
OPEN ALL FUEL VENTS AND SATURATE TARGET ZONE.

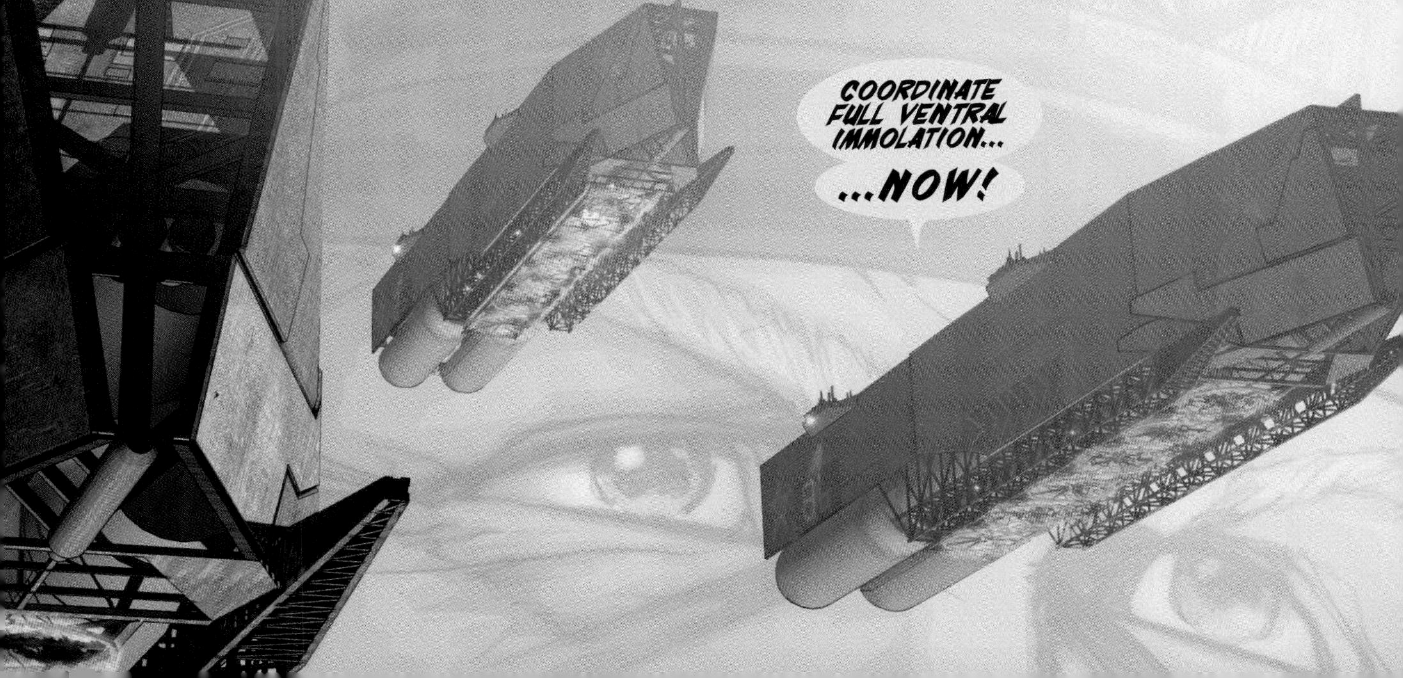
COORDINATE FULL VENTRAL IMMOLATION...
...NOW!

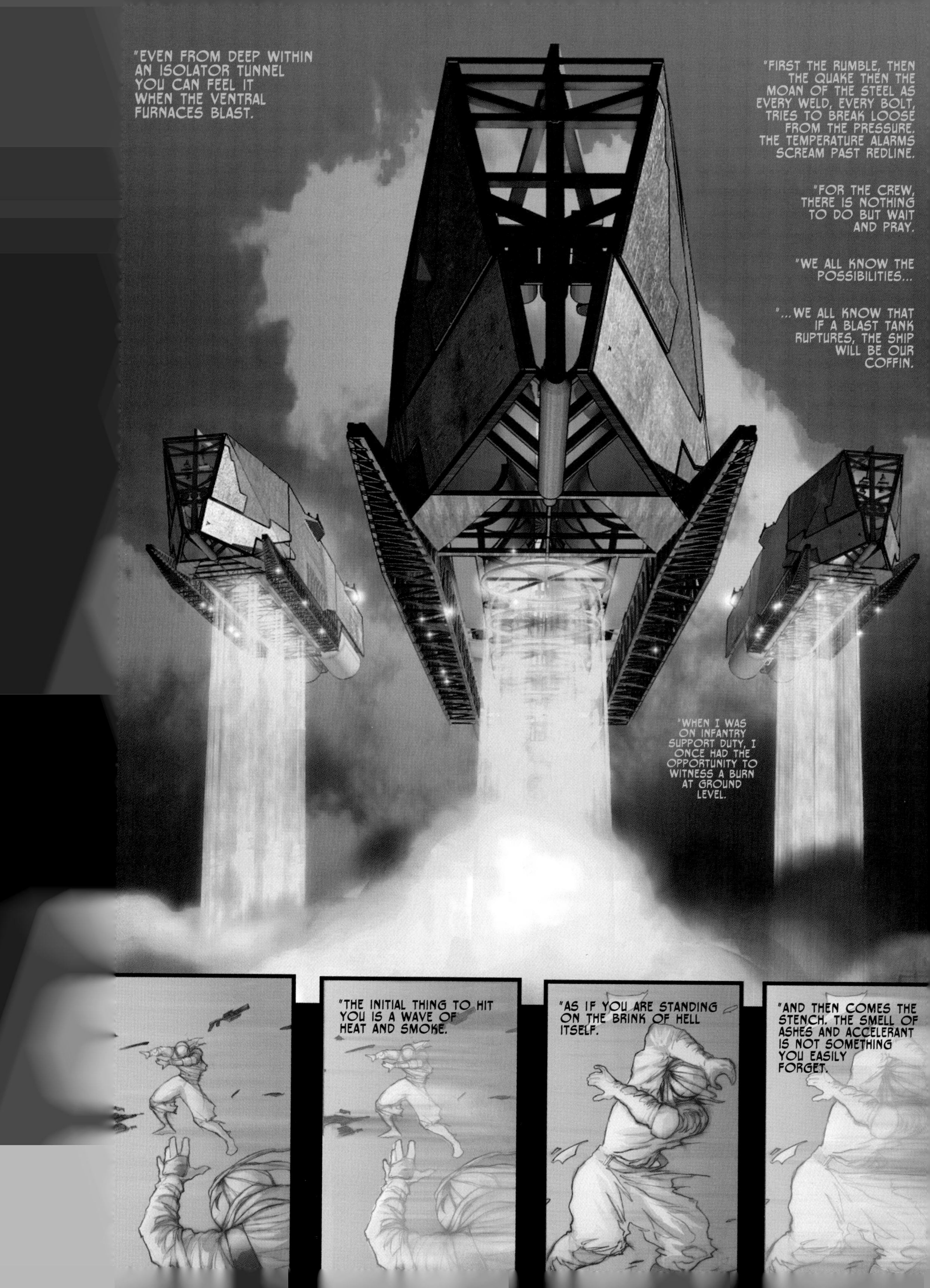
"EVEN FROM DEEP WITHIN AN ISOLATOR TUNNEL YOU CAN FEEL IT WHEN THE VENTRAL FURNACES BLAST.
"FIRST THE RUMBLE, THEN THE QUAKE THEN THE MOAN OF THE STEEL AS EVERY WELD, EVERY BOLT, TRIES TO BREAK LOOSE FROM THE PRESSURE. THE TEMPERATURE ALARMS SCREAM PAST REDLINE.
"FOR THE CREW, THERE IS NOTHING TO DO BUT WAIT AND PRAY.
"WE ALL KNOW THE POSSIBILITIES...
"...WE ALL KNOW THAT IF A BLAST TANK RUPTURES, THE SHIP WILL BE OUR COFFIN.
"WHEN I WAS ON INFANTRY SUPPORT DUTY, I ONCE HAD THE OPPORTUNITY TO WITNESS A BURN AT GROUND LEVEL.
"THE INITIAL THING TO HIT YOU IS A WAVE OF HEAT AND SMOKE.
"AS IF YOU ARE STANDING ON THE BRINK OF HELL ITSELF.
"AND THEN COMES THE STENCH. THE SMELL OF ASHES AND ACCELERANT IS NOT SOMETHING YOU EASILY FORGET.

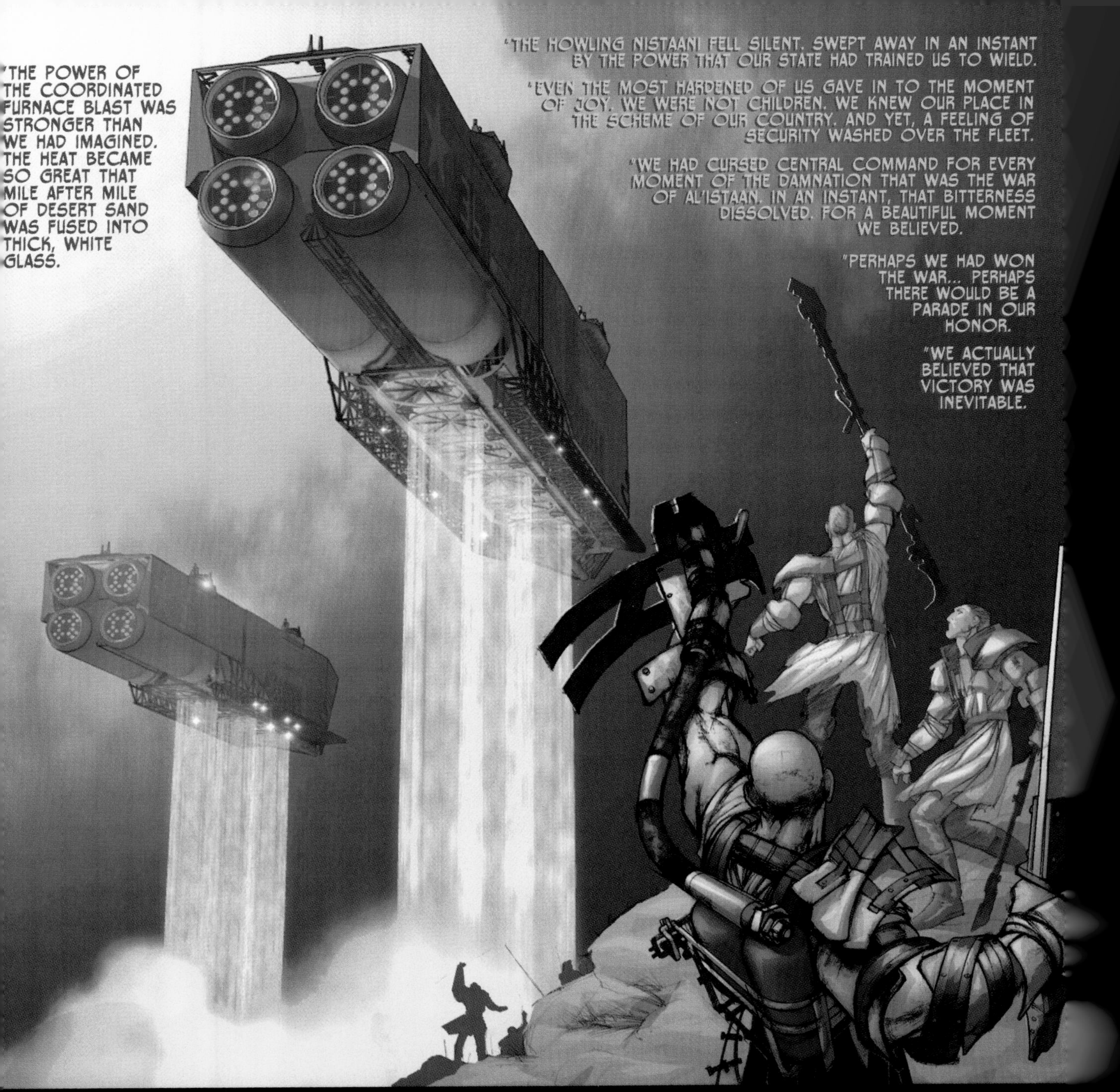
"THE POWER OF THE COORDINATED FURNACE BLAST WAS STRONGER THAN WE HAD IMAGINED. THE HEAT BECAME SO GREAT THAT MILE AFTER MILE OF DESERT SAND WAS FUSED INTO THICK, WHITE GLASS.
"THE HOWLING NISTAANI FELL SILENT. SWEPT AWAY IN AN INSTANT BY THE POWER THAT OUR STATE HAD TRAINED US TO WIELD.
"EVEN THE MOST HARDENED OF US GAVE IN TO THE MOMENT OF JOY. WE WERE NOT CHILDREN. WE KNEW OUR PLACE IN THE SCHEME OF OUR COUNTRY. AND YET, A FEELING OF SECURITY WASHED OVER THE FLEET.
"WE HAD CURSED CENTRAL COMMAND FOR EVERY MOMENT OF THE DAMNATION THAT WAS THE WAR OF AL'ISTAAN. IN AN INSTANT, THAT BITTERNESS DISSOLVED. FOR A BEAUTIFUL MOMENT WE BELIEVED.
"PERHAPS WE HAD WON THE WAR... PERHAPS THERE WOULD BE A PARADE IN OUR HONOR.
"WE ACTUALLY BELIEVED THAT VICTORY WAS INEVITABLE.

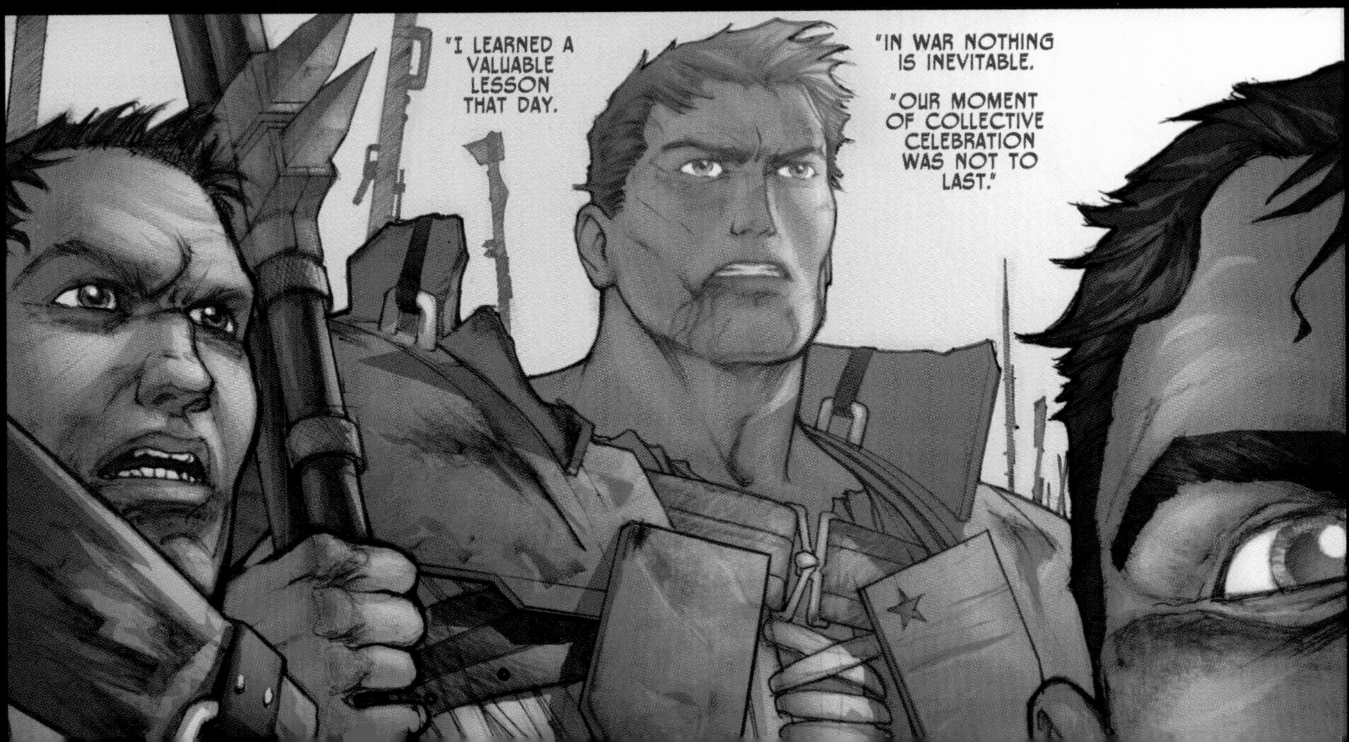
"I LEARNED A VALUABLE LESSON THAT DAY.
"IN WAR NOTHING IS INEVITABLE.
"OUR MOMENT OF COLLECTIVE CELEBRATION WAS NOT TO LAST."

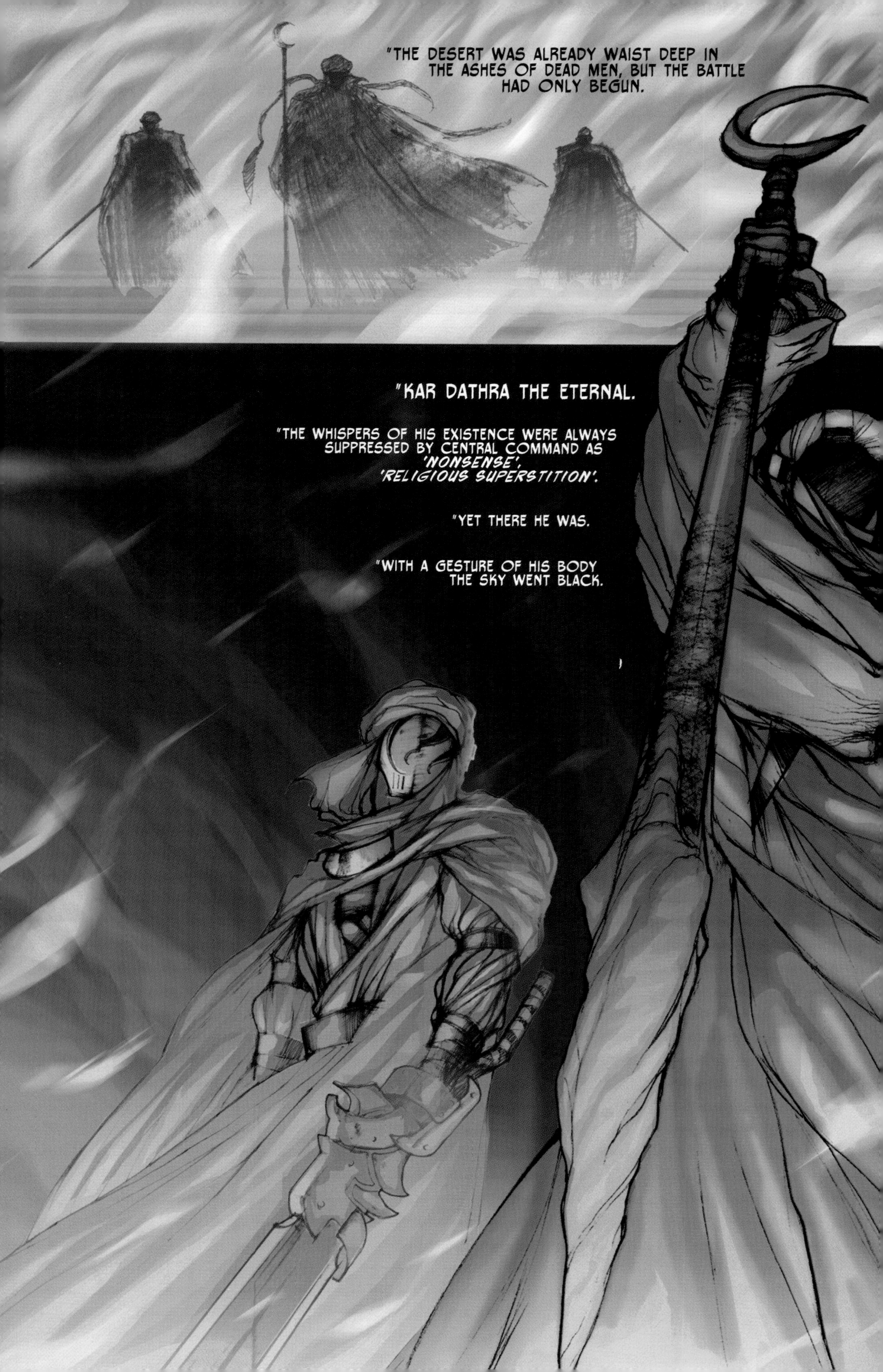
"THE DESERT WAS ALREADY WAIST DEEP IN THE ASHES OF DEAD MEN, BUT THE BATTLE HAD ONLY BEGUN.
"KAR DATHRA THE ETERNAL.
"THE WHISPERS OF HIS EXISTENCE WERE ALWAYS SUPPRESSED BY CENTRAL COMMAND AS 'NONSENSE', 'RELIGIOUS SUPERSTITION'.
"YET THERE HE WAS.
"WITH A GESTURE OF HIS BODY THE SKY WENT BLACK.

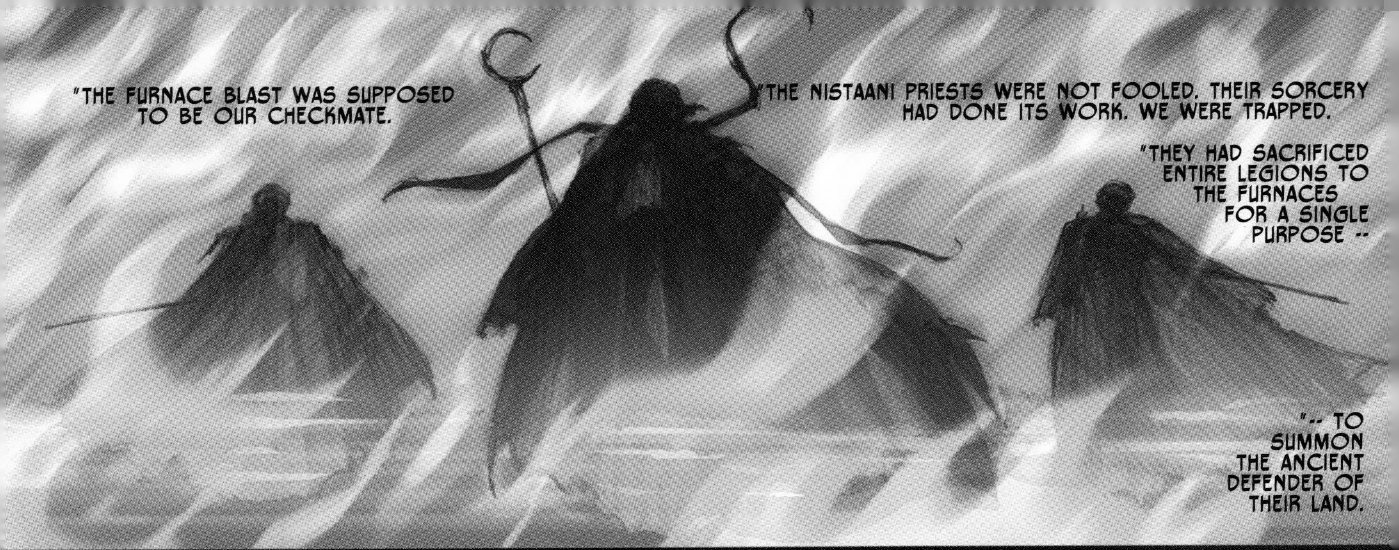
"THE FURNACE BLAST WAS SUPPOSED TO BE OUR CHECKMATE.
"THE NISTAANI PRIESTS WERE NOT FOOLED. THEIR SORCERY HAD DONE ITS WORK. WE WERE TRAPPED.
"THEY HAD SACRIFICED ENTIRE LEGIONS TO THE FURNACES FOR A SINGLE PURPOSE --
"-- TO SUMMON THE ANCIENT DEFENDER OF THEIR LAND.

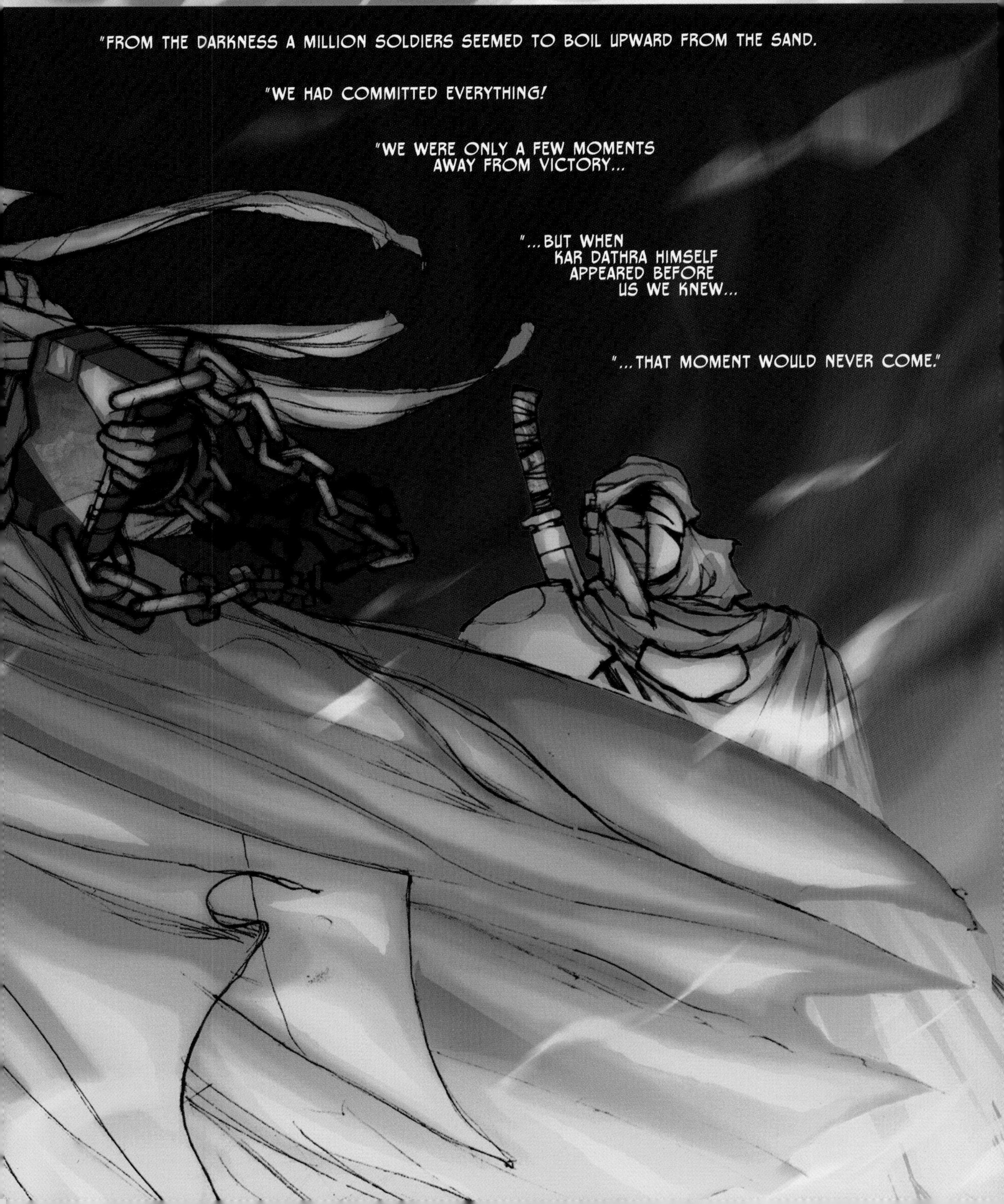
"FROM THE DARKNESS A MILLION SOLDIERS SEEMED TO BOIL UPWARD FROM THE SAND.
"WE HAD COMMITTED EVERYTHING!
"WE WERE ONLY A FEW MOMENTS AWAY FROM VICTORY...
"...BUT WHEN KAR DATHRA HIMSELF APPEARED BEFORE US WE KNEW...
"...THAT MOMENT WOULD NEVER COME."

BOOK TWO

WWW.THEREDSTAR.COM/TPB1/BOOK2.HTM

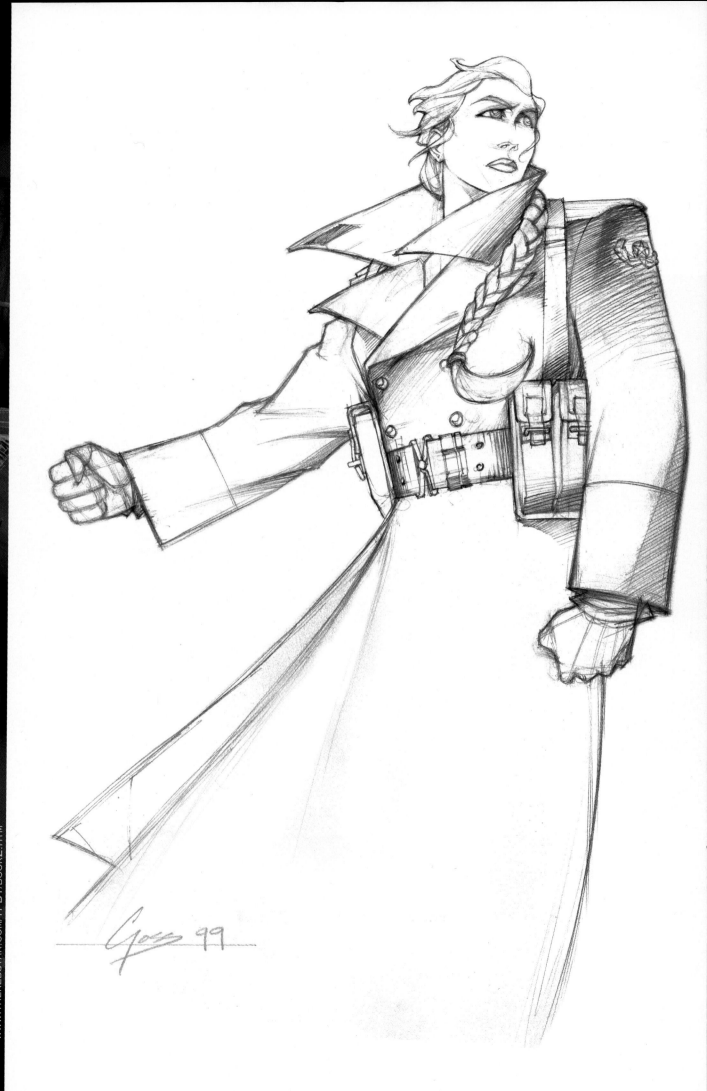

Goss 99

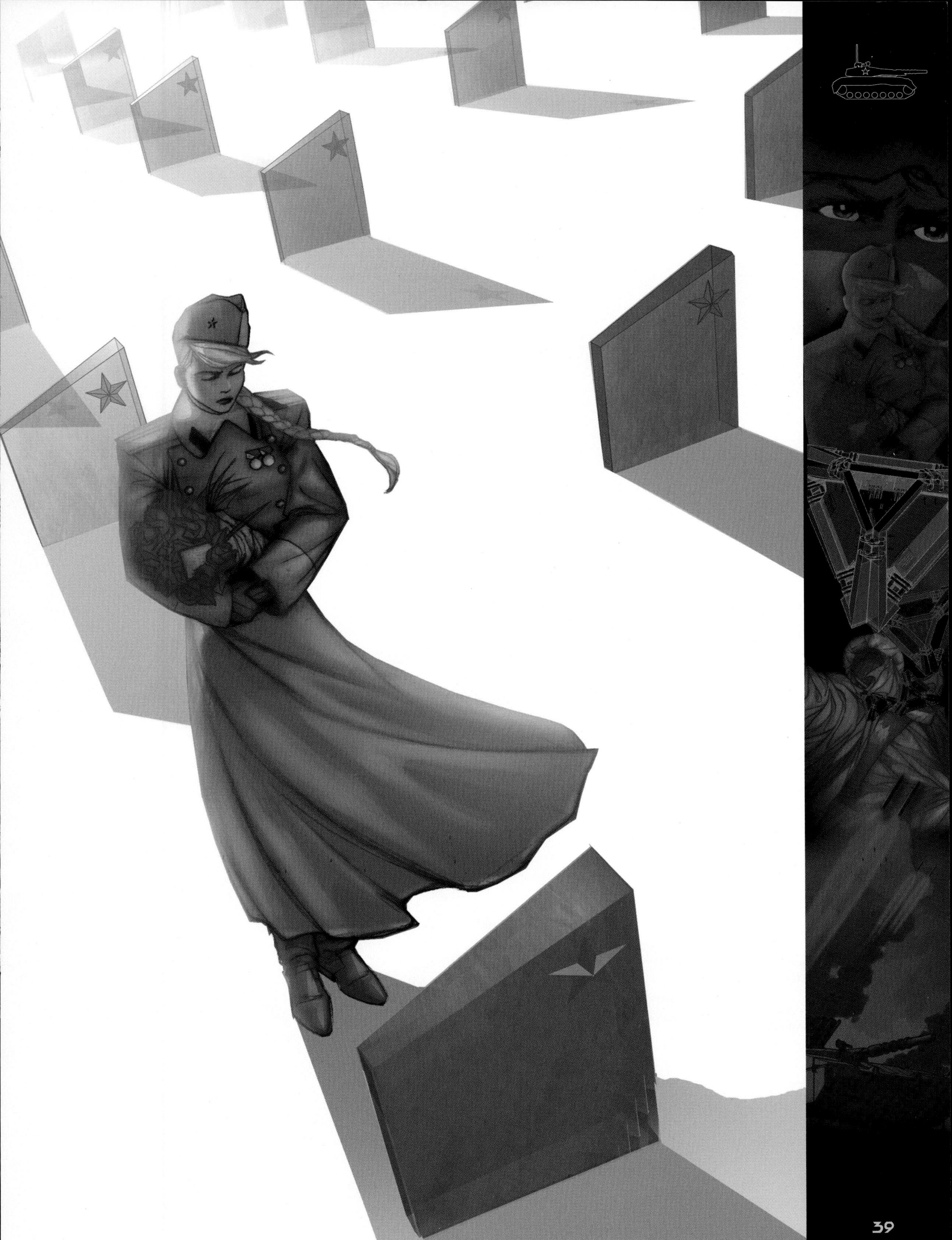

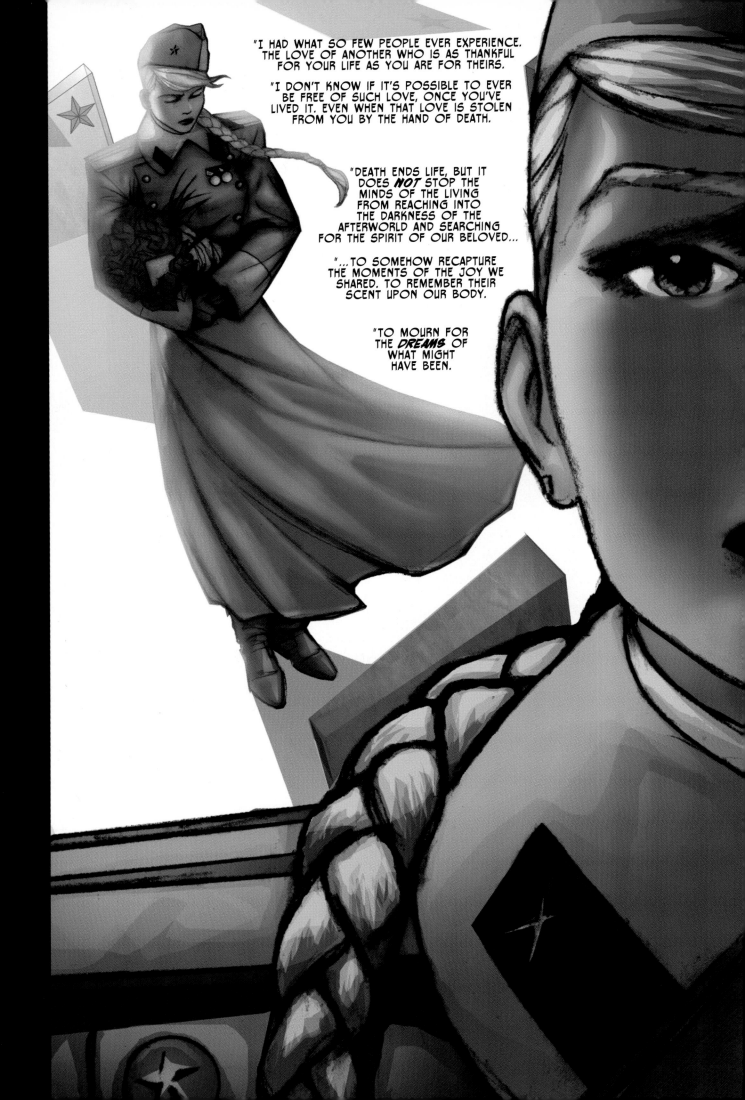

"I HAD WHAT SO FEW PEOPLE EVER EXPERIENCE. THE LOVE OF ANOTHER WHO IS AS THANKFUL FOR YOUR LIFE AS YOU ARE FOR THEIRS.

"I DON'T KNOW IF IT'S POSSIBLE TO EVER BE FREE OF SUCH LOVE, ONCE YOU'VE LIVED IT. EVEN WHEN THAT LOVE IS STOLEN FROM YOU BY THE HAND OF DEATH.

"DEATH ENDS LIFE, BUT IT DOES *NOT* STOP THE MINDS OF THE LIVING FROM REACHING INTO THE DARKNESS OF THE AFTERWORLD AND SEARCHING FOR THE SPIRIT OF OUR BELOVED...

"...TO SOMEHOW RECAPTURE THE MOMENTS OF THE JOY WE SHARED. TO REMEMBER THEIR SCENT UPON OUR BODY.

"TO MOURN FOR THE *DREAMS* OF WHAT MIGHT HAVE BEEN.

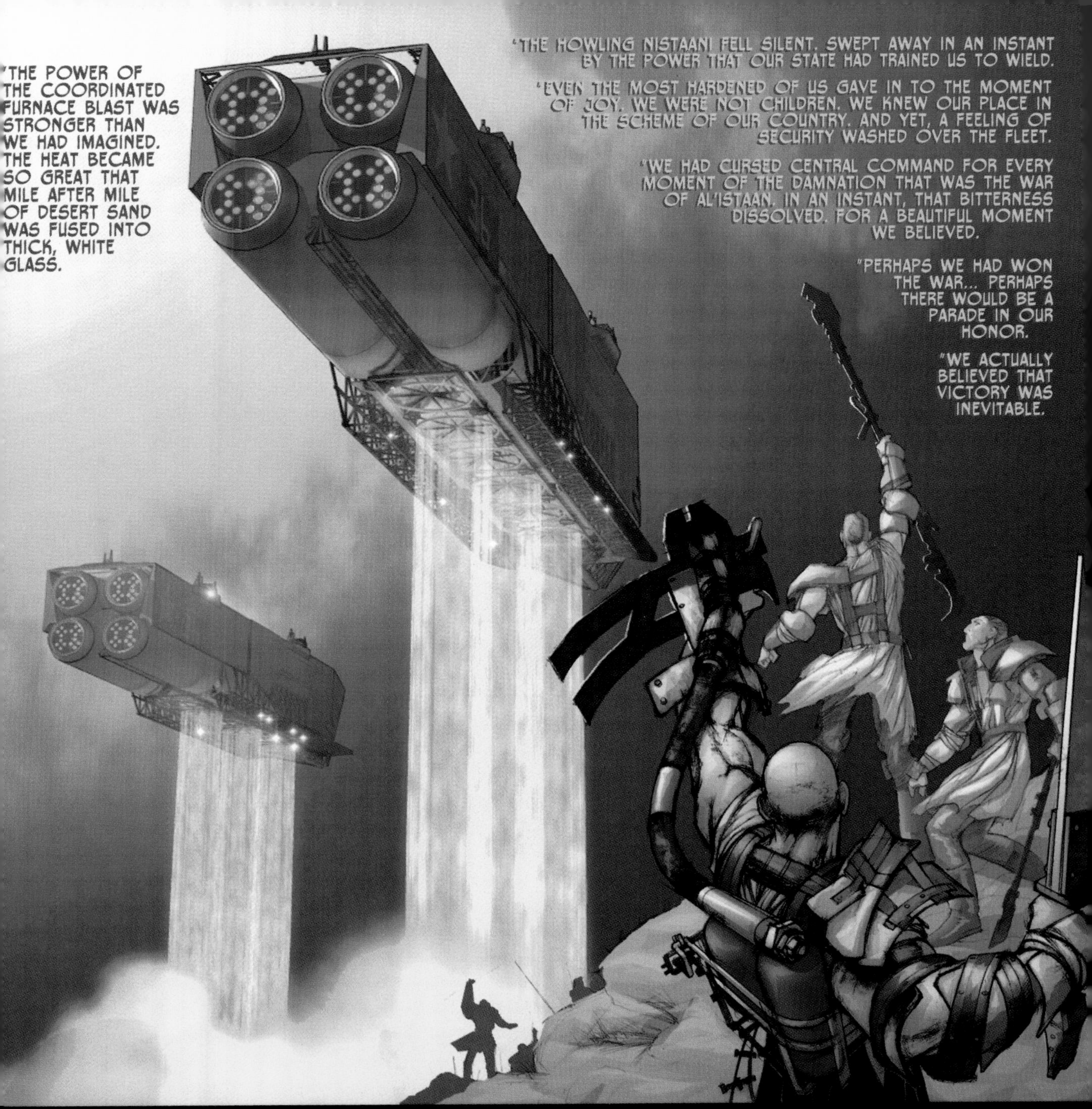
"THE POWER OF THE COORDINATED FURNACE BLAST WAS STRONGER THAN WE HAD IMAGINED. THE HEAT BECAME SO GREAT THAT MILE AFTER MILE OF DESERT SAND WAS FUSED INTO THICK, WHITE GLASS.
"THE HOWLING NISTAANI FELL SILENT. SWEPT AWAY IN AN INSTANT BY THE POWER THAT OUR STATE HAD TRAINED US TO WIELD.
"EVEN THE MOST HARDENED OF US GAVE IN TO THE MOMENT OF JOY. WE WERE NOT CHILDREN. WE KNEW OUR PLACE IN THE SCHEME OF OUR COUNTRY. AND YET, A FEELING OF SECURITY WASHED OVER THE FLEET.
"WE HAD CURSED CENTRAL COMMAND FOR EVERY MOMENT OF THE DAMNATION THAT WAS THE WAR OF AL'ISTAAN. IN AN INSTANT, THAT BITTERNESS DISSOLVED. FOR A BEAUTIFUL MOMENT WE BELIEVED.
"PERHAPS WE HAD WON THE WAR... PERHAPS THERE WOULD BE A PARADE IN OUR HONOR.
"WE ACTUALLY BELIEVED THAT VICTORY WAS INEVITABLE.

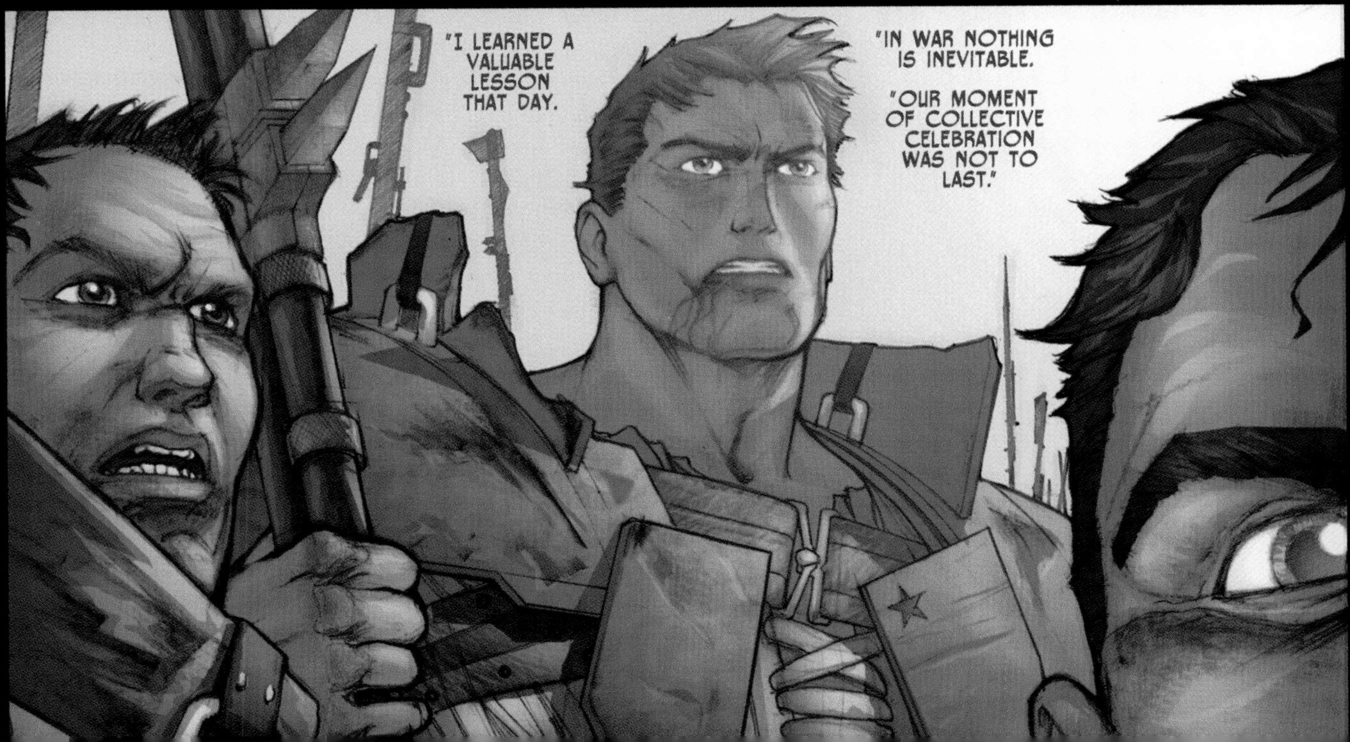
"I LEARNED A VALUABLE LESSON THAT DAY.
"IN WAR NOTHING IS INEVITABLE.
"OUR MOMENT OF COLLECTIVE CELEBRATION WAS NOT TO LAST."

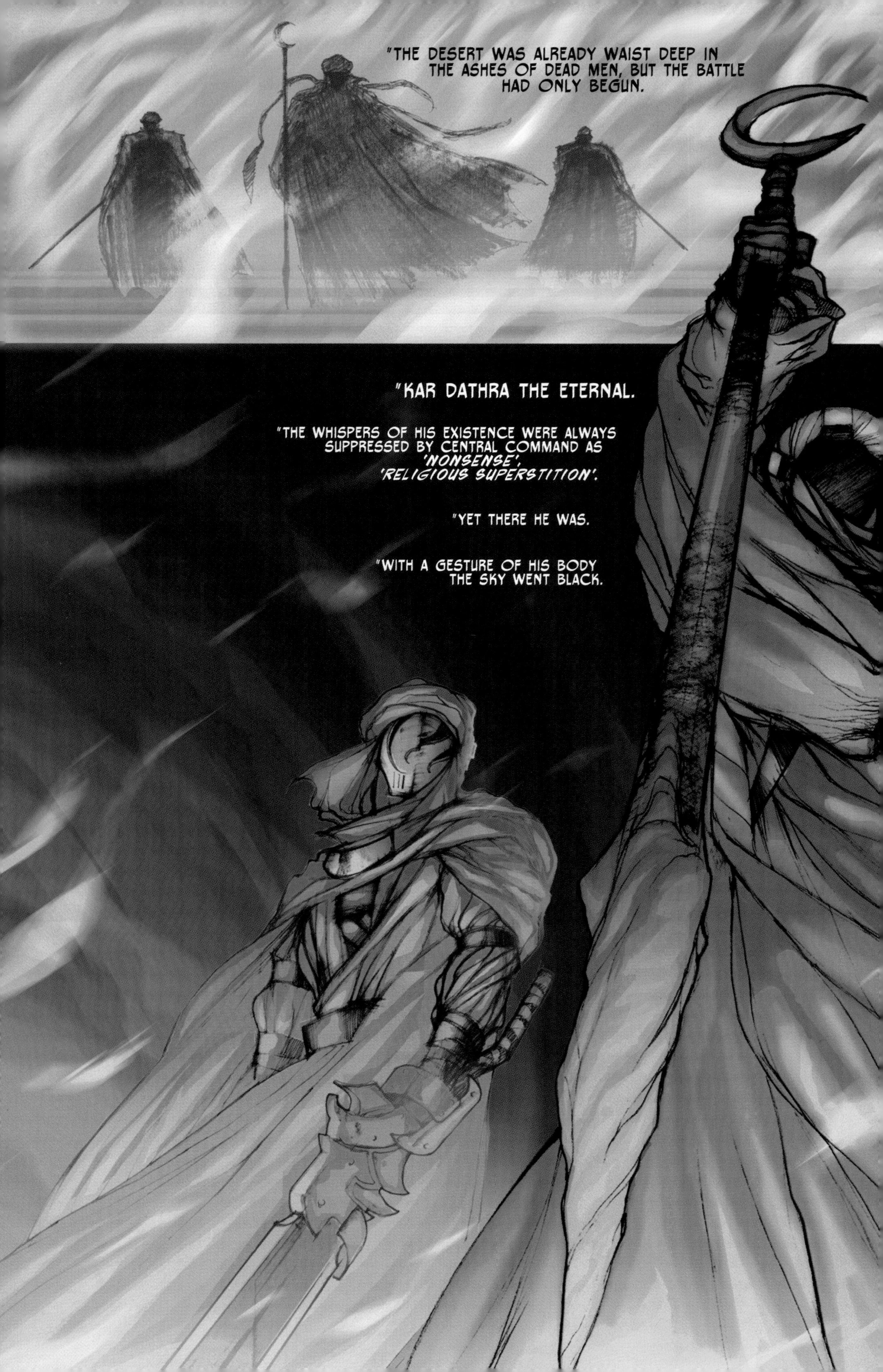
"THE DESERT WAS ALREADY WAIST DEEP IN THE ASHES OF DEAD MEN, BUT THE BATTLE HAD ONLY BEGUN.
"KAR DATHRA THE ETERNAL.
"THE WHISPERS OF HIS EXISTENCE WERE ALWAYS SUPPRESSED BY CENTRAL COMMAND AS 'NONSENSE', 'RELIGIOUS SUPERSTITION'.
"YET THERE HE WAS.
"WITH A GESTURE OF HIS BODY THE SKY WENT BLACK.

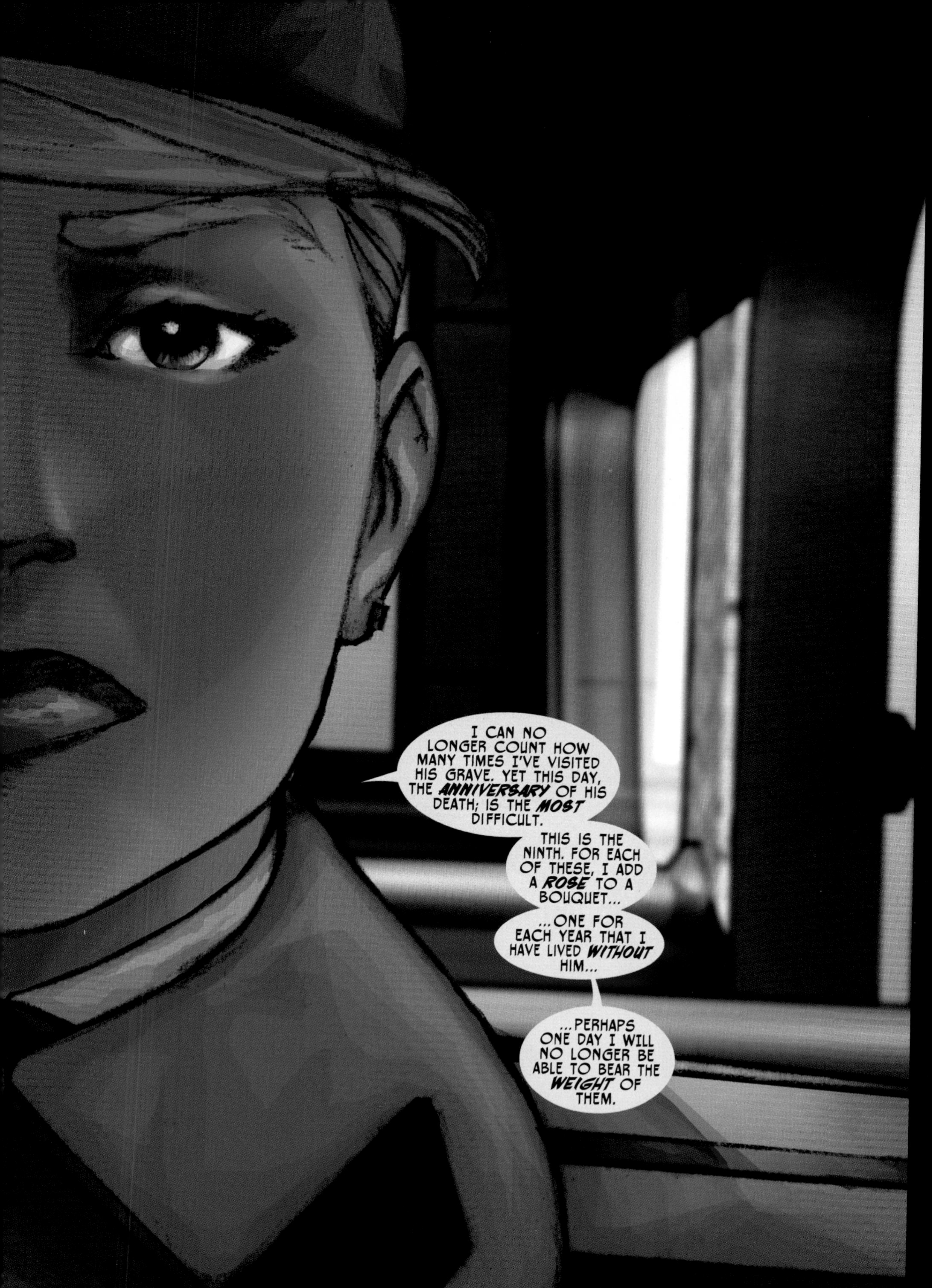
I CAN NO LONGER COUNT HOW MANY TIMES I'VE VISITED HIS GRAVE. YET THIS DAY, THE ANNIVERSARY OF HIS DEATH; IS THE MOST DIFFICULT.
THIS IS THE NINTH. FOR EACH OF THESE, I ADD A ROSE TO A BOUQUET...
...ONE FOR EACH YEAR THAT I HAVE LIVED WITHOUT HIM...
...PERHAPS ONE DAY I WILL NO LONGER BE ABLE TO BEAR THE WEIGHT OF THEM.

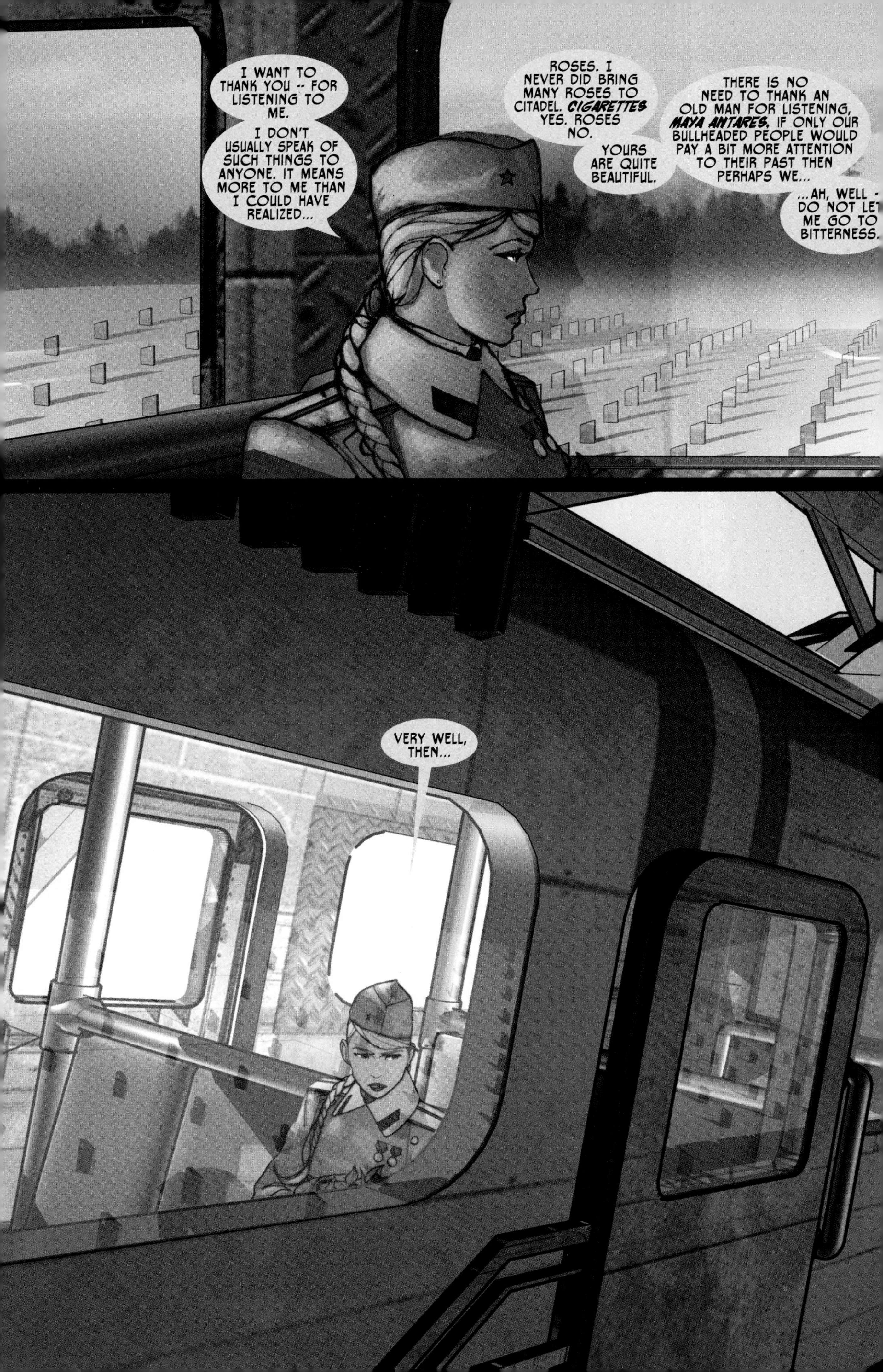
I WANT TO THANK YOU -- FOR LISTENING TO ME.
I DON'T USUALLY SPEAK OF SUCH THINGS TO ANYONE. IT MEANS MORE TO ME THAN I COULD HAVE REALIZED...
ROSES. I NEVER DID BRING MANY ROSES TO CITADEL. CIGARETTES YES. ROSES NO.
YOURS ARE QUITE BEAUTIFUL.
THERE IS NO NEED TO THANK AN OLD MAN FOR LISTENING, MAYA ANTARES. IF ONLY OUR BULLHEADED PEOPLE WOULD PAY A BIT MORE ATTENTION TO THEIR PAST THEN PERHAPS WE...
...AH, WELL - DO NOT LET ME GO TO BITTERNESS.
VERY WELL, THEN...

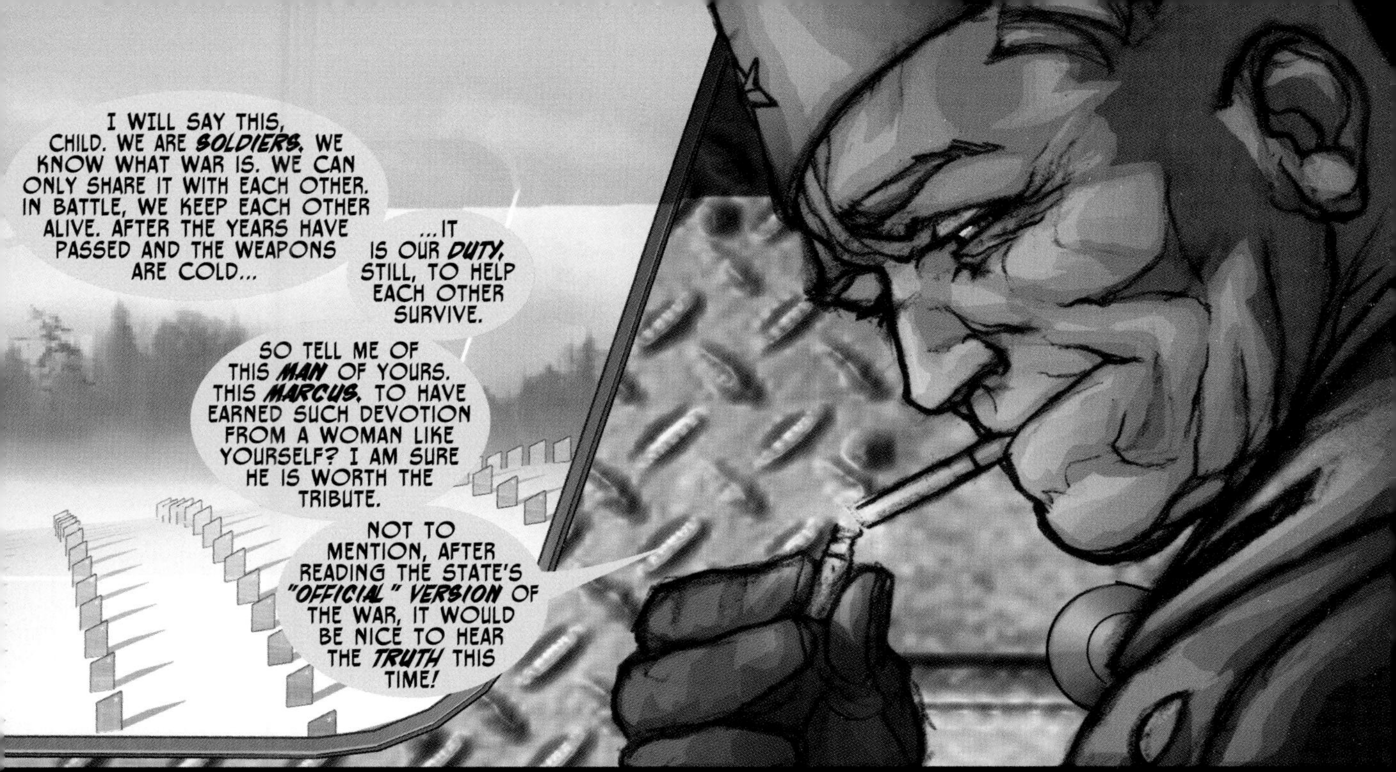
I WILL SAY THIS, CHILD. WE ARE SOLDIERS. WE KNOW WHAT WAR IS. WE CAN ONLY SHARE IT WITH EACH OTHER. IN BATTLE, WE KEEP EACH OTHER ALIVE. AFTER THE YEARS HAVE PASSED AND THE WEAPONS ARE COLD...
...IT IS OUR DUTY, STILL, TO HELP EACH OTHER SURVIVE.
SO TELL ME OF THIS MAN OF YOURS. THIS MARCUS. TO HAVE EARNED SUCH DEVOTION FROM A WOMAN LIKE YOURSELF? I AM SURE HE IS WORTH THE TRIBUTE.
NOT TO MENTION, AFTER READING THE STATE'S "OFFICIAL" VERSION OF THE WAR, IT WOULD BE NICE TO HEAR THE TRUTH THIS TIME!

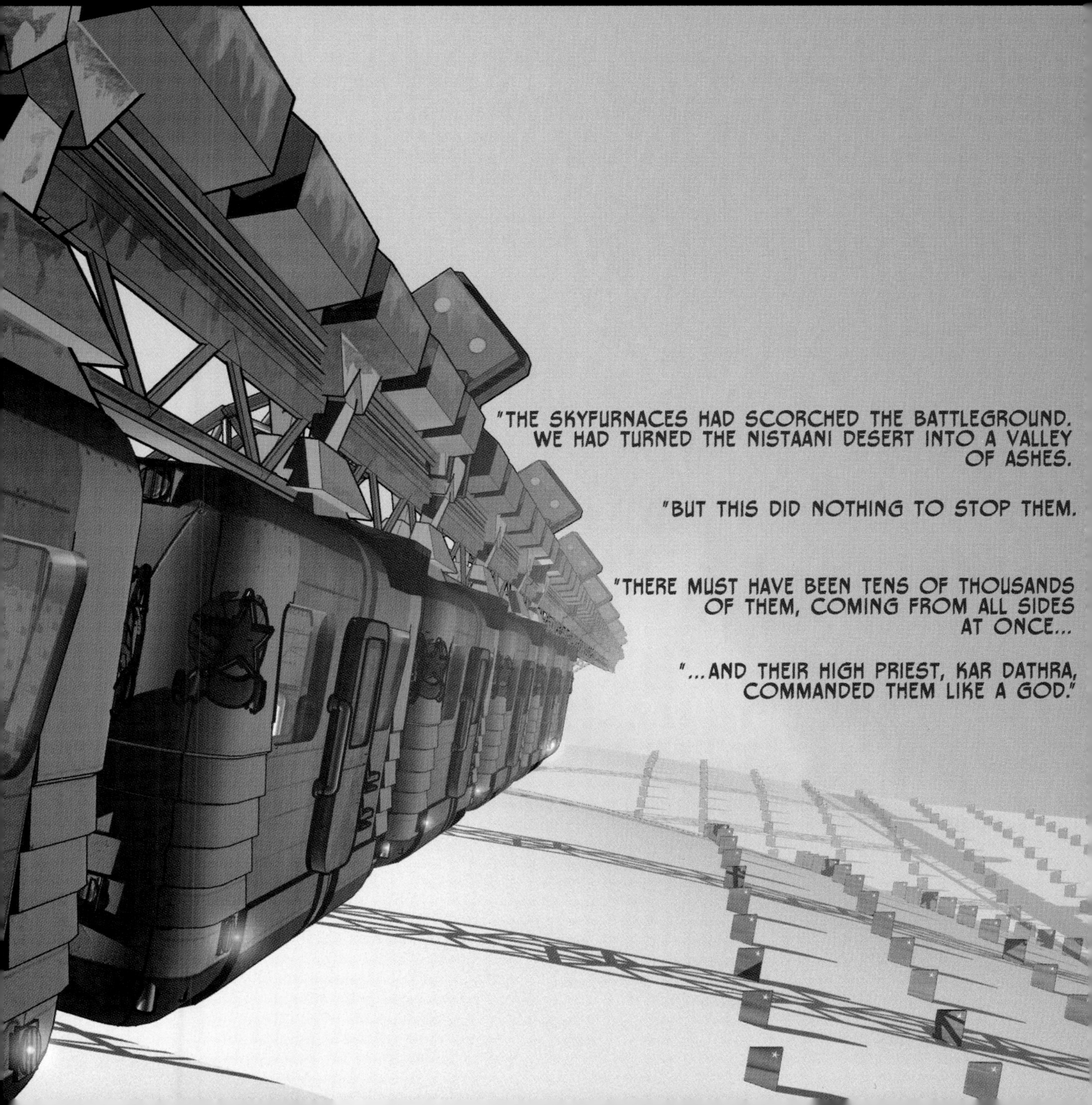
"THE SKYFURNACES HAD SCORCHED THE BATTLEGROUND. WE HAD TURNED THE NISTAANI DESERT INTO A VALLEY OF ASHES.
"BUT THIS DID NOTHING TO STOP THEM.
"THERE MUST HAVE BEEN TENS OF THOUSANDS OF THEM, COMING FROM ALL SIDES AT ONCE...
"...AND THEIR HIGH PRIEST, KAR DATHRA, COMMANDED THEM LIKE A GOD."

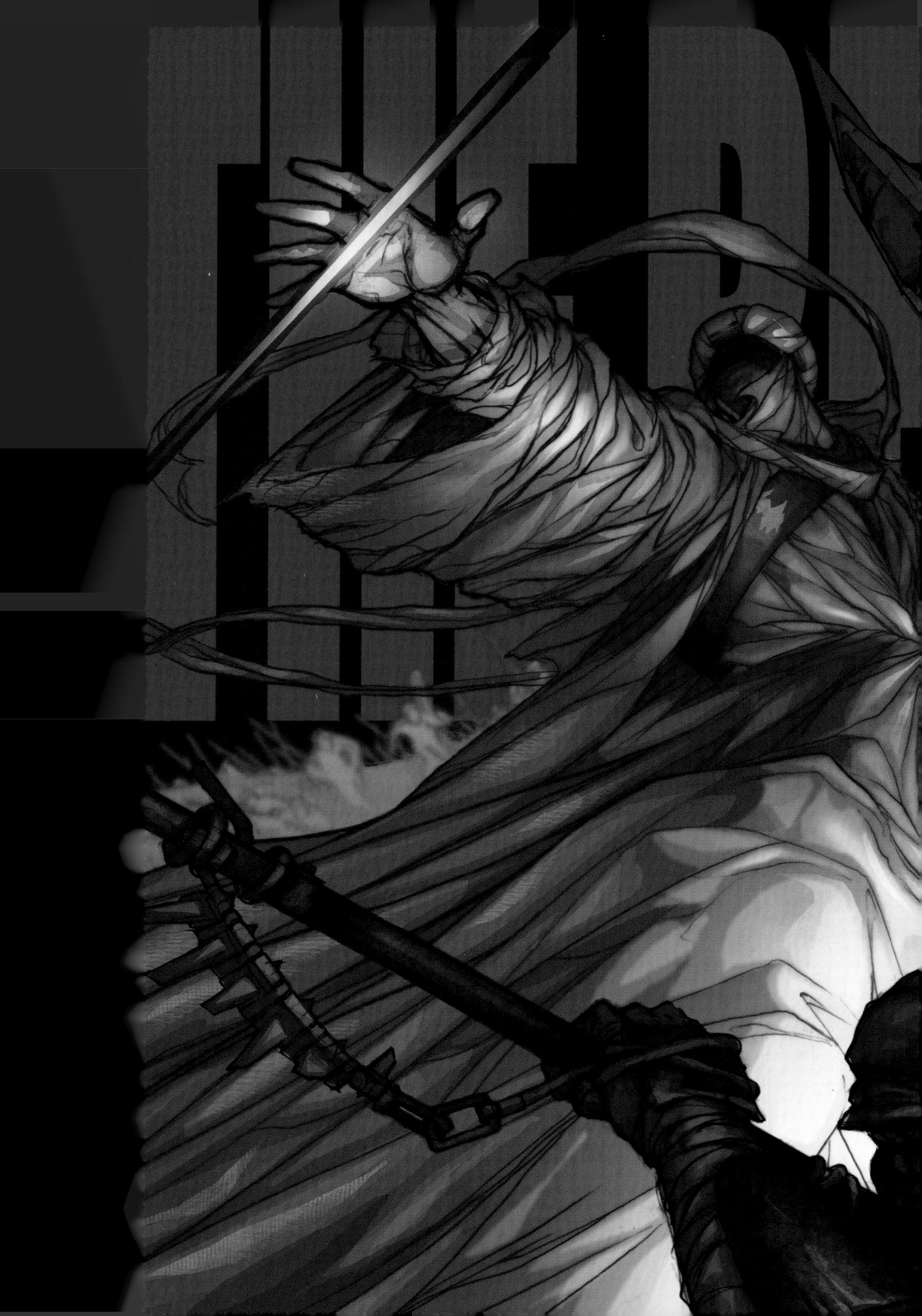

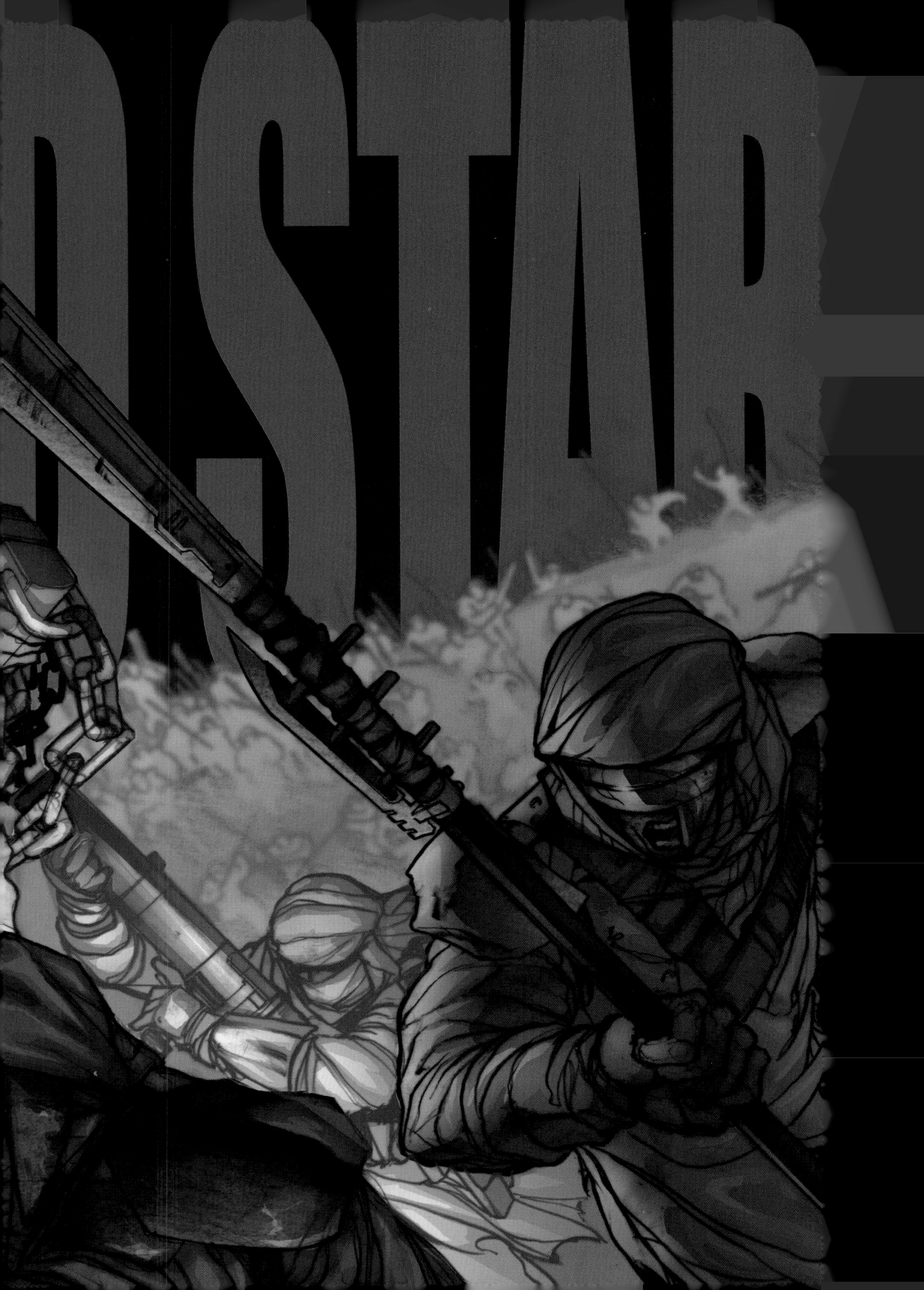

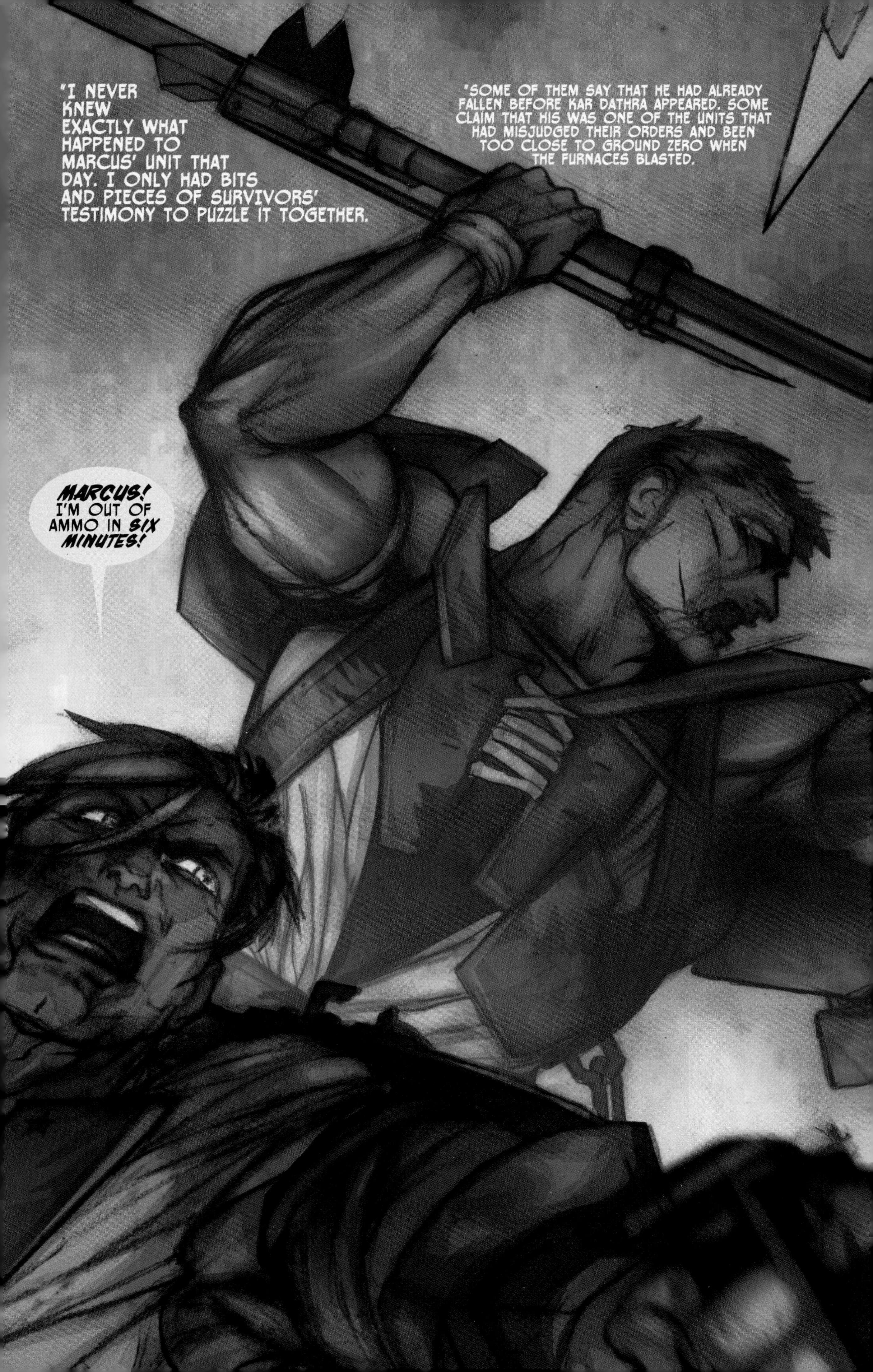
"I NEVER KNEW EXACTLY WHAT HAPPENED TO MARCUS' UNIT THAT DAY. I ONLY HAD BITS AND PIECES OF SURVIVORS' TESTIMONY TO PUZZLE IT TOGETHER.
"SOME OF THEM SAY THAT HE HAD ALREADY FALLEN BEFORE KAR DATHRA APPEARED. SOME CLAIM THAT HIS WAS ONE OF THE UNITS THAT HAD MISJUDGED THEIR ORDERS AND BEEN TOO CLOSE TO GROUND ZERO WHEN THE FURNACES BLASTED.
MARCUS! I'M OUT OF AMMO IN SIX MINUTES!

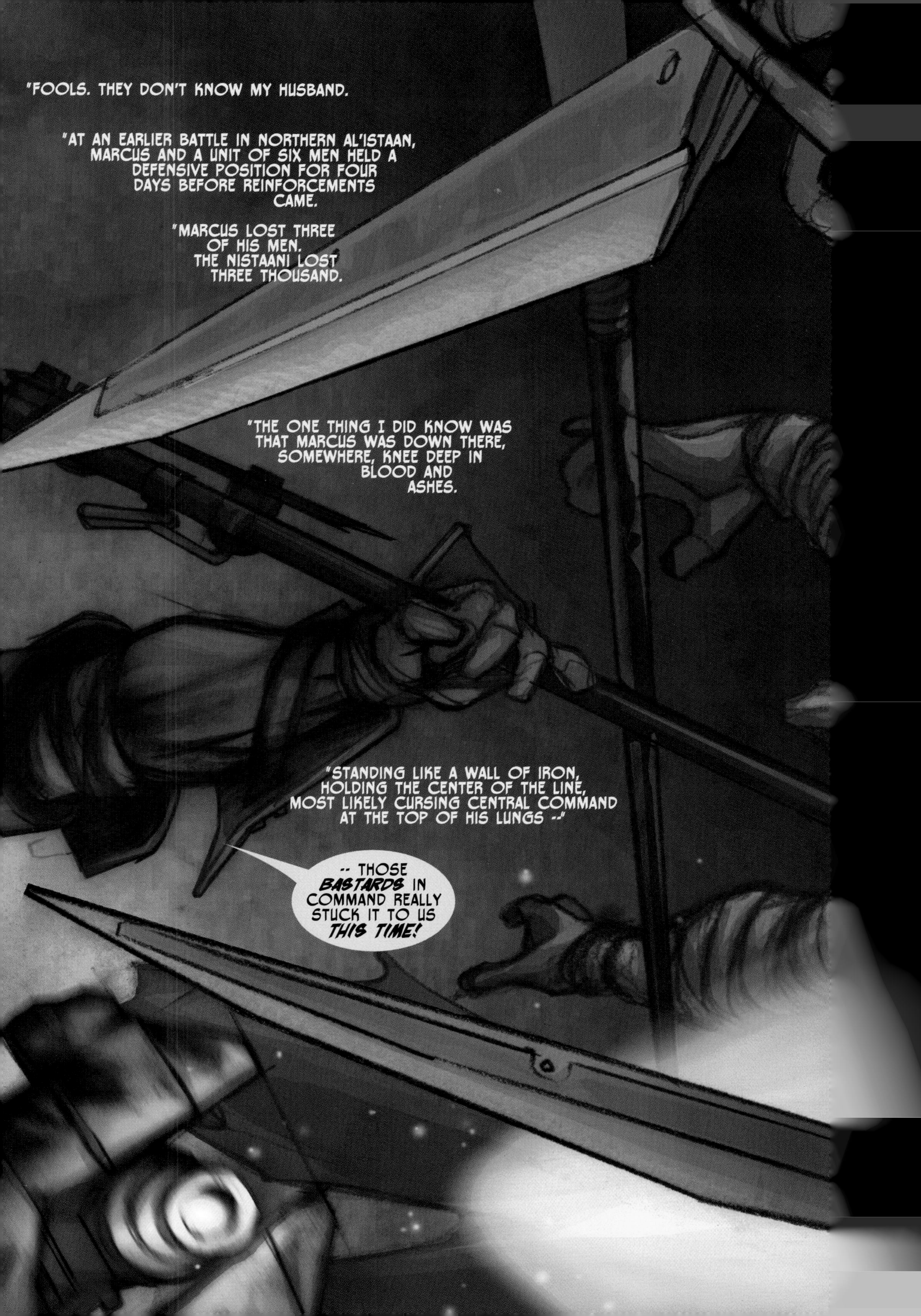
"FOOLS. THEY DON'T KNOW MY HUSBAND.
"AT AN EARLIER BATTLE IN NORTHERN AL'ISTAAN, MARCUS AND A UNIT OF SIX MEN HELD A DEFENSIVE POSITION FOR FOUR DAYS BEFORE REINFORCEMENTS CAME.
"MARCUS LOST THREE OF HIS MEN. THE NISTAANI LOST THREE THOUSAND.
"THE ONE THING I DID KNOW WAS THAT MARCUS WAS DOWN THERE, SOMEWHERE, KNEE DEEP IN BLOOD AND ASHES.
"STANDING LIKE A WALL OF IRON, HOLDING THE CENTER OF THE LINE, MOST LIKELY CURSING CENTRAL COMMAND AT THE TOP OF HIS LUNGS --"
-- THOSE *BASTARDS* IN COMMAND REALLY STUCK IT TO US *THIS TIME!*

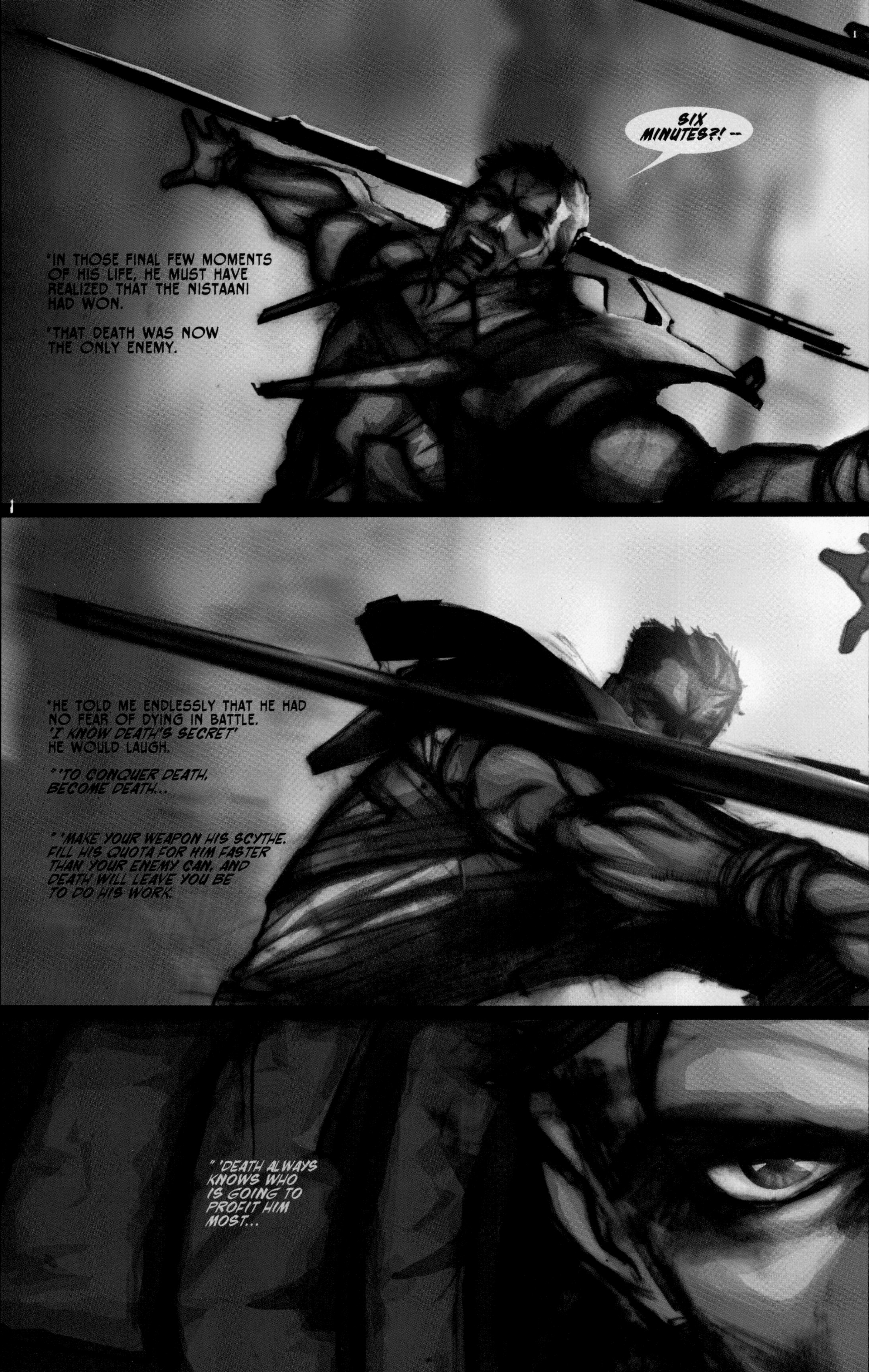
SIX MINUTES?! --
"IN THOSE FINAL FEW MOMENTS OF HIS LIFE, HE MUST HAVE REALIZED THAT THE NISTAANI HAD WON.
"THAT DEATH WAS NOW THE ONLY ENEMY.
"HE TOLD ME ENDLESSLY THAT HE HAD NO FEAR OF DYING IN BATTLE. 'I KNOW DEATH'S SECRET' HE WOULD LAUGH.
" 'TO CONQUER DEATH, BECOME DEATH...
" 'MAKE YOUR WEAPON HIS SCYTHE. FILL HIS QUOTA FOR HIM FASTER THAN YOUR ENEMY CAN, AND DEATH WILL LEAVE YOU BE TO DO HIS WORK.
" 'DEATH ALWAYS KNOWS WHO IS GOING TO PROFIT HIM MOST...

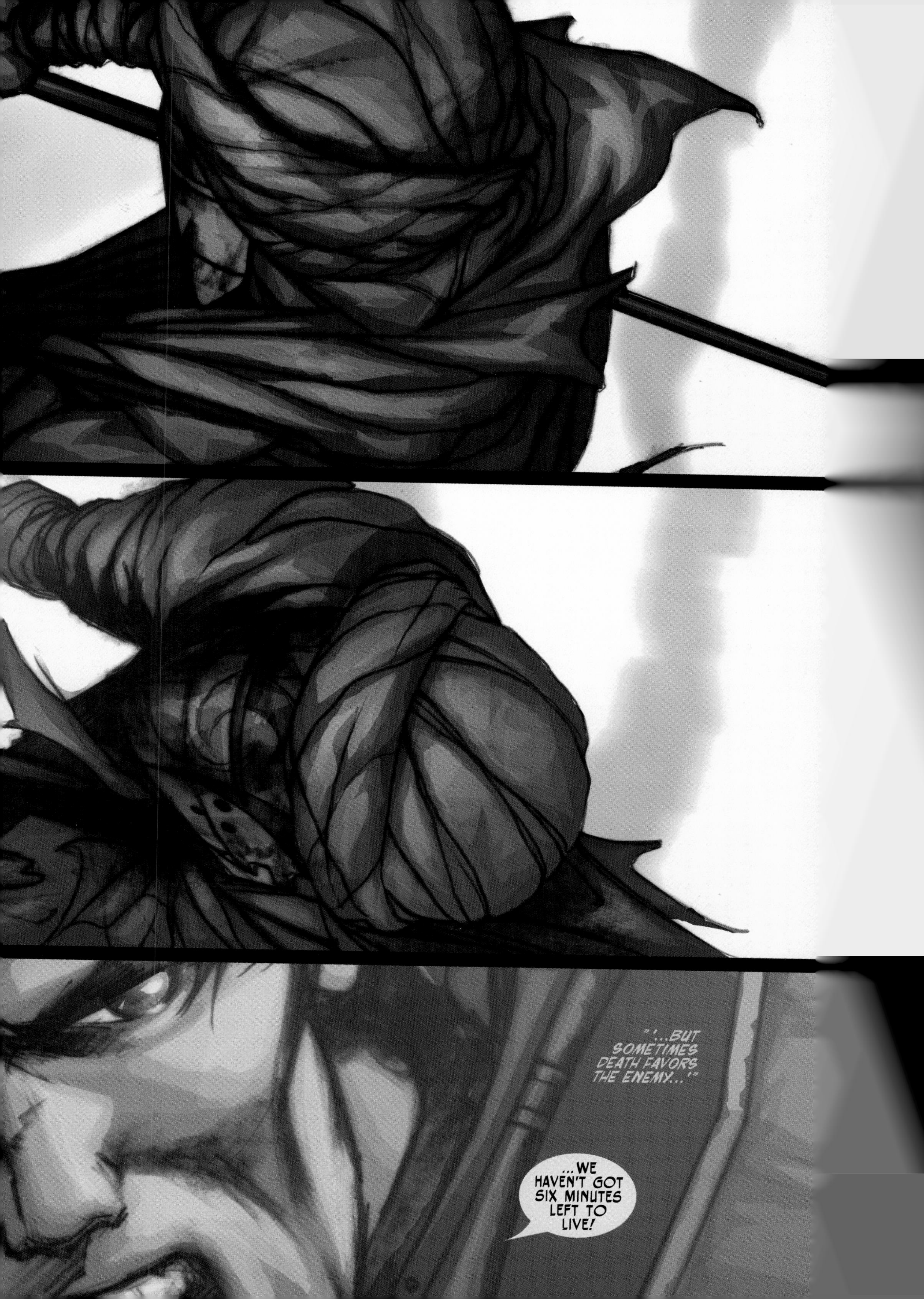
"'...BUT SOMETIMES DEATH FAVORS THE ENEMY...'"
...WE HAVEN'T GOT SIX MINUTES LEFT TO LIVE!

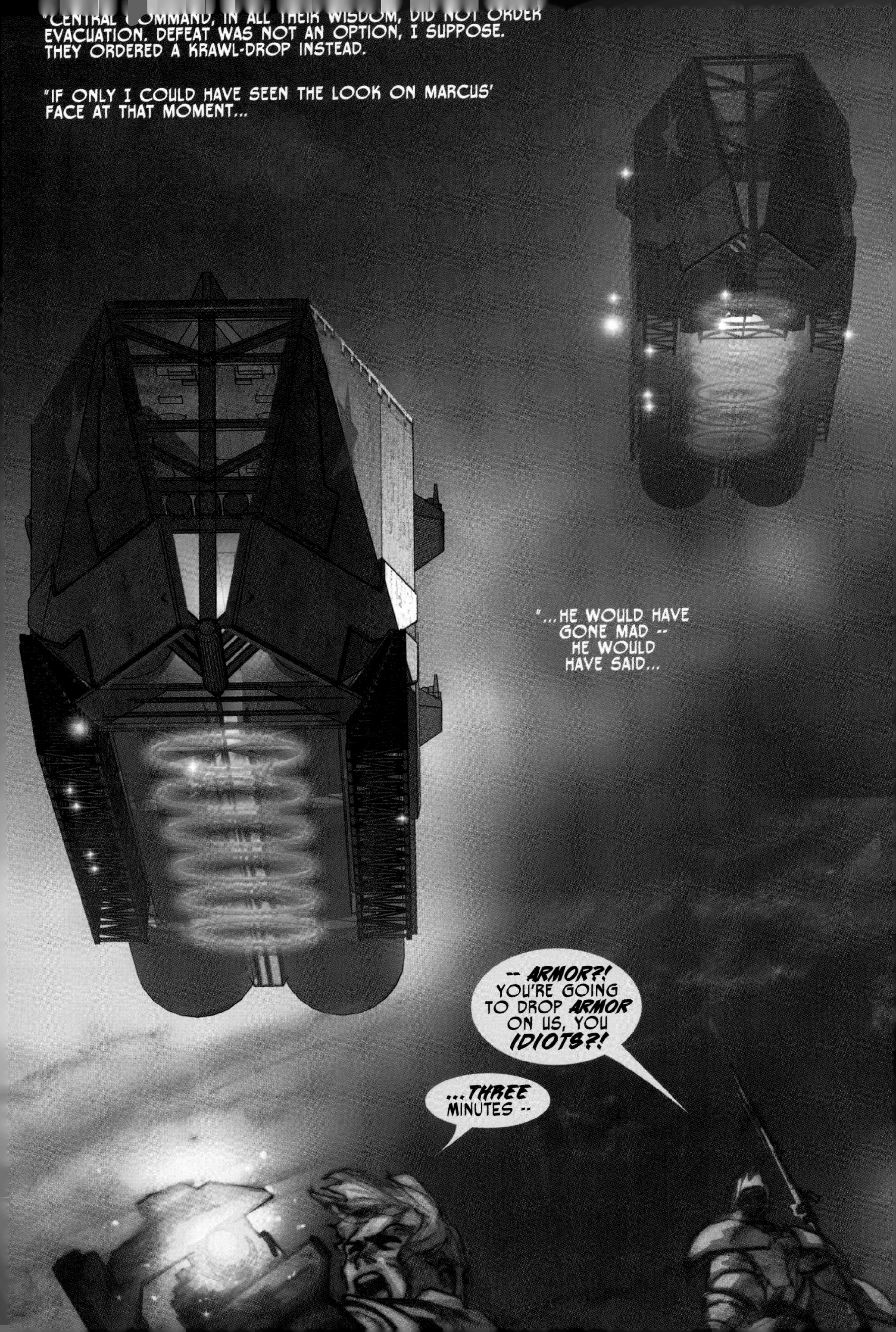
"CENTRAL COMMAND, IN ALL THEIR WISDOM, DID NOT ORDER EVACUATION. DEFEAT WAS NOT AN OPTION, I SUPPOSE. THEY ORDERED A KRAWL-DROP INSTEAD.
"IF ONLY I COULD HAVE SEEN THE LOOK ON MARCUS' FACE AT THAT MOMENT...
"...HE WOULD HAVE GONE MAD -- HE WOULD HAVE SAID...
-- ARMOR?! YOU'RE GOING TO DROP ARMOR ON US, YOU IDIOTS?!
...THREE MINUTES --

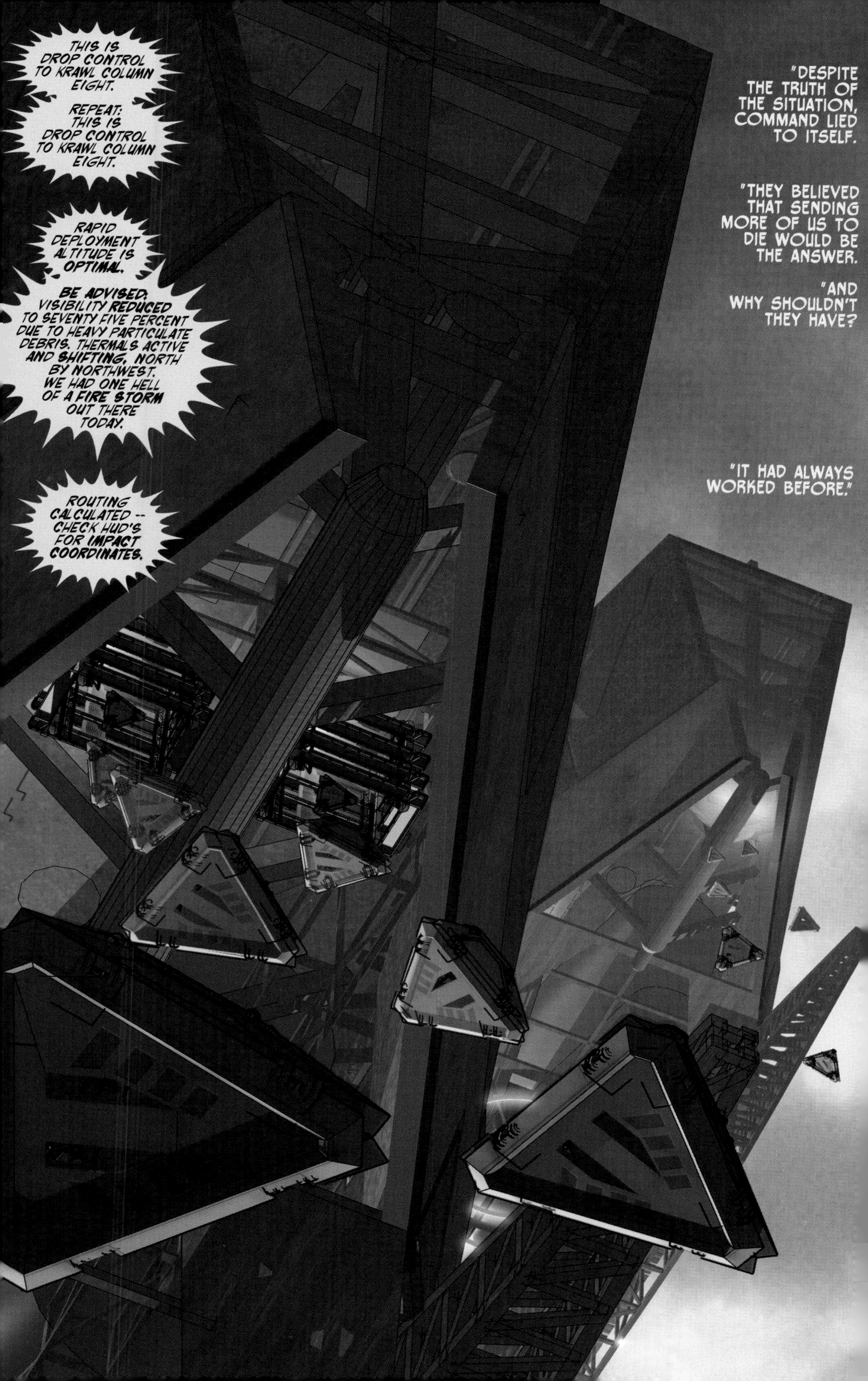
THIS IS DROP CONTROL TO KRAWL COLUMN EIGHT.
REPEAT: THIS IS DROP CONTROL TO KRAWL COLUMN EIGHT.
RAPID DEPLOYMENT ALTITUDE IS OPTIMAL.
BE ADVISED: VISIBILITY REDUCED TO SEVENTY FIVE PERCENT DUE TO HEAVY PARTICULATE DEBRIS. THERMALS ACTIVE AND SHIFTING, NORTH BY NORTHWEST. WE HAD ONE HELL OF A FIRE STORM OUT THERE TODAY.
ROUTING CALCULATED -- CHECK HUD'S FOR IMPACT COORDINATES.
"DESPITE THE TRUTH OF THE SITUATION, COMMAND LIED TO ITSELF.
"THEY BELIEVED THAT SENDING MORE OF US TO DIE WOULD BE THE ANSWER.
"AND WHY SHOULDN'T THEY HAVE?
"IT HAD ALWAYS WORKED BEFORE."

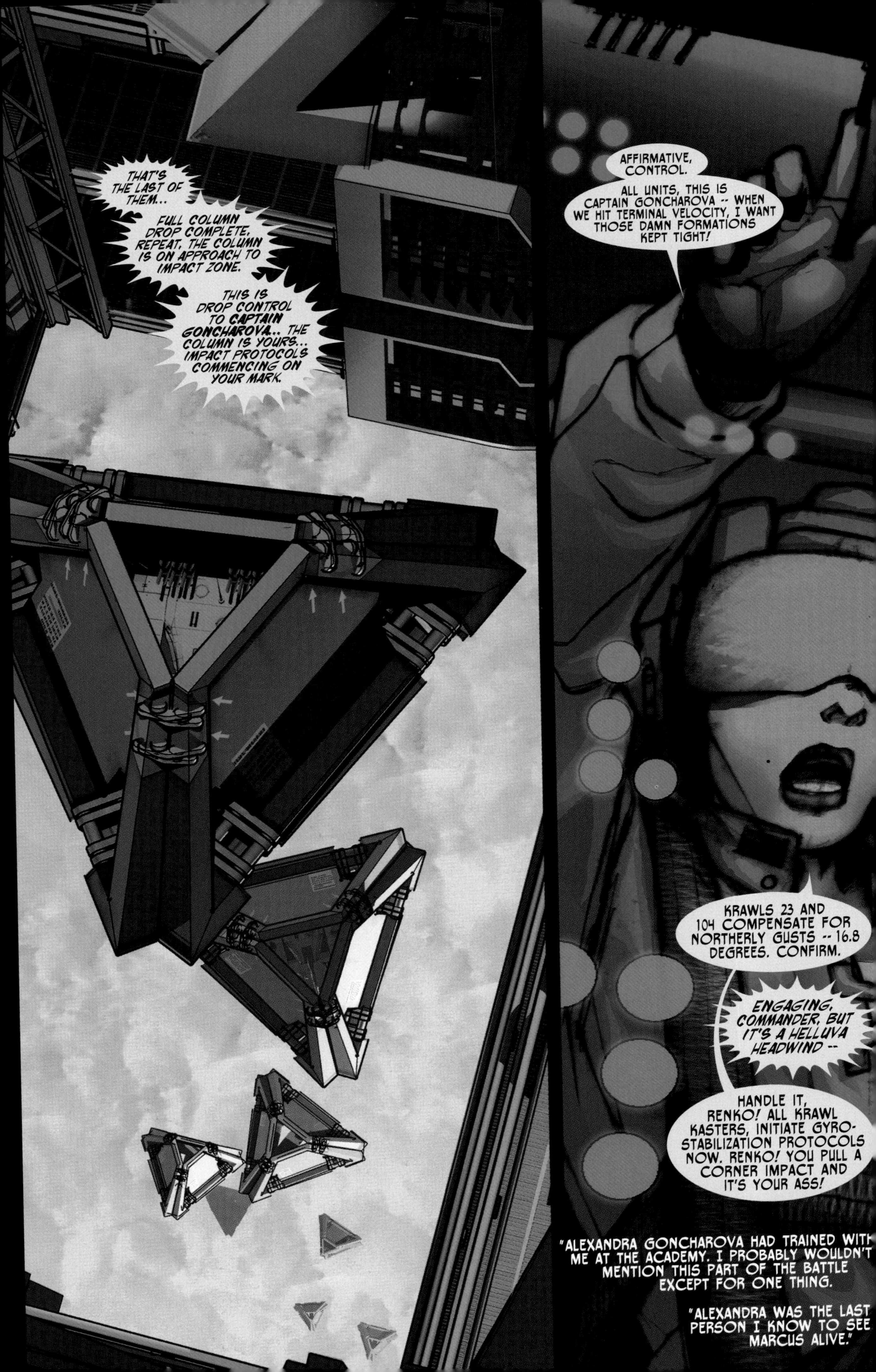
THAT'S THE LAST OF THEM...
FULL COLUMN DROP COMPLETE, REPEAT, THE COLUMN IS ON APPROACH TO IMPACT ZONE.
THIS IS DROP CONTROL TO CAPTAIN GONCHAROVA... THE COLUMN IS YOURS... IMPACT PROTOCOLS COMMENCING ON YOUR MARK.
AFFIRMATIVE, CONTROL.
ALL UNITS, THIS IS CAPTAIN GONCHAROVA -- WHEN WE HIT TERMINAL VELOCITY, I WANT THOSE DAMN FORMATIONS KEPT TIGHT!
KRAWLS 23 AND 104 COMPENSATE FOR NORTHERLY GUSTS -- 16.8 DEGREES. CONFIRM.
ENGAGING, COMMANDER, BUT IT'S A HELLUVA HEADWIND --
HANDLE IT, RENKO! ALL KRAWL KASTERS, INITIATE GYRO-STABILIZATION PROTOCOLS NOW. RENKO! YOU PULL A CORNER IMPACT AND IT'S YOUR ASS!
"ALEXANDRA GONCHAROVA HAD TRAINED WITH ME AT THE ACADEMY. I PROBABLY WOULDN'T MENTION THIS PART OF THE BATTLE EXCEPT FOR ONE THING.
"ALEXANDRA WAS THE LAST PERSON I KNOW TO SEE MARCUS ALIVE."

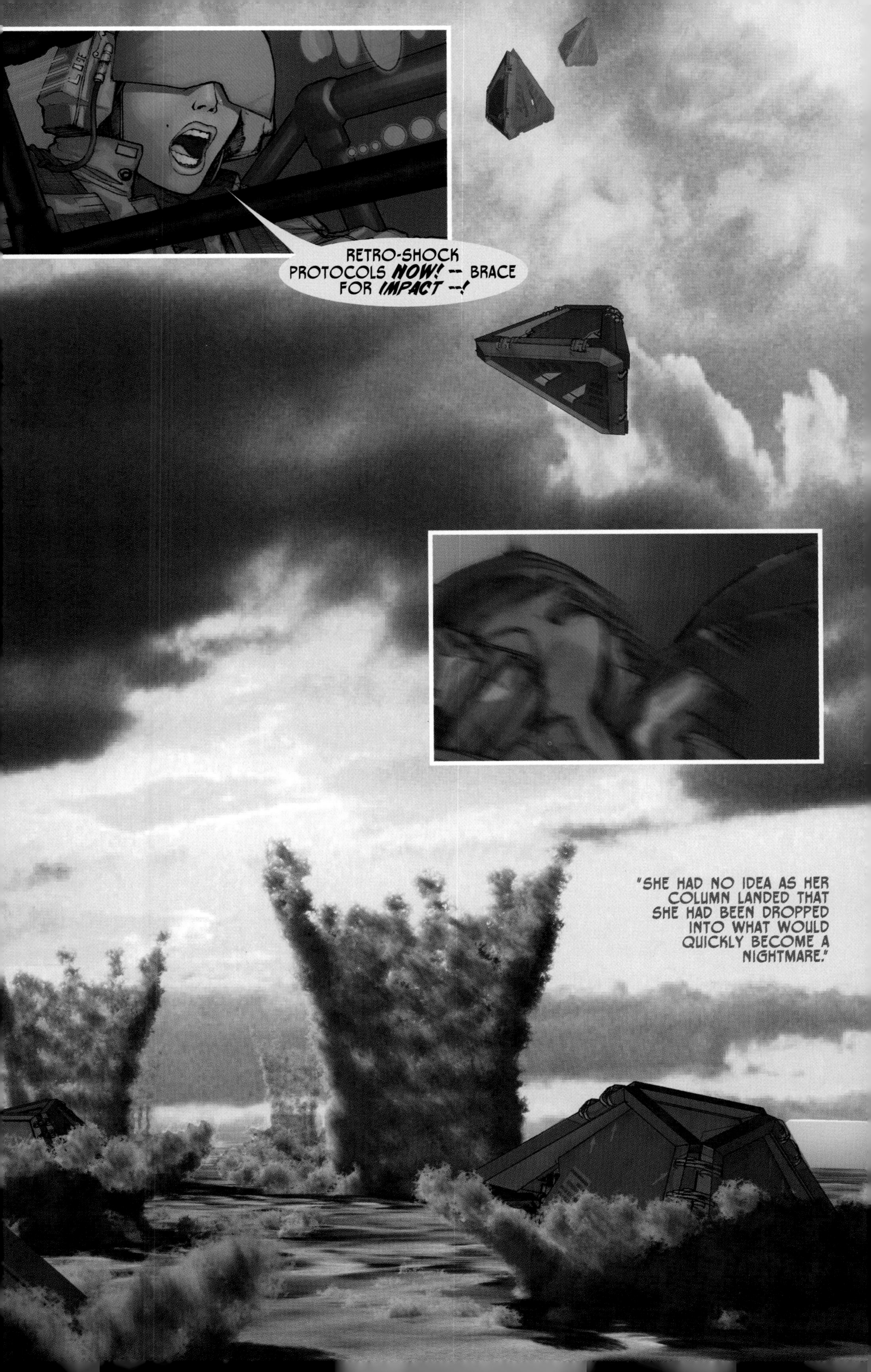
RETRO-SHOCK PROTOCOLS NOW! -- BRACE FOR IMPACT --!
"SHE HAD NO IDEA AS HER COLUMN LANDED THAT SHE HAD BEEN DROPPED INTO WHAT WOULD QUICKLY BECOME A NIGHTMARE."

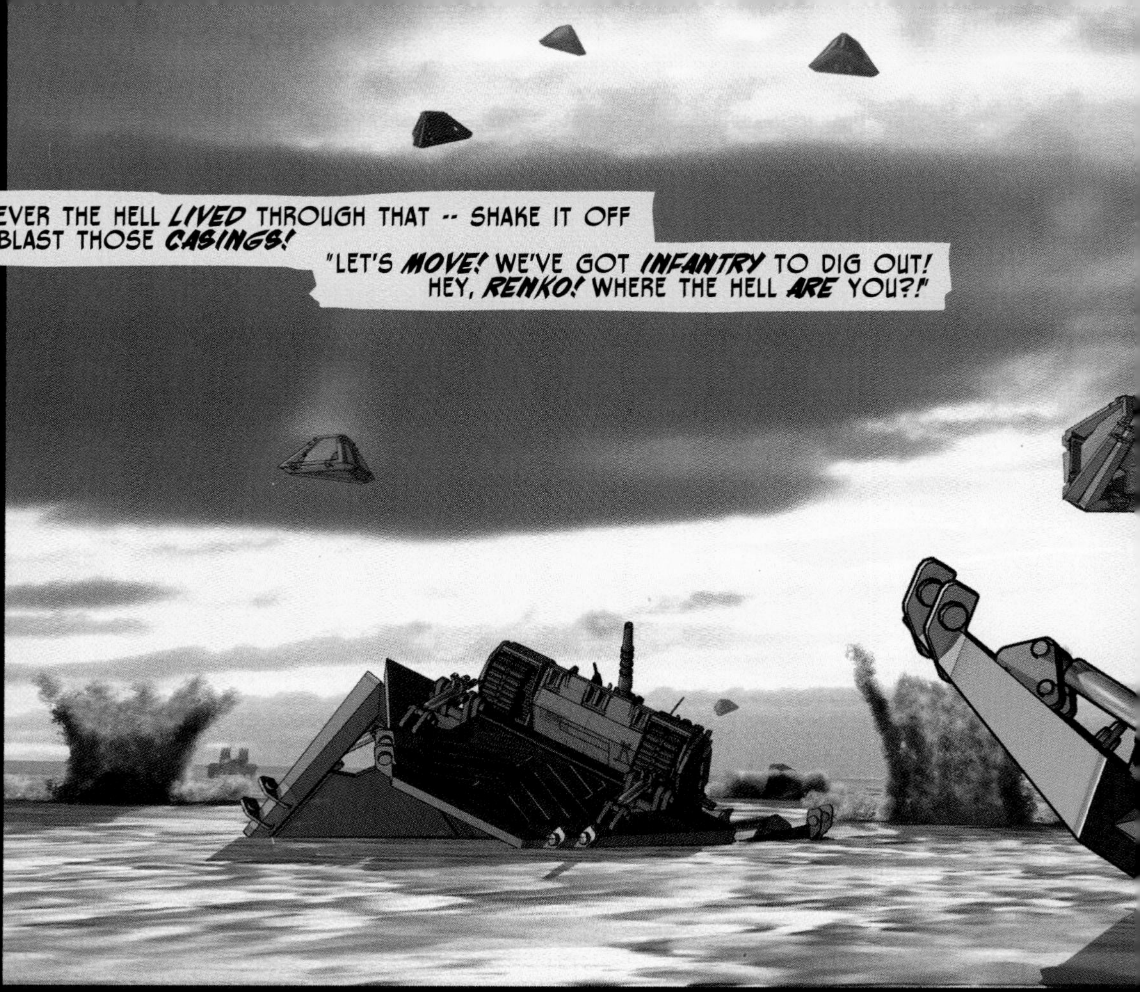
"WHOEVER THE HELL LIVED THROUGH THAT -- SHAKE IT OFF AND BLAST THOSE CASINGS!
"LET'S MOVE! WE'VE GOT INFANTRY TO DIG OUT! HEY, RENKO! WHERE THE HELL ARE YOU?!"

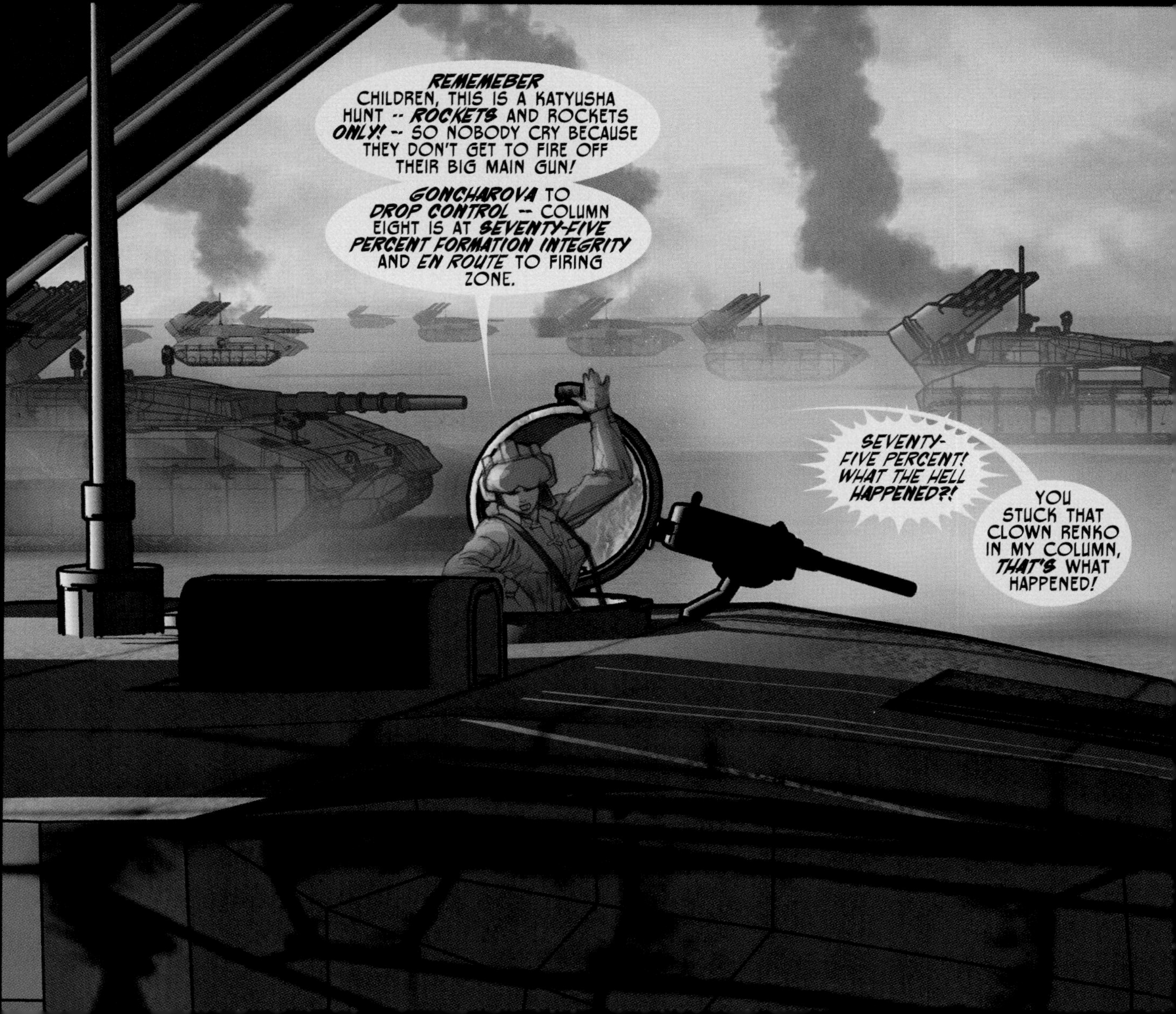
REMEMEBER CHILDREN, THIS IS A KATYUSHA HUNT -- ROCKETS AND ROCKETS ONLY! -- SO NOBODY CRY BECAUSE THEY DON'T GET TO FIRE OFF THEIR BIG MAIN GUN!
GONCHAROVA TO DROP CONTROL -- COLUMN EIGHT IS AT SEVENTY-FIVE PERCENT FORMATION INTEGRITY AND EN ROUTE TO FIRING ZONE.
SEVENTY-FIVE PERCENT! WHAT THE HELL HAPPENED?!
YOU STUCK THAT CLOWN RENKO IN MY COLUMN, THAT'S WHAT HAPPENED!

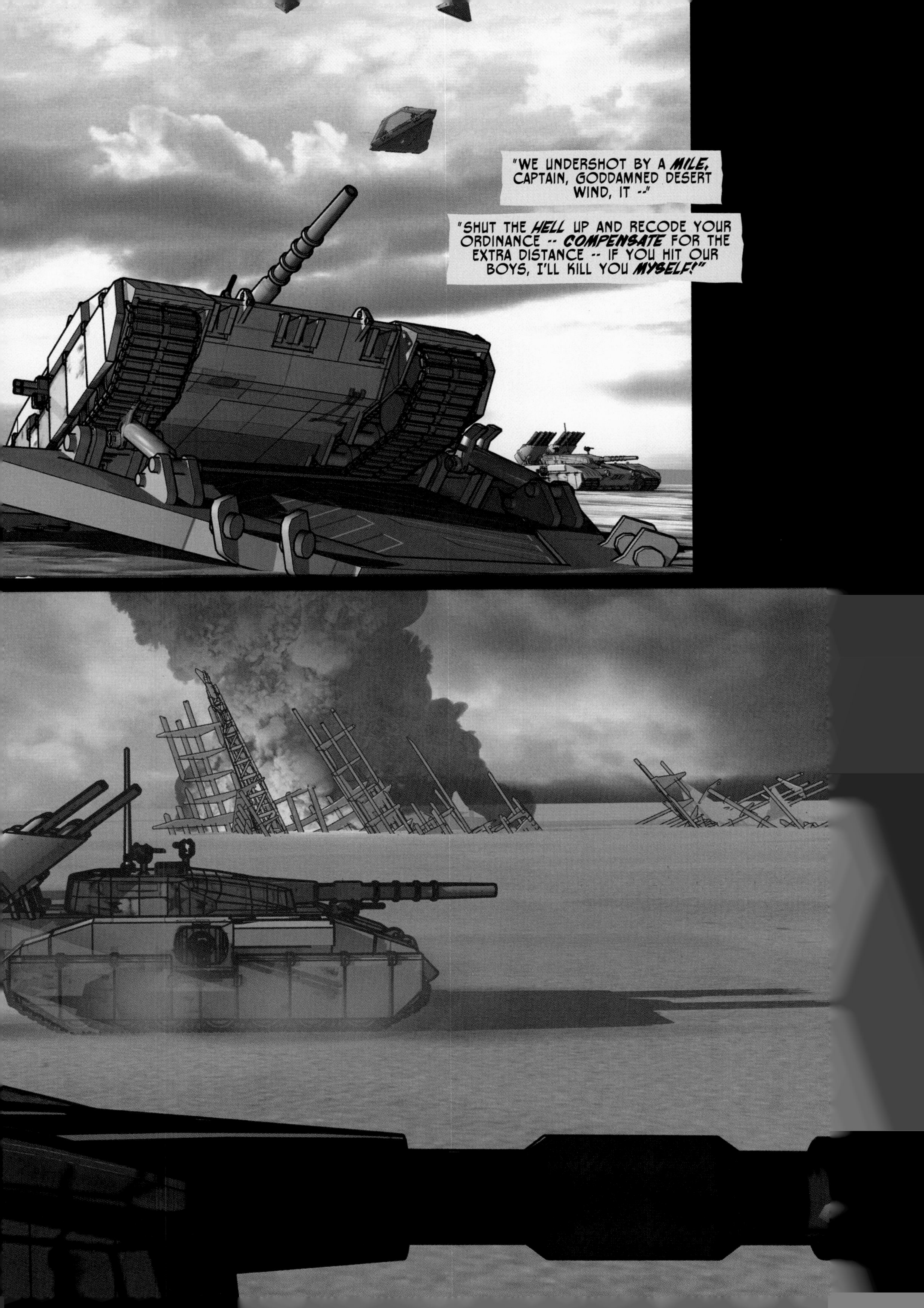
"WE UNDERSHOT BY A MILE, CAPTAIN, GODDAMNED DESERT WIND, IT --"
"SHUT THE HELL UP AND RECODE YOUR ORDINANCE -- COMPENSATE FOR THE EXTRA DISTANCE -- IF YOU HIT OUR BOYS, I'LL KILL YOU MYSELF!"

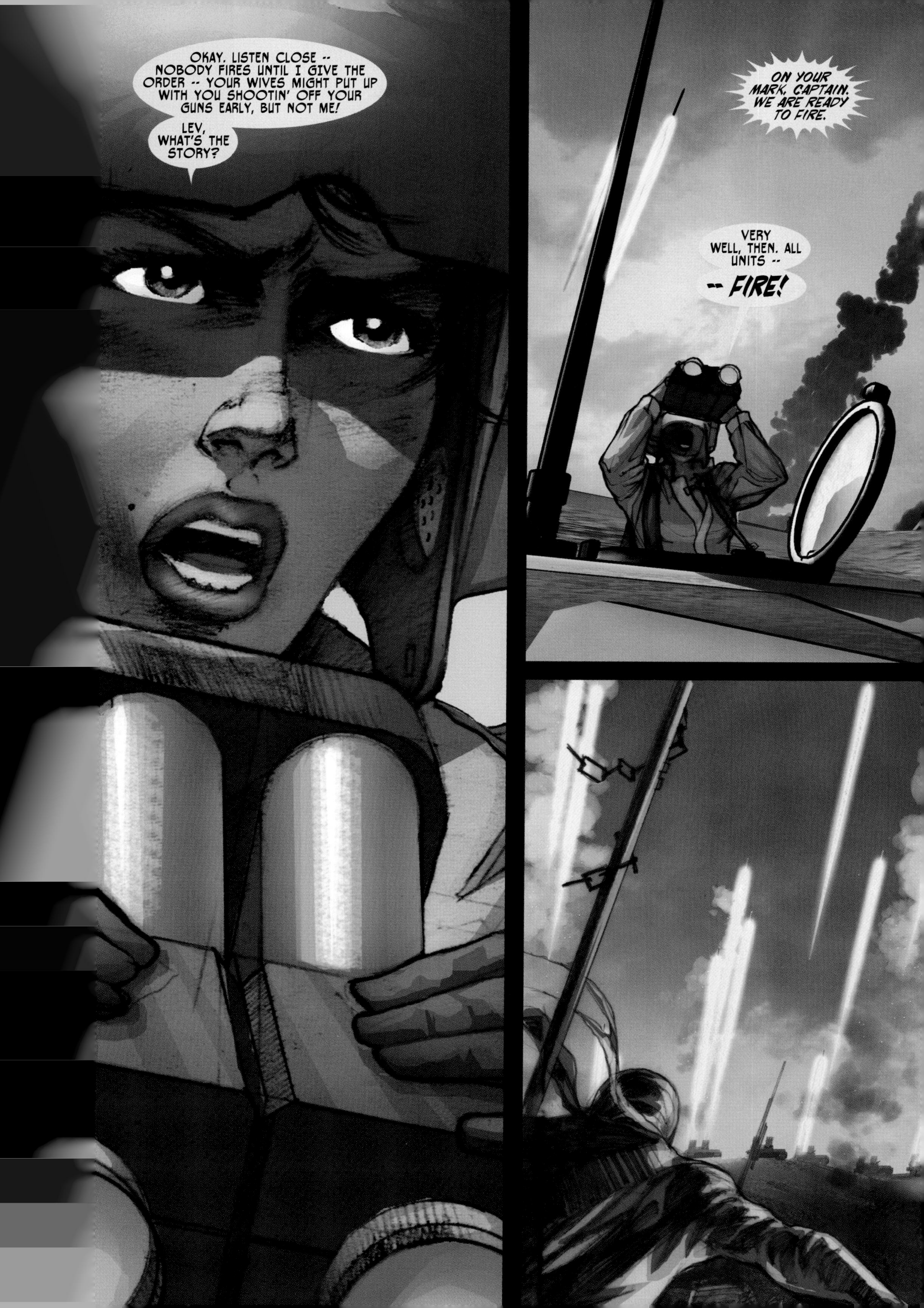
OKAY. LISTEN CLOSE -- NOBODY FIRES UNTIL I GIVE THE ORDER -- YOUR WIVES MIGHT PUT UP WITH YOU SHOOTIN' OFF YOUR GUNS EARLY, BUT NOT ME!
LEV, WHAT'S THE STORY?
ON YOUR MARK, CAPTAIN. WE ARE READY TO FIRE.
VERY WELL, THEN. ALL UNITS --
-- FIRE!

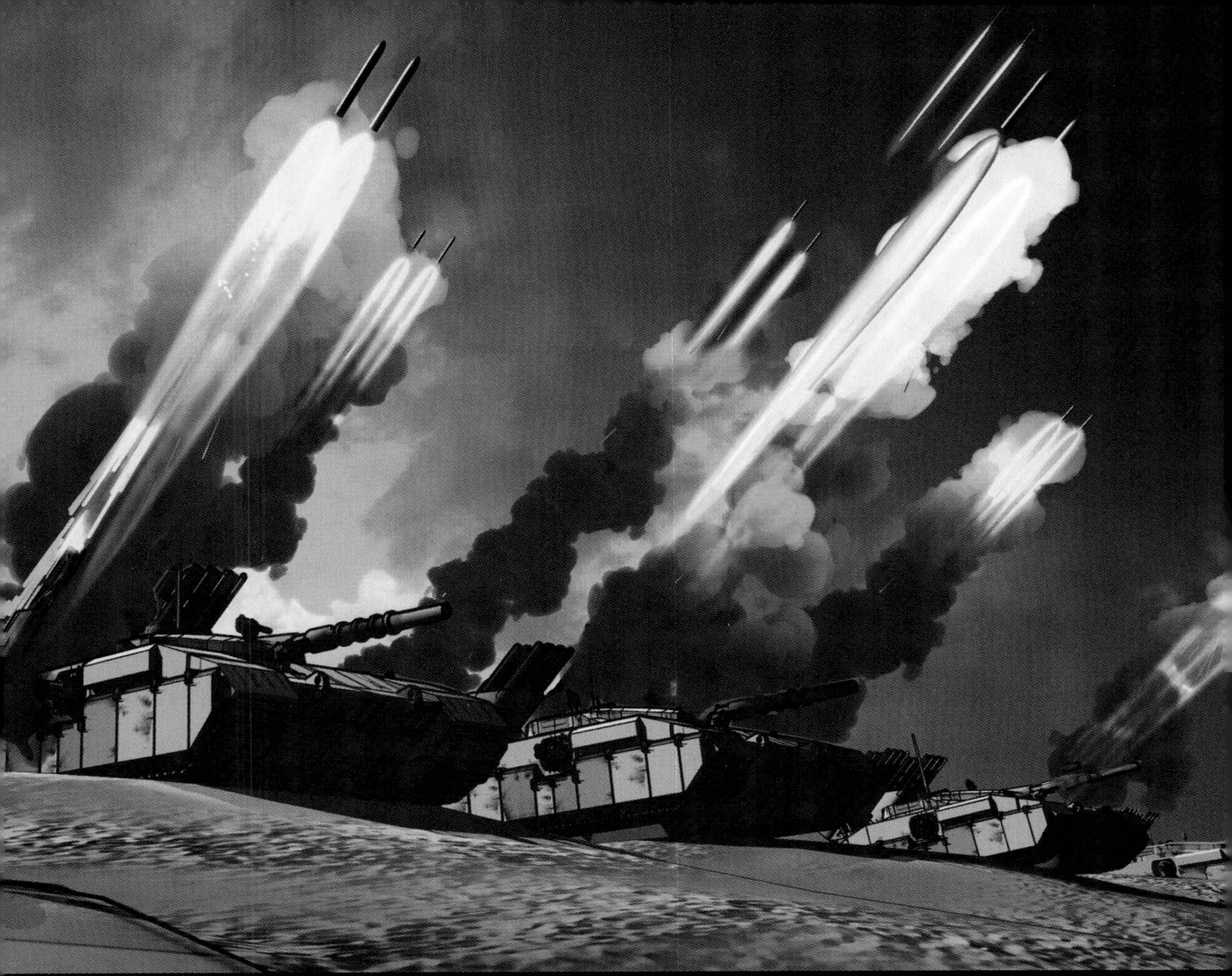

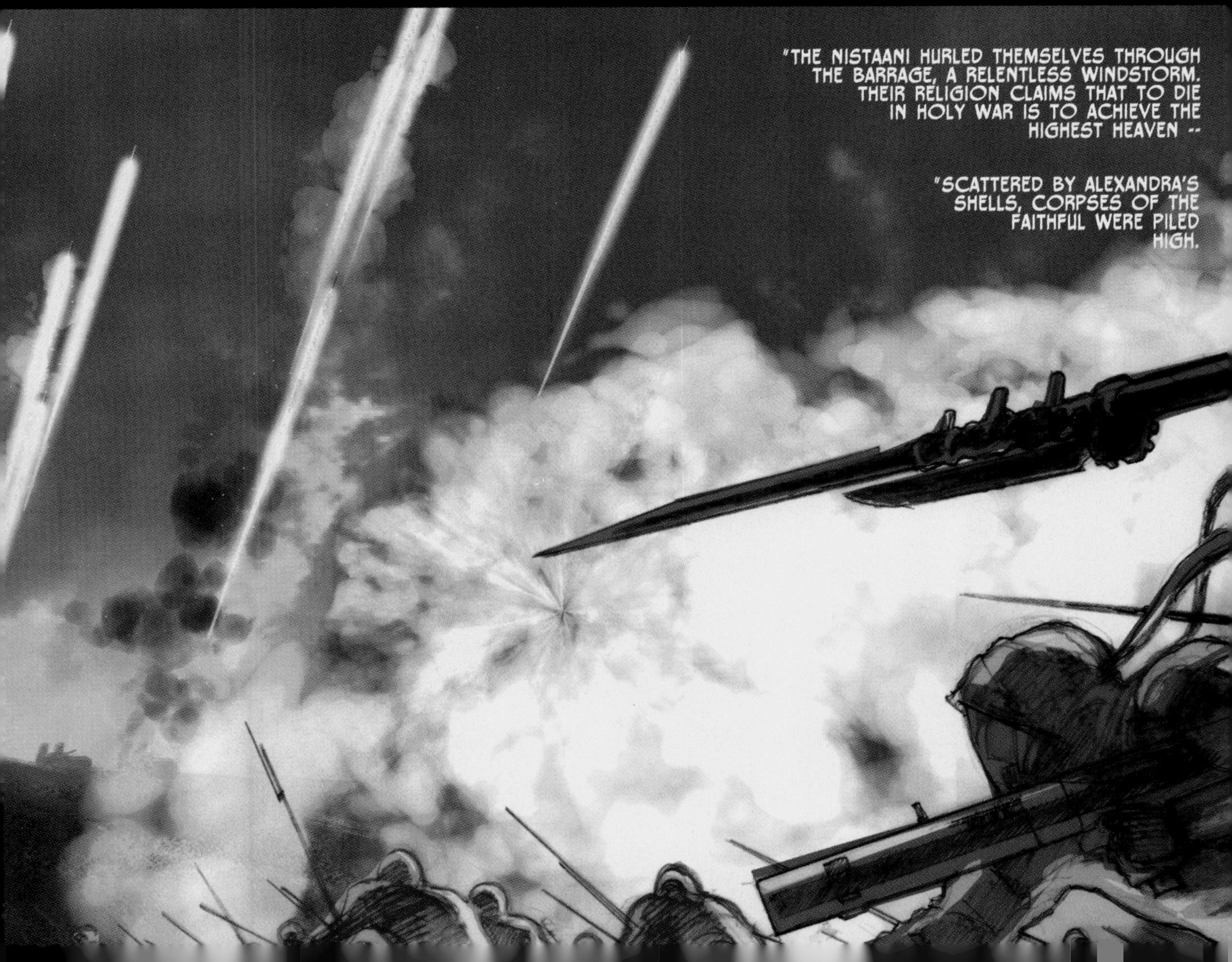
"THE NISTAANI HURLED THEMSELVES THROUGH THE BARRAGE, A RELENTLESS WINDSTORM. THEIR RELIGION CLAIMS THAT TO DIE IN HOLY WAR IS TO ACHIEVE THE HIGHEST HEAVEN --
"SCATTERED BY ALEXANDRA'S SHELLS, CORPSES OF THE FAITHFUL WERE PILED HIGH.

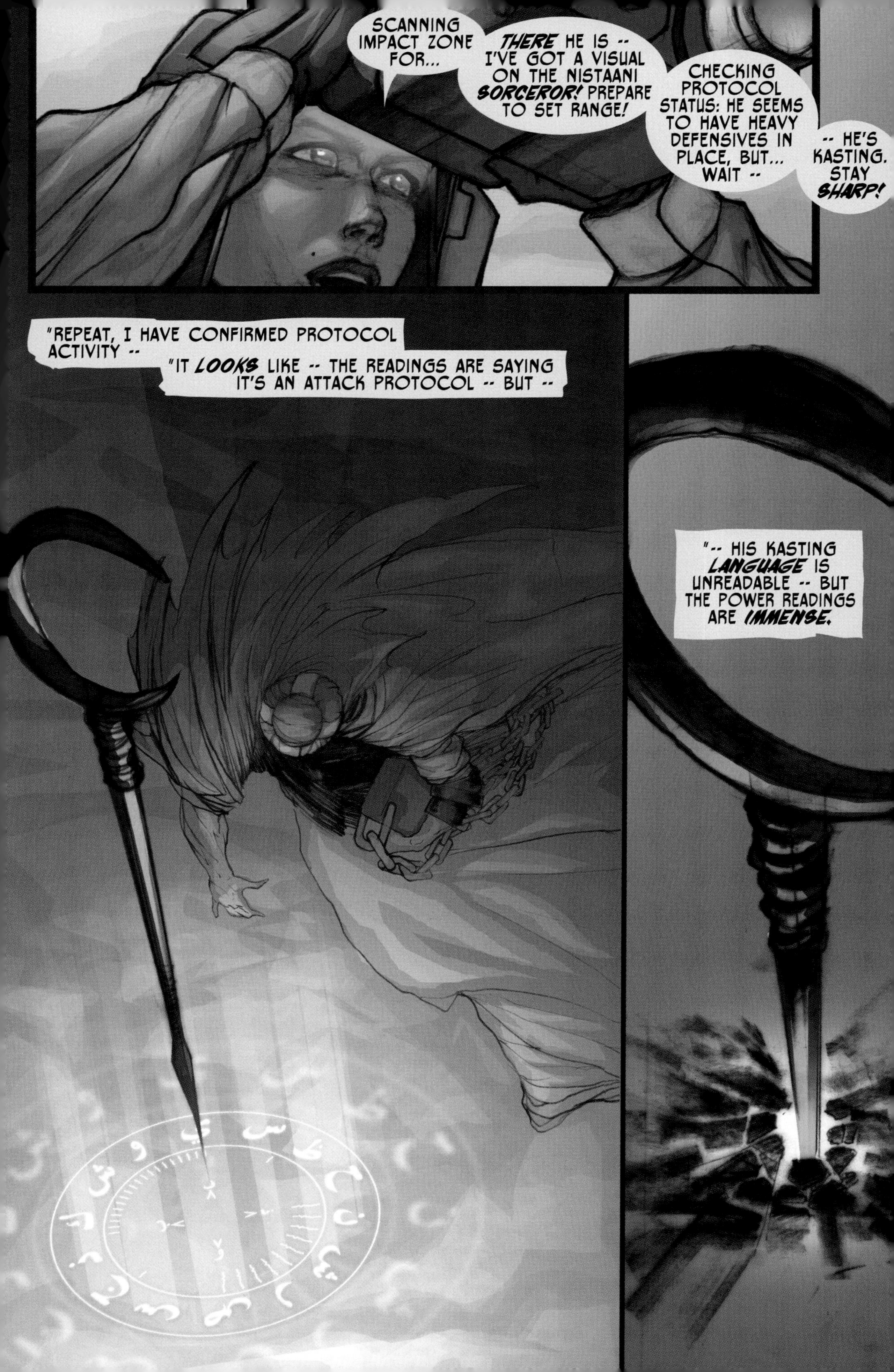
SCANNING IMPACT ZONE FOR...
THERE HE IS -- I'VE GOT A VISUAL ON THE NISTAANI SORCEROR! PREPARE TO SET RANGE!
CHECKING PROTOCOL STATUS: HE SEEMS TO HAVE HEAVY DEFENSIVES IN PLACE, BUT... WAIT --
-- HE'S KASTING. STAY SHARP!
"REPEAT, I HAVE CONFIRMED PROTOCOL ACTIVITY --
"IT LOOKS LIKE -- THE READINGS ARE SAYING IT'S AN ATTACK PROTOCOL -- BUT --
"-- HIS KASTING LANGUAGE IS UNREADABLE -- BUT THE POWER READINGS ARE IMMENSE.

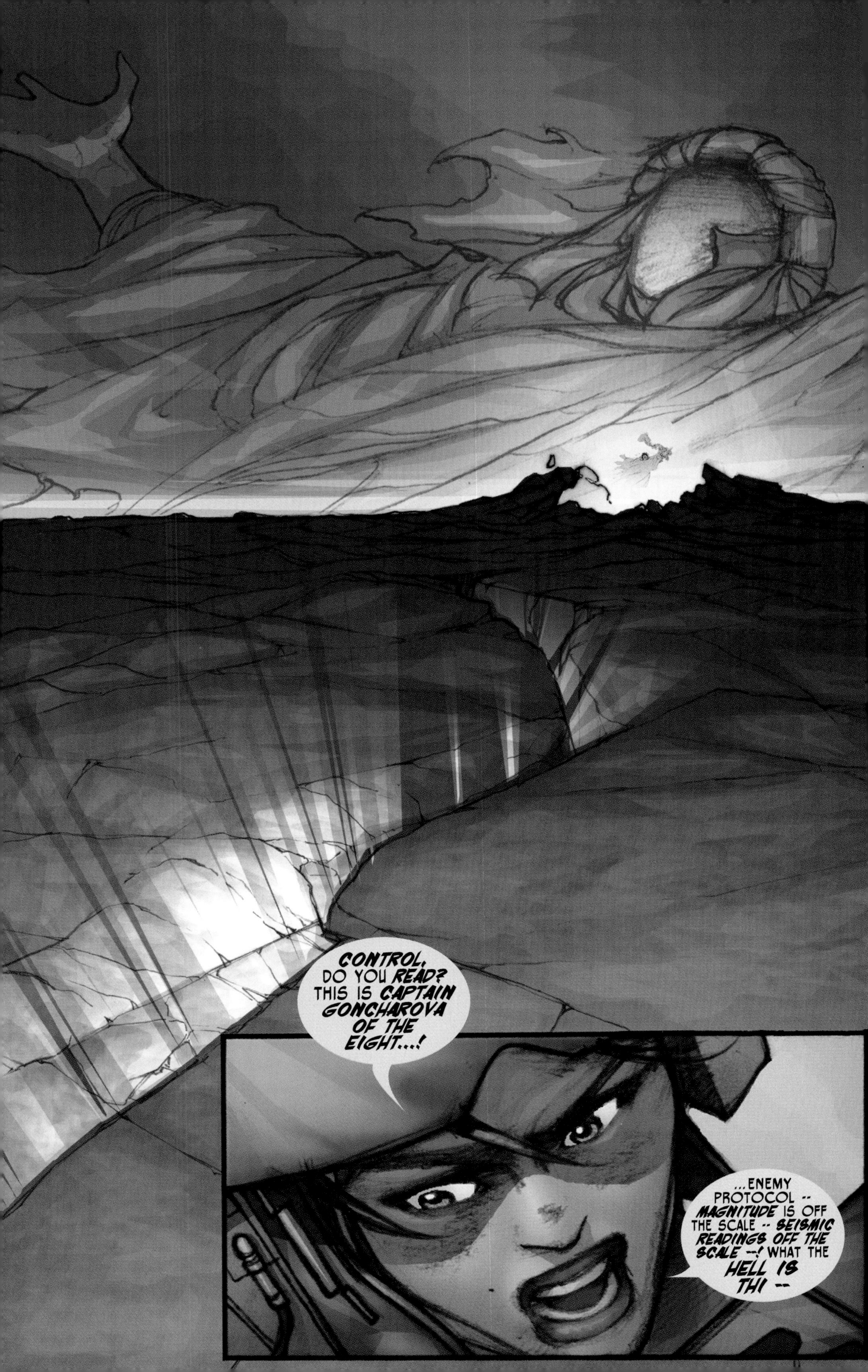
CONTROL, DO YOU READ? THIS IS CAPTAIN GONCHAROVA OF THE EIGHT...!
...ENEMY PROTOCOL -- MAGNITUDE IS OFF THE SCALE -- SEISMIC READINGS OFF THE SCALE --! WHAT THE HELL IS THI --

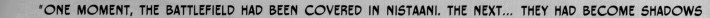

"ONE MOMENT, THE BATTLEFIELD HAD BEEN COVERED IN NISTAANI. THE NEXT... THEY HAD BECOME SHADOWS

"-- THEIR BATTLE CRIES COULD BE HEARD, BUT NOT SEEN. FROM OUT OF THE DUST AND SMOKE A BLADE WOULD TAKE ANOTHER RED TROOPER'S LIFE, AND THEN VANISH INTO THE AIR.

"IT WAS AS IF WE HAD ANGERED NOT ONLY KAR DATHRA, BUT THE VERY SOIL OF AL'ISTAAN ITSELF. THE LAND AND SKY BUCKLED AND ROARED AT HIS COMMAND.

"A POWER EXPLODED FORTH FROM HIM THAT THREW OUR FORCES INTO PANICKED CHAOS.

"ACCORDING TO ALEXANDRA, THIS IS WHEN SHE FIRST MADE CONTACT WITH MARCUS.

THIS IS *CAPTAIN ANTARES* TO THE *KRAWL COLUMN* -- REPEAT, THIS IS CAPTAIN ANTARES REQUESTING *IMMEDIATE EXTRACTION!*

MARCUS -- IS THAT YOU?! DO YOU SEE THIS?! MY GOD -- THE POWER -- IT'S IMPOSSI --*
ALEXANDRA! LISTEN TO ME -- GET US THE HELL OUT OF HERE -- IT'S ALL OVER! ALEXA --*
I'M ON MY WAY, ANTARES, ACTIVATE YOUR LOCATION MARKER -- I'M EN ROUTE NOW!

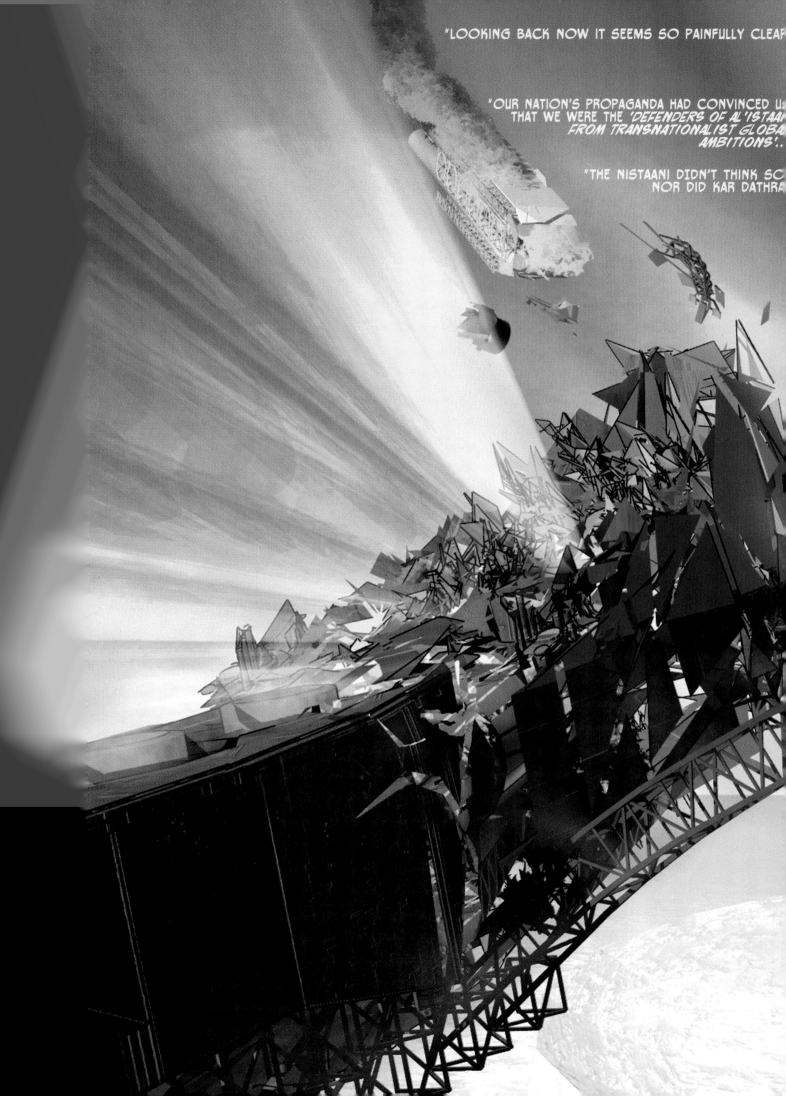

"LOOKING BACK NOW IT SEEMS SO PAINFULLY CLEAR

"OUR NATION'S PROPAGANDA HAD CONVINCED U:
THAT WE WERE THE *DEFENDERS OF AL'ISTAAN
FROM TRANSNATIONALIST GLOBA
AMBITIONS'*..

"THE NISTAANI DIDN'T THINK SC
NOR DID KAR DATHRA

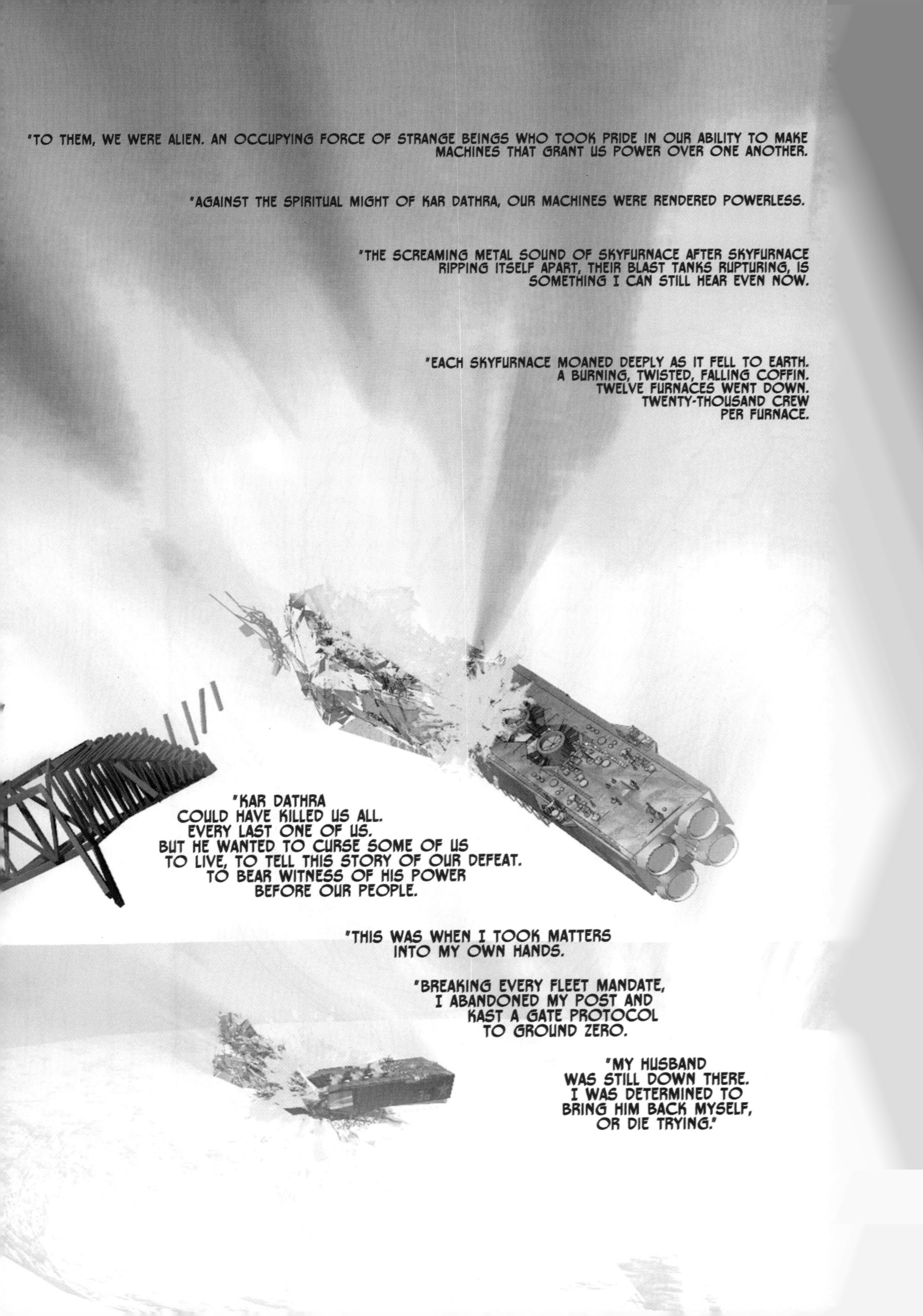
"TO THEM, WE WERE ALIEN. AN OCCUPYING FORCE OF STRANGE BEINGS WHO TOOK PRIDE IN OUR ABILITY TO MAKE MACHINES THAT GRANT US POWER OVER ONE ANOTHER.
"AGAINST THE SPIRITUAL MIGHT OF KAR DATHRA, OUR MACHINES WERE RENDERED POWERLESS.
"THE SCREAMING METAL SOUND OF SKYFURNACE AFTER SKYFURNACE RIPPING ITSELF APART, THEIR BLAST TANKS RUPTURING, IS SOMETHING I CAN STILL HEAR EVEN NOW.
"EACH SKYFURNACE MOANED DEEPLY AS IT FELL TO EARTH. A BURNING, TWISTED, FALLING COFFIN. TWELVE FURNACES WENT DOWN. TWENTY-THOUSAND CREW PER FURNACE.
"KAR DATHRA COULD HAVE KILLED US ALL. EVERY LAST ONE OF US. BUT HE WANTED TO CURSE SOME OF US TO LIVE, TO TELL THIS STORY OF OUR DEFEAT. TO BEAR WITNESS OF HIS POWER BEFORE OUR PEOPLE.
"THIS WAS WHEN I TOOK MATTERS INTO MY OWN HANDS.
"BREAKING EVERY FLEET MANDATE, I ABANDONED MY POST AND KAST A GATE PROTOCOL TO GROUND ZERO.
"MY HUSBAND WAS STILL DOWN THERE. I WAS DETERMINED TO BRING HIM BACK MYSELF, OR DIE TRYING."

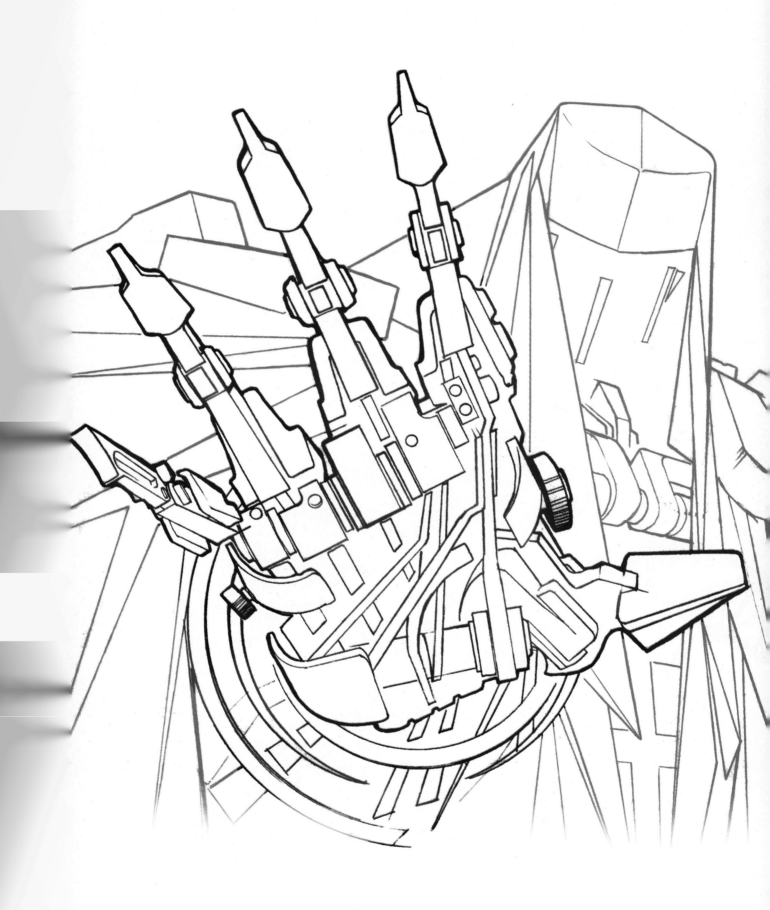

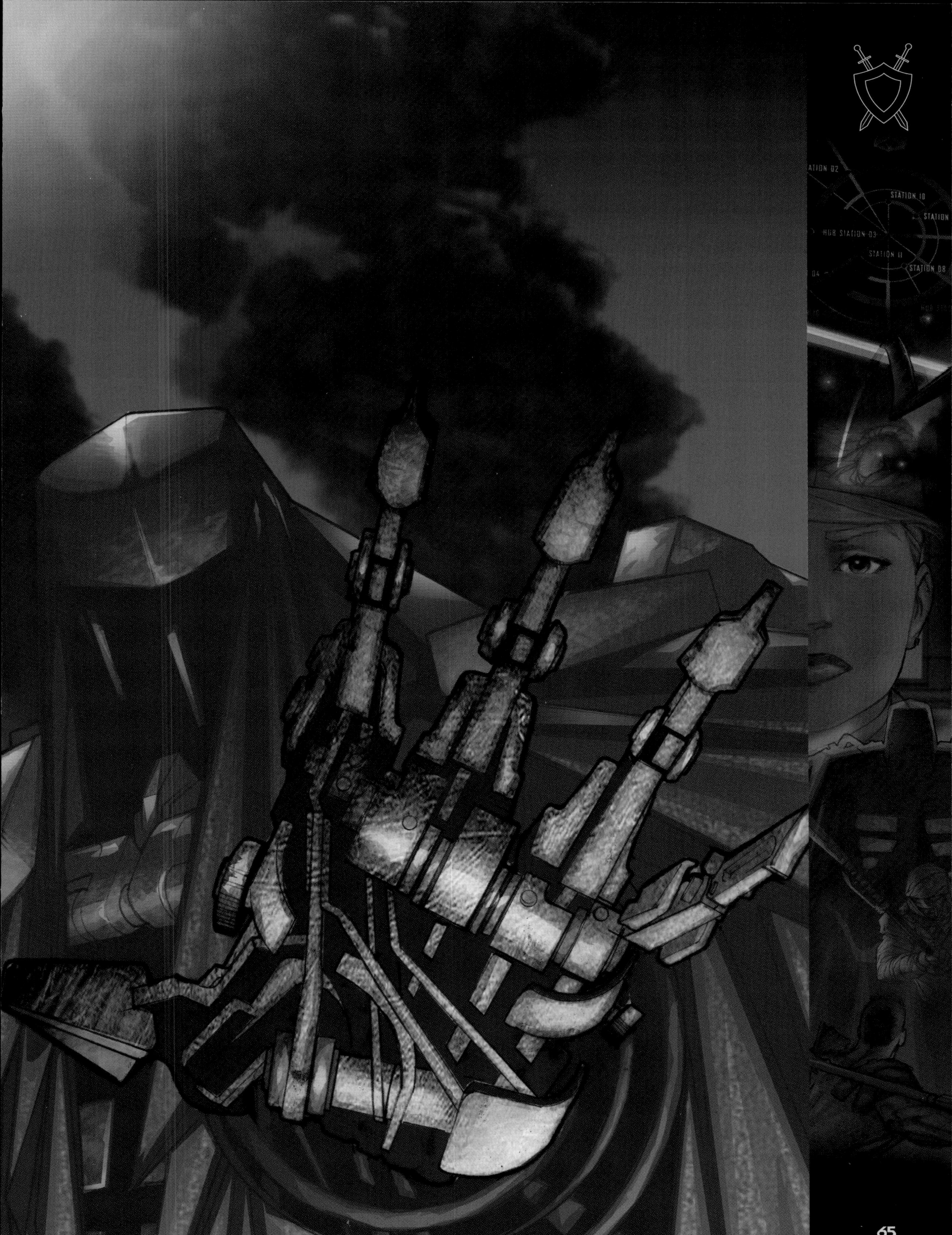
STATION 10
HUB STATION 03
STATION 11
STATION 08

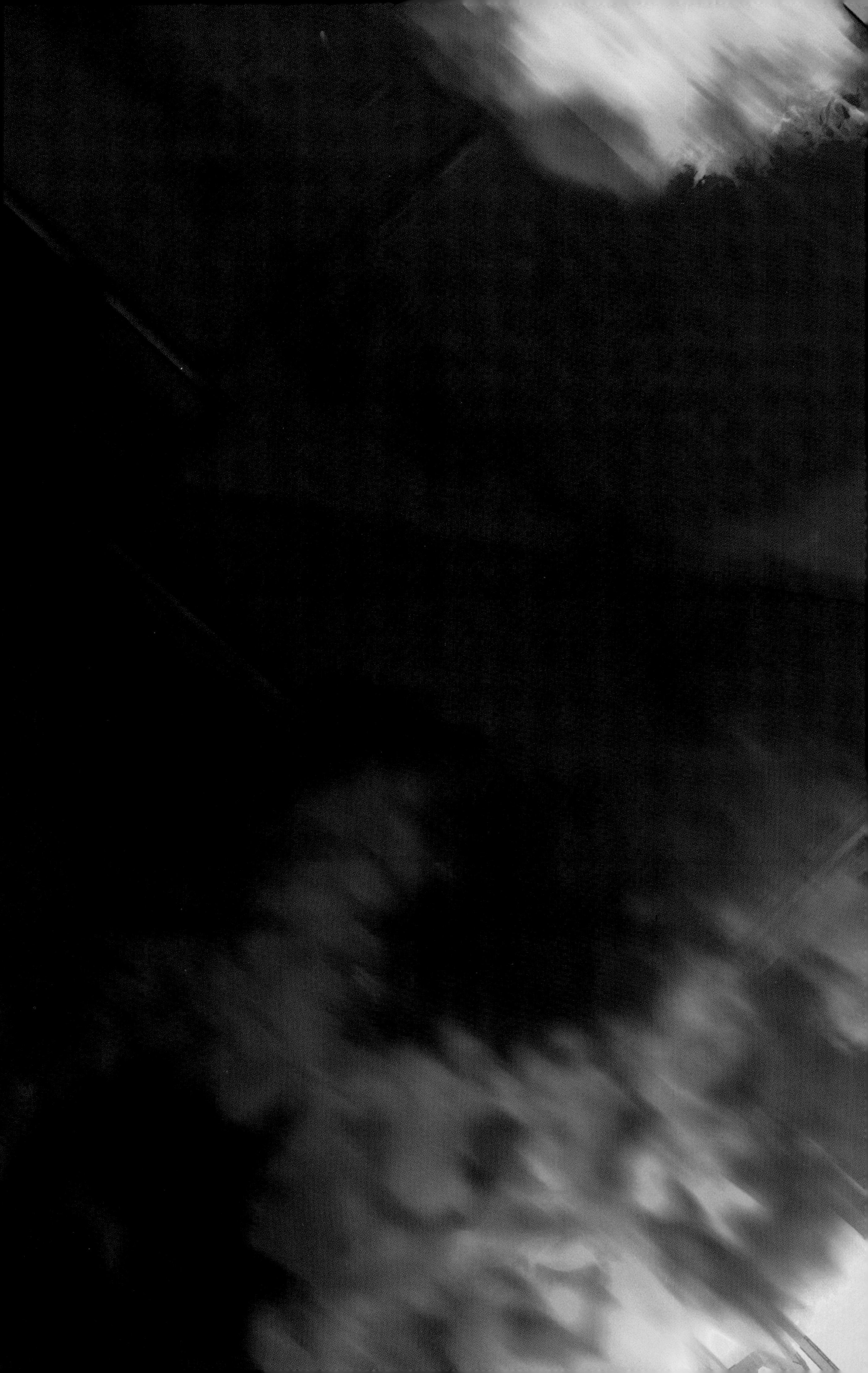

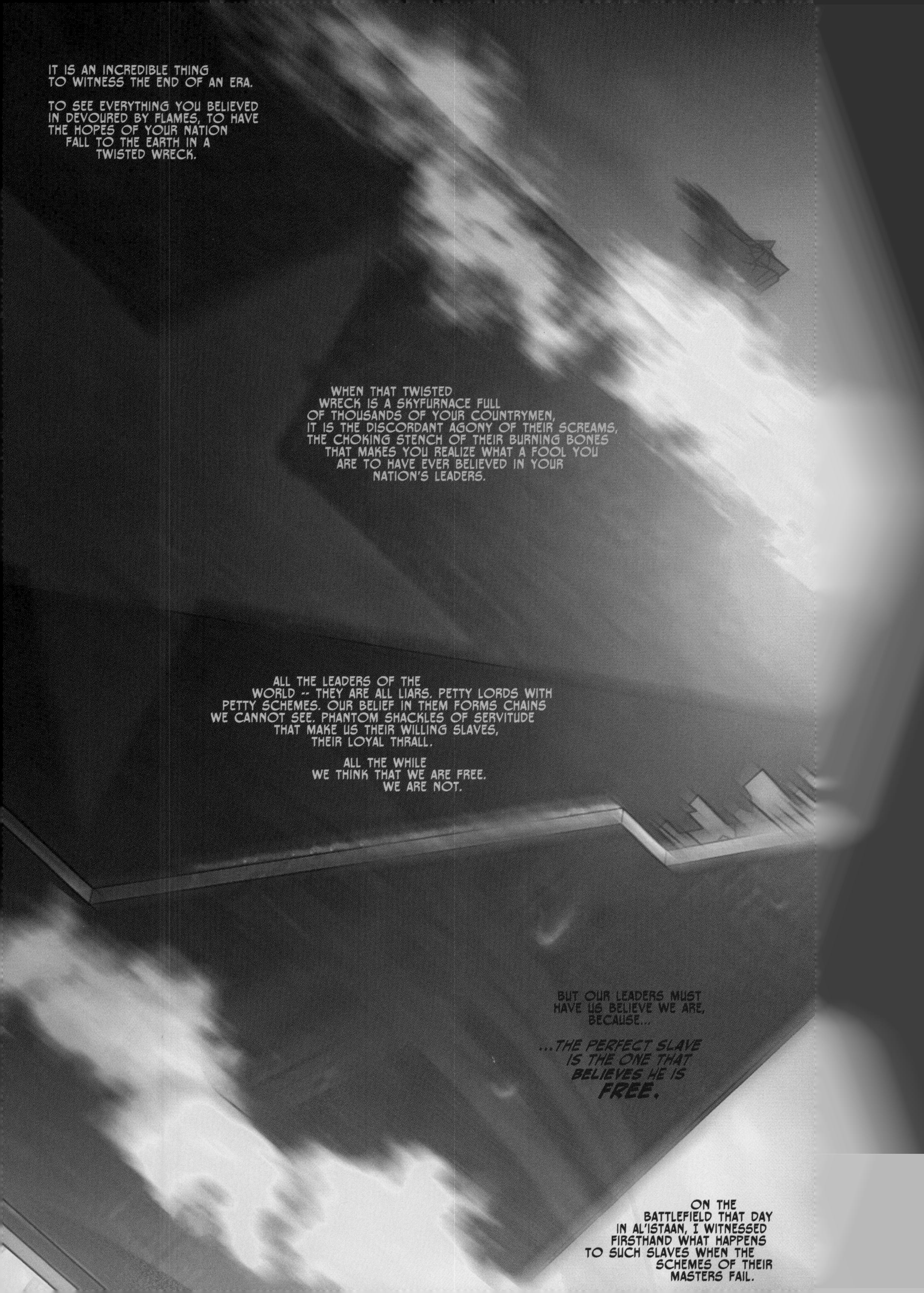
IT IS AN INCREDIBLE THING TO WITNESS THE END OF AN ERA.
TO SEE EVERYTHING YOU BELIEVED IN DEVOURED BY FLAMES, TO HAVE THE HOPES OF YOUR NATION FALL TO THE EARTH IN A TWISTED WRECK.
WHEN THAT TWISTED WRECK IS A SKYFURNACE FULL OF THOUSANDS OF YOUR COUNTRYMEN, IT IS THE DISCORDANT AGONY OF THEIR SCREAMS, THE CHOKING STENCH OF THEIR BURNING BONES THAT MAKES YOU REALIZE WHAT A FOOL YOU ARE TO HAVE EVER BELIEVED IN YOUR NATION'S LEADERS.
ALL THE LEADERS OF THE WORLD -- THEY ARE ALL LIARS. PETTY LORDS WITH PETTY SCHEMES. OUR BELIEF IN THEM FORMS CHAINS WE CANNOT SEE. PHANTOM SHACKLES OF SERVITUDE THAT MAKE US THEIR WILLING SLAVES, THEIR LOYAL THRALL.
ALL THE WHILE WE THINK THAT WE ARE FREE. WE ARE NOT.
BUT OUR LEADERS MUST HAVE US BELIEVE WE ARE, BECAUSE...
...*THE PERFECT SLAVE IS THE ONE THAT BELIEVES HE IS* ***FREE.***
ON THE BATTLEFIELD THAT DAY IN AL'ISTAAN, I WITNESSED FIRSTHAND WHAT HAPPENS TO SUCH SLAVES WHEN THE SCHEMES OF THEIR MASTERS FAIL.

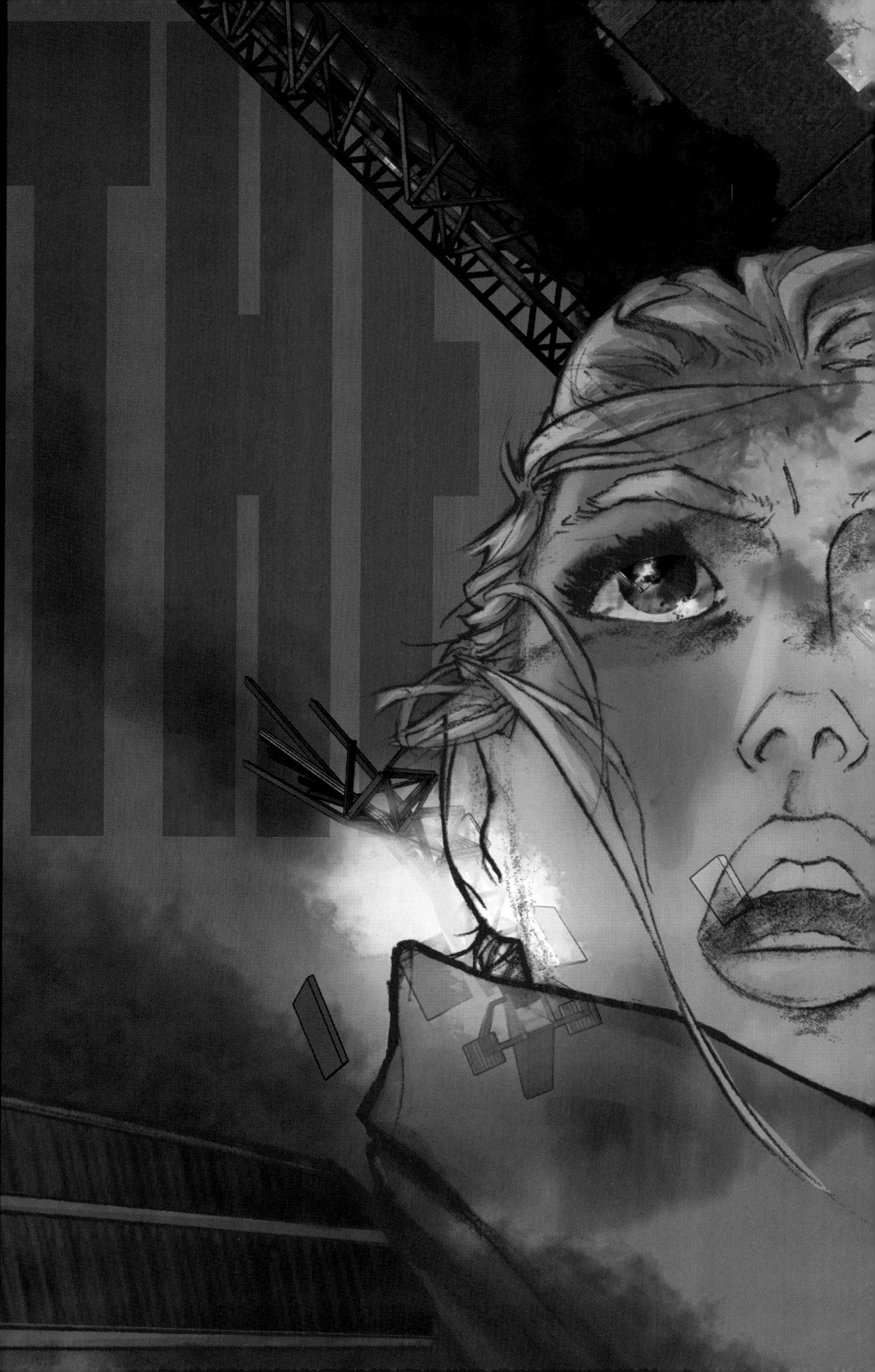
THE

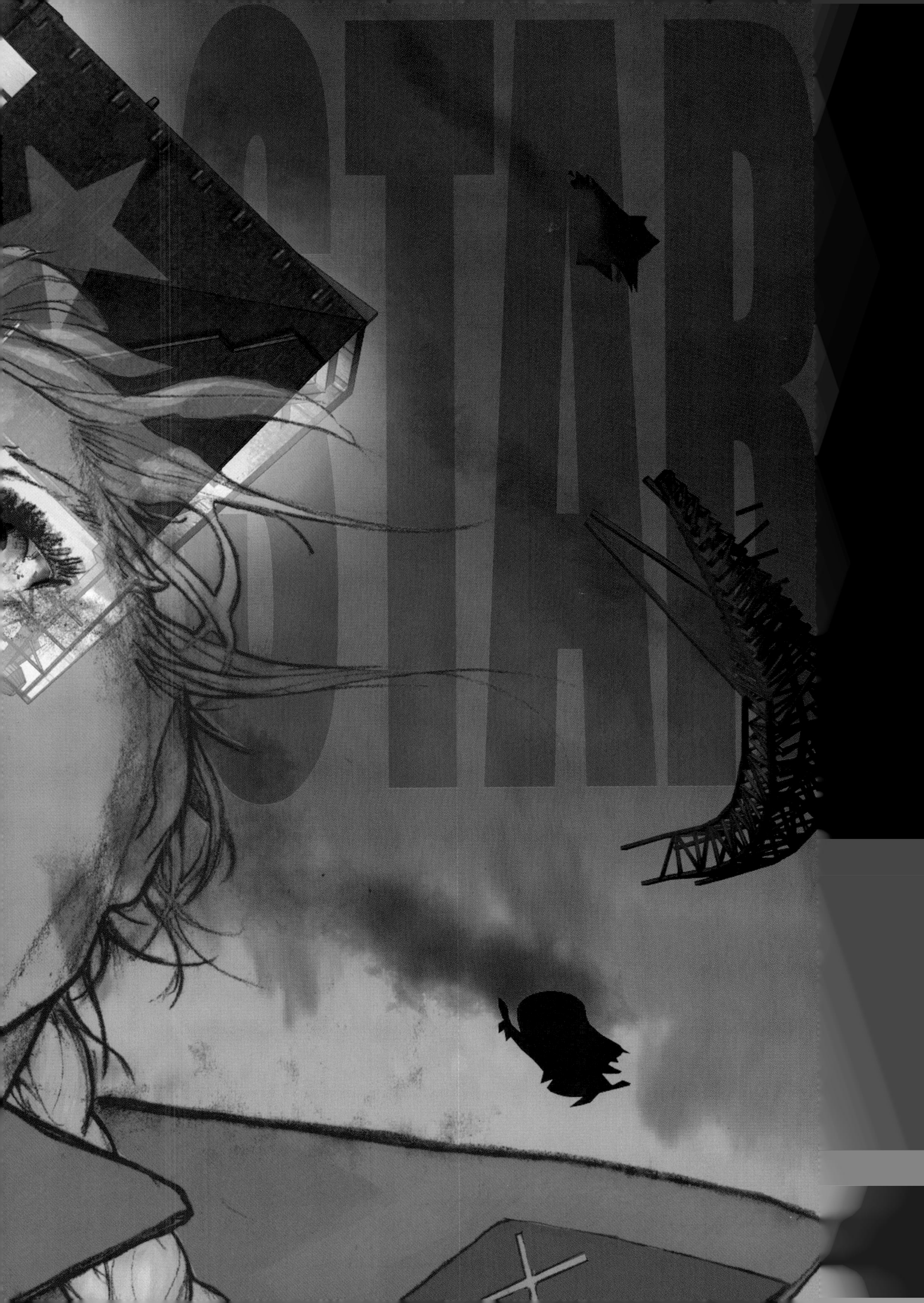

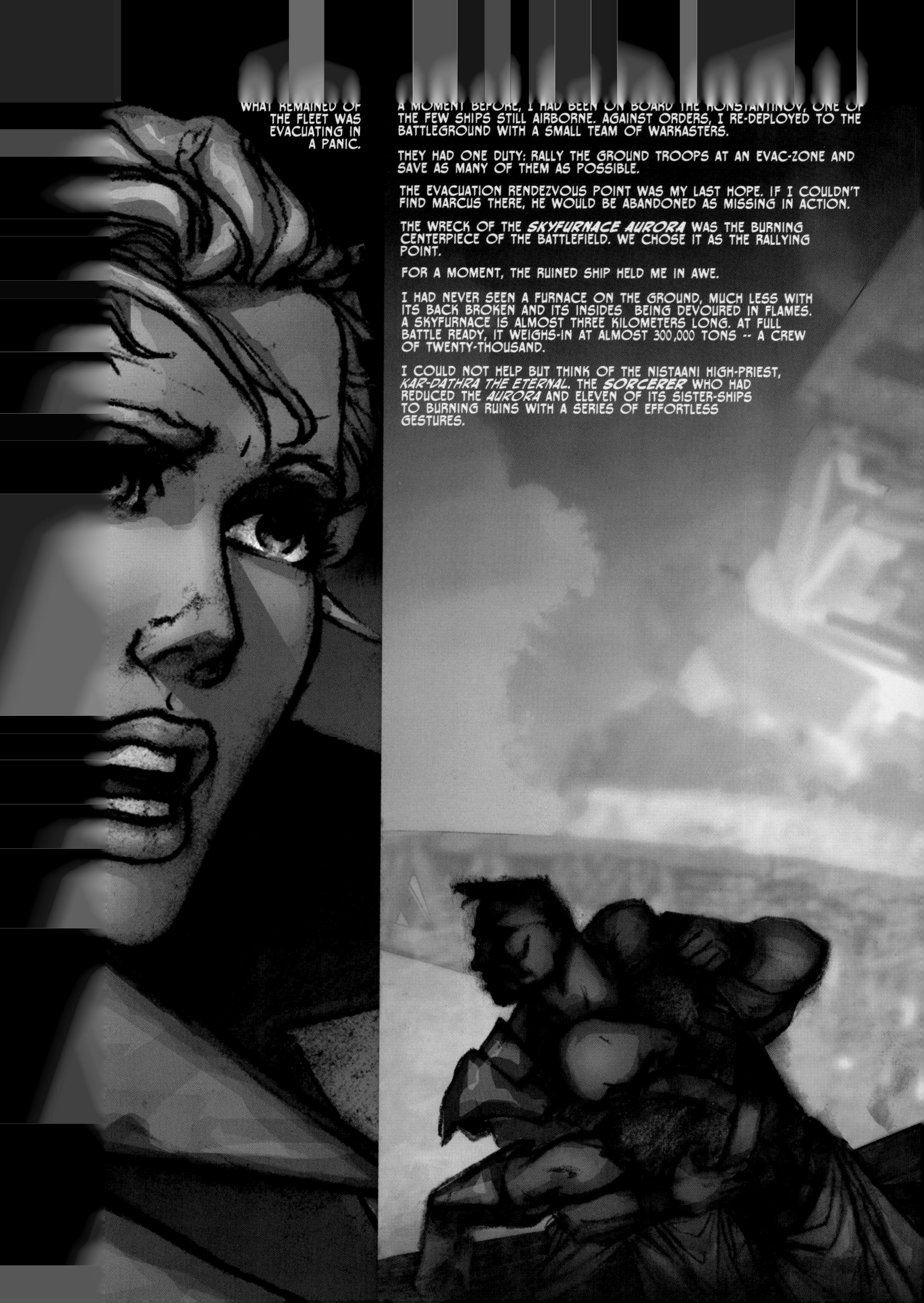

WHAT REMAINED OF THE FLEET WAS EVACUATING IN A PANIC.
A MOMENT BEFORE, I HAD BEEN ON BOARD THE KONSTANTINOV, ONE OF THE FEW SHIPS STILL AIRBORNE. AGAINST ORDERS, I RE-DEPLOYED TO THE BATTLEGROUND WITH A SMALL TEAM OF WARKASTERS.
THEY HAD ONE DUTY: RALLY THE GROUND TROOPS AT AN EVAC-ZONE AND SAVE AS MANY OF THEM AS POSSIBLE.
THE EVACUATION RENDEZVOUS POINT WAS MY LAST HOPE. IF I COULDN'T FIND MARCUS THERE, HE WOULD BE ABANDONED AS MISSING IN ACTION.
THE WRECK OF THE *SKYFURNACE AURORA* WAS THE BURNING CENTERPIECE OF THE BATTLEFIELD. WE CHOSE IT AS THE RALLYING POINT.
FOR A MOMENT, THE RUINED SHIP HELD ME IN AWE.
I HAD NEVER SEEN A FURNACE ON THE GROUND, MUCH LESS WITH ITS BACK BROKEN AND ITS INSIDES BEING DEVOURED IN FLAMES. A SKYFURNACE IS ALMOST THREE KILOMETERS LONG. AT FULL BATTLE READY, IT WEIGHS-IN AT ALMOST 300,000 TONS -- A CREW OF TWENTY-THOUSAND.
I COULD NOT HELP BUT THINK OF THE NISTAANI HIGH-PRIEST, *KAR-DATHRA THE ETERNAL*. THE *SORCERER* WHO HAD REDUCED THE *AURORA* AND ELEVEN OF ITS SISTER-SHIPS TO BURNING RUINS WITH A SERIES OF EFFORTLESS GESTURES.

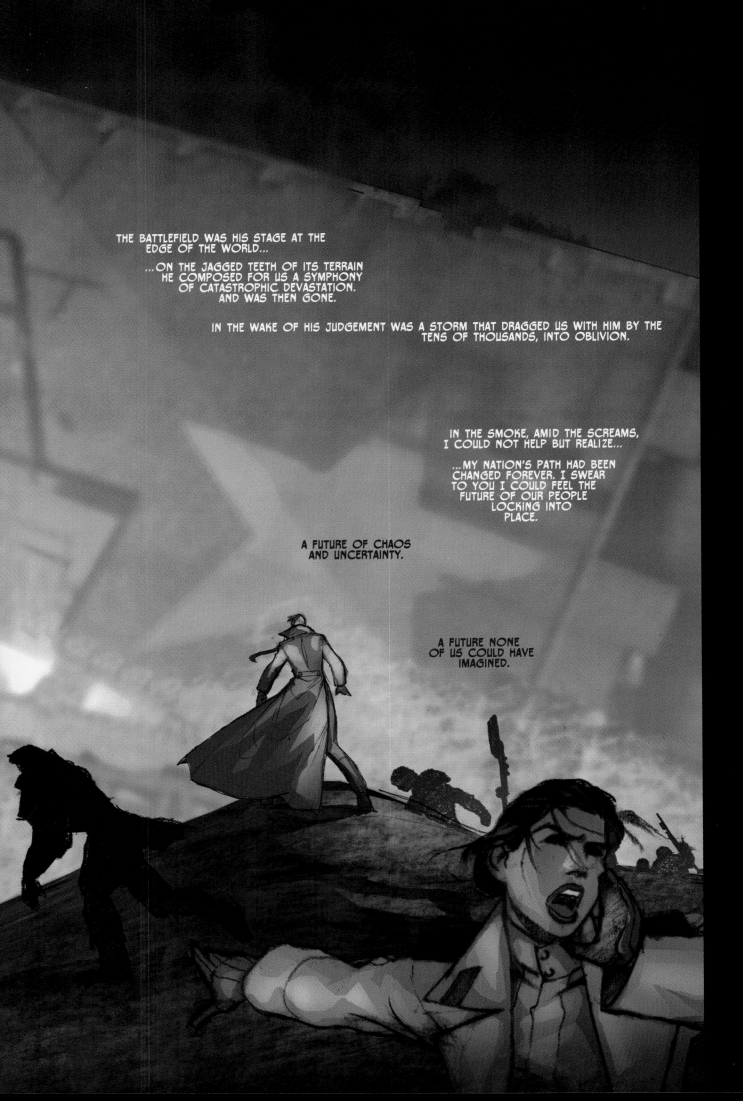

THE BATTLEFIELD WAS HIS STAGE AT THE EDGE OF THE WORLD...

...ON THE JAGGED TEETH OF ITS TERRAIN HE COMPOSED FOR US A SYMPHONY OF CATASTROPHIC DEVASTATION. AND WAS THEN GONE.

IN THE WAKE OF HIS JUDGEMENT WAS A STORM THAT DRAGGED US WITH HIM BY THE TENS OF THOUSANDS, INTO OBLIVION.

IN THE SMOKE, AMID THE SCREAMS, I COULD NOT HELP BUT REALIZE...

...MY NATION'S PATH HAD BEEN CHANGED FOREVER. I SWEAR TO YOU I COULD FEEL THE FUTURE OF OUR PEOPLE LOCKING INTO PLACE.

A FUTURE OF CHAOS AND UNCERTAINTY.

A FUTURE NONE OF US COULD HAVE IMAGINED.

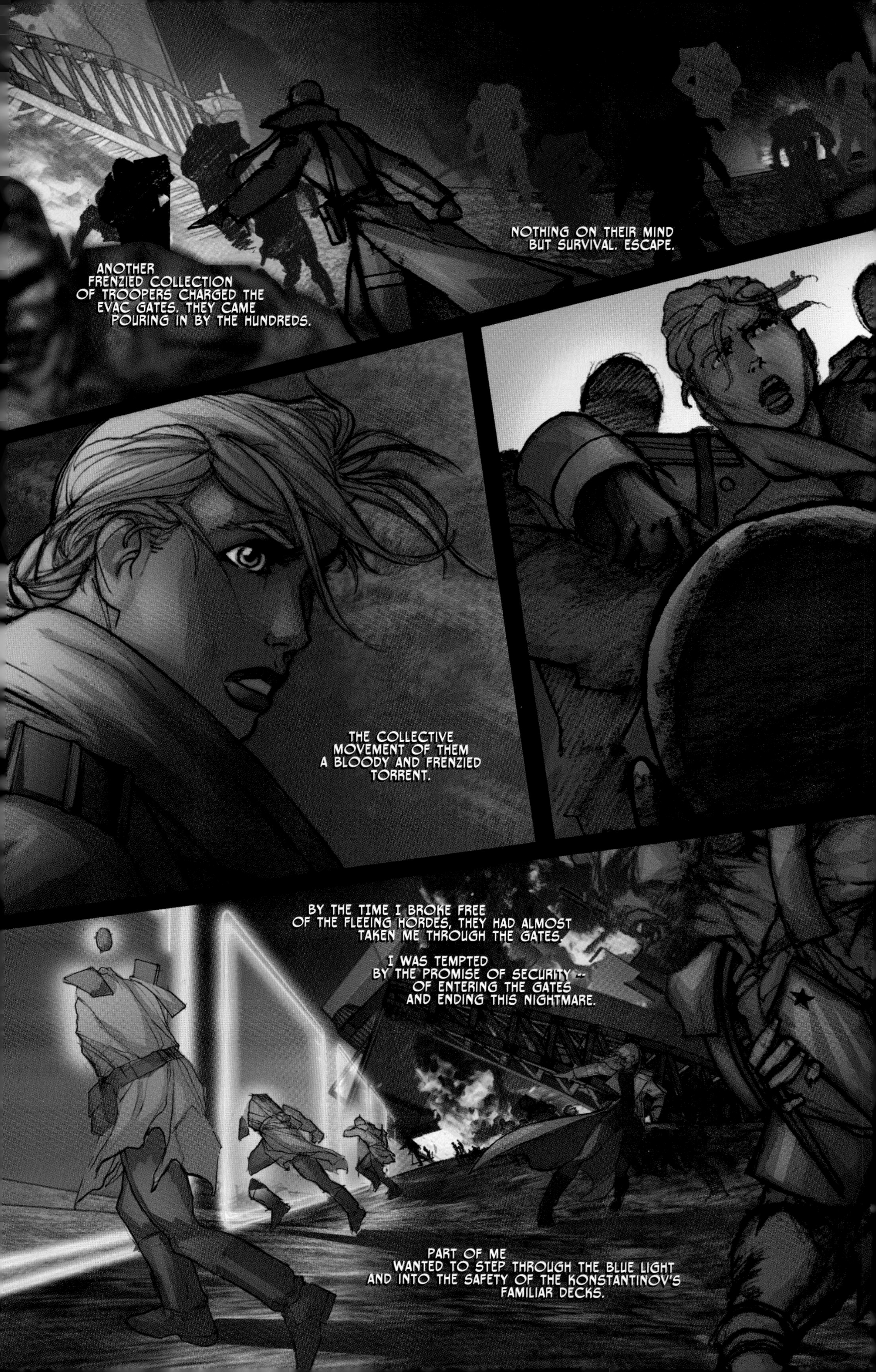

ANOTHER FRENZIED COLLECTION OF TROOPERS CHARGED THE EVAC GATES. THEY CAME POURING IN BY THE HUNDREDS.
NOTHING ON THEIR MIND BUT SURVIVAL. ESCAPE.
THE COLLECTIVE MOVEMENT OF THEM A BLOODY AND FRENZIED TORRENT.
BY THE TIME I BROKE FREE OF THE FLEEING HORDES, THEY HAD ALMOST TAKEN ME THROUGH THE GATES.
I WAS TEMPTED BY THE PROMISE OF SECURITY -- OF ENTERING THE GATES AND ENDING THIS NIGHTMARE.
PART OF ME WANTED TO STEP THROUGH THE BLUE LIGHT AND INTO THE SAFETY OF THE KONSTANTINOV'S FAMILIAR DECKS.

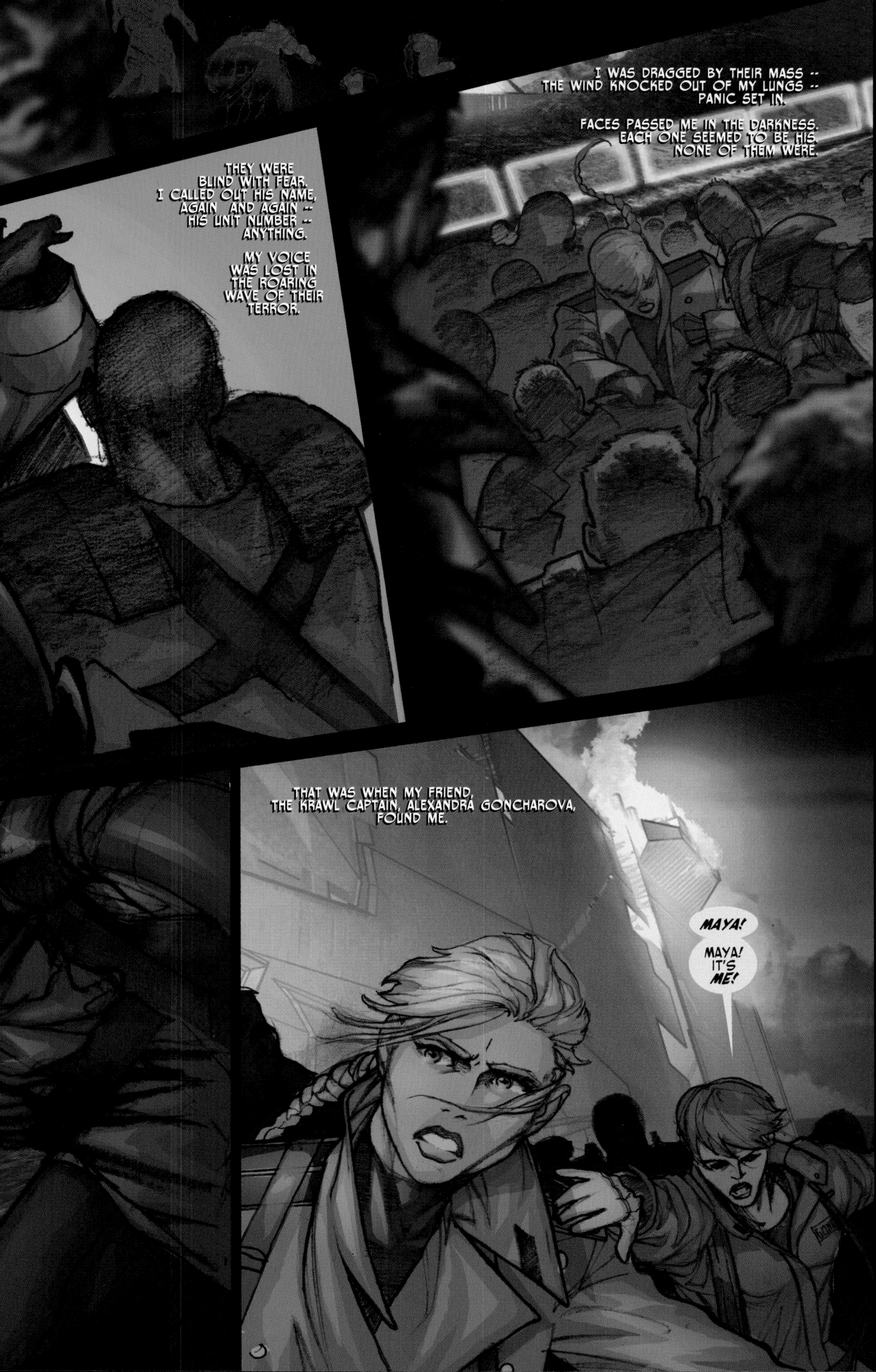

THEY WERE BLIND WITH FEAR. I CALLED OUT HIS NAME, AGAIN AND AGAIN -- HIS UNIT NUMBER -- ANYTHING.
MY VOICE WAS LOST IN THE ROARING WAVE OF THEIR TERROR.
I WAS DRAGGED BY THEIR MASS -- THE WIND KNOCKED OUT OF MY LUNGS -- PANIC SET IN.
FACES PASSED ME IN THE DARKNESS. EACH ONE SEEMED TO BE HIS. NONE OF THEM WERE.
THAT WAS WHEN MY FRIEND, THE KRAWL CAPTAIN, ALEXANDRA GONCHAROVA, FOUND ME.
MAYA!
MAYA! IT'S ME!

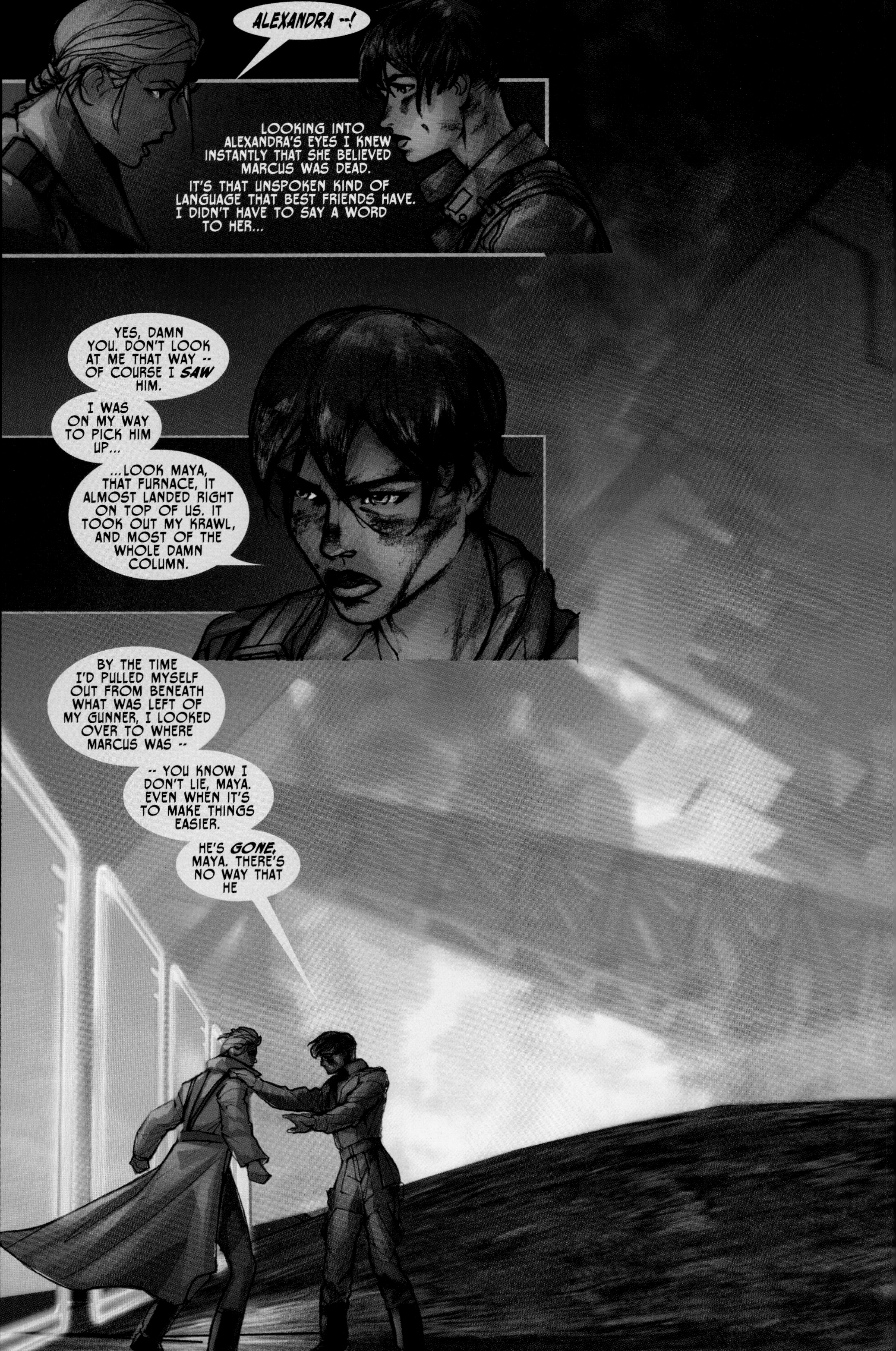

ALEXANDRA --!
LOOKING INTO ALEXANDRA'S EYES I KNEW INSTANTLY THAT SHE BELIEVED MARCUS WAS DEAD.
IT'S THAT UNSPOKEN KIND OF LANGUAGE THAT BEST FRIENDS HAVE. I DIDN'T HAVE TO SAY A WORD TO HER...
YES, DAMN YOU. DON'T LOOK AT ME THAT WAY -- OF COURSE I SAW HIM.
I WAS ON MY WAY TO PICK HIM UP...
...LOOK MAYA, THAT FURNACE, IT ALMOST LANDED RIGHT ON TOP OF US. IT TOOK OUT MY KRAWL, AND MOST OF THE WHOLE DAMN COLUMN.
BY THE TIME I'D PULLED MYSELF OUT FROM BENEATH WHAT WAS LEFT OF MY GUNNER, I LOOKED OVER TO WHERE MARCUS WAS --
-- YOU KNOW I DON'T LIE, MAYA. EVEN WHEN IT'S TO MAKE THINGS EASIER.
HE'S GONE, MAYA. THERE'S NO WAY THAT HE

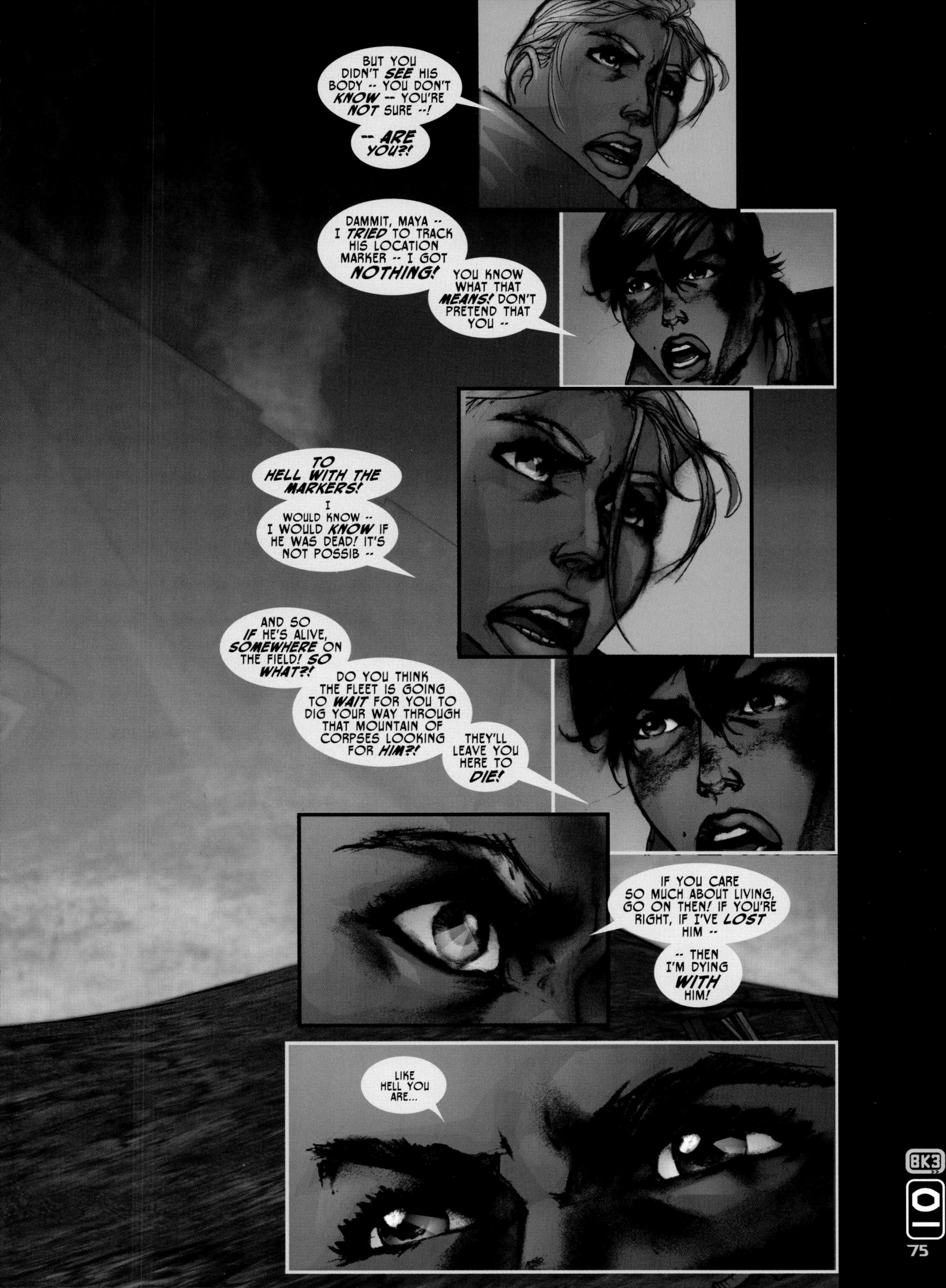
BUT YOU DIDN'T SEE HIS BODY -- YOU DON'T KNOW -- YOU'RE NOT SURE --!
-- ARE YOU?!
DAMMIT, MAYA -- I TRIED TO TRACK HIS LOCATION MARKER -- I GOT NOTHING!
YOU KNOW WHAT THAT MEANS! DON'T PRETEND THAT YOU --
TO HELL WITH THE MARKERS!
I WOULD KNOW -- I WOULD KNOW IF HE WAS DEAD! IT'S NOT POSSIB --
AND SO IF HE'S ALIVE, SOMEWHERE ON THE FIELD! SO WHAT?!
DO YOU THINK THE FLEET IS GOING TO WAIT FOR YOU TO DIG YOUR WAY THROUGH THAT MOUNTAIN OF CORPSES LOOKING FOR HIM?!
THEY'LL LEAVE YOU HERE TO DIE!
IF YOU CARE SO MUCH ABOUT LIVING, GO ON THEN! IF YOU'RE RIGHT, IF I'VE LOST HIM --
-- THEN I'M DYING WITH HIM!
LIKE HELL YOU ARE...

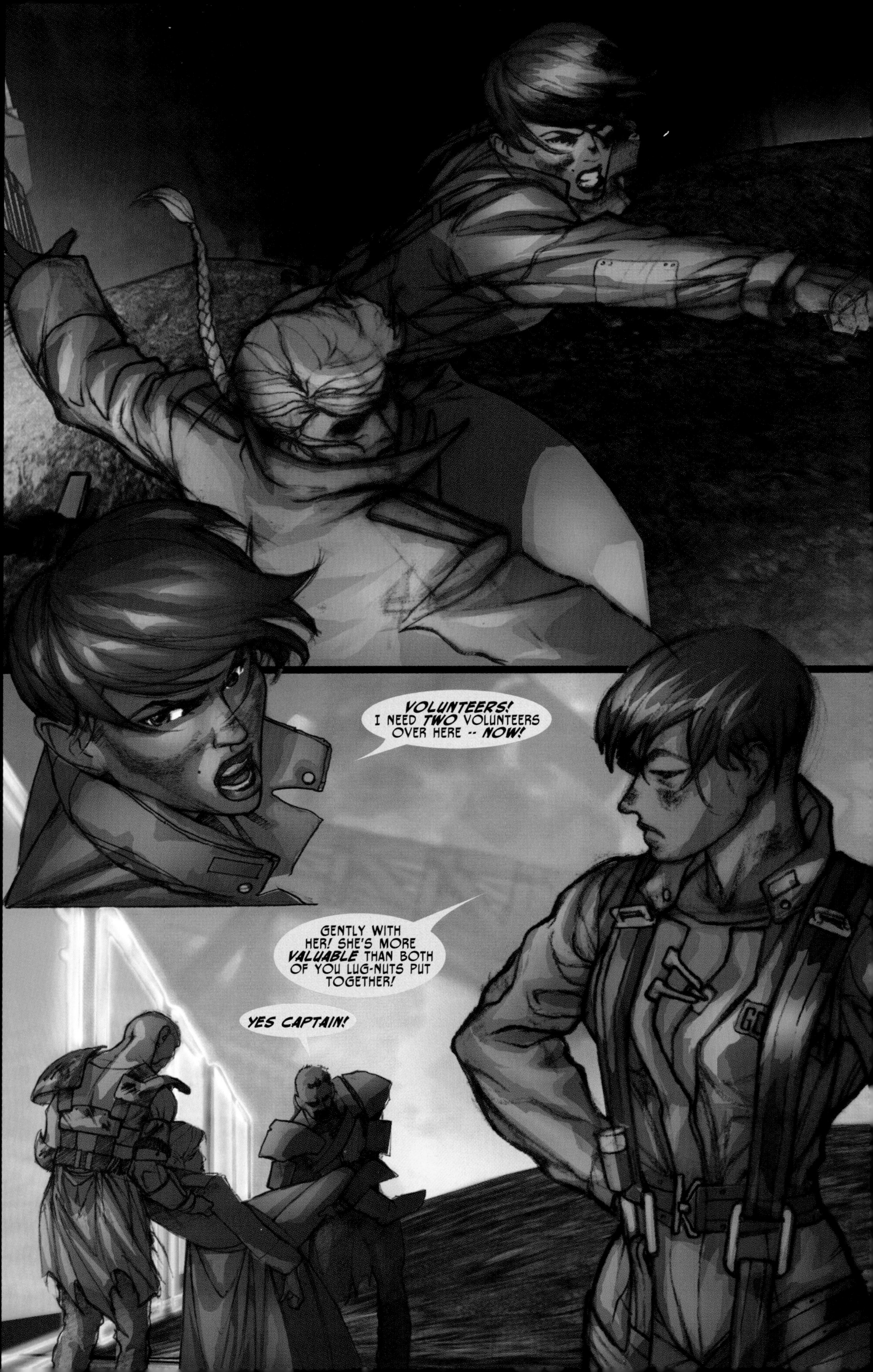
VOLUNTEERS! I NEED TWO VOLUNTEERS OVER HERE -- NOW!
GENTLY WITH HER! SHE'S MORE VALUABLE THAN BOTH OF YOU LUG-NUTS PUT TOGETHER!
YES CAPTAIN!

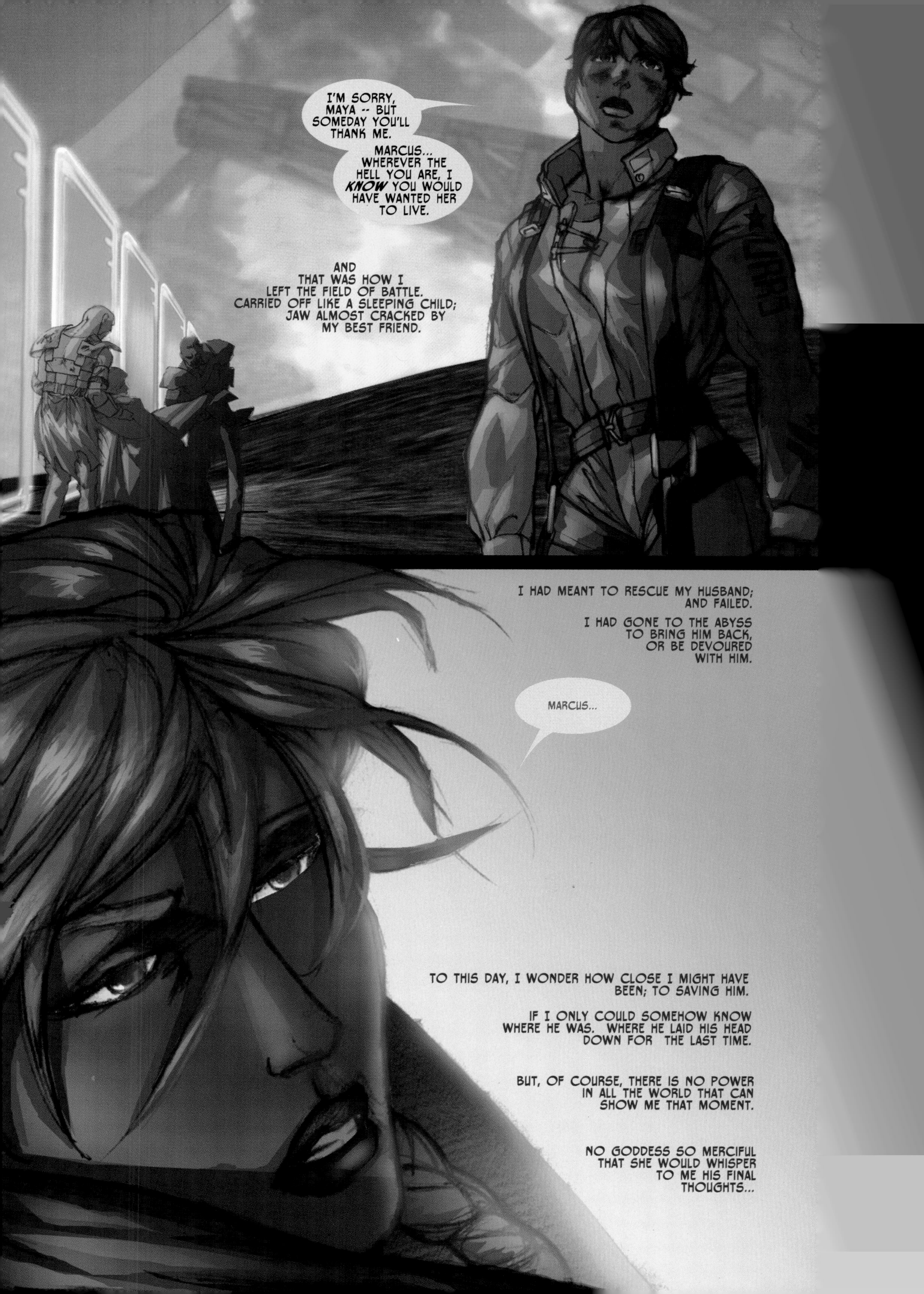
I'M SORRY, MAYA -- BUT SOMEDAY YOU'LL THANK ME.
MARCUS... WHEREVER THE HELL YOU ARE, I KNOW YOU WOULD HAVE WANTED HER TO LIVE.
AND THAT WAS HOW I LEFT THE FIELD OF BATTLE. CARRIED OFF LIKE A SLEEPING CHILD; JAW ALMOST CRACKED BY MY BEST FRIEND.
I HAD MEANT TO RESCUE MY HUSBAND; AND FAILED.
I HAD GONE TO THE ABYSS TO BRING HIM BACK, OR BE DEVOURED WITH HIM.
MARCUS...
TO THIS DAY, I WONDER HOW CLOSE I MIGHT HAVE BEEN; TO SAVING HIM.
IF I ONLY COULD SOMEHOW KNOW WHERE HE WAS. WHERE HE LAID HIS HEAD DOWN FOR THE LAST TIME.
BUT, OF COURSE, THERE IS NO POWER IN ALL THE WORLD THAT CAN SHOW ME THAT MOMENT.
NO GODDESS SO MERCIFUL THAT SHE WOULD WHISPER TO ME HIS FINAL THOUGHTS...

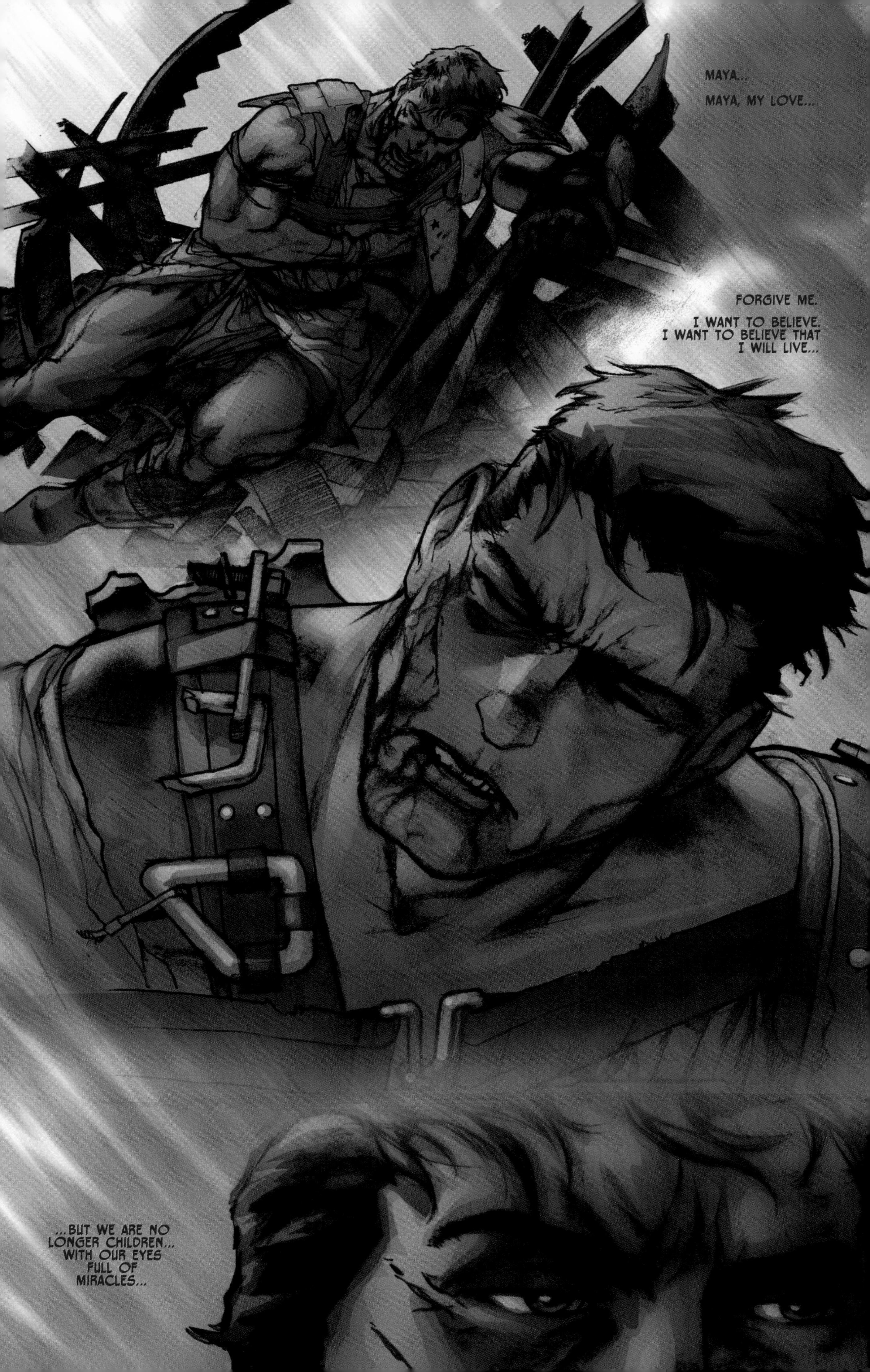
MAYA...
MAYA, MY LOVE...
FORGIVE ME.
I WANT TO BELIEVE. I WANT TO BELIEVE THAT I WILL LIVE...
...BUT WE ARE NO LONGER CHILDREN... WITH OUR EYES FULL OF MIRACLES...

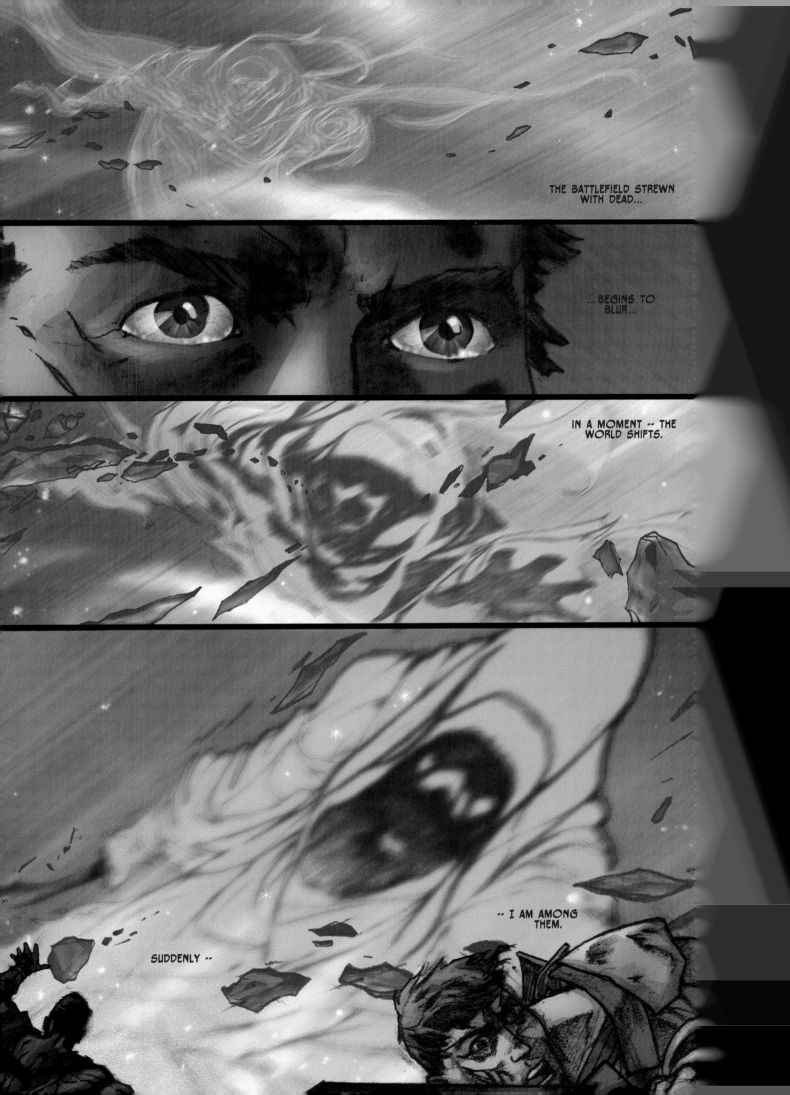

THE BATTLEFIELD STREWN WITH DEAD...

...BEGINS TO BLUR...

IN A MOMENT -- THE WORLD SHIFTS.

-- I AM AMONG THEM.

SUDDENLY --

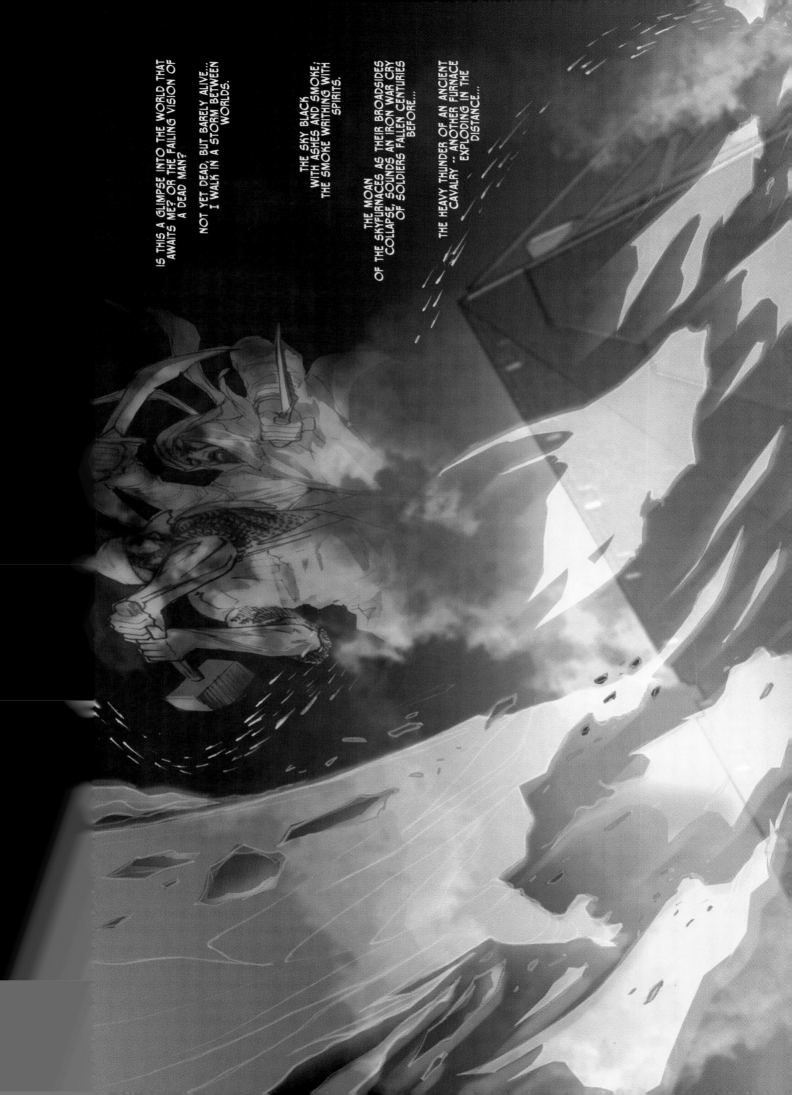

IS THIS A GLIMPSE INTO THE WORLD THAT AWAITS ME? OR THE FAILING VISION OF A DEAD MAN?

NOT YET DEAD, BUT BARELY ALIVE... I WALK IN A STORM BETWEEN WORLDS.

THE SKY BLACK WITH ASHES AND SMOKE; THE SMOKE WRITHING WITH SPIRITS.

THE MOAN OF THE SKYFURNACES AS THEIR BROADSIDES COLLAPSE, SOUNDS AN IRON WAR CRY OF SOLDIERS FALLEN CENTURIES BEFORE...

THE HEAVY THUNDER OF AN ANCIENT CAVALRY -- ANOTHER FURNACE EXPLODING IN THE DISTANCE...

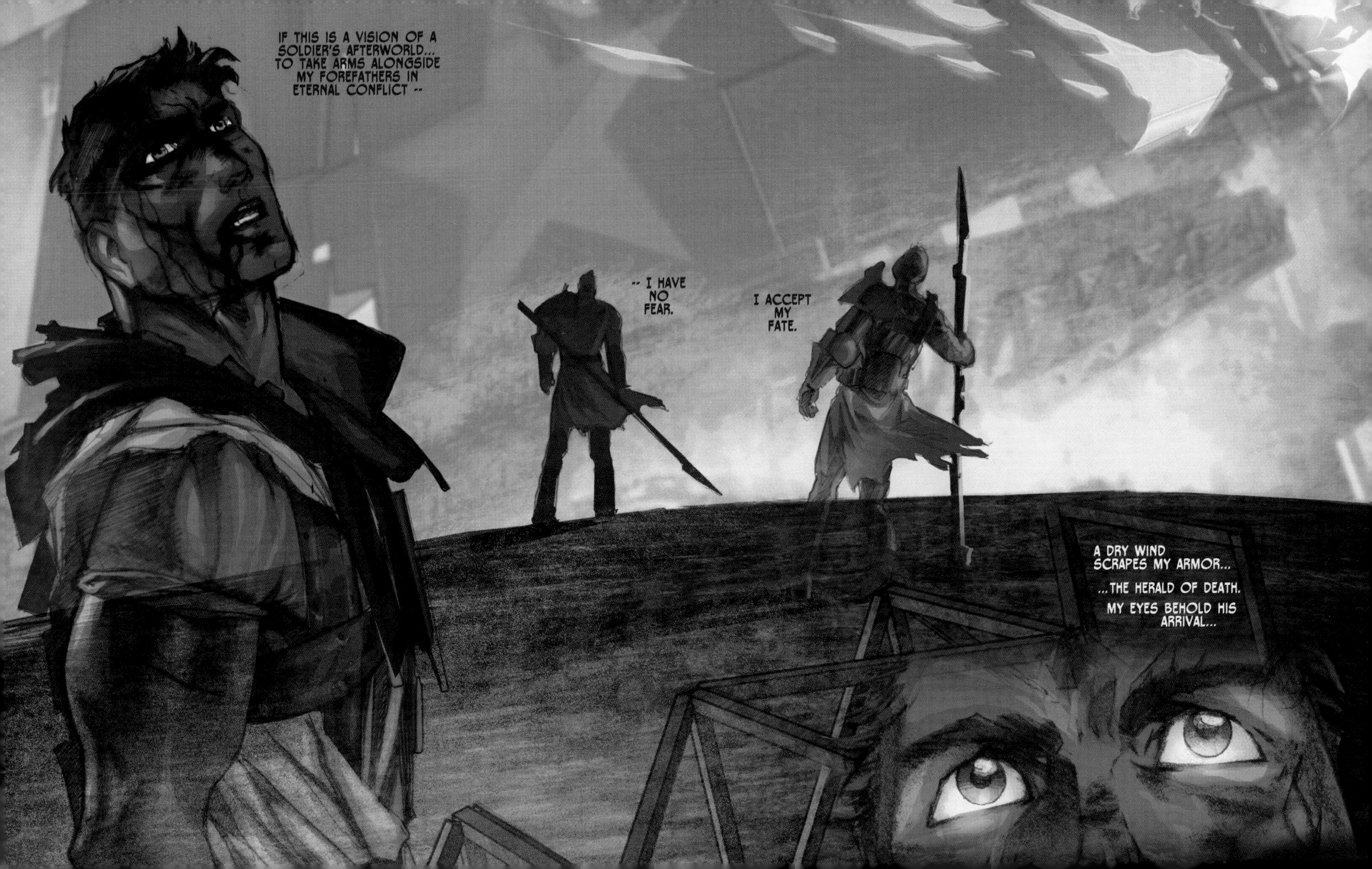
IF THIS IS A VISION OF A SOLDIER'S AFTERWORLD... TO TAKE ARMS ALONGSIDE MY FOREFATHERS IN ETERNAL CONFLICT --
-- I HAVE NO FEAR.
I ACCEPT MY FATE.
A DRY WIND SCRAPES MY ARMOR...
...THE HERALD OF DEATH.
MY EYES BEHOLD HIS ARRIVAL...

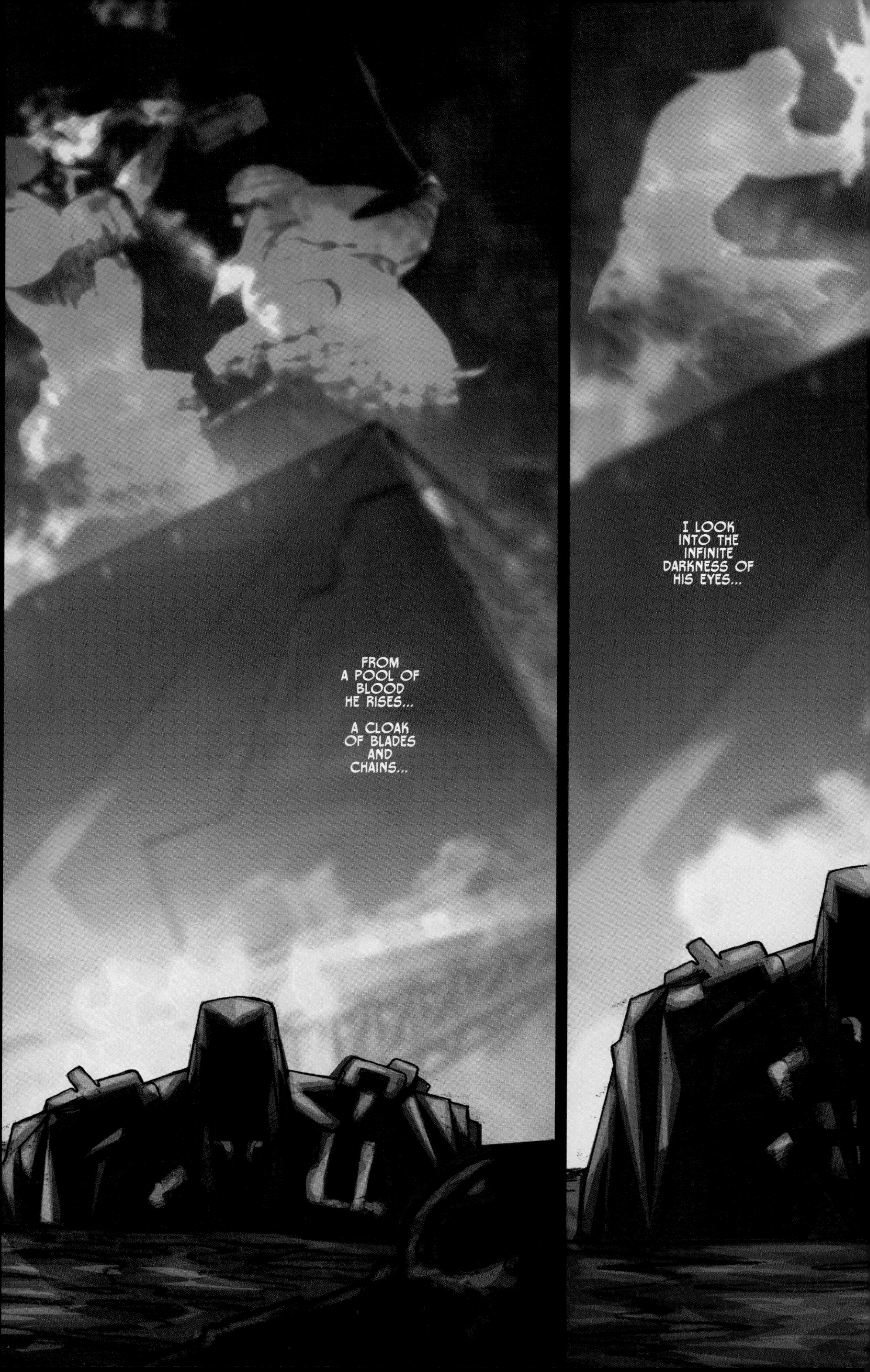
FROM A POOL OF BLOOD HE RISES...
A CLOAK OF BLADES AND CHAINS...
I LOOK INTO THE INFINITE DARKNESS OF HIS EYES...

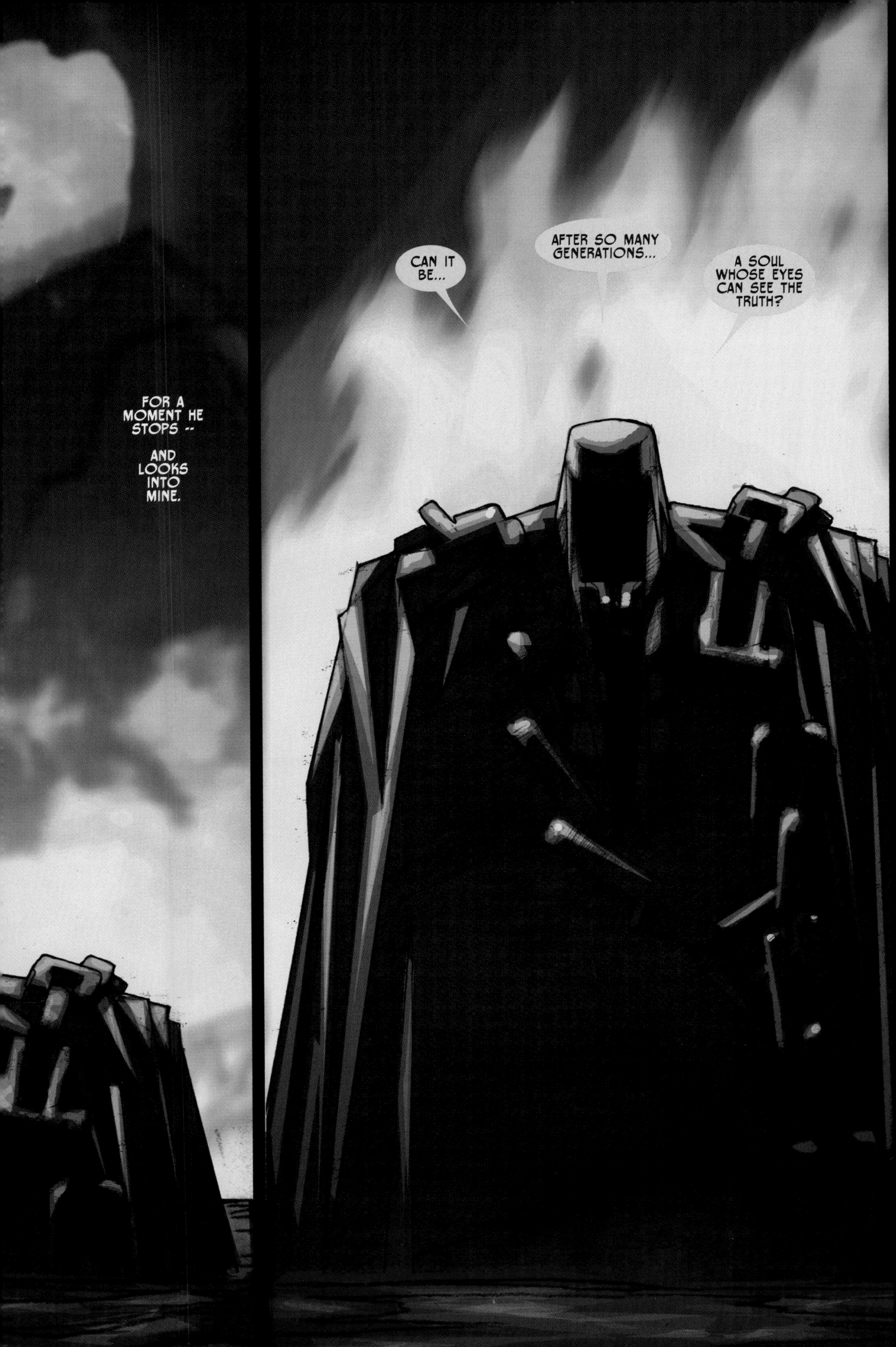
FOR A MOMENT HE STOPS --
AND LOOKS INTO MINE.
CAN IT BE...
AFTER SO MANY GENERATIONS...
A SOUL WHOSE EYES CAN SEE THE TRUTH?
BK3
8

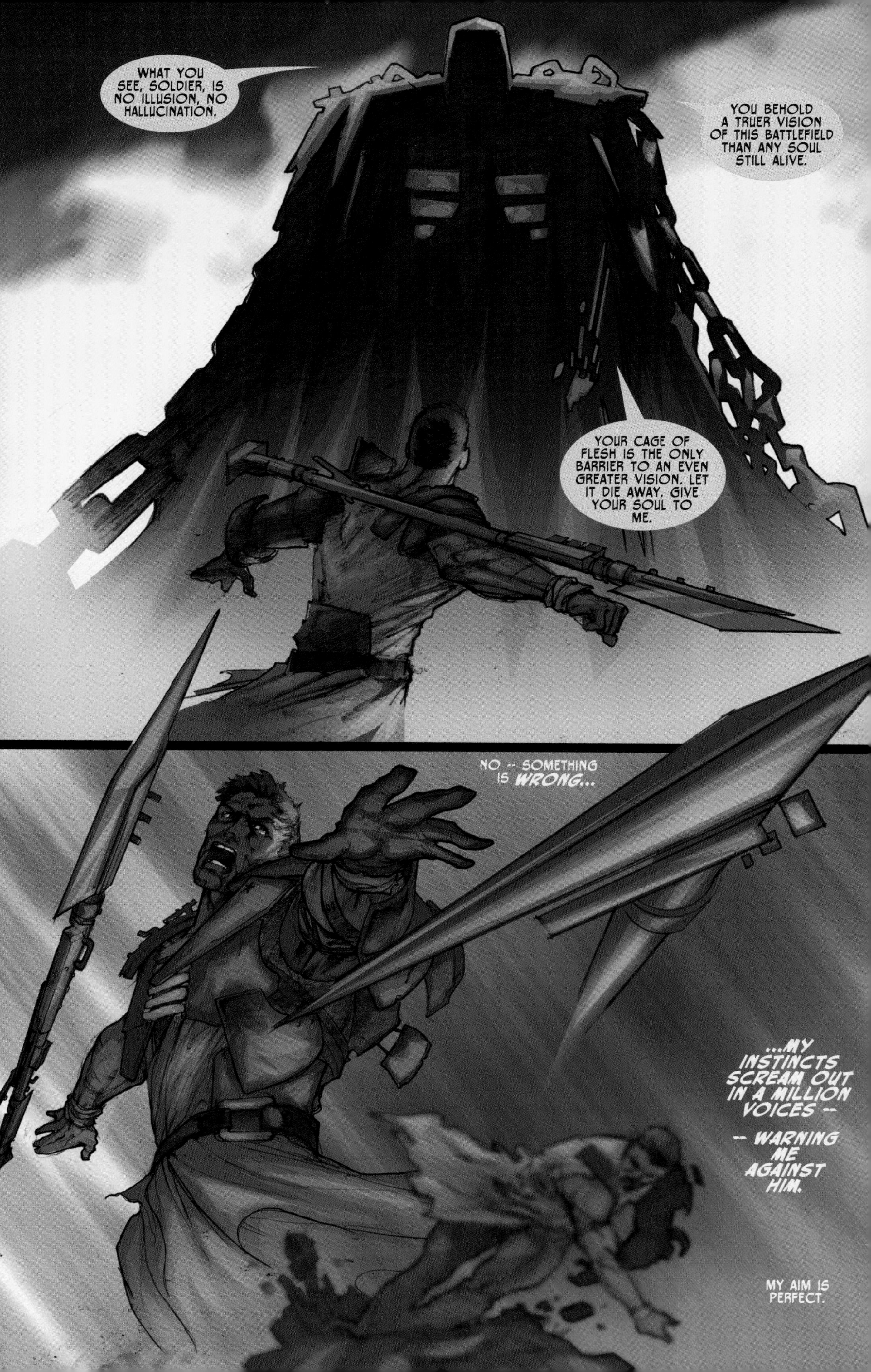
WHAT YOU SEE, SOLDIER, IS NO ILLUSION, NO HALLUCINATION.
YOU BEHOLD A TRUER VISION OF THIS BATTLEFIELD THAN ANY SOUL STILL ALIVE.
YOUR CAGE OF FLESH IS THE ONLY BARRIER TO AN EVEN GREATER VISION. LET IT DIE AWAY. GIVE YOUR SOUL TO ME.
NO -- SOMETHING IS *WRONG*...
...MY INSTINCTS SCREAM OUT IN A MILLION VOICES --
-- WARNING ME AGAINST HIM.
MY AIM IS PERFECT.

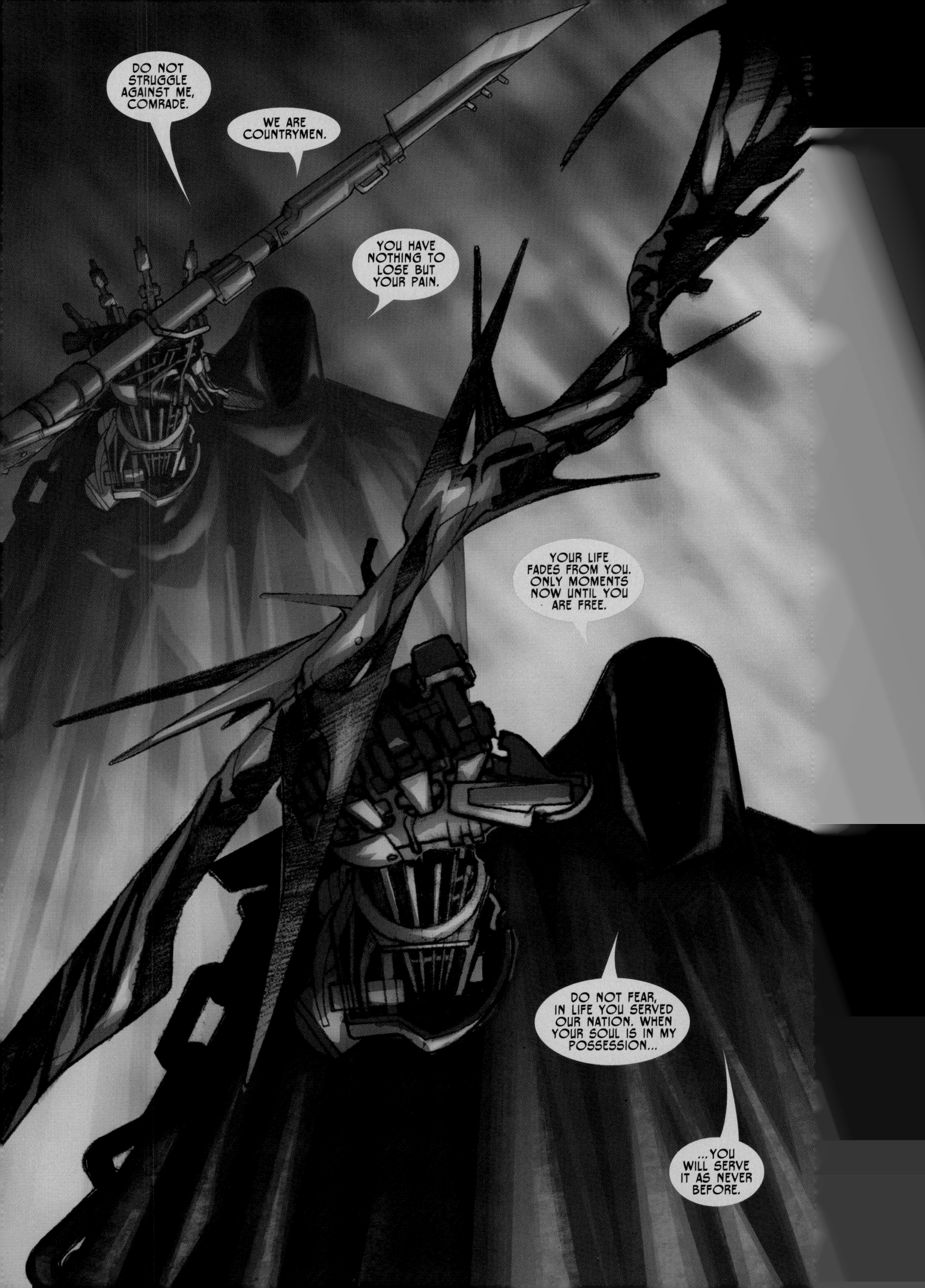
DO NOT STRUGGLE AGAINST ME, COMRADE.
WE ARE COUNTRYMEN.
YOU HAVE NOTHING TO LOSE BUT YOUR PAIN.
YOUR LIFE FADES FROM YOU. ONLY MOMENTS NOW UNTIL YOU ARE FREE.
DO NOT FEAR, IN LIFE YOU SERVED OUR NATION. WHEN YOUR SOUL IS IN MY POSSESSION...
...YOU WILL SERVE IT AS NEVER BEFORE.

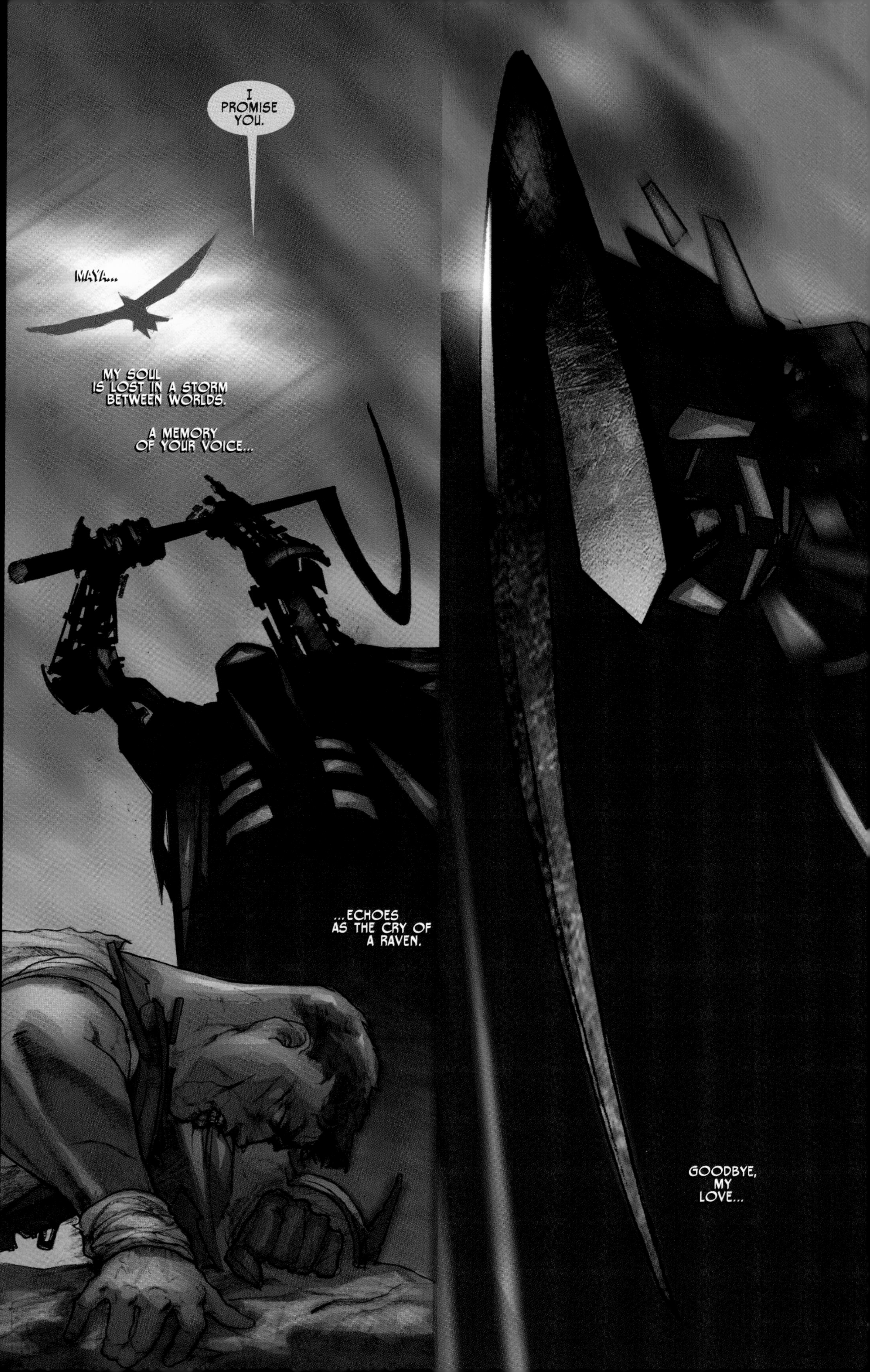
I PROMISE YOU.
MAYA...
MY SOUL IS LOST IN A STORM BETWEEN WORLDS.
A MEMORY OF YOUR VOICE...
...ECHOES AS THE CRY OF A RAVEN.
GOODBYE, MY LOVE...

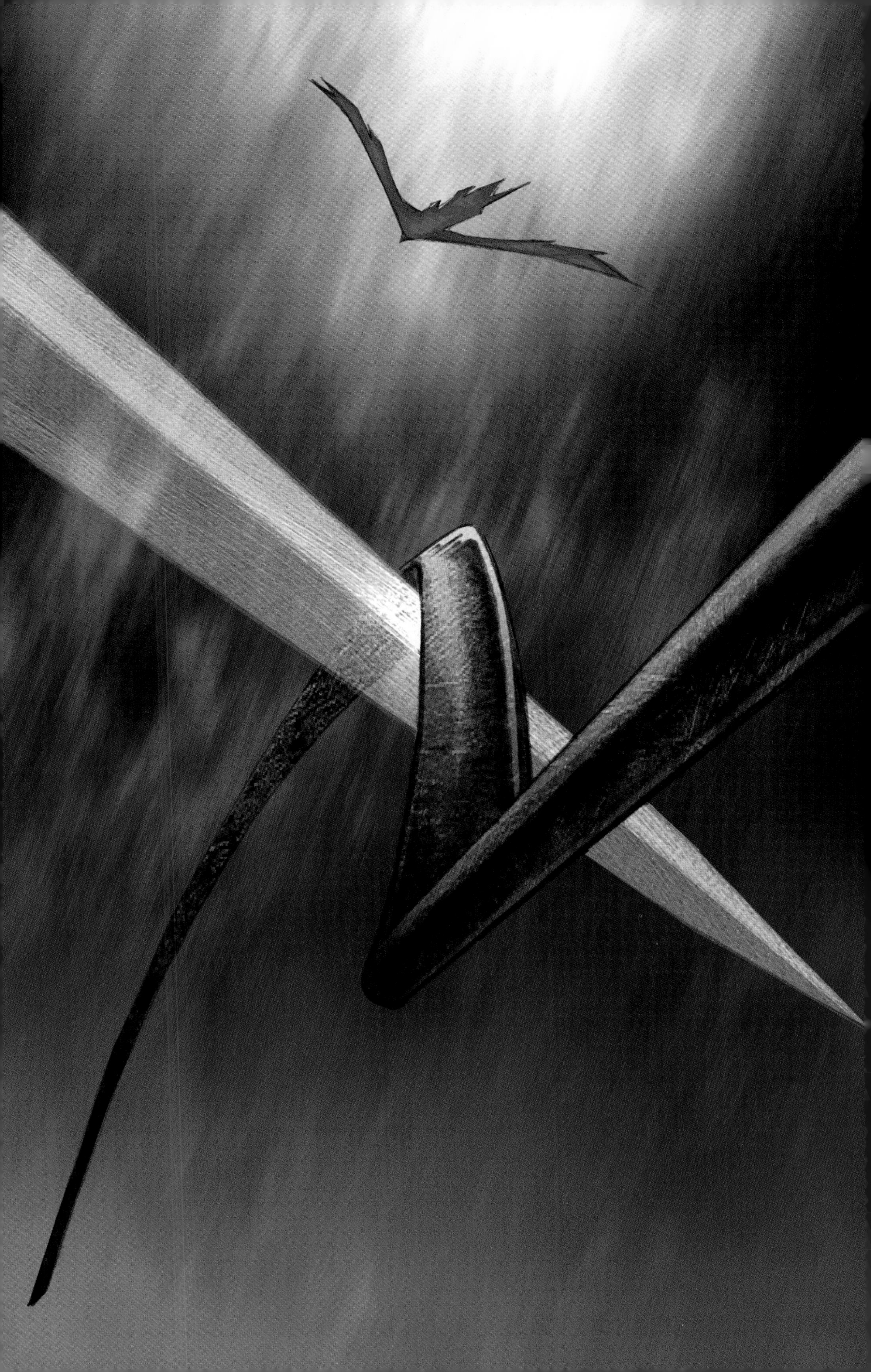

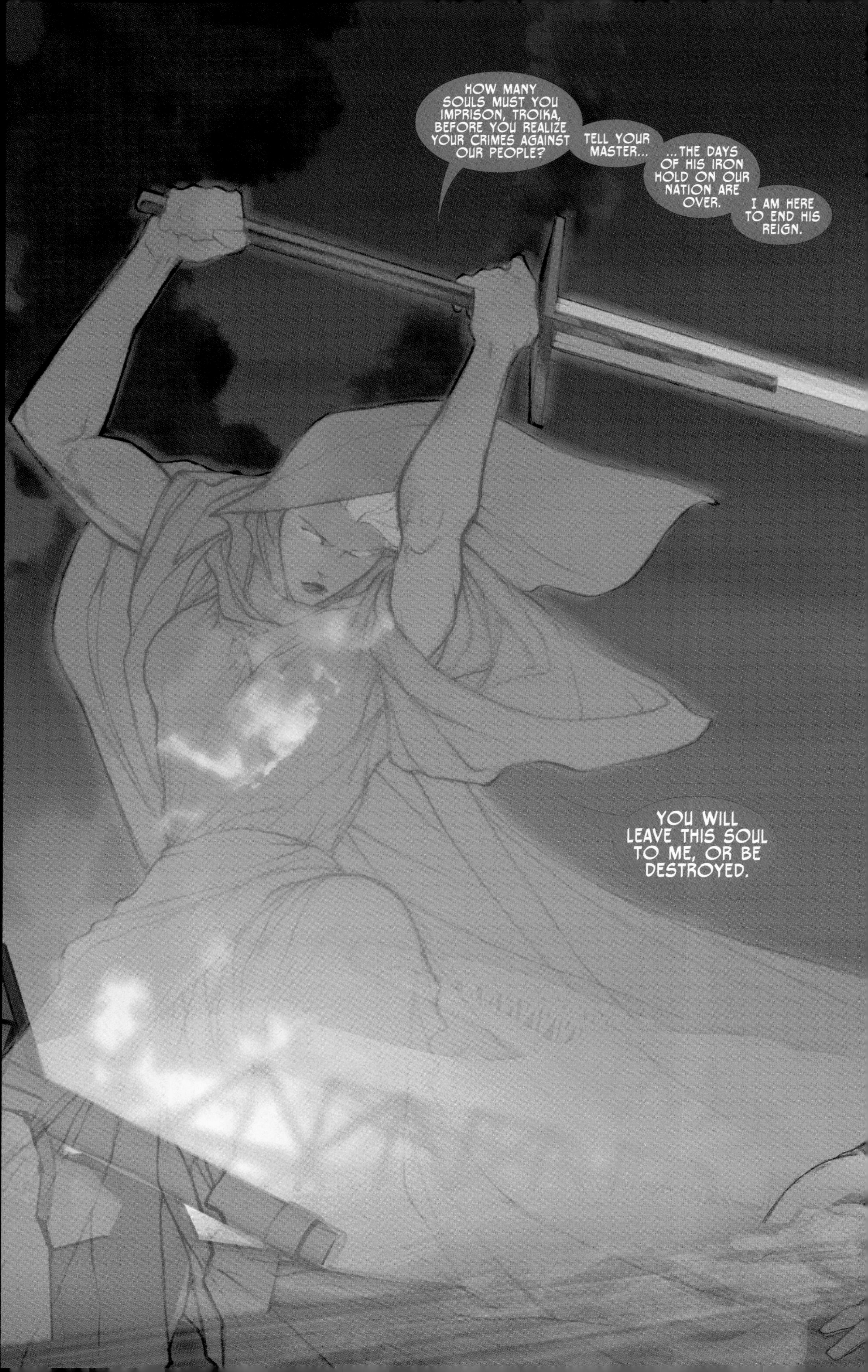
HOW MANY SOULS MUST YOU IMPRISON, TROIKA, BEFORE YOU REALIZE YOUR CRIMES AGAINST OUR PEOPLE?
TELL YOUR MASTER...
...THE DAYS OF HIS IRON HOLD ON OUR NATION ARE OVER.
I AM HERE TO END HIS REIGN.
YOU WILL LEAVE THIS SOUL TO ME, OR BE DESTROYED.

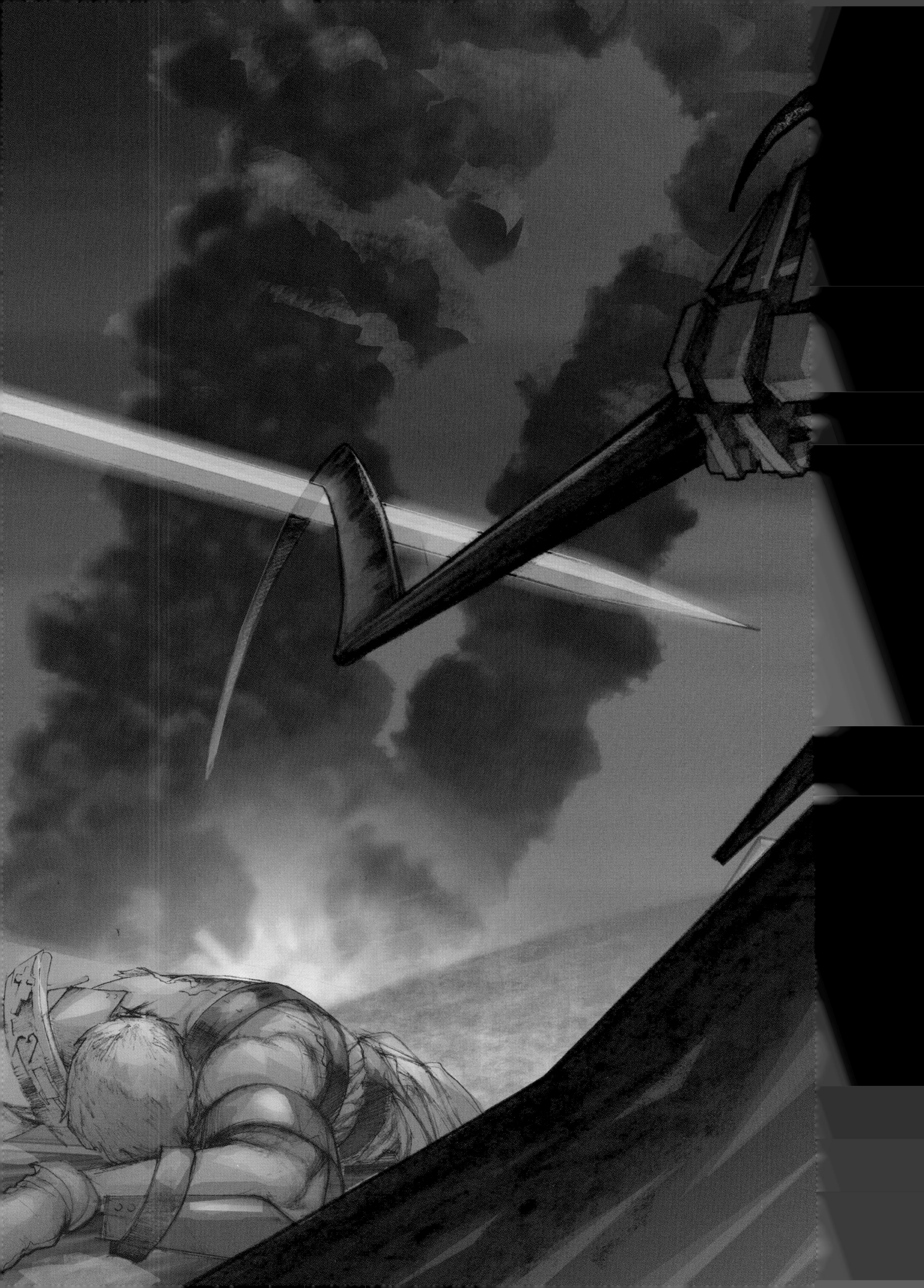

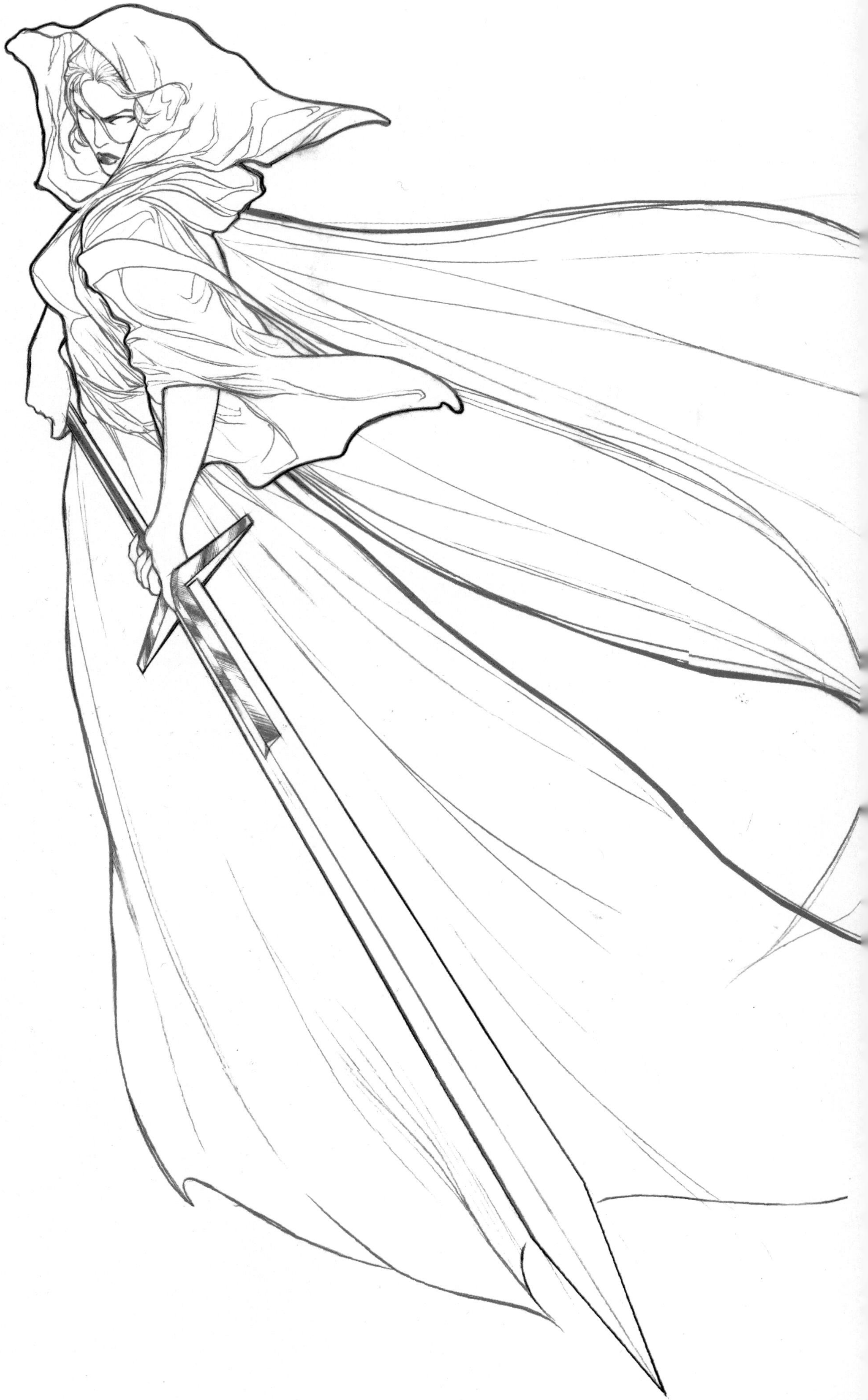

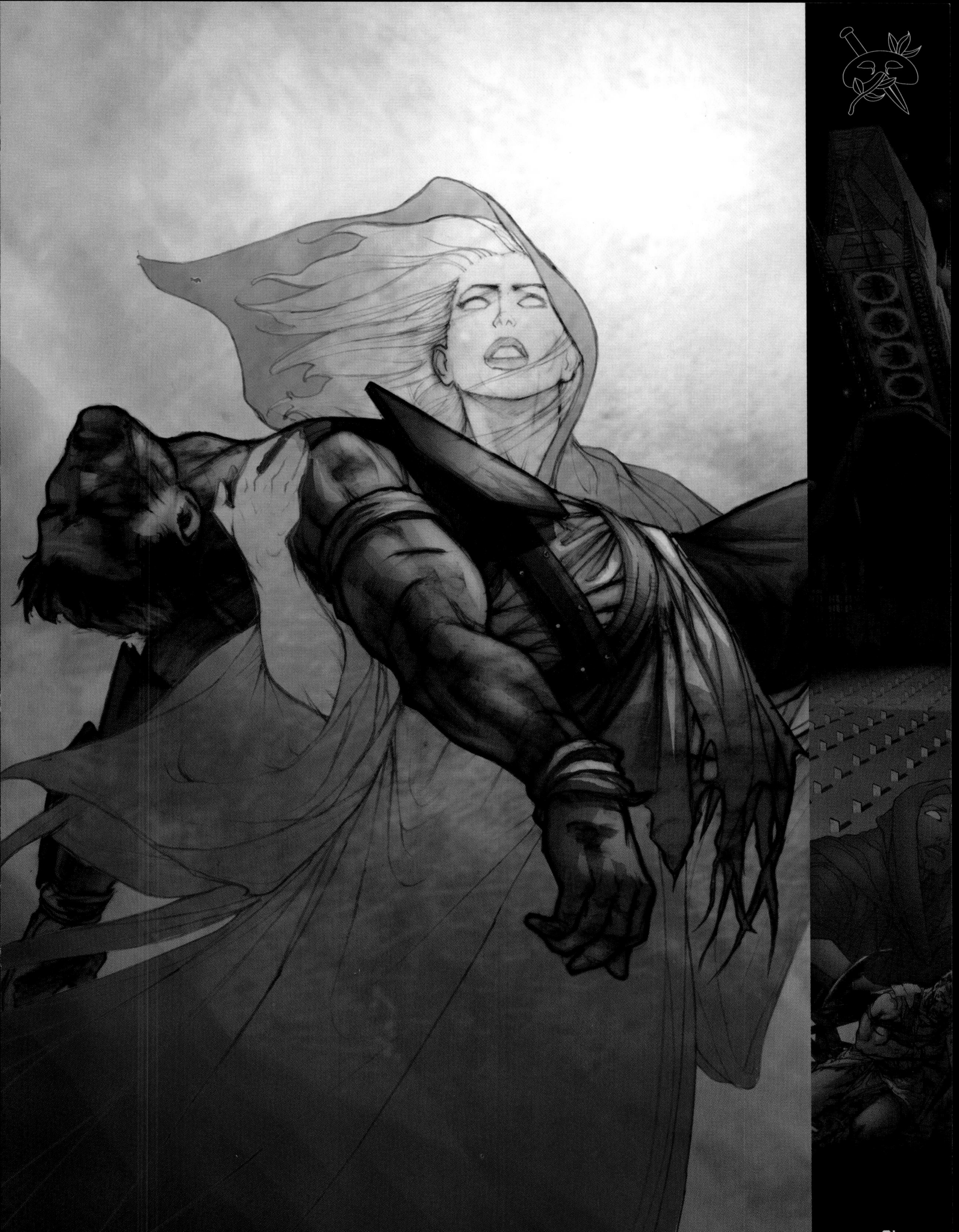

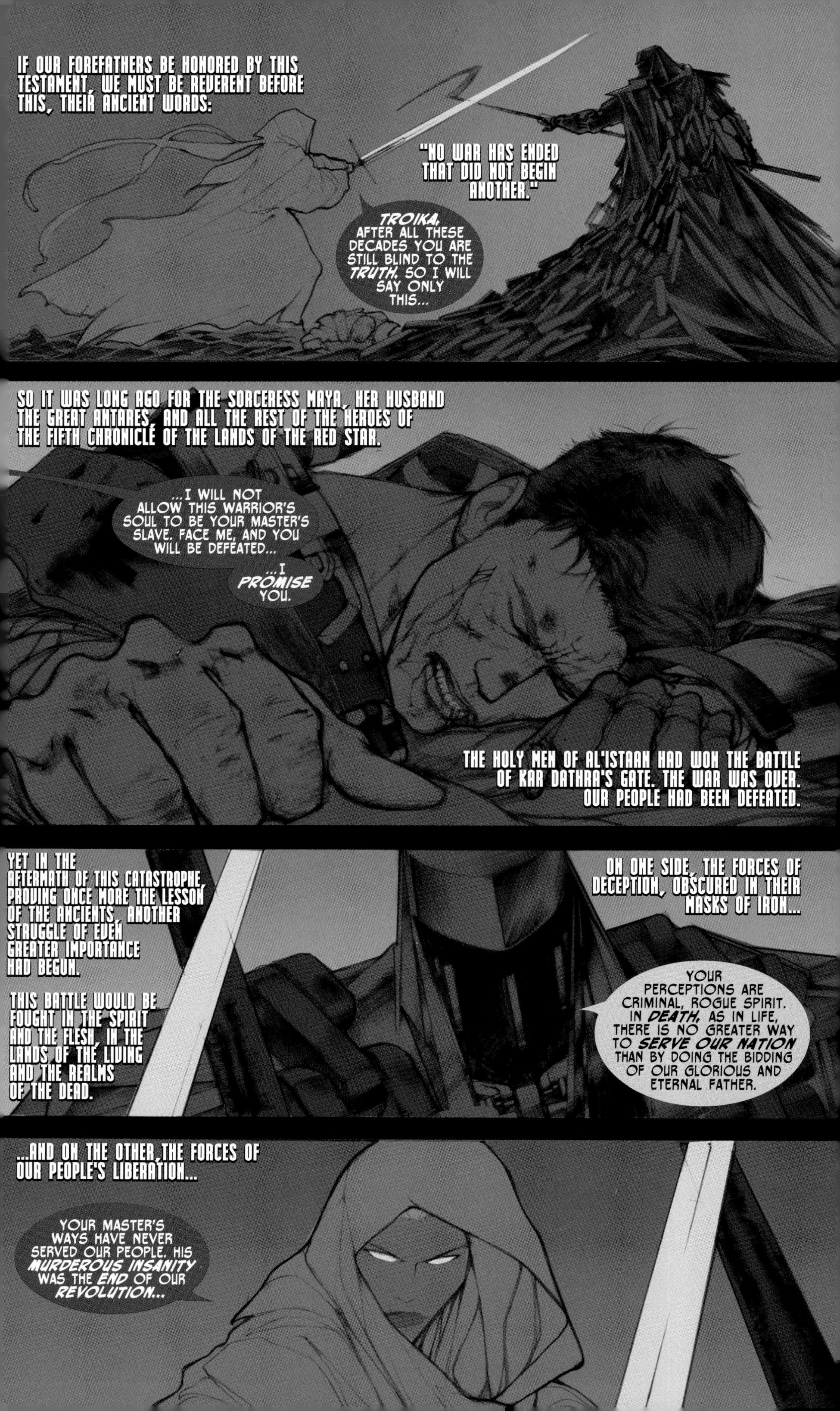

IF OUR FOREFATHERS BE HONORED BY THIS TESTAMENT, WE MUST BE REVERENT BEFORE THIS, THEIR ANCIENT WORDS:
"NO WAR HAS ENDED THAT DID NOT BEGIN ANOTHER."
TROIKA, AFTER ALL THESE DECADES YOU ARE STILL BLIND TO THE TRUTH, SO I WILL SAY ONLY THIS...
SO IT WAS LONG AGO FOR THE SORCERESS MAYA, HER HUSBAND THE GREAT ANTARES, AND ALL THE REST OF THE HEROES OF THE FIFTH CHRONICLE OF THE LANDS OF THE RED STAR.
...I WILL NOT ALLOW THIS WARRIOR'S SOUL TO BE YOUR MASTER'S SLAVE. FACE ME, AND YOU WILL BE DEFEATED...
...I PROMISE YOU.
THE HOLY MEN OF AL'ISTAAN HAD WON THE BATTLE OF KAR DATHRA'S GATE. THE WAR WAS OVER. OUR PEOPLE HAD BEEN DEFEATED.
YET IN THE AFTERMATH OF THIS CATASTROPHE, PROVING ONCE MORE THE LESSON OF THE ANCIENTS, ANOTHER STRUGGLE OF EVEN GREATER IMPORTANCE HAD BEGUN.
THIS BATTLE WOULD BE FOUGHT IN THE SPIRIT AND THE FLESH, IN THE LANDS OF THE LIVING AND THE REALMS OF THE DEAD.
ON ONE SIDE, THE FORCES OF DECEPTION, OBSCURED IN THEIR MASKS OF IRON...
YOUR PERCEPTIONS ARE CRIMINAL, ROGUE SPIRIT. IN DEATH, AS IN LIFE, THERE IS NO GREATER WAY TO SERVE OUR NATION THAN BY DOING THE BIDDING OF OUR GLORIOUS AND ETERNAL FATHER.
...AND ON THE OTHER, THE FORCES OF OUR PEOPLE'S LIBERATION...
YOUR MASTER'S WAYS HAVE NEVER SERVED OUR PEOPLE. HIS MURDEROUS INSANITY WAS THE END OF OUR REVOLUTION...

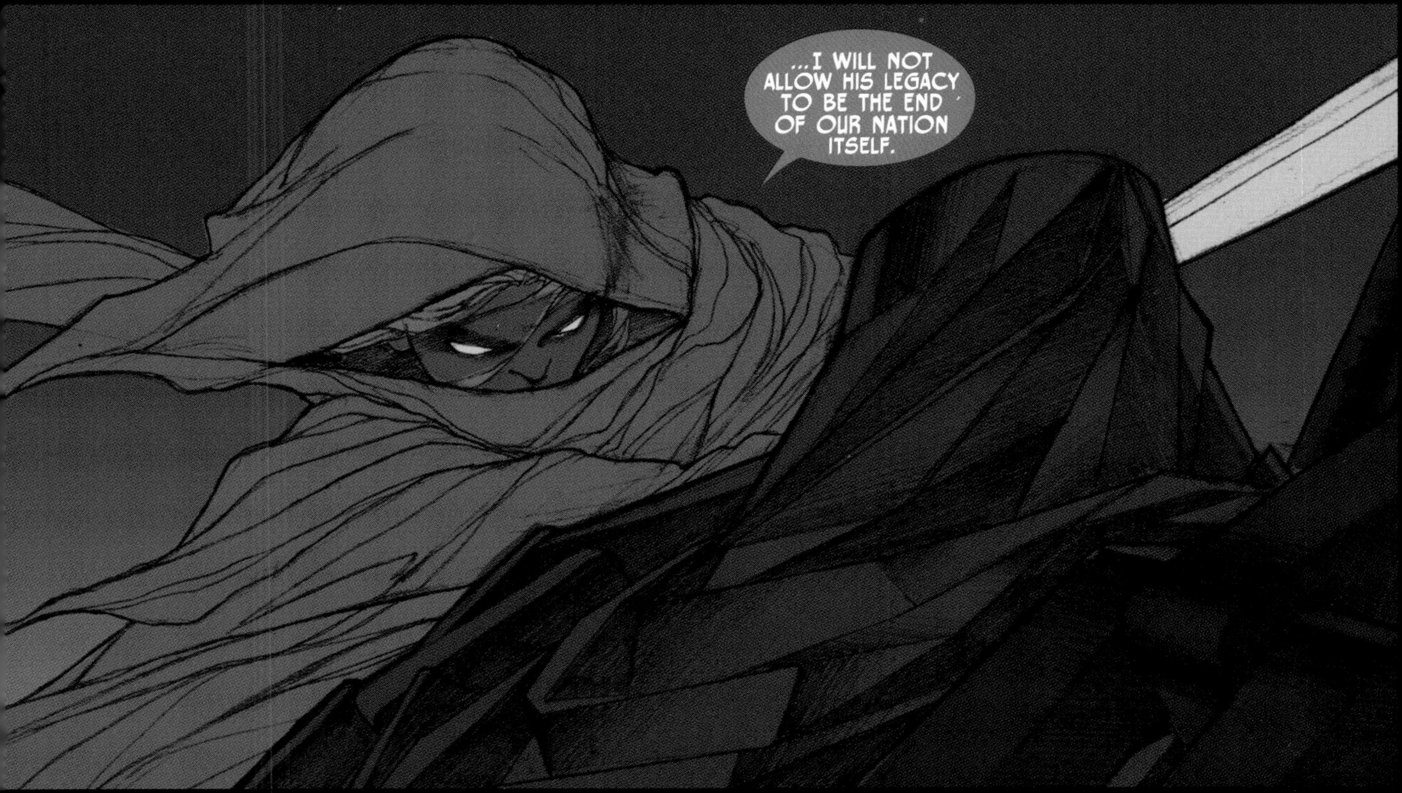
...I WILL NOT ALLOW HIS LEGACY TO BE THE END OF OUR NATION ITSELF.

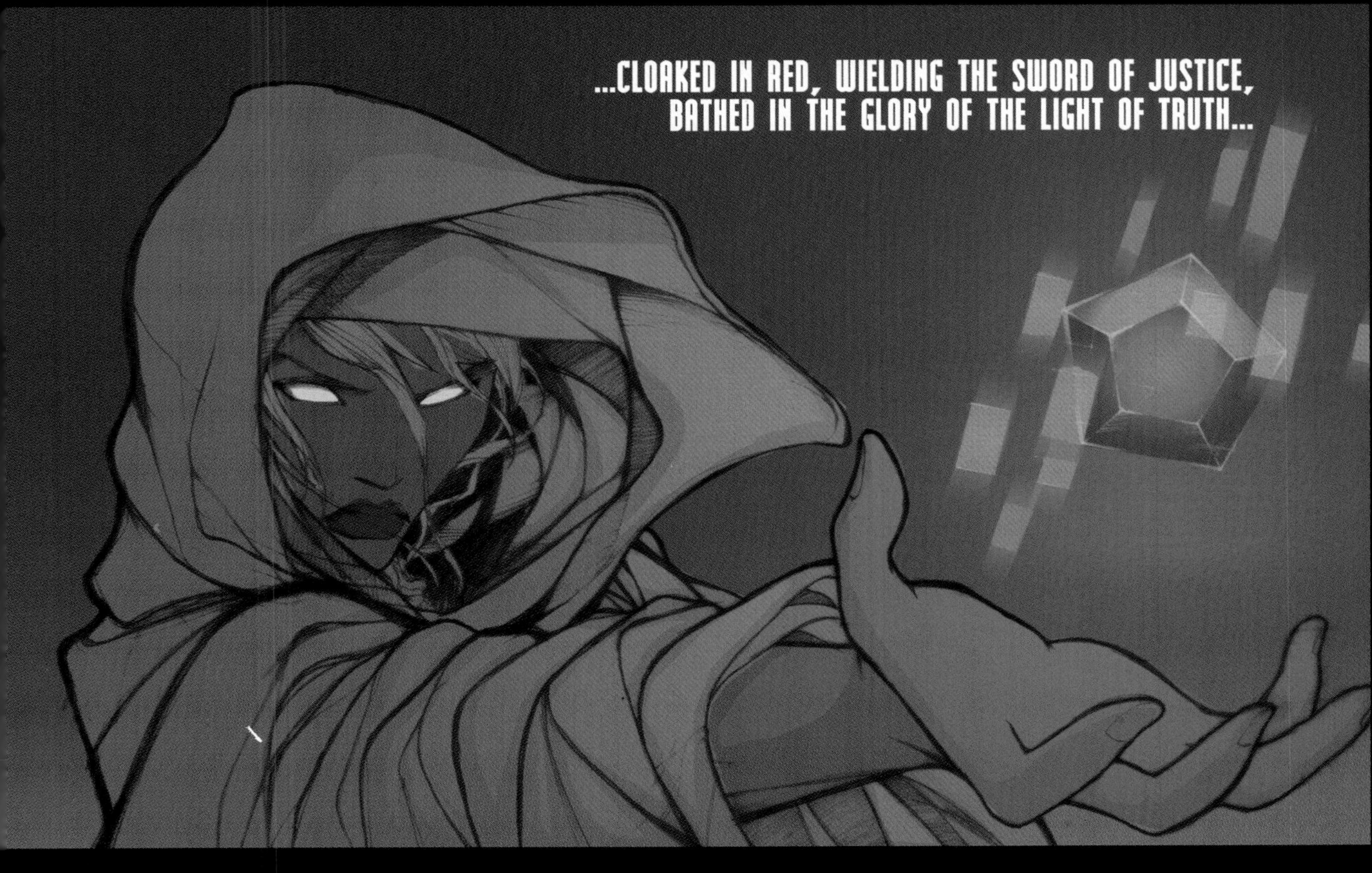
...CLOAKED IN RED, WIELDING THE SWORD OF JUSTICE, BATHED IN THE GLORY OF THE LIGHT OF TRUTH...

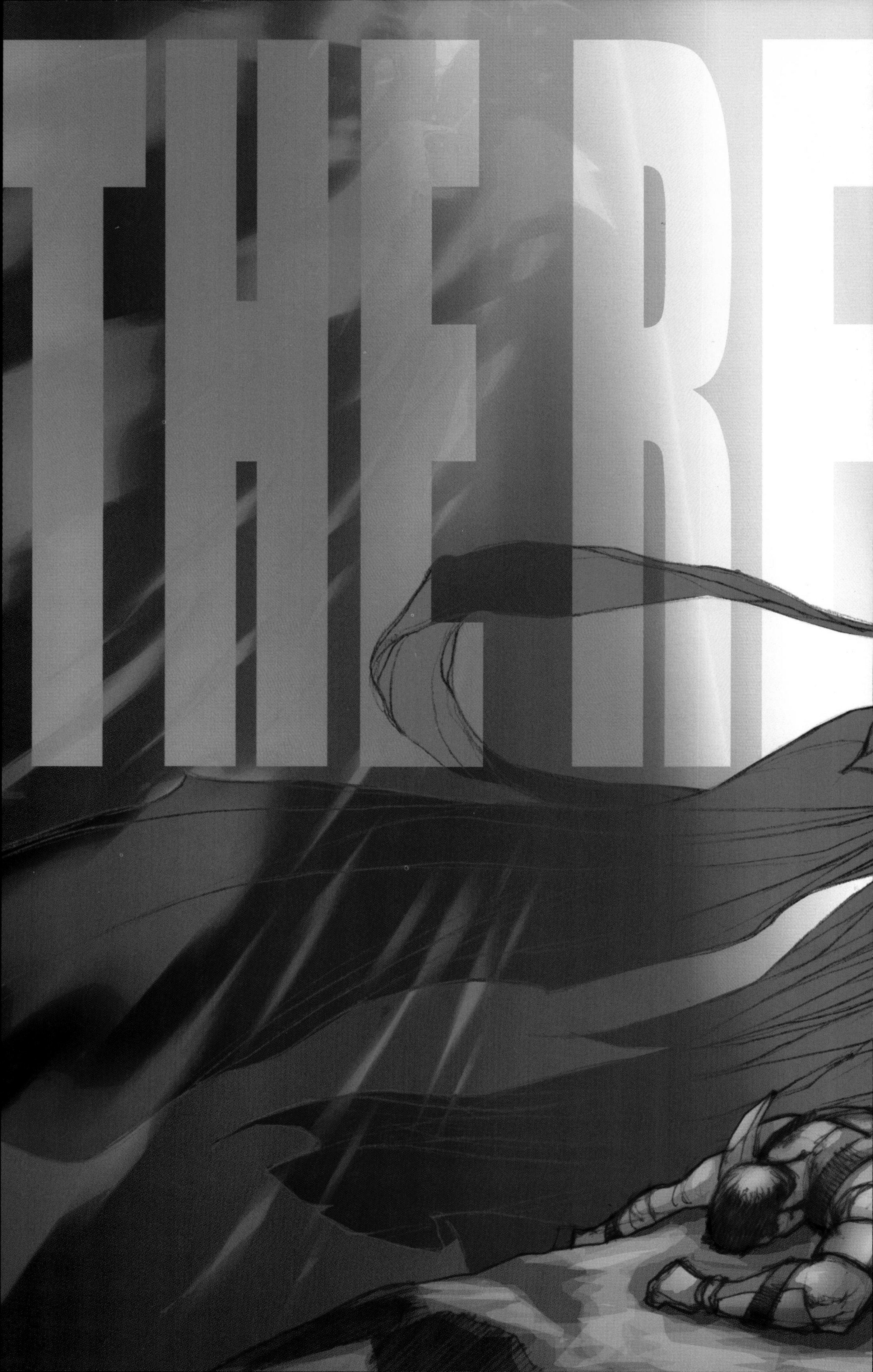
THE RE

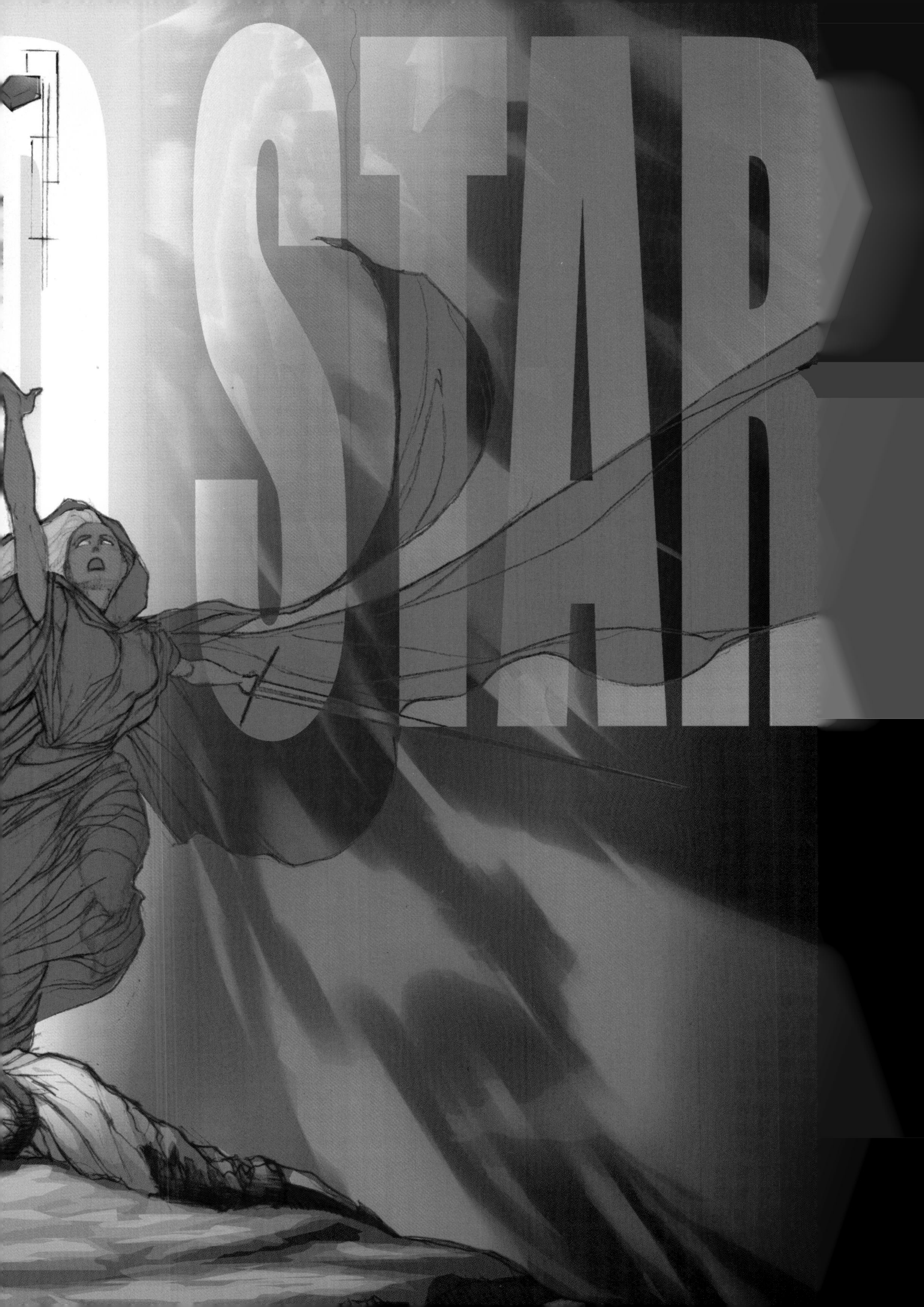
STAR

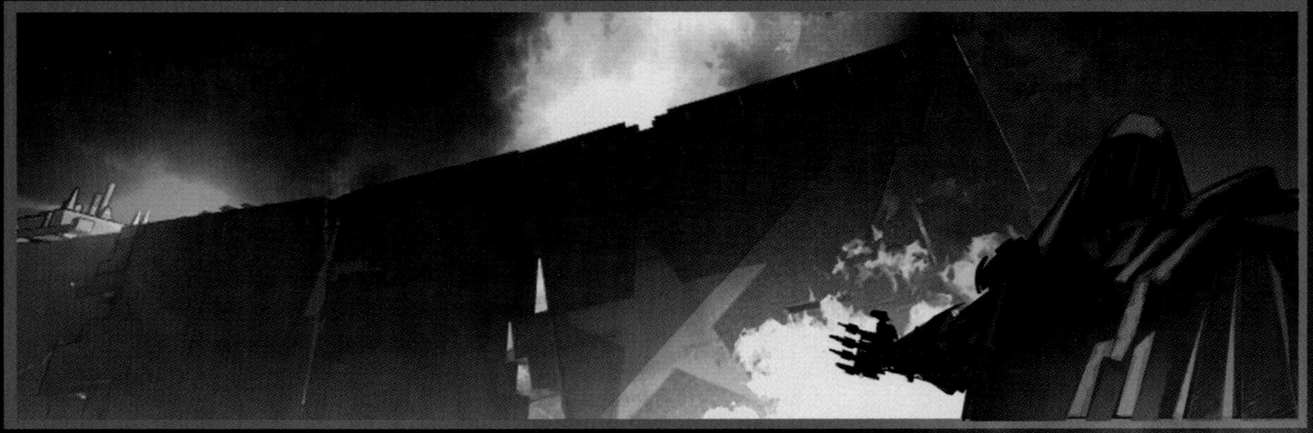

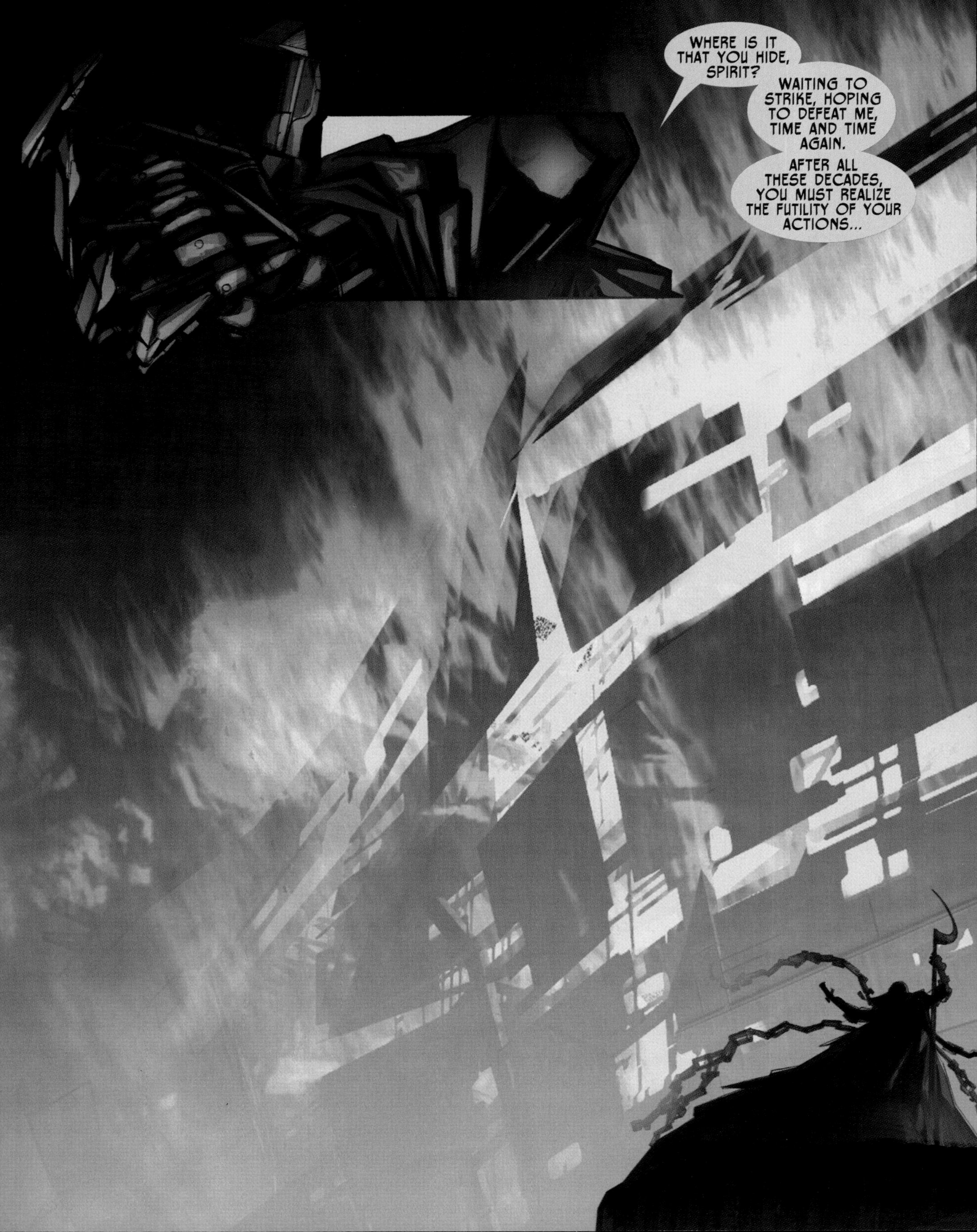

WHERE IS IT THAT YOU HIDE, SPIRIT?
WAITING TO STRIKE, HOPING TO DEFEAT ME, TIME AND TIME AGAIN.
AFTER ALL THESE DECADES, YOU MUST REALIZE THE FUTILITY OF YOUR ACTIONS...

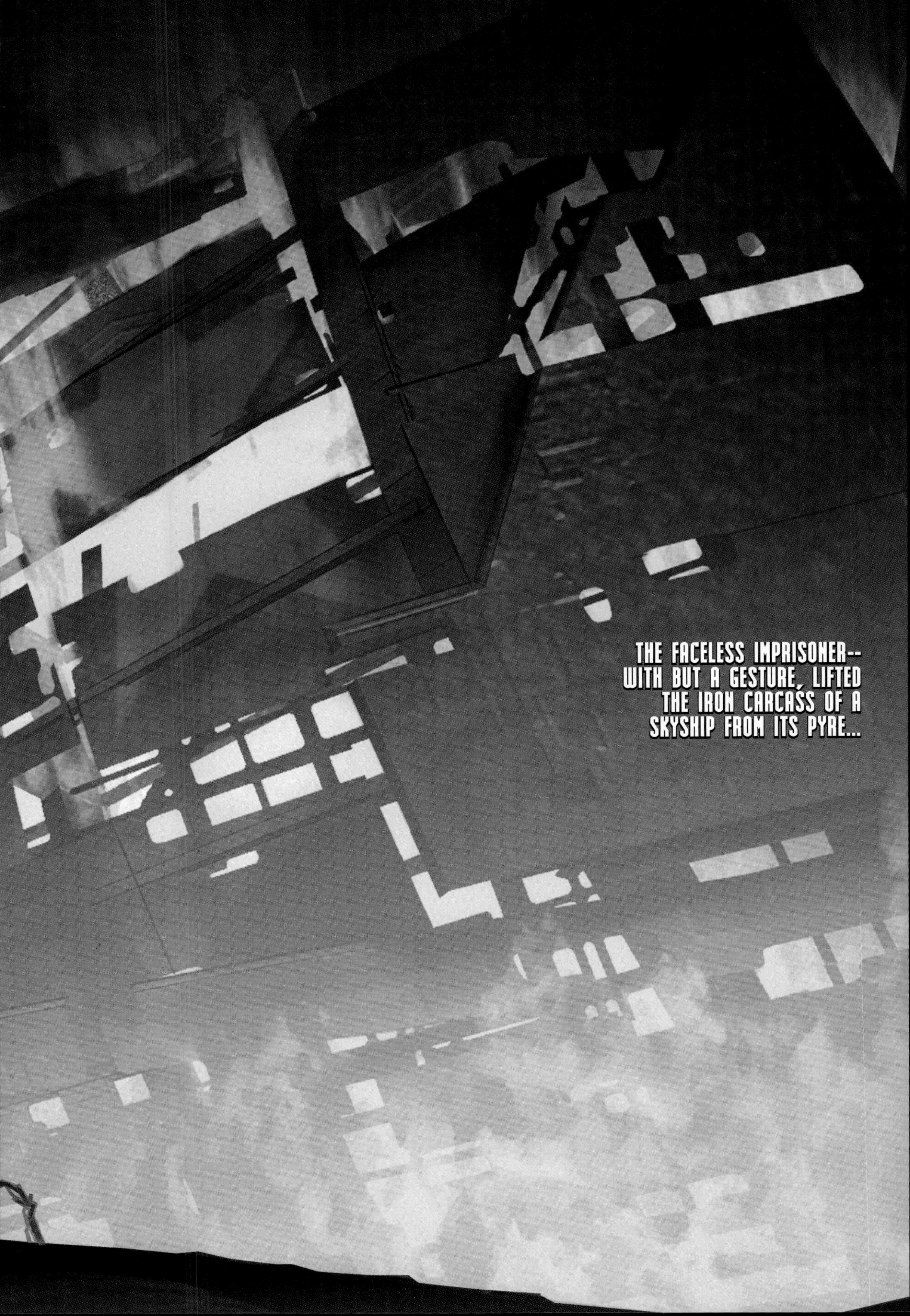
THE FACELESS IMPRISONER-- WITH BUT A GESTURE, LIFTED THE IRON CARCASS OF A SKYSHIP FROM ITS PYRE...

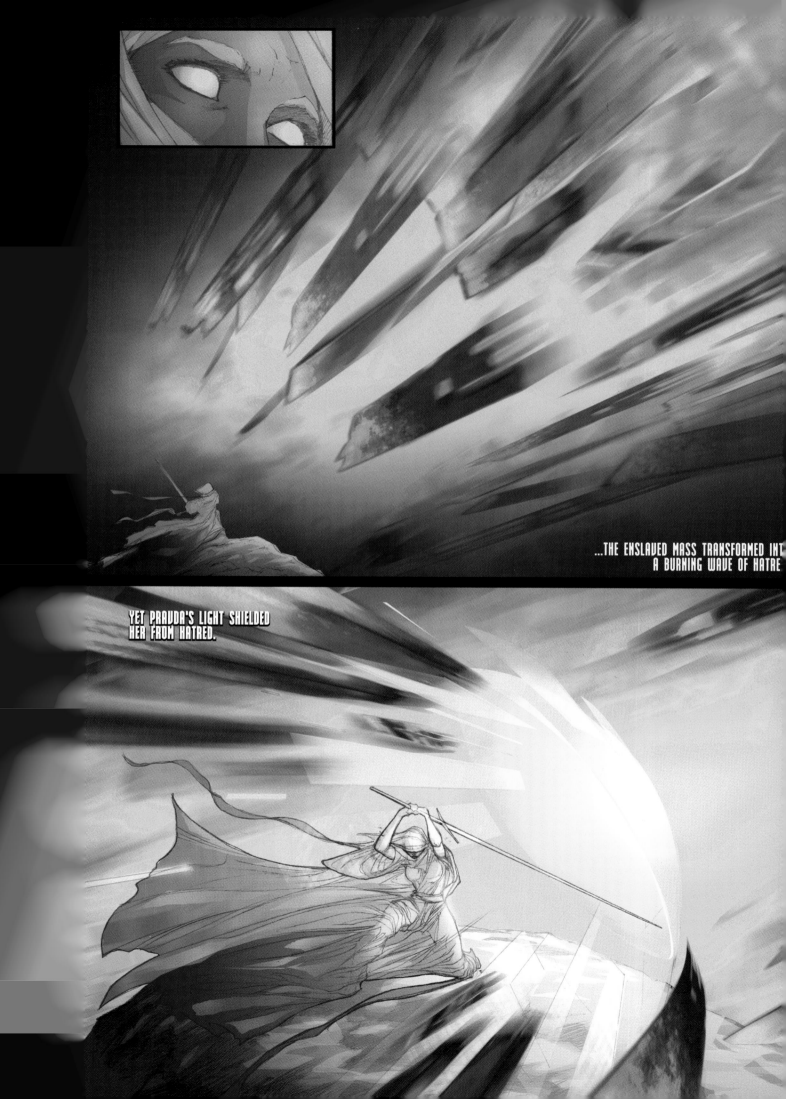

...THE ENSLAVED MASS TRANSFORMED INT
A BURNING WAVE OF HATRE

YET PRAVDA'S LIGHT SHIELDED
HER FROM HATRED.

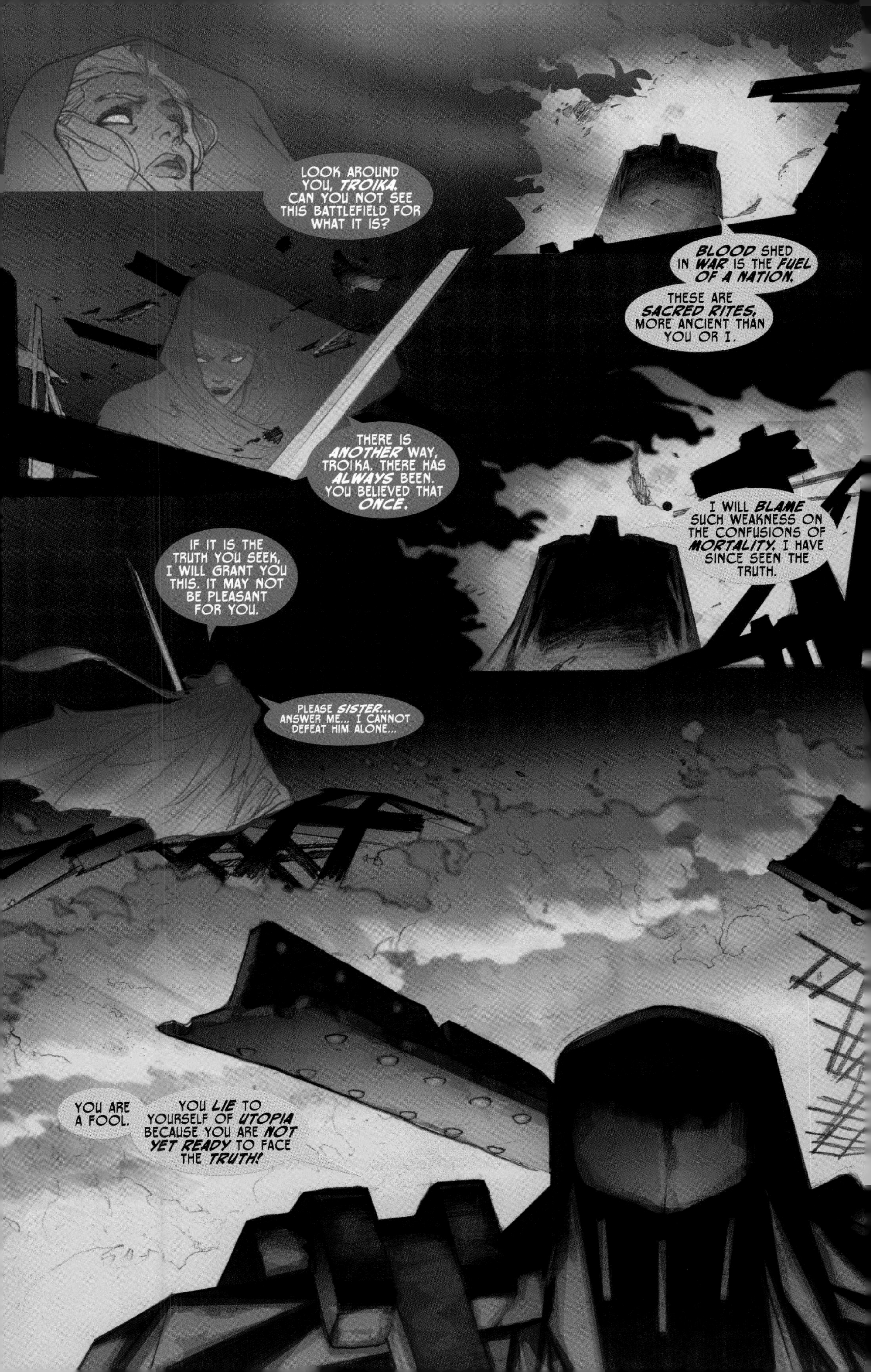
LOOK AROUND YOU, TROIKA. CAN YOU NOT SEE THIS BATTLEFIELD FOR WHAT IT IS?
BLOOD SHED IN WAR IS THE FUEL OF A NATION.
THESE ARE SACRED RITES, MORE ANCIENT THAN YOU OR I.
THERE IS ANOTHER WAY, TROIKA. THERE HAS ALWAYS BEEN. YOU BELIEVED THAT ONCE.
I WILL BLAME SUCH WEAKNESS ON THE CONFUSIONS OF MORTALITY. I HAVE SINCE SEEN THE TRUTH.
IF IT IS THE TRUTH YOU SEEK, I WILL GRANT YOU THIS. IT MAY NOT BE PLEASANT FOR YOU.
PLEASE SISTER... ANSWER ME... I CANNOT DEFEAT HIM ALONE...
YOU ARE A FOOL.
YOU LIE TO YOURSELF OF UTOPIA BECAUSE YOU ARE NOT YET READY TO FACE THE TRUTH!

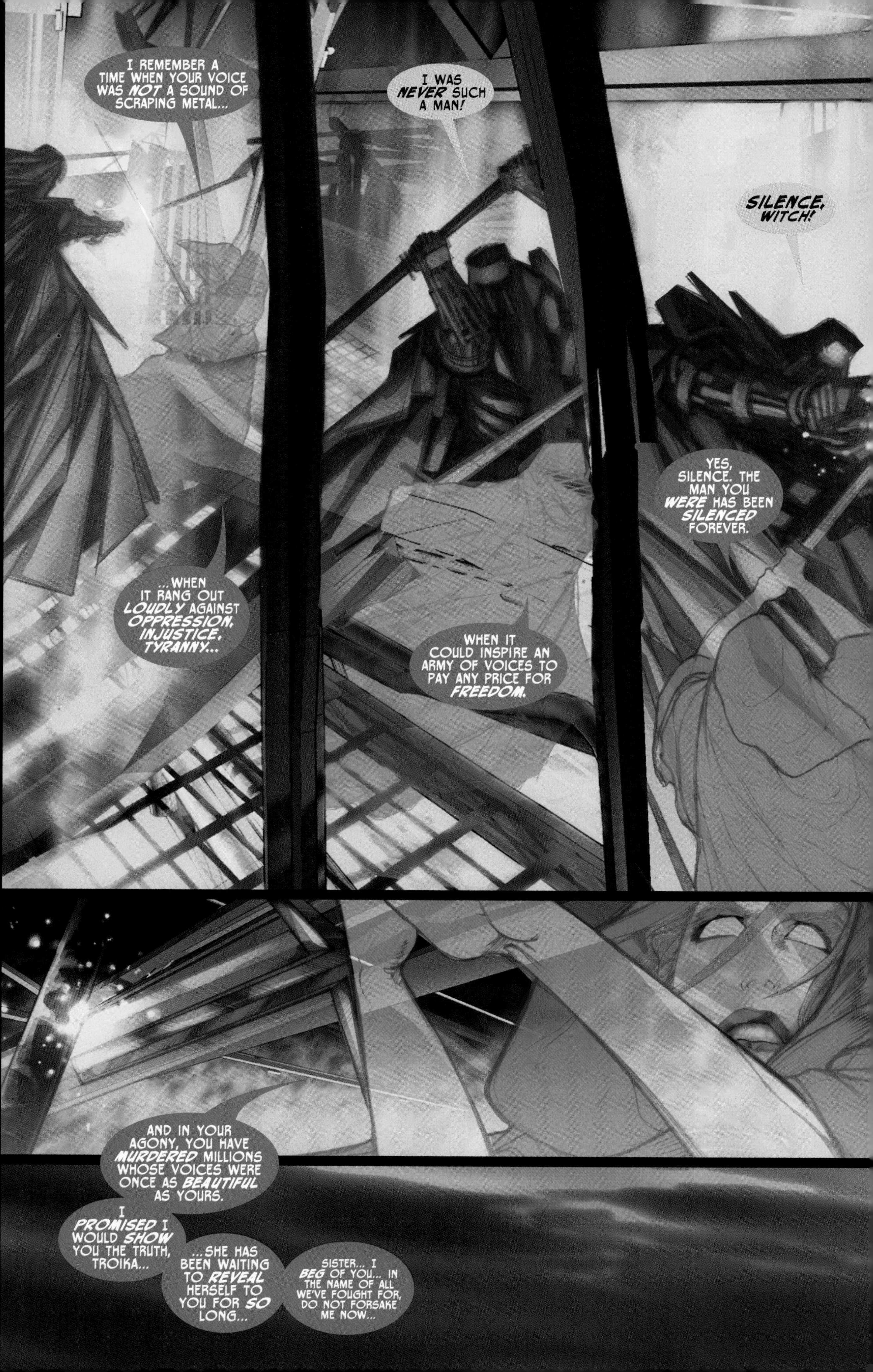
I REMEMBER A TIME WHEN YOUR VOICE WAS NOT A SOUND OF SCRAPING METAL...
I WAS NEVER SUCH A MAN!
SILENCE, WITCH!
...WHEN IT RANG OUT LOUDLY AGAINST OPPRESSION, INJUSTICE, TYRANNY...
WHEN IT COULD INSPIRE AN ARMY OF VOICES TO PAY ANY PRICE FOR FREEDOM.
YES, SILENCE. THE MAN YOU WERE HAS BEEN SILENCED FOREVER.
AND IN YOUR AGONY, YOU HAVE MURDERED MILLIONS WHOSE VOICES WERE ONCE AS BEAUTIFUL AS YOURS.
I PROMISED I WOULD SHOW YOU THE TRUTH, TROIKA...
...SHE HAS BEEN WAITING TO REVEAL HERSELF TO YOU FOR SO LONG...
SISTER... I BEG OF YOU... IN THE NAME OF ALL WE'VE FOUGHT FOR, DO NOT FORSAKE ME NOW...

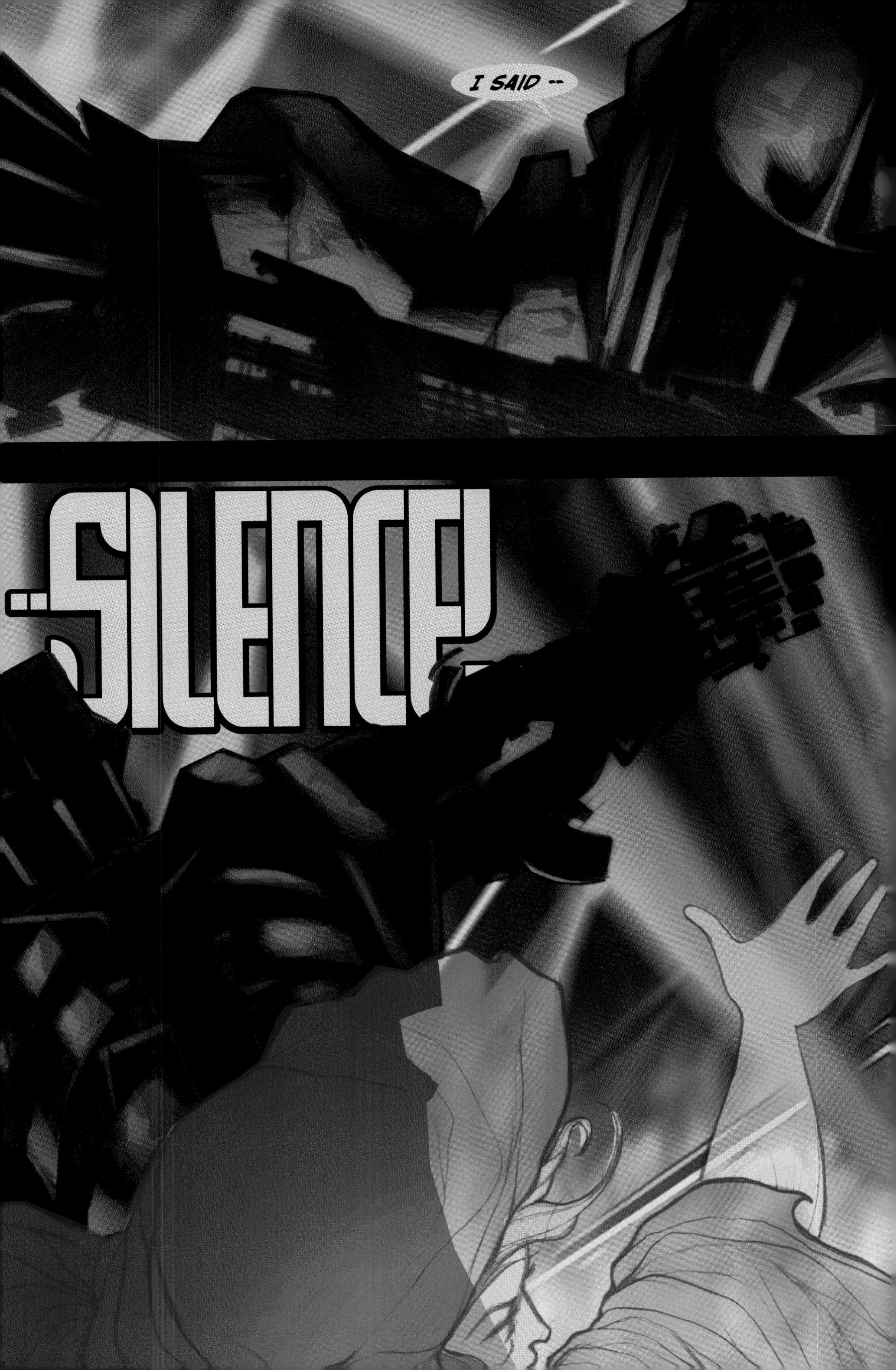
I SAID --
--SILENCE!

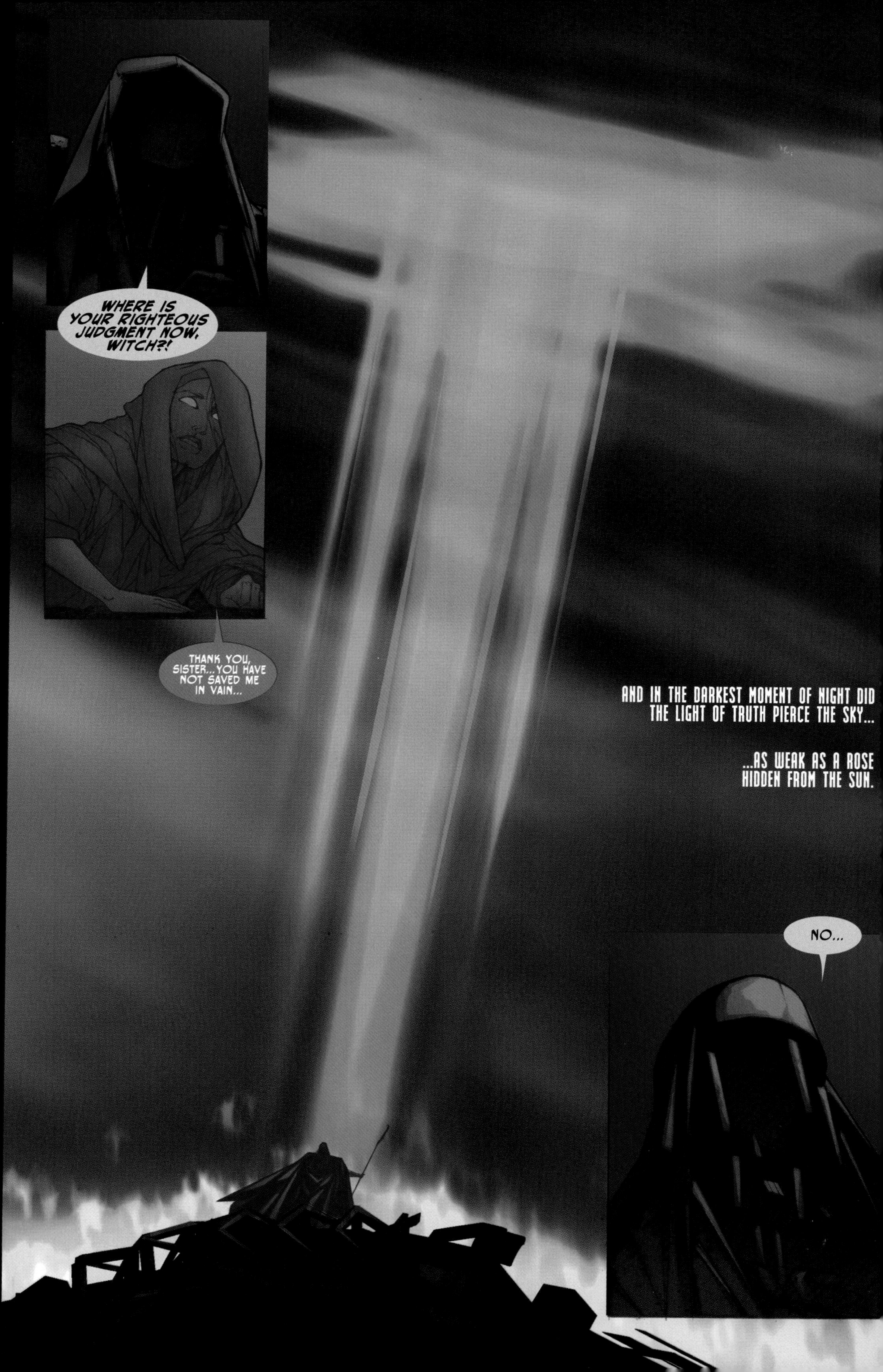
WHERE IS YOUR RIGHTEOUS JUDGMENT NOW, WITCH?!
THANK YOU, SISTER... YOU HAVE NOT SAVED ME IN VAIN...
AND IN THE DARKEST MOMENT OF NIGHT DID THE LIGHT OF TRUTH PIERCE THE SKY...
...AS WEAK AS A ROSE HIDDEN FROM THE SUN.
NO...

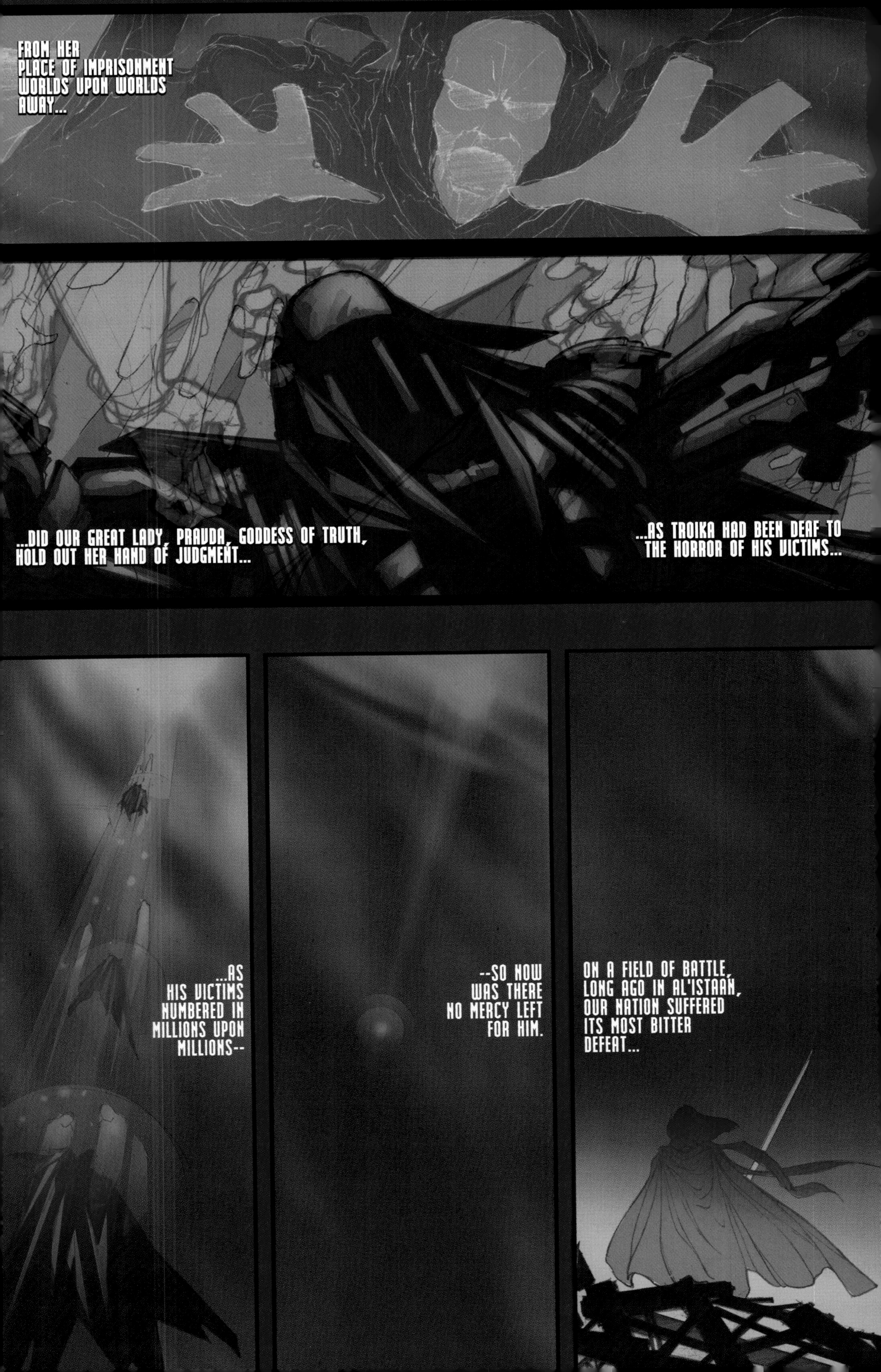
FROM HER PLACE OF IMPRISONMENT WORLDS UPON WORLDS AWAY...
...DID OUR GREAT LADY, PRAVDA, GODDESS OF TRUTH, HOLD OUT HER HAND OF JUDGMENT...
...AS TROIKA HAD BEEN DEAF TO THE HORROR OF HIS VICTIMS...
...AS HIS VICTIMS NUMBERED IN MILLIONS UPON MILLIONS--
--SO NOW WAS THERE NO MERCY LEFT FOR HIM.
ON A FIELD OF BATTLE, LONG AGO IN AL'ISTAAN, OUR NATION SUFFERED ITS MOST BITTER DEFEAT...

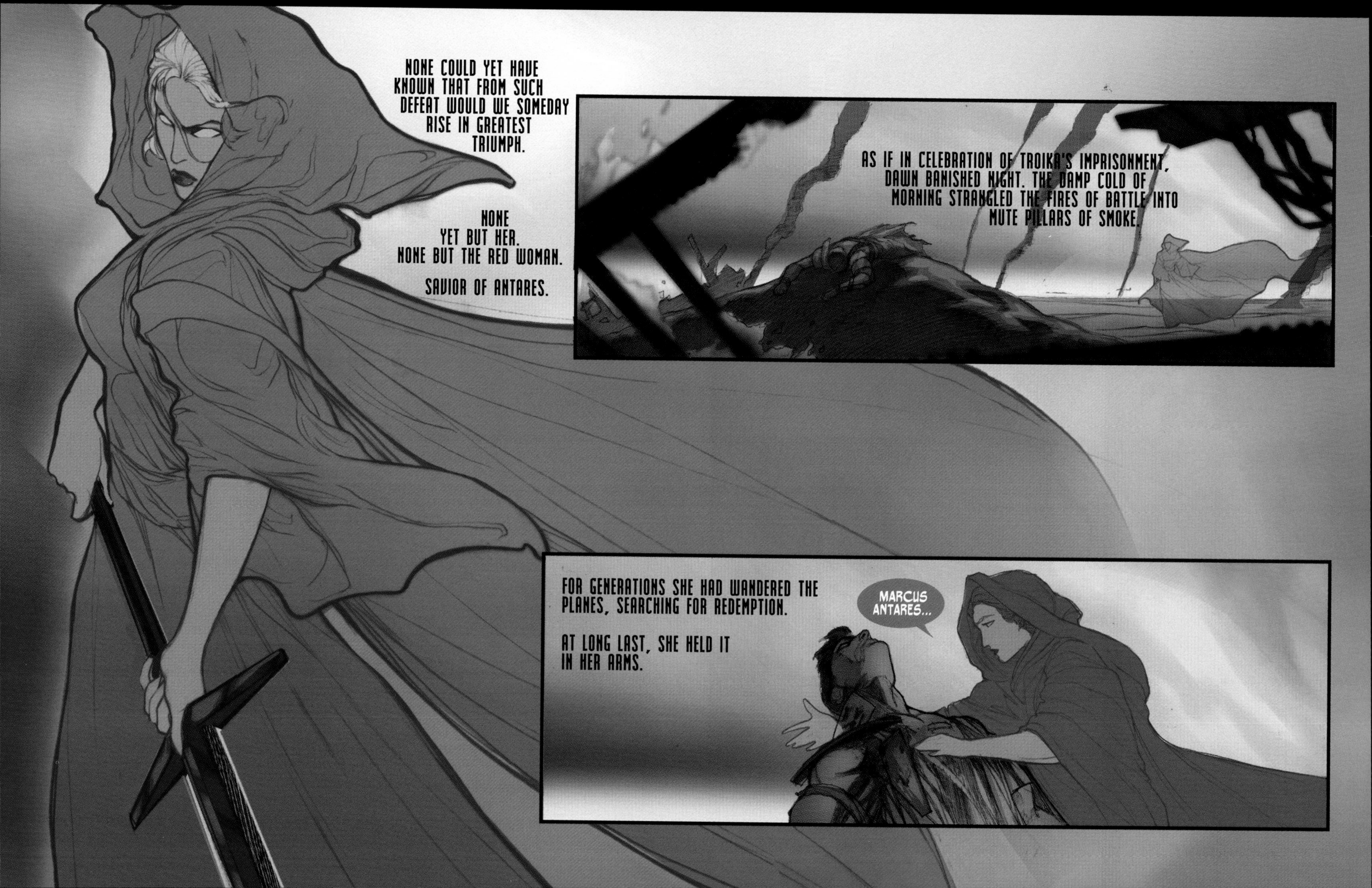
NONE COULD YET HAVE KNOWN THAT FROM SUCH DEFEAT WOULD WE SOMEDAY RISE IN GREATEST TRIUMPH.
NONE YET BUT HER. NONE BUT THE RED WOMAN.
SAVIOR OF ANTARES.
AS IF IN CELEBRATION OF TROIKA'S IMPRISONMENT, DAWN BANISHED NIGHT. THE DAMP COLD OF MORNING STRANGLED THE FIRES OF BATTLE INTO MUTE PILLARS OF SMOKE.
FOR GENERATIONS SHE HAD WANDERED THE PLANES, SEARCHING FOR REDEMPTION.
AT LONG LAST, SHE HELD IT IN HER ARMS.
MARCUS ANTARES...

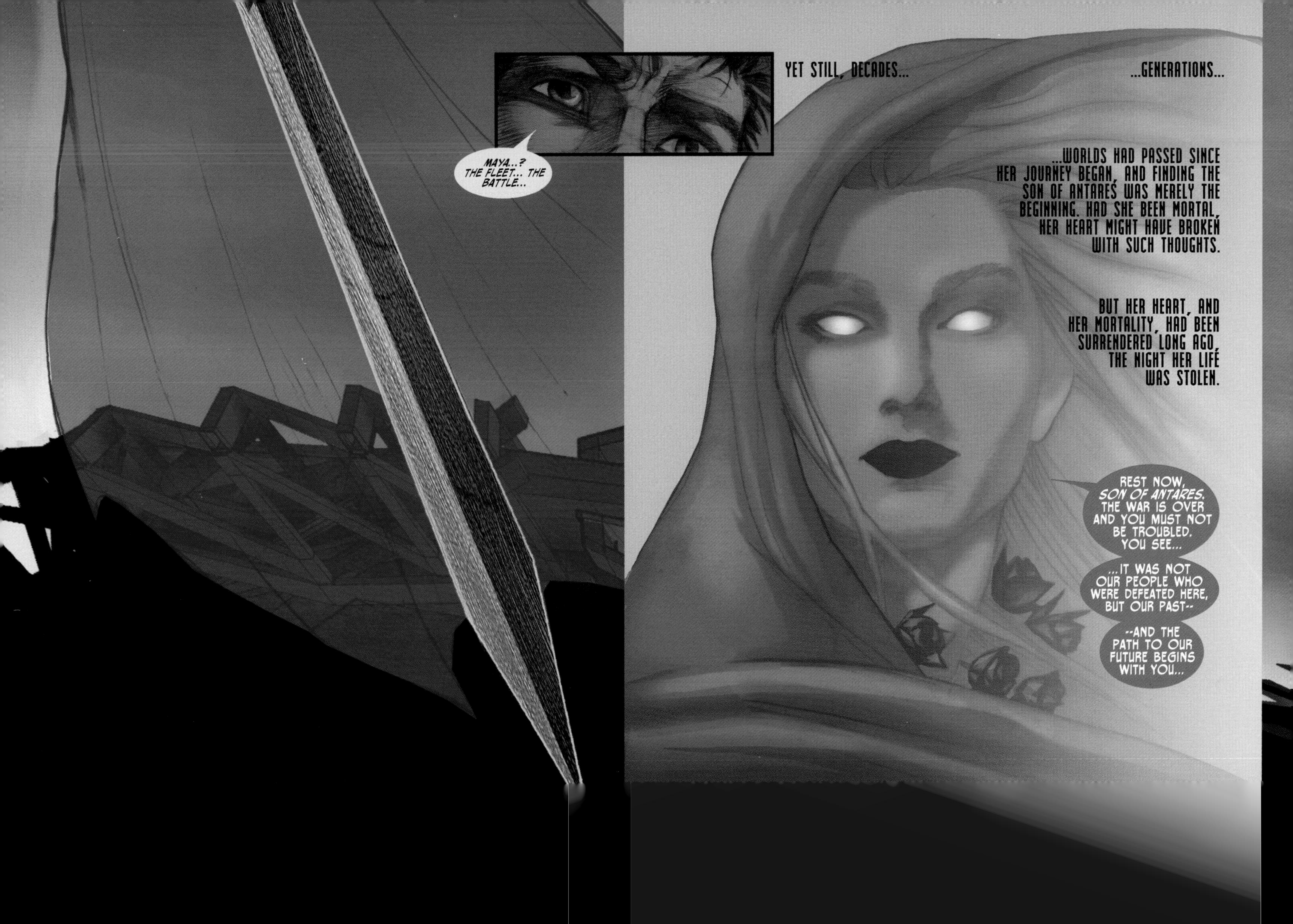
MAYA...? THE FLEET... THE BATTLE...
YET STILL, DECADES...
...GENERATIONS...
...WORLDS HAD PASSED SINCE HER JOURNEY BEGAN, AND FINDING THE SON OF ANTARES WAS MERELY THE BEGINNING. HAD SHE BEEN MORTAL, HER HEART MIGHT HAVE BROKEN WITH SUCH THOUGHTS.
BUT HER HEART, AND HER MORTALITY, HAD BEEN SURRENDERED LONG AGO, THE NIGHT HER LIFE WAS STOLEN.
REST NOW, SON OF ANTARES. THE WAR IS OVER AND YOU MUST NOT BE TROUBLED. YOU SEE...
...IT WAS NOT OUR PEOPLE WHO WERE DEFEATED HERE, BUT OUR PAST--
--AND THE PATH TO OUR FUTURE BEGINS WITH YOU...

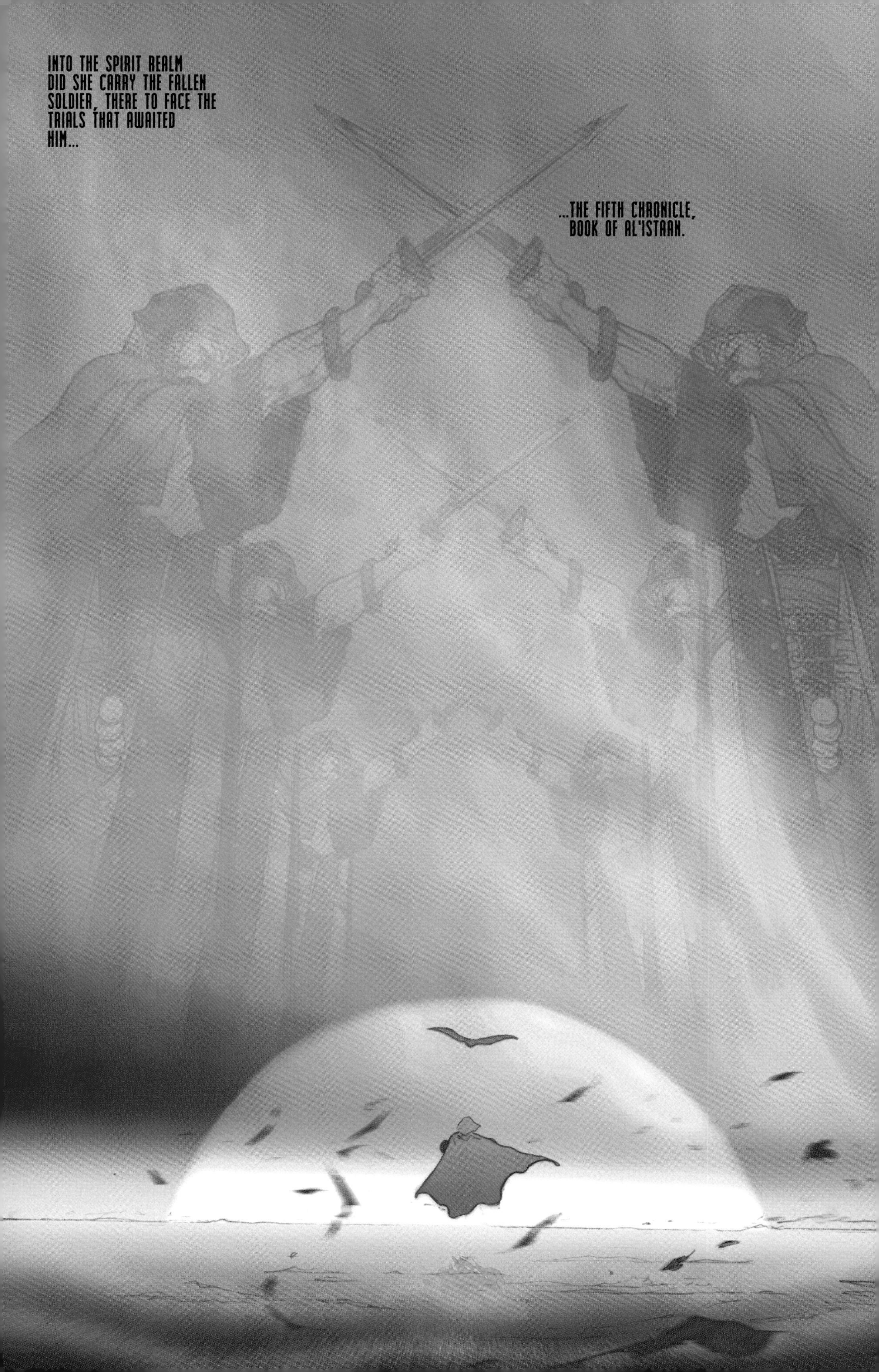

INTO THE SPIRIT REALM DID SHE CARRY THE FALLEN SOLDIER, THERE TO FACE THE TRIALS THAT AWAITED HIM...
...THE FIFTH CHRONICLE, BOOK OF AL'ISTAAN.

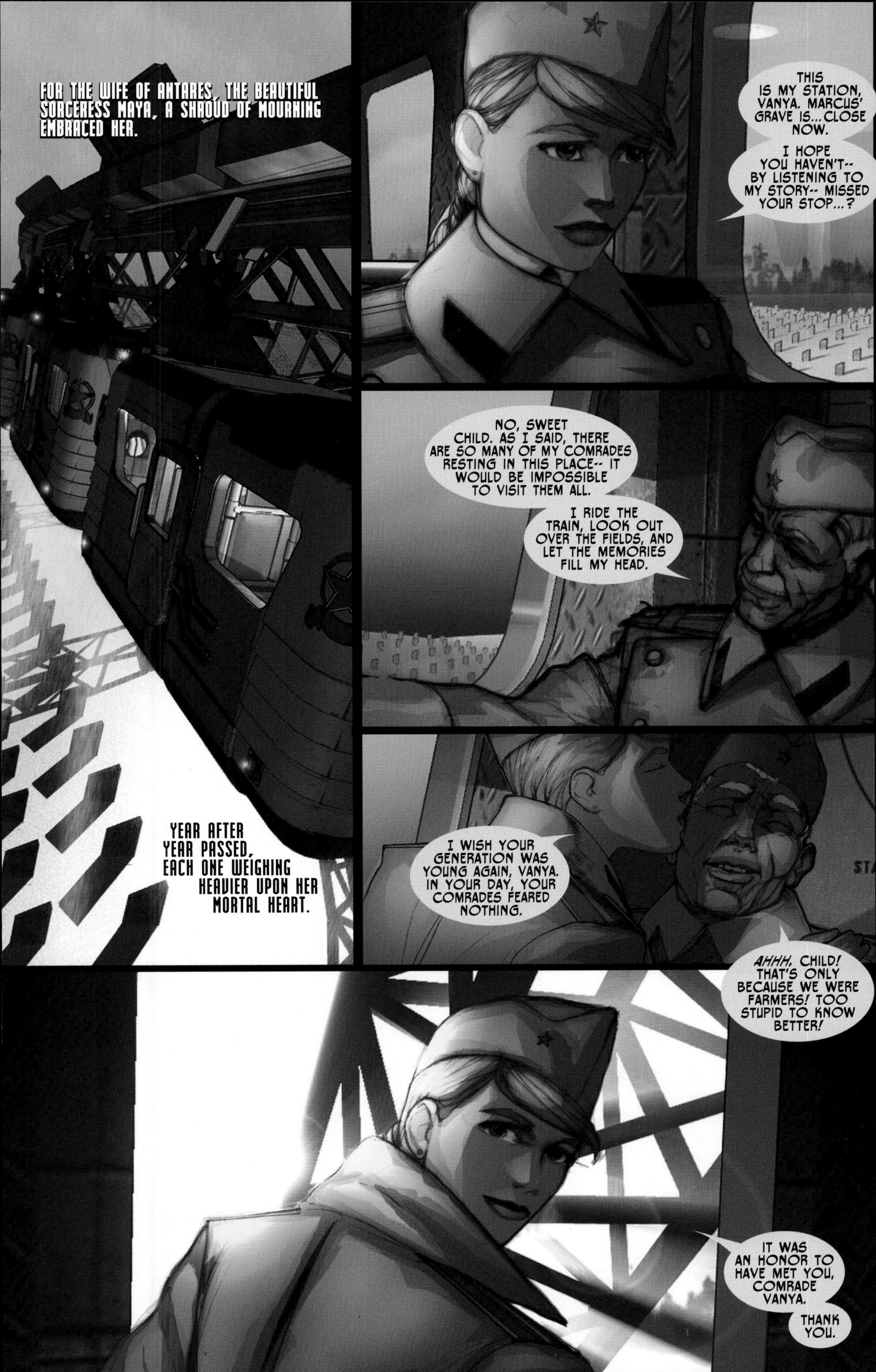

FOR THE WIFE OF ANTARES, THE BEAUTIFUL SORCERESS MAYA, A SHROUD OF MOURNING EMBRACED HER.
THIS IS MY STATION, VANYA. MARCUS' GRAVE IS...CLOSE NOW.
I HOPE YOU HAVEN'T-- BY LISTENING TO MY STORY-- MISSED YOUR STOP...?
NO, SWEET CHILD. AS I SAID, THERE ARE SO MANY OF MY COMRADES RESTING IN THIS PLACE-- IT WOULD BE IMPOSSIBLE TO VISIT THEM ALL.
I RIDE THE TRAIN, LOOK OUT OVER THE FIELDS, AND LET THE MEMORIES FILL MY HEAD.
YEAR AFTER YEAR PASSED, EACH ONE WEIGHING HEAVIER UPON HER MORTAL HEART.
I WISH YOUR GENERATION WAS YOUNG AGAIN, VANYA. IN YOUR DAY, YOUR COMRADES FEARED NOTHING.
AHHH, CHILD! THAT'S ONLY BECAUSE WE WERE FARMERS! TOO STUPID TO KNOW BETTER!
IT WAS AN HONOR TO HAVE MET YOU, COMRADE VANYA.
THANK YOU.

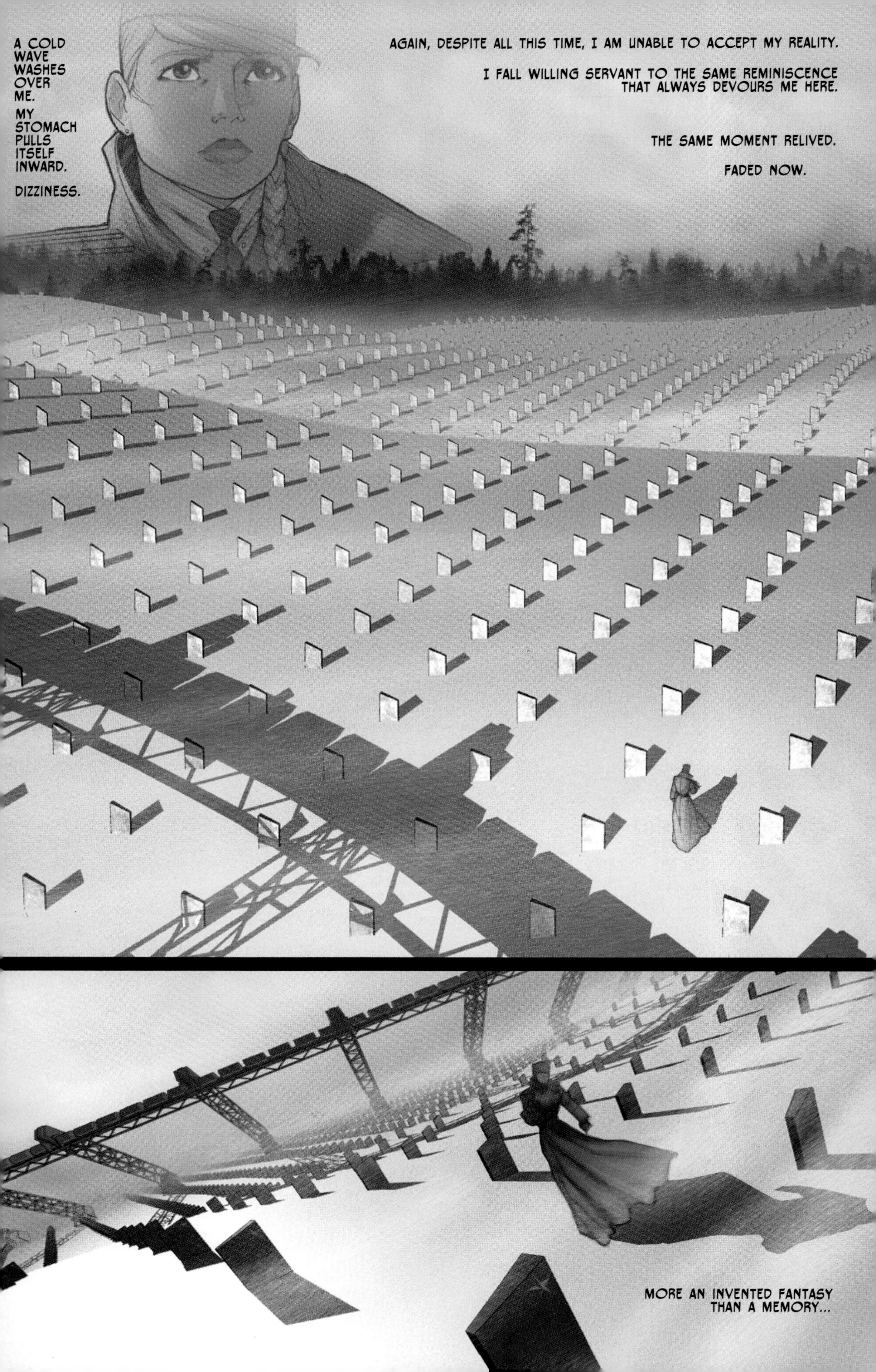
A COLD WAVE WASHES OVER ME.
MY STOMACH PULLS ITSELF INWARD.
DIZZINESS.
AGAIN, DESPITE ALL THIS TIME, I AM UNABLE TO ACCEPT MY REALITY.
I FALL WILLING SERVANT TO THE SAME REMINISCENCE THAT ALWAYS DEVOURS ME HERE.
THE SAME MOMENT RELIVED.
FADED NOW.
MORE AN INVENTED FANTASY THAN A MEMORY...

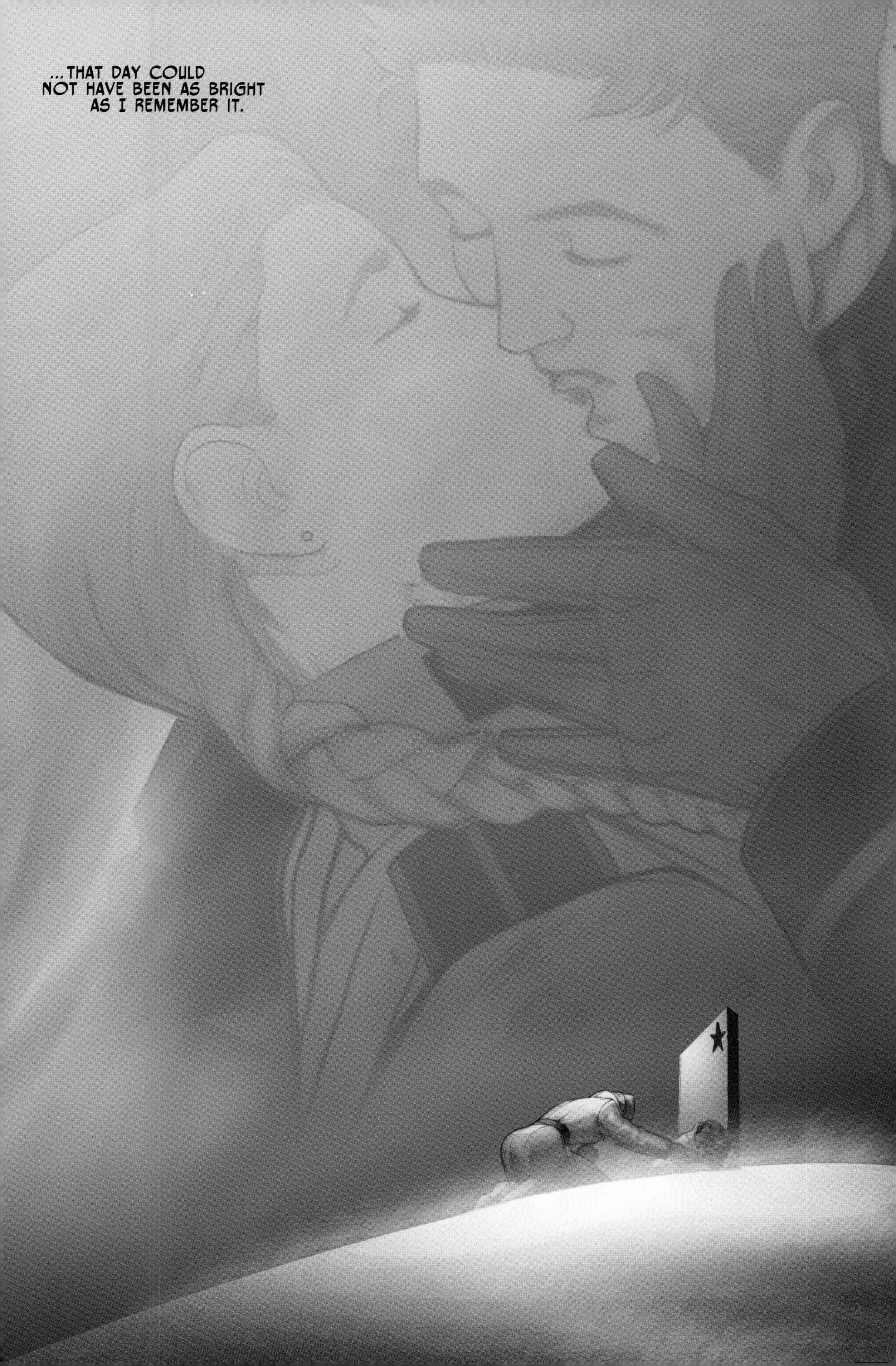
...THAT DAY COULD NOT HAVE BEEN AS BRIGHT AS I REMEMBER IT.

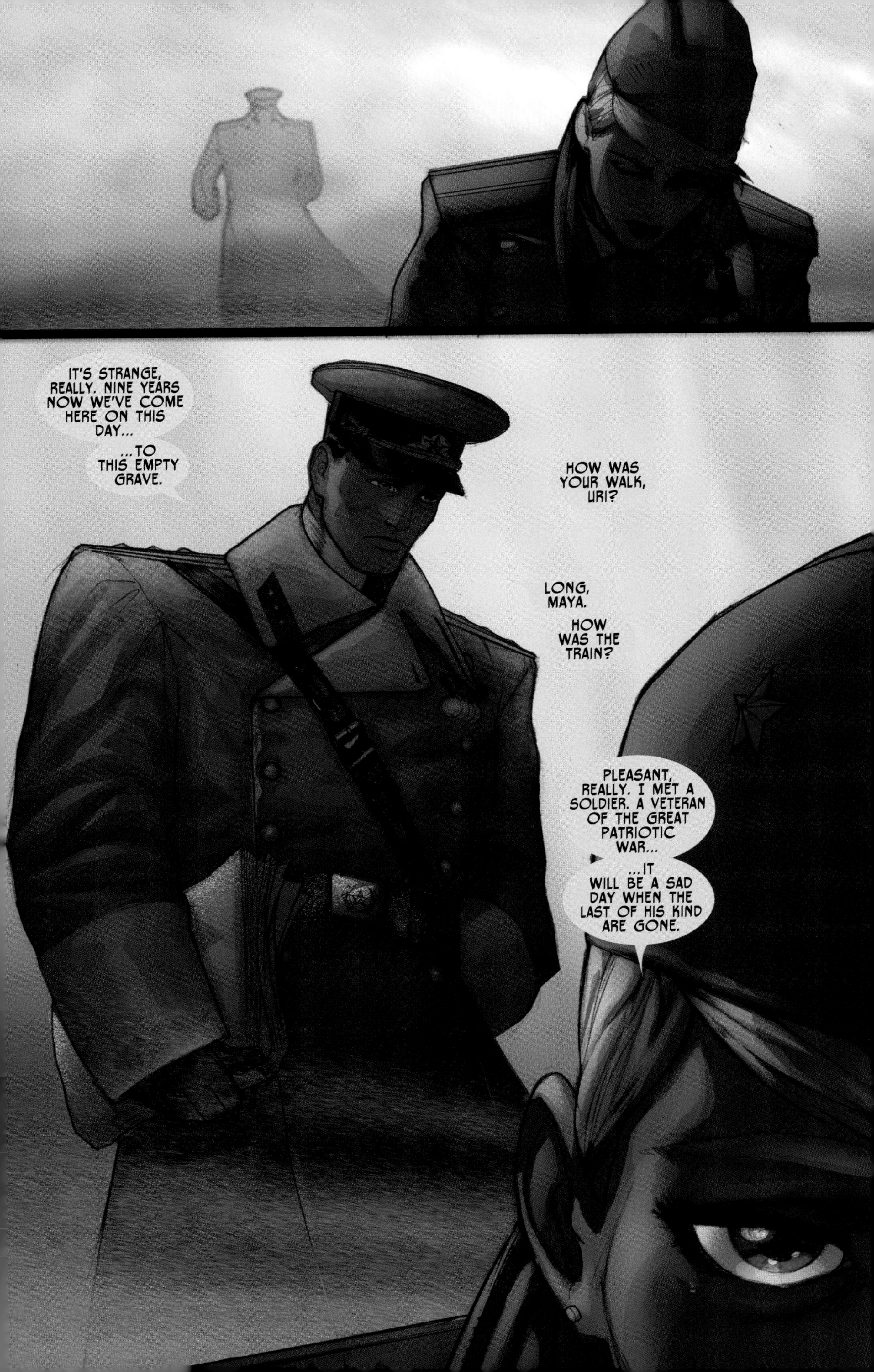
IT'S STRANGE, REALLY. NINE YEARS NOW WE'VE COME HERE ON THIS DAY...
...TO THIS EMPTY GRAVE.
HOW WAS YOUR WALK, URI?
LONG, MAYA.
HOW WAS THE TRAIN?
PLEASANT, REALLY. I MET A SOLDIER. A VETERAN OF THE GREAT PATRIOTIC WAR...
...IT WILL BE A SAD DAY WHEN THE LAST OF HIS KIND ARE GONE.

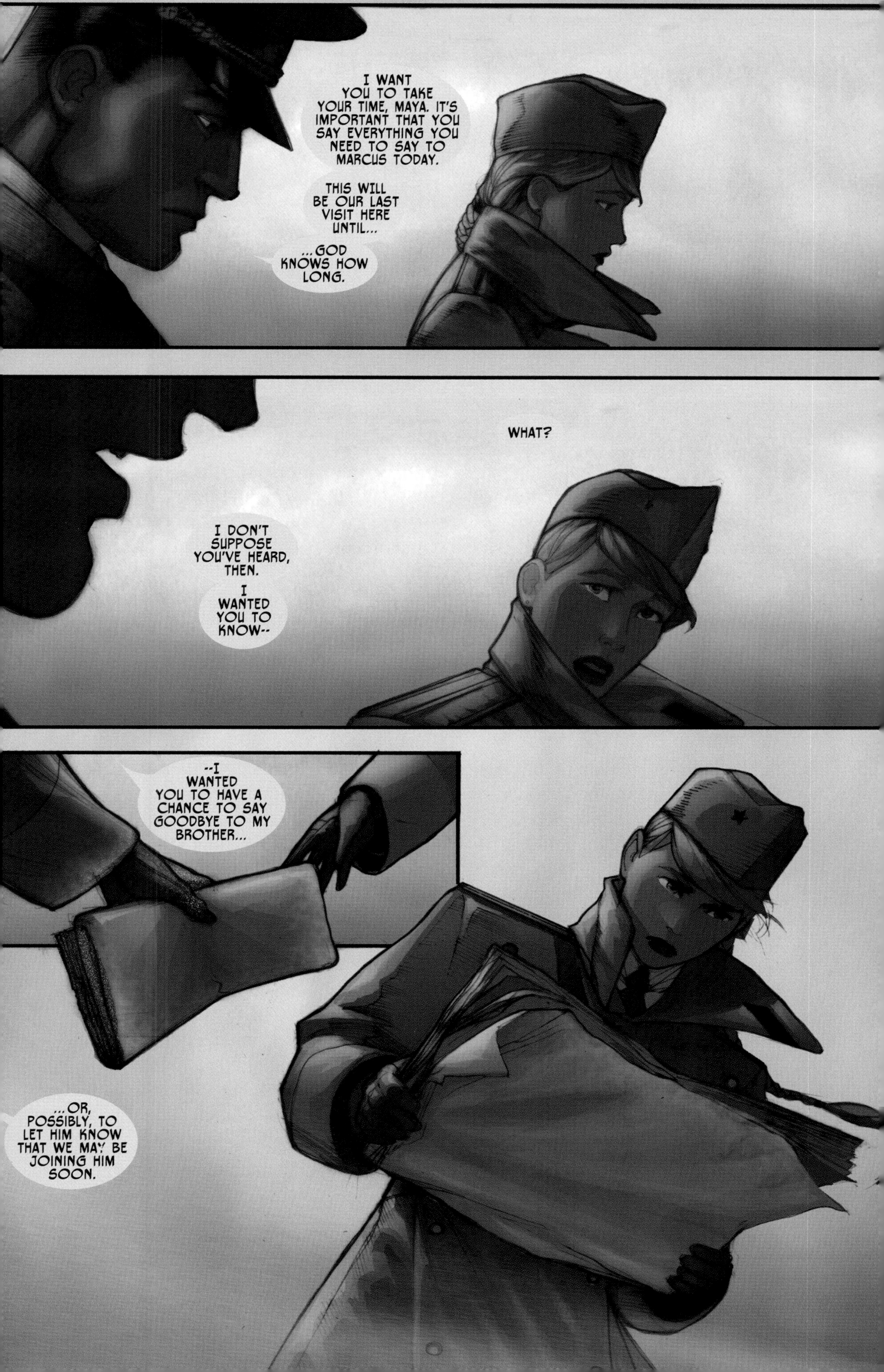
I WANT YOU TO TAKE YOUR TIME, MAYA. IT'S IMPORTANT THAT YOU SAY EVERYTHING YOU NEED TO SAY TO MARCUS TODAY.
THIS WILL BE OUR LAST VISIT HERE UNTIL...
...GOD KNOWS HOW LONG.
WHAT?
I DON'T SUPPOSE YOU'VE HEARD, THEN.
I WANTED YOU TO KNOW--
--I WANTED YOU TO HAVE A CHANCE TO SAY GOODBYE TO MY BROTHER...
...OR, POSSIBLY, TO LET HIM KNOW THAT WE MAY BE JOINING HIM SOON.

KRASNAYA
WAR IN N

BAHAMUT, Nokgorka.

For centuries, the mountainous region of Nokgorka has been a province under the leadership of the lands of the Red Star. Yesterday, in an attempt to gain their independence from their former rulers, Nokgorka's leaders declared themselves a sovereign nation.

The government of the former United Republics of the Red Star immediately refused to accept this decision, ordering Nokgorka's rebellious leaders to surrender what they call a "Threat to the territorial integrity of the nation that will be suppressed by any and all means at our disposal."

This statement of position was then followed with a declaration of war. Forces of the Red Fleet have been mobilized, and have orders to crush Nokgorka for its defiance. The exact size of the deployment force is not yet known, but sources confirm that this is the largest military operation since the catastrophic war of

Standing against the red fleet will be the irregular forces of the Nokgorka resistance militia. Mainly a small guerilla force, the people of Nokgorka are nonetheless united in their belief that they no longer have any need of the government of the former U.R.R.S. and are willing to wage war, if need be, to be free of their rule once and for all.

Western reaction has been mixed, with leaders of most of the transnationalist countries not wanting any part of what they consider a highly complex situation. A spokesman for the western transnationalist alliance had cautious words for the press, "Although a peaceful resolution is always preferential, the current world climate is one of sometimes tumultuous transition, and does not always offer such alternatives. In light of this, it is our position that the conflict in Nokgorka be left to the leaders of the region to decide. This is an internal conflict, and the

DEPUT
MINIST
OPI
NON

CITADEL
Star.

"Had the p
deploymer
secret from
voiced my
sooner." T
words of
Minister
hearing of
by centr
mobilize
rebel factic

"Just as
military op
and short
for Nokgc
clearly d
continued
likelihood
use force
spur of the
thought of
the troops
Nokgorka
morally pr
fighting s
now, w
considered
have we le
the battle
Gate?"

Chigayev
any way
Nokgorka

ZVYEZDA
OKGORKA

ENSE
ICES
N
A

the Red

s for this
en kept
uld have
n much
he angry
Defense
upon
ncement
and to
inst the
gorka.

aan, the
ng term
gic goals
not been
Chigayev
e in all
cision to
on the
with little
Many of
ding into
r from
deal with
o, until
been
ntrymen.
ing from
Dathra's

s not see
ing the
by force

LYULIN CALLS NOKGORKA REBELS A CRIMINAL REGIME

CITADEL, Lands of the Red Star.

Minister of state affairs, Aleksei G. Lyulin stressed that the Nokgorka issue is a prime example of the secessionist trend which the former United Republics of the Red Star must overcome.

"If necessary the government will use force in any and all provinces threatening to secede to preserve our territorial integrity," said Lyulin today. Lyulin went on to say that he considers the calls to settle the Nokgorka crisis through peaceful means weak and ultimately hypocritical. "No peaceful means will ever help us deal with a criminal regime which is armed to the teeth," said Lyulin. He argued that comrades of the former U.R.R.S. must view their motherland first and foremost as an indivisible power. *cont on page 4*

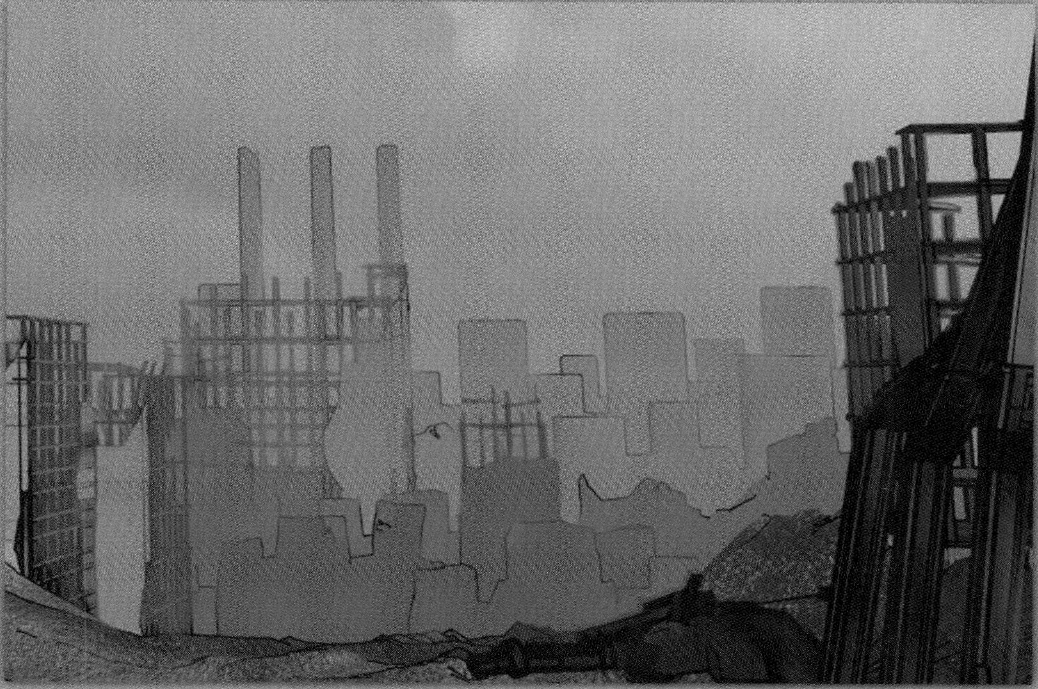

IN OUR EDITORIAL SECTION: NINE YEARS AFTER KAR DATHRA'S GATE... THE GHOSTS OF AL'ISTAAN

As things change, so do they stay the same. It is almost twenty years since the first shots were fired in the war of Al'istaan. by the time the conflict ended in the decisive battle of Kar Dathra's

Others claim that such platitudes are the obsolete rhetoric of an empire that could no longer sustain itself. For them, the Ghosts of Al'istaan have yet to be put to rest, and the war in

MY MIND TRANSPORTS ITSELF TO THE PLACE IN THE PHOTOGRAPH.

NOKGORKA.
A PLACE THAT WILL SOON BE AS COLD AND LADEN WITH DEATH AS THE GRAVEYARD IN WHICH I STAND.

TRAINED AS A SOLDIER, MY MIND IMMEDIATELY ARMS ITSELF WITH THOUGHTS OF
DUTY, COUNTRY, SURVIVAL.
TRAINED AS A WIDOW, MY MIND CAN NOW SEE THESE WEAPONS AS SOMETHING MORE THAN
INSTRUMENTS OF MY OWN PROTECTION.

THEY SEEM MORE LIKE A CAGE NOW.
A COMPLEX SYSTEM OF MENTAL IMPRISONMENT THAT I WILL NEED TO FIND A WAY TO BELIEVE IN ONCE AGAIN.

OR I WILL DIE IN NOKGORKA.

THE SOLDIER'S EYES MUST BE VEILED TO THE TRUTH BEHIND THEIR LICENSE FOR SLAUGHTER.
WE MUST FIND A WAY TO BELIEVE THAT WHAT WE ARE FIGHTING FOR IS WORTH DYING FOR.

IF AN ARMY CANNOT FIND TRUTH, OR AT VERY LEAST HOPE, IN THEIR COUNTRY'S
PROPAGANDA... THEY WILL BE DESTROYED.

THE PERCEPTIONS MUST BE CONSTRAINED IN THIS WAY.
WHERE ONCE EVERY COLOR OF THE PRISM EXISTED, THERE CAN BE ONLY THE BLACK ABSENCE OF ALL LIGHT--
OTHER THAN THE MUZZLE FLASH OF AUTOMATIC FIRE...

...OR THE BLINDING BURSTS OF A KAST PROTOCOL.

MY COUNTRY, AT THIS MOMENT, IS TOO PLAGUED AND CORRUPT TO WIN ANY WAR.
BUT TO ACCEPT THIS IS TO BECOME THE IMPERFECT SOLDIER-- THE SOLDIER OF DOUBT--
SOLDIERS MADE OF SUCH ARMIES ARE PAWNS MARCHED TO SLAUGHTER.

ON THIS UNSTABLE PRECIPICE DO I STAND.

THE SOLDIER IN ME CURSES MY THOUGHTS. STRUGGLES TO MAKE ME ACCEPT WHAT I AM.
THE WIDOW IS NOT SURE OF ANYTHING. SHE PLEADS WITH ME TO ESCAPE THIS FATE.

ON THE ONE SIDE OF THIS DARK TUNNEL, IN THE FUTURE,
STANDS THE DIM WINTER LIGHT OF NOKGORKA.

ON THE OTHER, IN THE PAST...

...AL'ISTAAN BURNS.

AL'ISTAAN.
THE PLACE THAT CLAIMED MY HUSBAND.

I WAS LITTLE MORE THAN A CHILD WHEN I ENTERED THAT WAR.
ONLY A NEWLY MARRIED BRIDE WHEN I WAS TRAINED TO TRANSFORM MYSELF INTO A PILLAR OF LIGHT
THAT COULD DESTROY ANYTHING IN MY NATION'S PATH.

NO THOUGHT PLAGUED ME THEN.
NO CONSCIOUSNESS OF WHAT I WAS PART OF.

I WAS THE HEAT OF MY NATION'S ANGER
THE BURNING WILL OF THE STATE.
I WAS AN INFERNO, CLEARING THE PATH OF THOSE WHO RESISTED.

NOW, YEARS LATER, THE DAMAGE DONE...
I MAKE MY DECISION.

THE WIDOW, HER EYES SHADOWED, HIDES IN THE DARKNESS.
THE SOLDIER STANDS BOLDLY AT ATTENTION IN THE FOREFRONT OF MY MIND.

I AM *MAYA ANTARES*, SORCERESS-MAJOR
OF THE RED STAR SKYFURNACE *KONSTANTINOV* OF THE *RED FLEET*.

IN MY NATION'S SERVICE,
I WEAR PROUDLY UPON MY UNIFORM THE ORDER OF *IMBOHL*-- GLORIOUS FATHER OF
THE *REVOLUTION* IN WHICH OUR NATION WAS BORN, AND THE ORDER OF THE RED STAR--
THE SYMBOL OF OUR ANCIENT LANDS.

NO WEAKNESS WILL
CONSUME ME.

NO FEAR WILL
LURE ME INTO PARALYSIS.

IF I AM TO DIE IN NOKGORKA,
SO BE IT.

FROM BEHIND THE SOLDIER, IN THE DARKNESS OF MY MIND'S FEAR, THE WIDOW WAILS IN PROTEST.
SHE HOLDS IN HER ARMS A CHILD WITH HAIR THAT SHINES LIKE SPUN GOLD.
A CHILD WITH BLUE EYES FULL OF MIRACLES.

I HAVE NOT BEEN THAT CHILD SINCE THE DAY I BECAME THAT WIDOW.
THERE IS ONLY THE SOLDIER NOW.

WITH EACH MOMENT, THIS SOLDIER'S FATE APPROACHES
NOKGORKA.

THERE ARE CHILDREN THERE.
I SHALL ORPHAN THEM.

THERE ARE WOMEN THERE WHOM
I SHALL WIDOW.

AS I STAND WITH MY BOOTS IN THE SNOW BEFORE MY HUSBAND'S GRAVE,
THEY ARE PREPARING NOW, FOR MY ARRIVAL.

THEIR BATTLE CRIES FILL THE AIR...

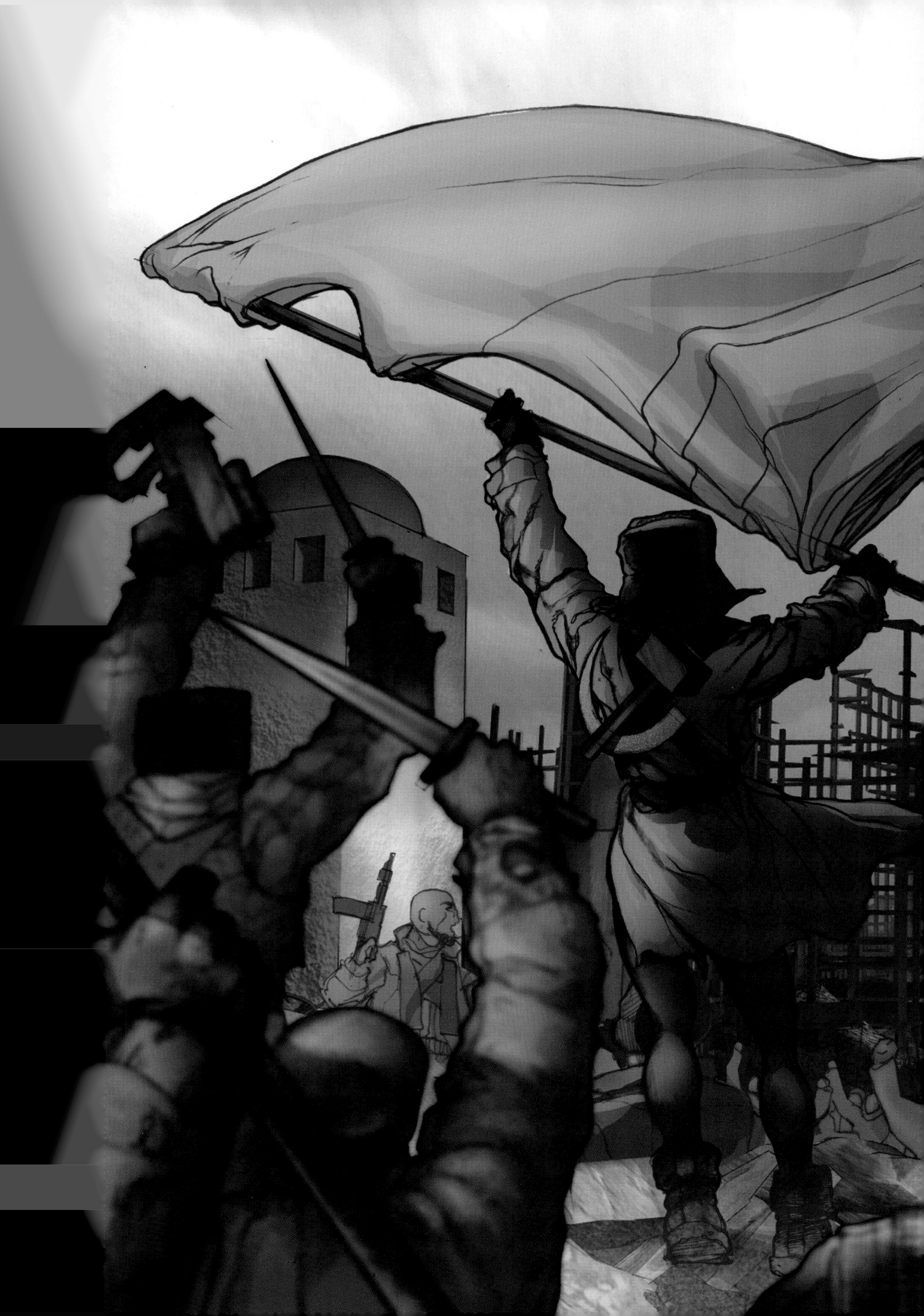

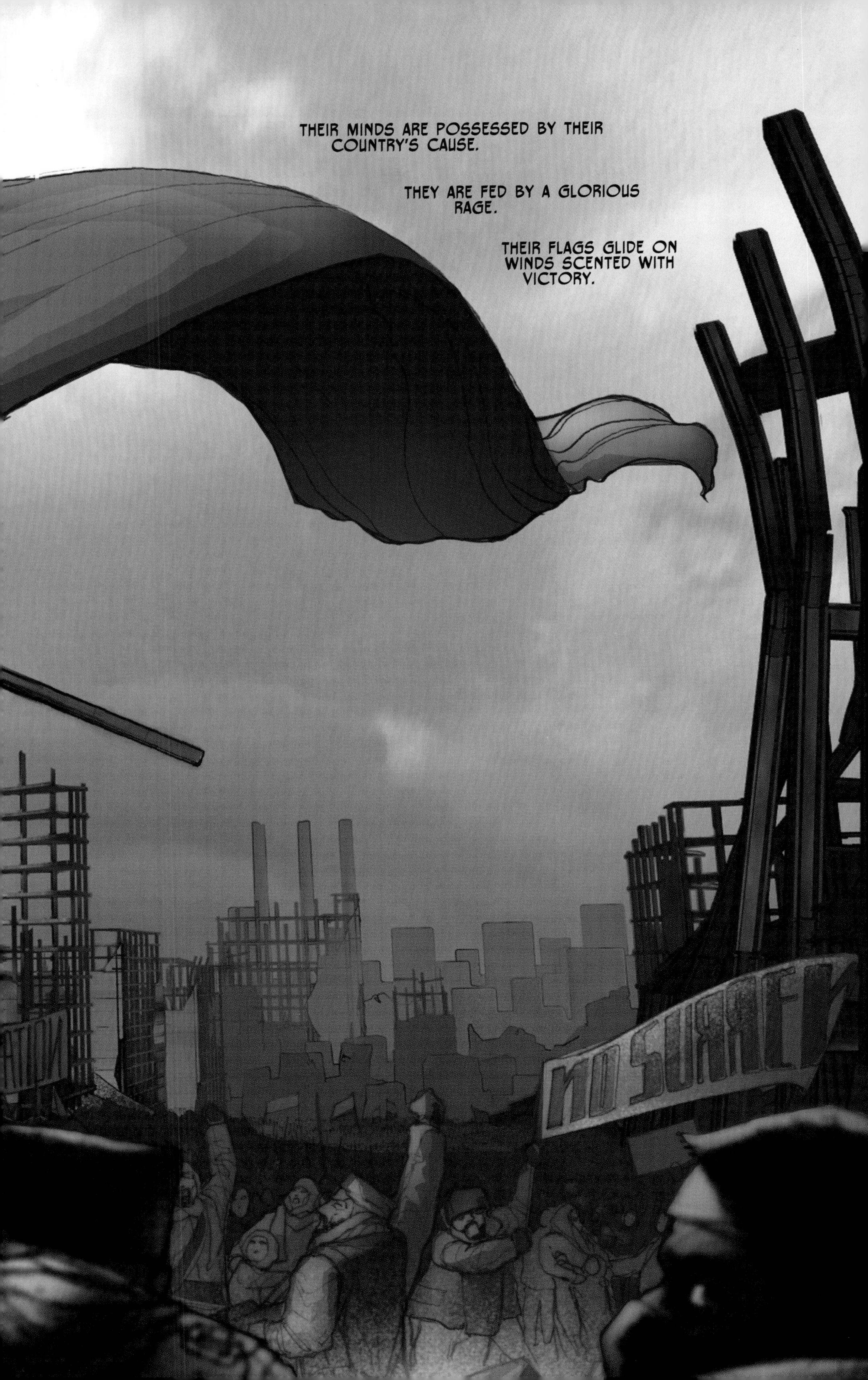
THEIR MINDS ARE POSSESSED BY THEIR COUNTRY'S CAUSE.
THEY ARE FED BY A GLORIOUS RAGE.
THEIR FLAGS GLIDE ON WINDS SCENTED WITH VICTORY.

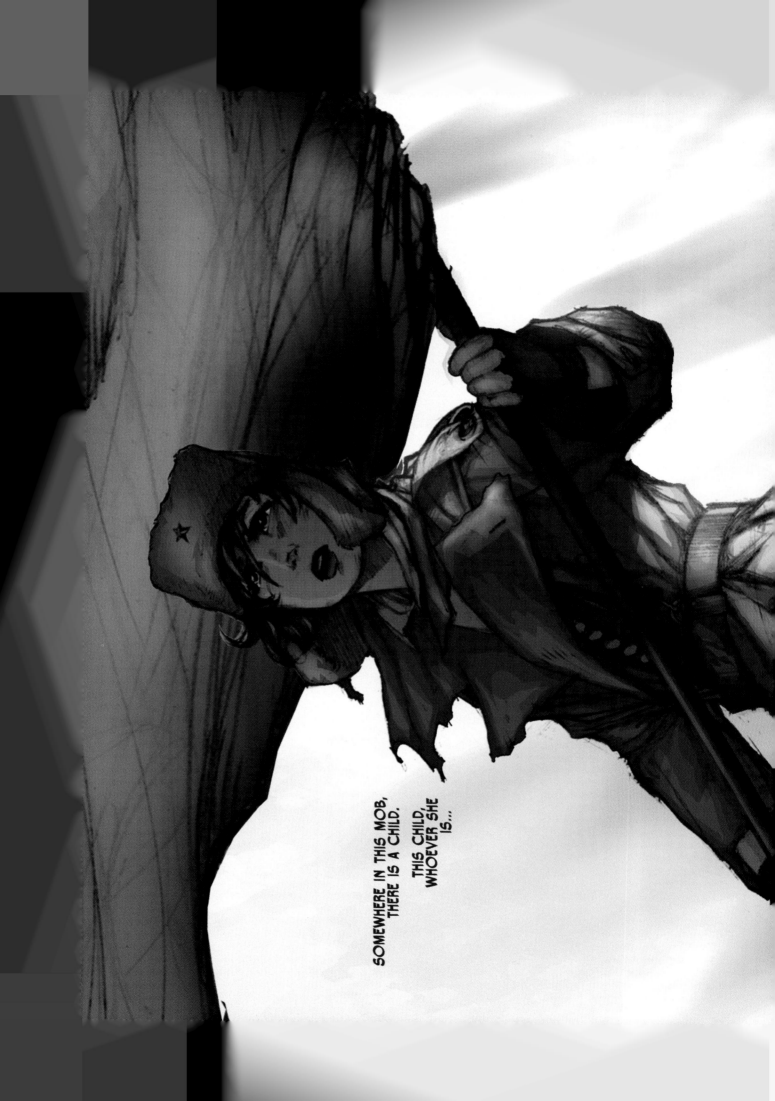

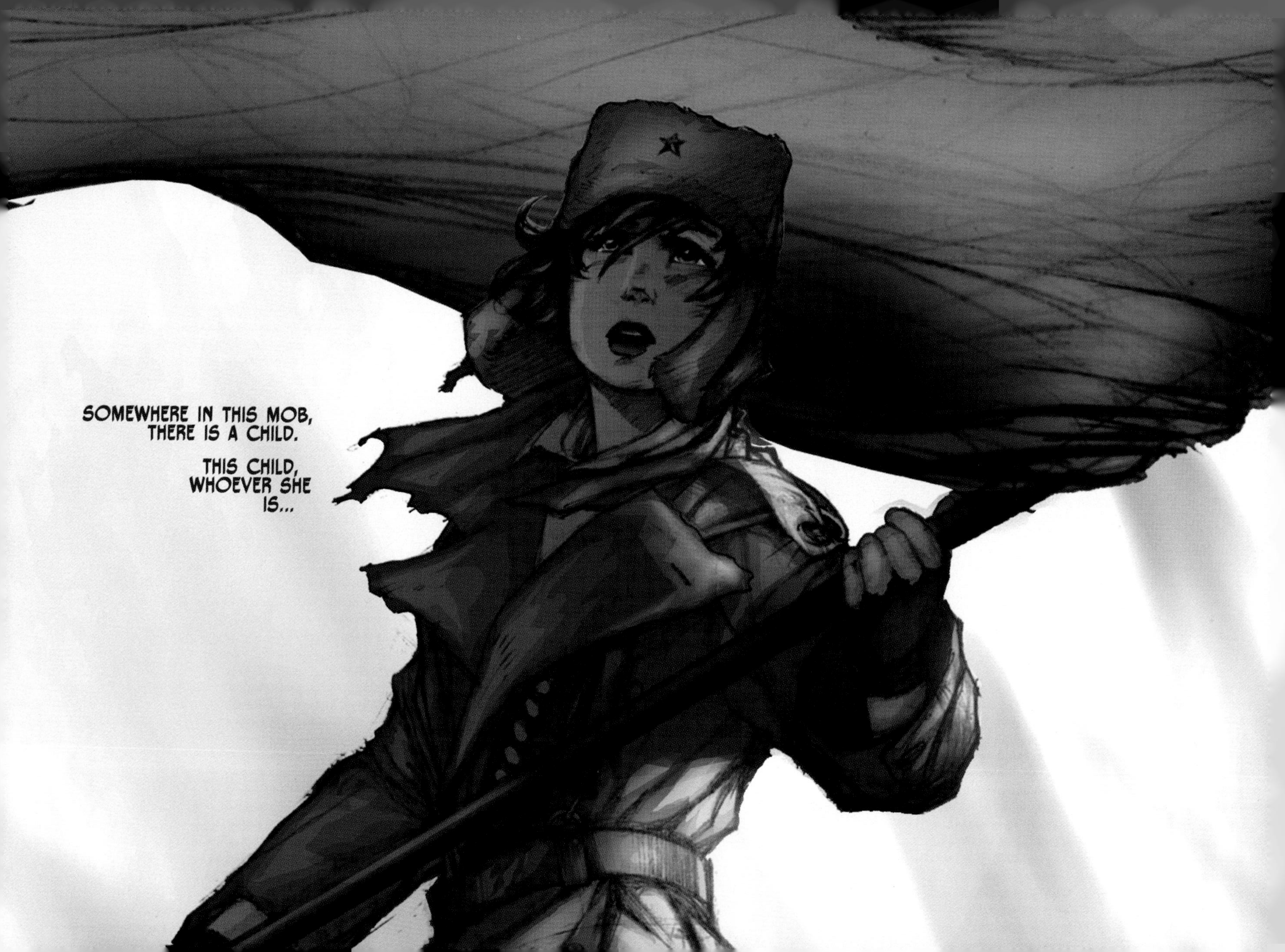
SOMEWHERE IN THIS MOB, THERE IS A CHILD.
THIS CHILD, WHOEVER SHE IS...

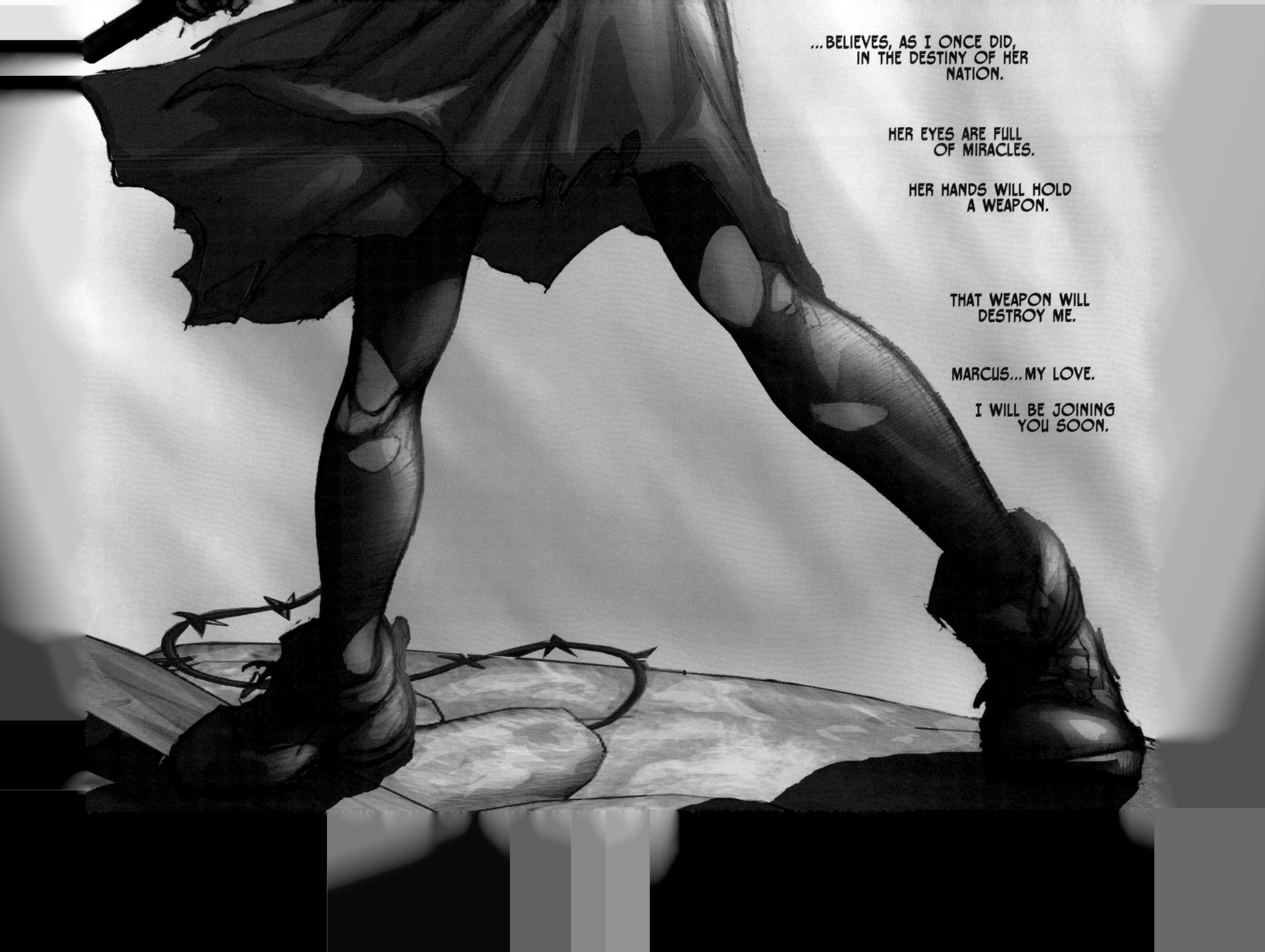
...BELIEVES, AS I ONCE DID, IN THE DESTINY OF HER NATION.
HER EYES ARE FULL OF MIRACLES.
HER HANDS WILL HOLD A WEAPON.
THAT WEAPON WILL DESTROY ME.
MARCUS...MY LOVE.
I WILL BE JOINING YOU SOON.

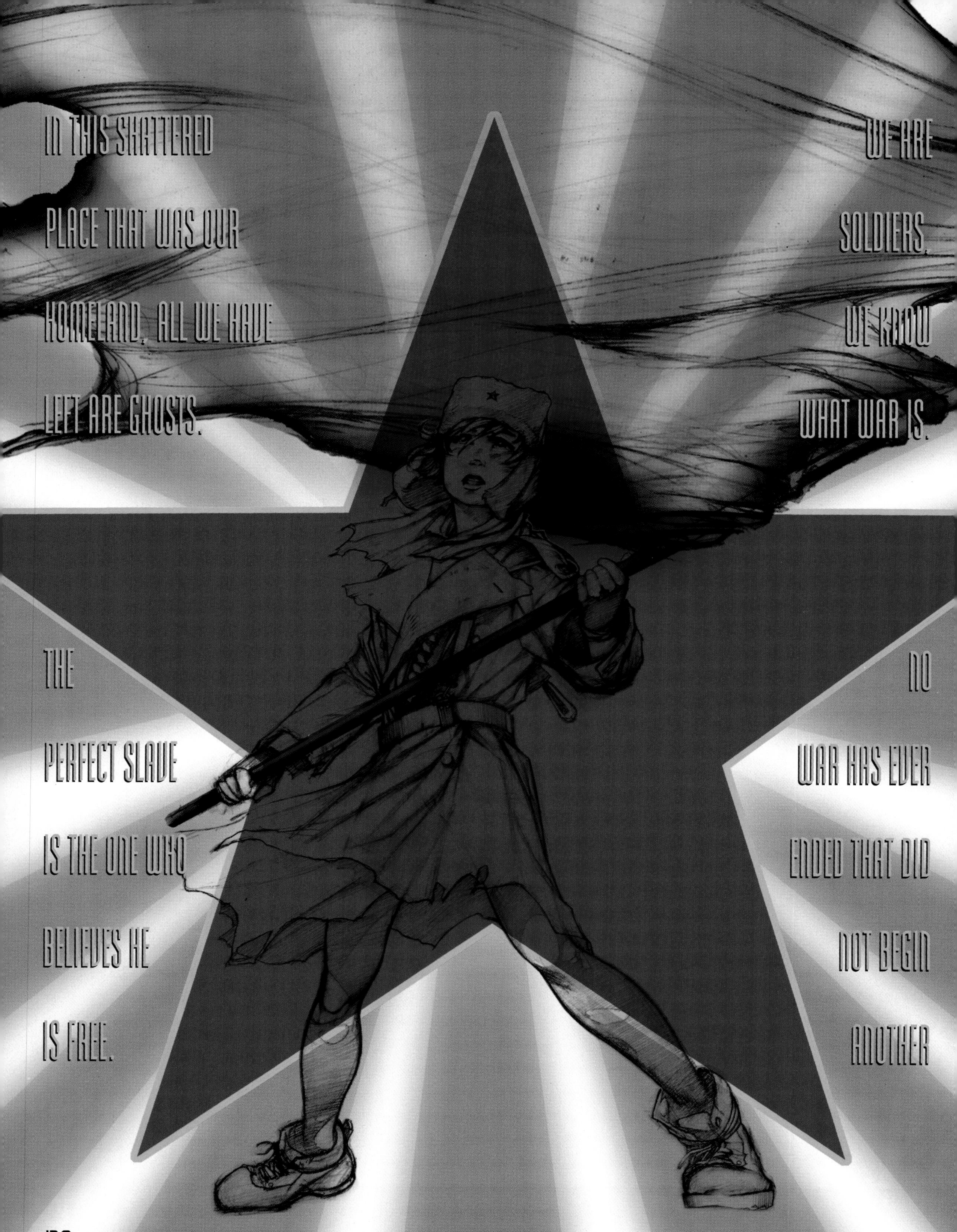
IN THIS SHATTERED PLACE THAT WAS OUR HOMELAND, ALL WE HAVE LEFT ARE GHOSTS.
WE ARE SOLDIERS, WE KNOW WHAT WAR IS.
THE PERFECT SLAVE IS THE ONE WHO BELIEVES HE IS FREE.
NO WAR HAS EVER ENDED THAT DID NOT BEGIN ANOTHER

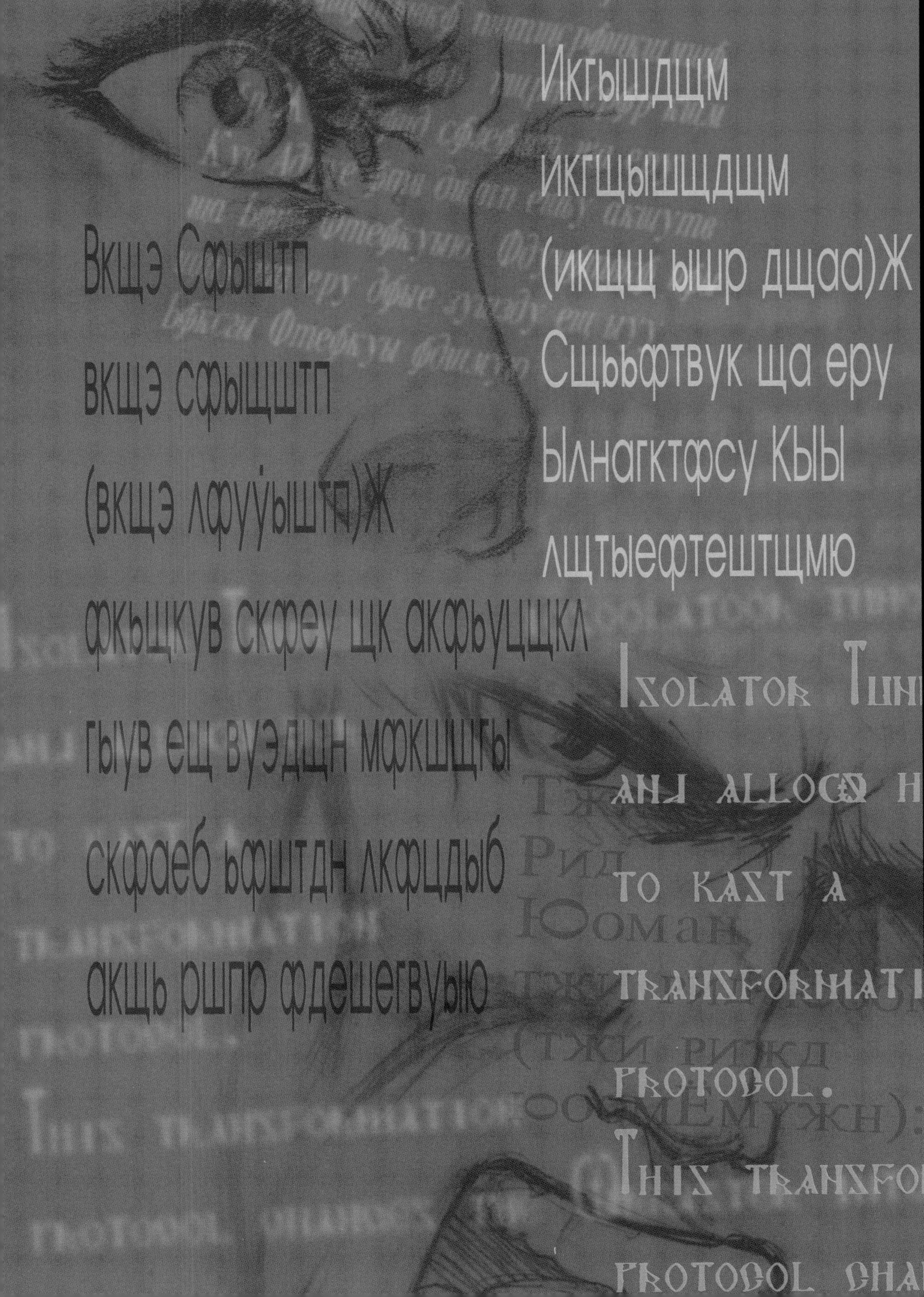

Ал Ыстаан алоысотаан (ажл ызтажн):
Ноунтрй соутж оф тжи УРРС; жоми оф тжи Нустааны ъаррыор.

Икгышдщм
икгщышщдщм
(икщщ ышр дщаа)Ж
Сщььфтвук ща еру
Ылнагктфсу КЫЫ
лщтыефтештщмю

Вкщэ Сфыштп
вкщэ сфыщштп
(вкщэ лфуўыштп)Ж
фкьщкув скфеу щк акфьуцщкл
гыув ещ вуэдщн мфкшщгы
скфаеб ьфштдн лкфцдыб
акщь ршпр фдешегвуыю

Izolator Tunn
and allows h
to kast a
transformati
protocol.
This transfor
protocol chan

LEXICON

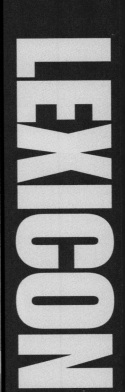

AL' ISTAAN – AL•IS•TAAN (AHL'IZTAHN): COUNTRY SOUTH OF THE URRS; HOME OF THE NISTAANI WARRIOR.

ALEXANDRA GONCHAROVA – AL•EX•AN•DRA GON•CHA•ROV•A (AL EX AN' DRAH GOHN CHAH ROV' AH): KRAWL CAPTAIN OF THE RED FLEET AND LONG TIME FRIEND OF MAYA ANTARES. ALEXANDRA WAS ONE OF THE LAST PEOPLE TO SEE MARCUS ANTARES ALIVE.

SKYMARSHALL A. A. BRUSILOV – BRU•SI•LOV (BROO'SIH LOFF): COMMANDER OF THE SKYFURNACE RSS KONSTANTINOV.

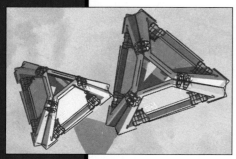

DROP CASING — DROP CAS•ING (DROP KAE'SING): ARMORED CRATE OR FRAMEWORK USED TO DEPLOY VARIOUS CRAFT, MAINLY KRAWLS, FROM HIGH ALTITUDES.

GATE TRANSFER PROTOCOL - GATE TRANS•FER PRO•TO•COL (GAYT TRANS'FUR PROH'TAH KOL): PROTOCOL THAT OPENS A TWO-WAY GATE CAPABLE OF TRANSPORTING TROOPS AND EQUIPMENT GREAT DISTANCES WITH MINIMAL EFFORT.

HAILER – HAIL•ER (HAY'LER): 1. A HEAVY CALIBER AUTOMATIC WEAPON CARRIED BY A SPECIAL CLASS OF INFANTRYMAN WITHIN THE RED FLEET. 2. MILITARY TERM FOR A SKILLED SOLDIER WHO OPERATES A HAILER WEAPON, AND WHO IS CHARGED WITH THE SOLE DUTY OF DEFENDING AN ASSIGNED WARKASTER.

HOOK – HOOK: HEAVY INFANTRY WEAPON WIELDED BY SOLDIERS OF THE RED FLEET; INFANTRYMEN HAVE LIMITED

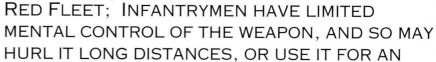

MENTAL CONTROL OF THE WEAPON, AND SO MAY HURL IT LONG DISTANCES, OR USE IT FOR AN ARRAY OF OTHER OFFENSIVE TASKS.

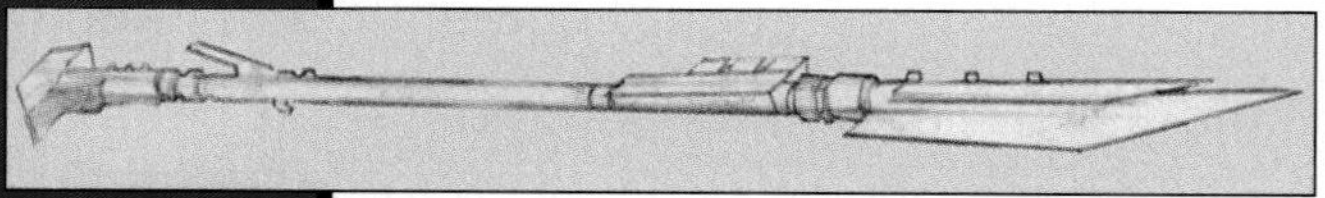

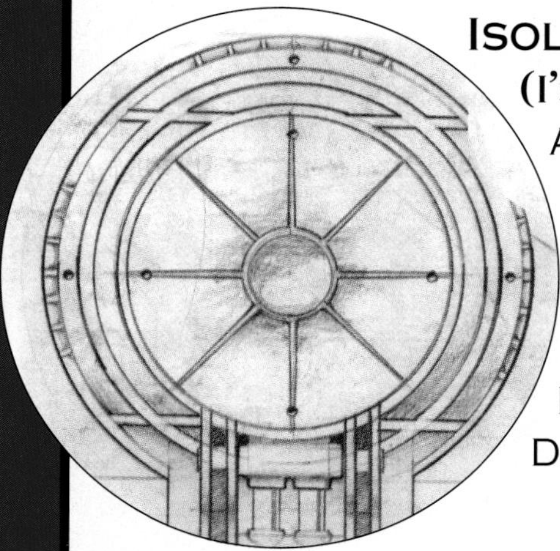

ISOLATOR TUNNEL – I•SO•LATO•R TUN•NEL (I'SO LAY TOR TUN'EL): STRUCTURE FOUND ONBOARD A SKYFURNACE THAT, DURING BATTLE, HOUSES A WARKASTER AND ALLOWS HER TO KAST A TRANSFORMATION PROTOCOL. THIS TRANSFORMATION PROTOCOL CHANGES THE WARKASTER INTO A PILLAR OF ENERGY WHICH, WHEN KAST CORRECTLY, CAN DELIVER GRAVE AMOUNTS OF DAMAGE TO ENEMY CRAFT.

KAR DATHRA'S GATE – KAR DATH•RAS GATE (KAR' DA' THRUHS GAYT): 1. AREA NAMED AFTER KAR DATHRA THE ETERNAL DEFENDER, A HIGH PRIEST REVERED BY THE NISTAANI PEOPLE. THIS REGION IS ONE OF THE MOST SACRED WITHIN AL' ISTAAN. 2. BATTLE SITE WHERE THE RED FLEET MET WITH HEAVY DEFEAT AT THE HANDS OF THE NISTAANI.

KONSTANTINOV – KON•STAN•TIN•OV (KAHN STAN TEEN' OFF): SKYFURNACE FLAGSHIP OF THE RED FLEET; CURRENTLY COMMANDED BY SKYMARSHALL BRUSILOV.

KRAWL – KRAWL (KRAHL): HEAVY OFFENSIVE COMBAT VEHICLE OF THE RED FLEET ARMED WITH CANNONS AND MACHINE GUNS WHICH MOVES ON CATERPILLAR TREAD. KRAWLS ARE DEPLOYED INTO BATTLE VIA STRATEGIC SKYFURNACE DROP AT AN RDA OR RAPID DEPLOYMENT ALTITUDE.

MARCUS ANTARES – MAR•CUS AN•TAR•ES (MAR'KUS AN TAR'EEZ): INFANTRY CAPTAIN OF THE RED FLEET; HUSBAND TO MAYA ANTARES.

MAYA ANTARES – MA•YA AN•TAR•ES (MÄ'YAH AN TAR'EEZ): WARKASTER OF THE RED FLEET, SORCERESS MAJOR; WIFE TO MARCUS ANTARES.

NISTAANI – NIS•TAA•NI (NIHS TAHN'EE): HARDENED DESERT WARRIORS OF AL' ISTAAN.

PROTOCOL – PRO•TO•COL (PROH'TAH KOL): MILITARY TERMINOLOGY FOR A SPELL OR ENCHANTMENT.

THE RED WOMAN – THE RED WO•MAN (THE REHD WOOM'MUHN): THE MYSTERIOUS IMAGE OF THE RED WOMAN HAS SELDOM BEEN WITNESSED. TESTIMONY OF THOSE THAT HAVE SEEN THIS ENIGMATIC FIGURE OFTEN REPORT NOTICING HER WEEP AT THE GRAVES OF FALLEN SOLDIERS.

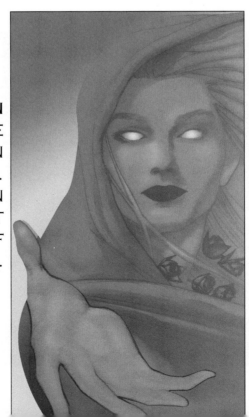

TROIKA – TROI•KA (TROI´KAH):
1. TRADITIONALLY A GROUP OR ASSOCIATION OF THREE OPERATIVES OR INTERROGATORS. 2. THE NAME OF IMBOHL'S MAIN LIEUTENANT AND FEARED ASSASSIN. LEGEND SPEAKS OF TROIKA'S HEINOUS ABILITY TO HARVEST THE SOULS OF THE FALLEN AND DELIVER THEM TO HIS LIEGE LORD FOR JUDGEMENT.

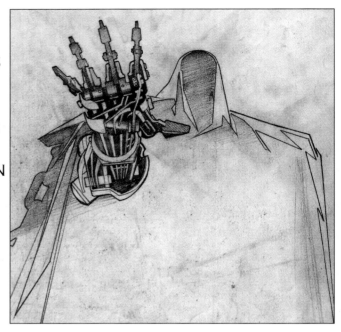

SKYFURNACE –
SKY•FUR•NACE (SKY'FUHR'NUS): A 1. MILE LONG HEAVILY ARMORED WARSHIP DESIGNED MAINLY FOR RAPID DEPLOYMENT OF INFANTRY AND VARIOUS CRAFT, AND MASSIVE SIEGE OPERATIONS.

URRS – U•R•R•S: UNITED REPUBLICS OF THE RED STAR.

VANYA – VAN•YA (VAHN'YAH): AN AGED VETERAN OF THE GREAT PATRIOTIC WAR.

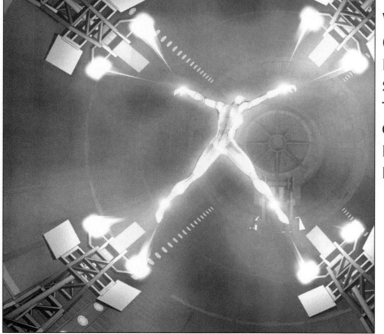

WARKASTER – WAR•KAS•TER (WOHR'KAS TUR): RED FLEET MILITARY TERMINOLOGY FOR A SORCERESS, OR SOMEONE TRAINED IN THE SORCERY CORPS. CAPABLE OF KASTING PROTOCOLS OF A MAINLY DESTRUCTIVE NATURE.

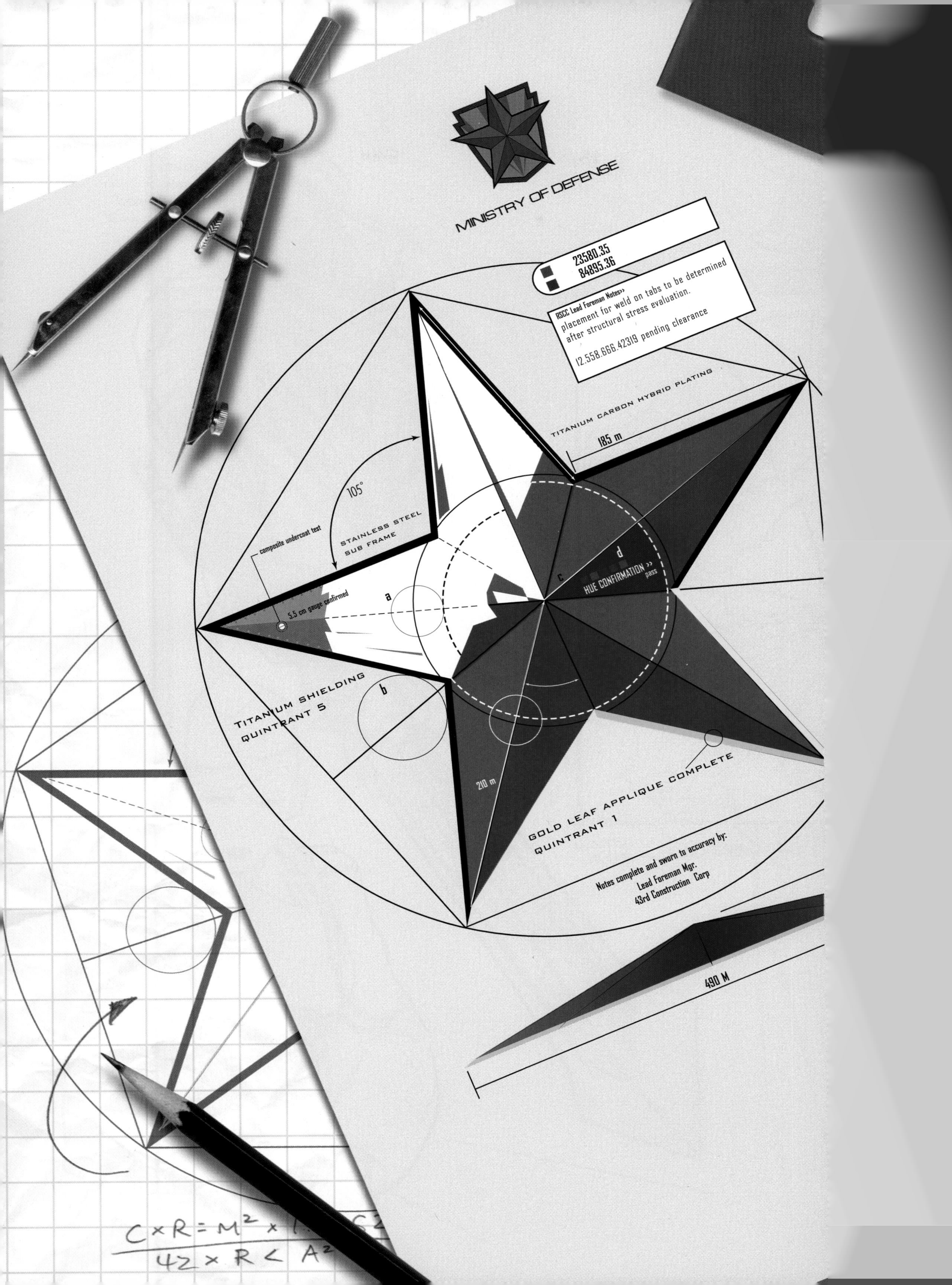
MINISTRY OF DEFENSE
23580.35
84895.36
RSCC Lead Foreman Notes>>
placement for weld on tabs to be determined
after structural stress evaluation.
12.558.666.42319 pending clearance
TITANIUM CARBON HYBRID PLATING
185 m
105°
STAINLESS STEEL
SUB FRAME
composite undercoat test
5.5 cm gauge confirmed
a
b
c
d
HUE CONFIRMATION >>
pass
TITANIUM SHIELDING
QUINTRANT 5
210 m
GOLD LEAF APPLIQUE COMPLETE
QUINTRANT 1
Notes complete and sworn to accuracy by:
Lead Foreman Mgr.
43rd Construction Corp
490 M

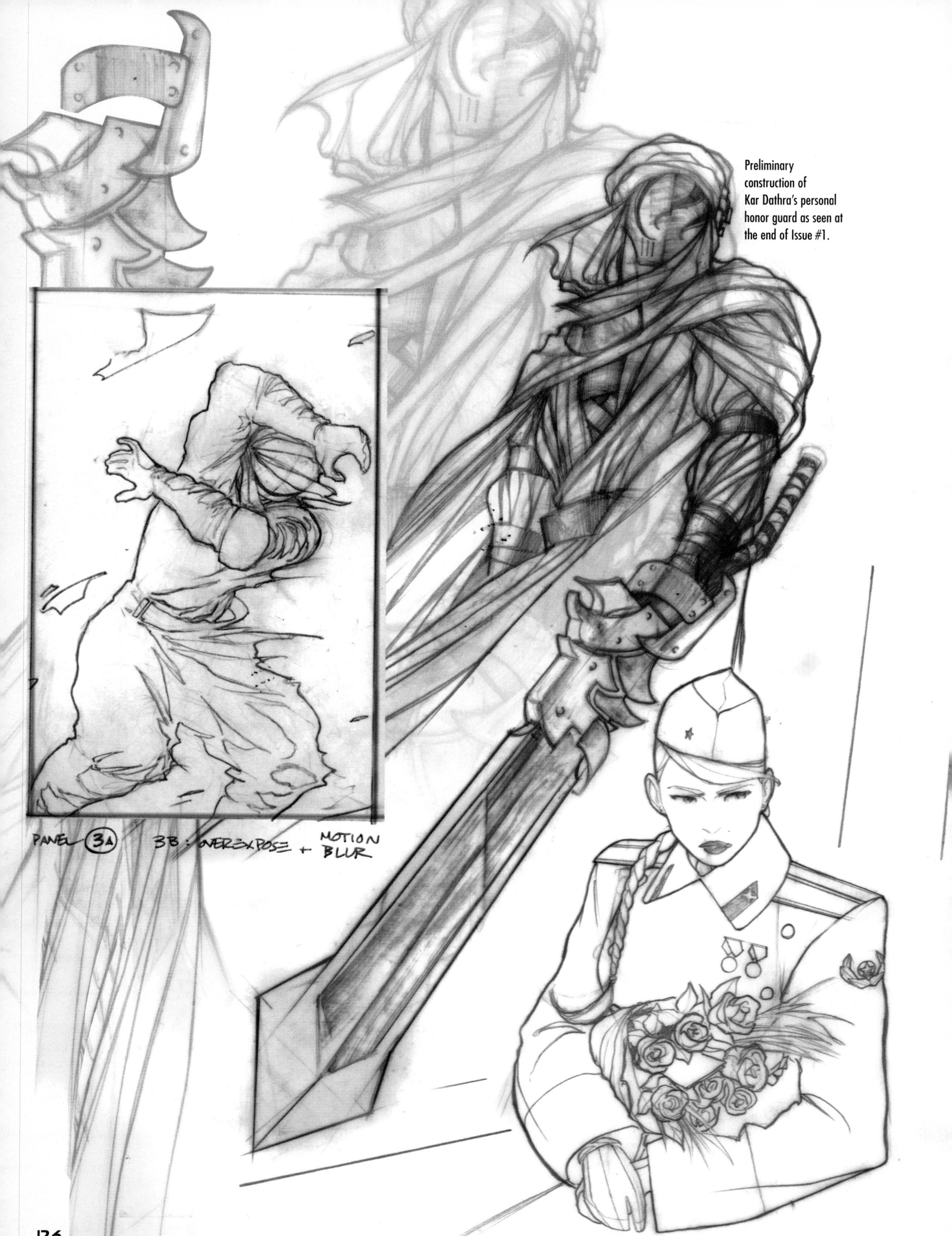
PANEL 3A
3B: OVEREXPOSE + MOTION BLUR

Preliminary construction of Kar Dathra's personal honor guard as seen at the end of Issue #1.

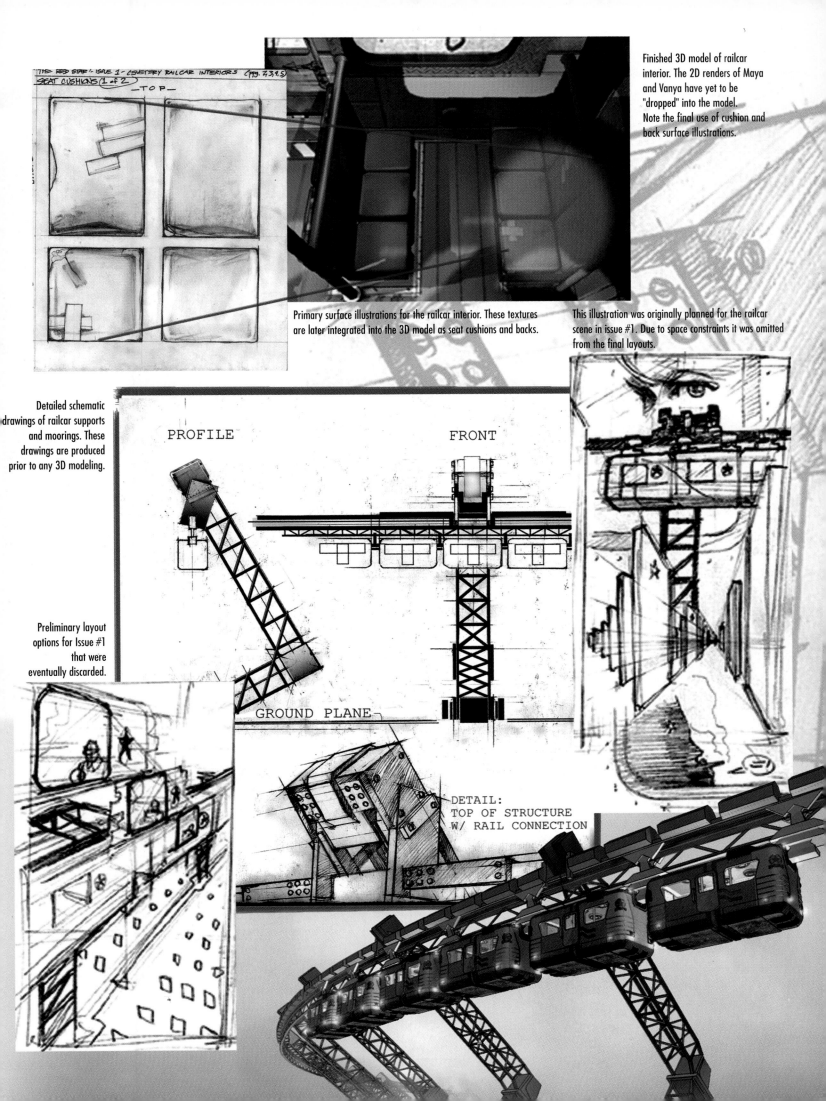

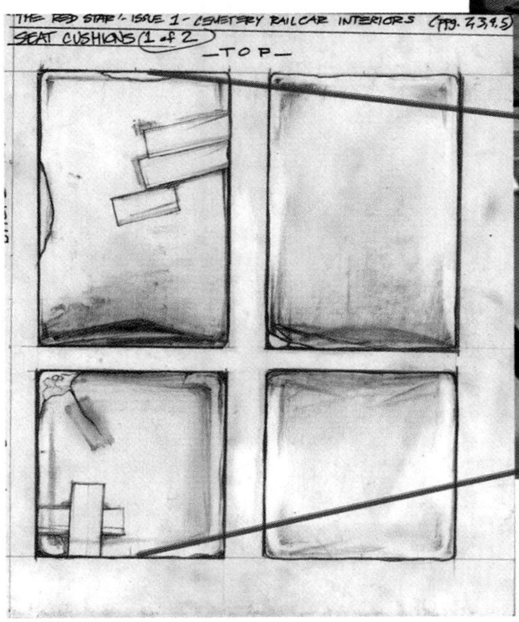
THE RED STAR - ISSUE 1 - CEMETERY RAILCAR INTERIORS (PGS. 2,3,4,5)
SEAT CUSHIONS (1 of 2)
—TOP—

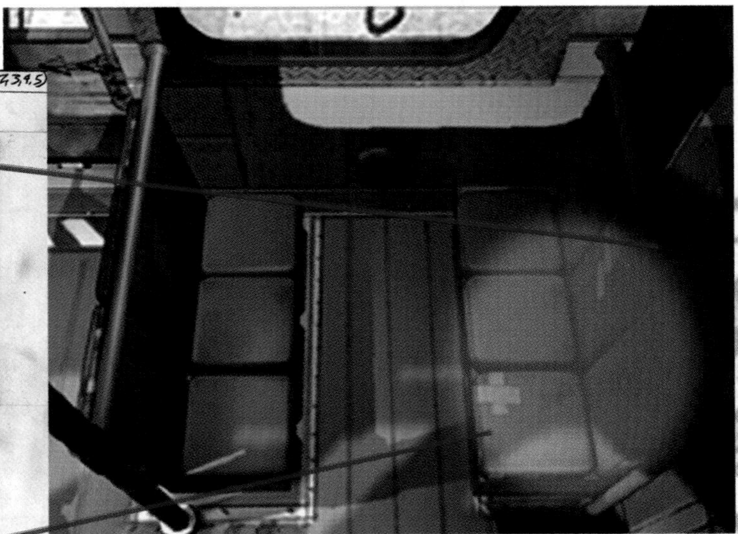

Finished 3D model of railcar interior. The 2D renders of Maya and Vanya have yet to be "dropped" into the model.
Note the final use of cushion and back surface illustrations.

Primary surface illustrations for the railcar interior. These textures are later integrated into the 3D model as seat cushions and backs.

This illustration was originally planned for the railcar scene in issue #1. Due to space constraints it was omitted from the final layouts.

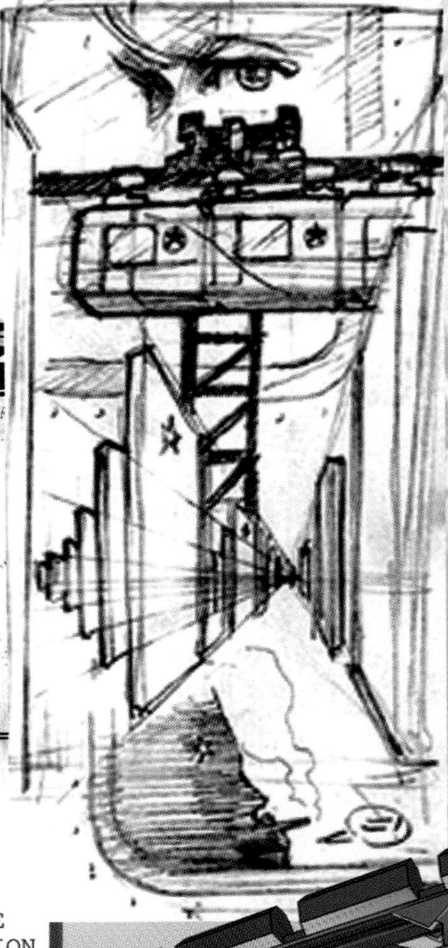

Detailed schematic drawings of railcar supports and moorings. These drawings are produced prior to any 3D modeling.

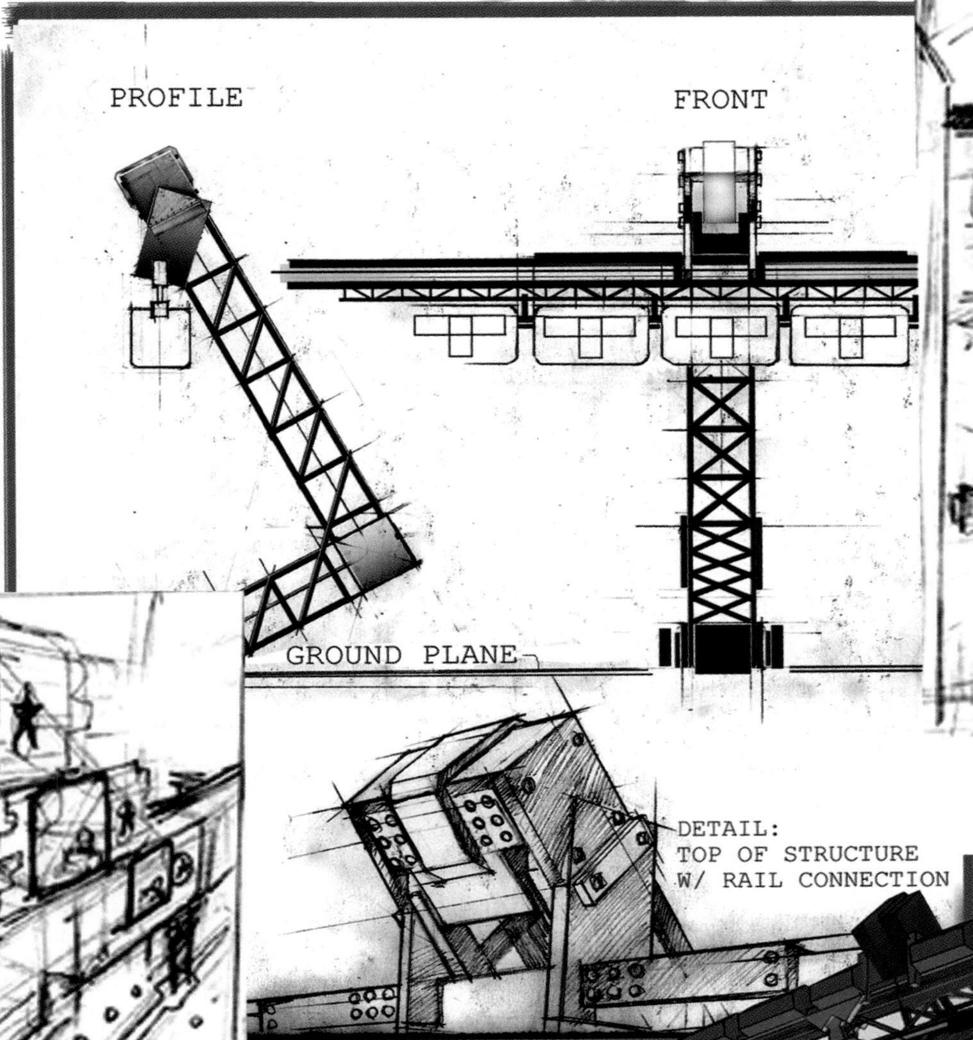
PROFILE
FRONT
GROUND PLANE
DETAIL:
TOP OF STRUCTURE
W/ RAIL CONNECTION

Preliminary layout options for Issue #1 that were eventually discarded.

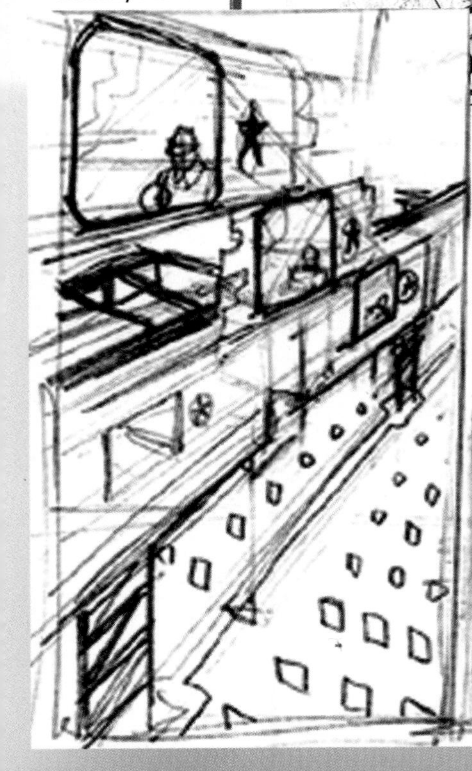

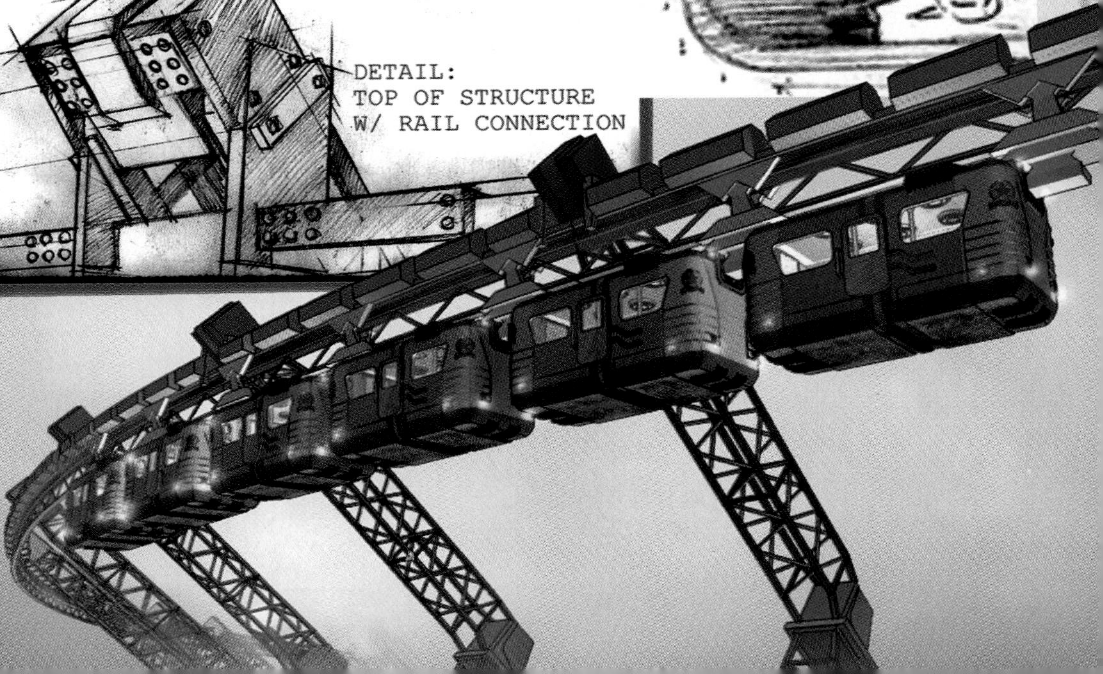

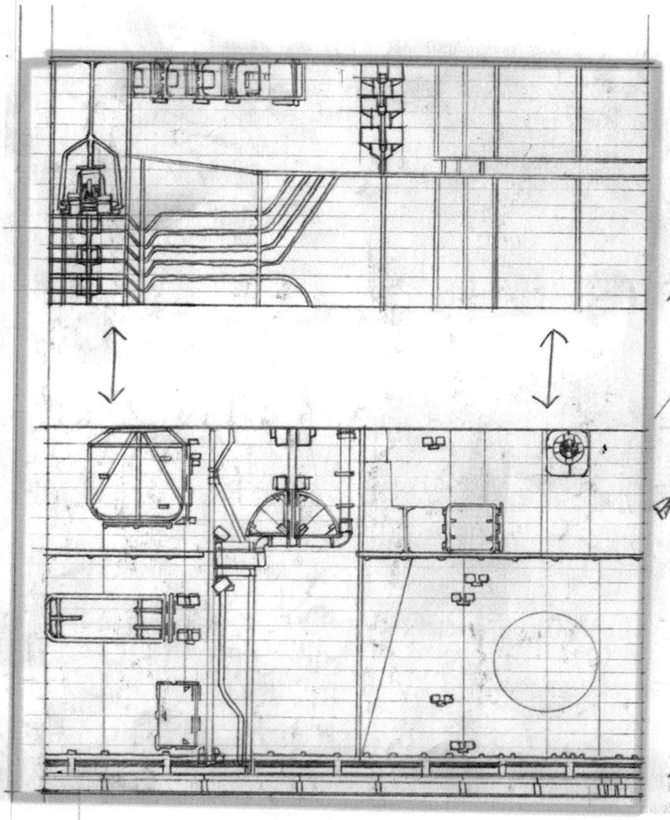

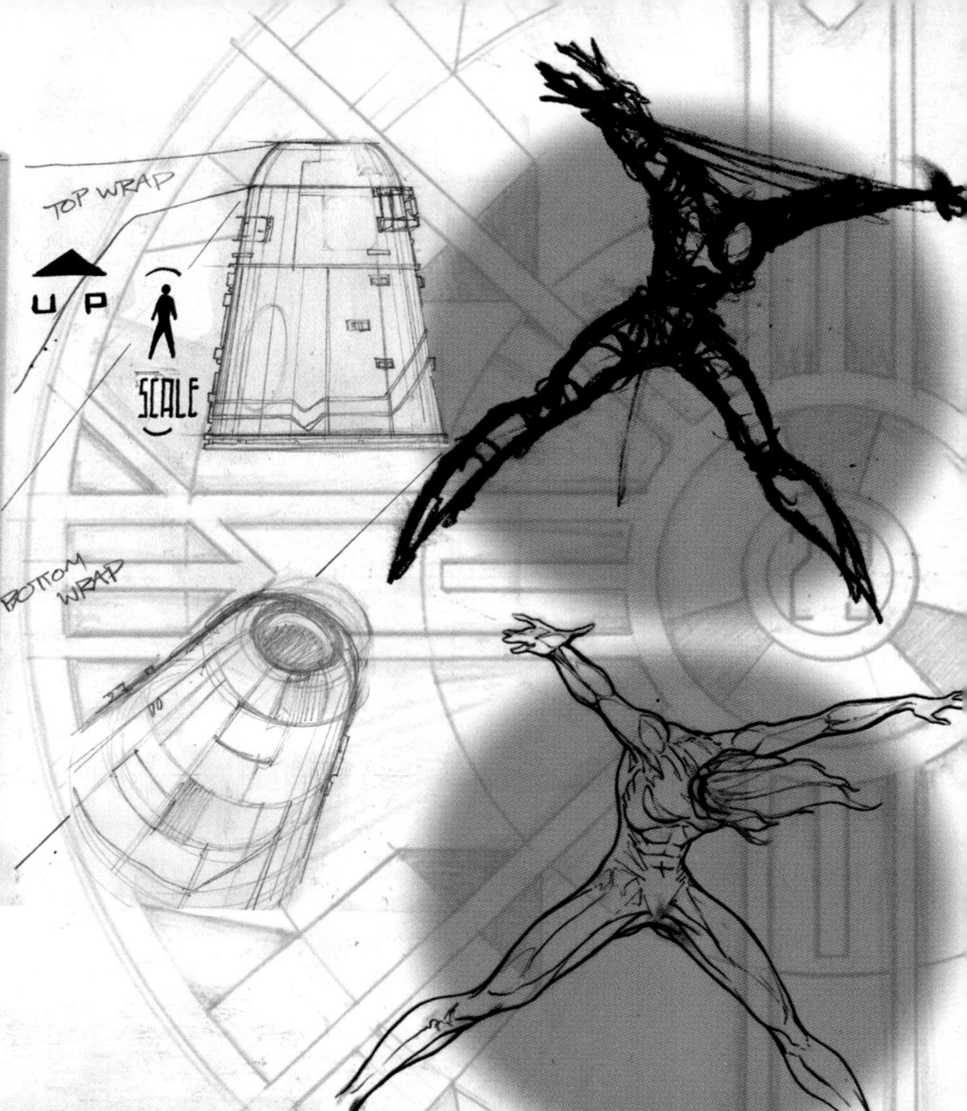

TOP WRAP
UP
SCALE
BOTTOM WRAP

Some surface illustrations are designed intentionally to be "wrapped" around a 3D model-- in this case, an isolator tunnel.

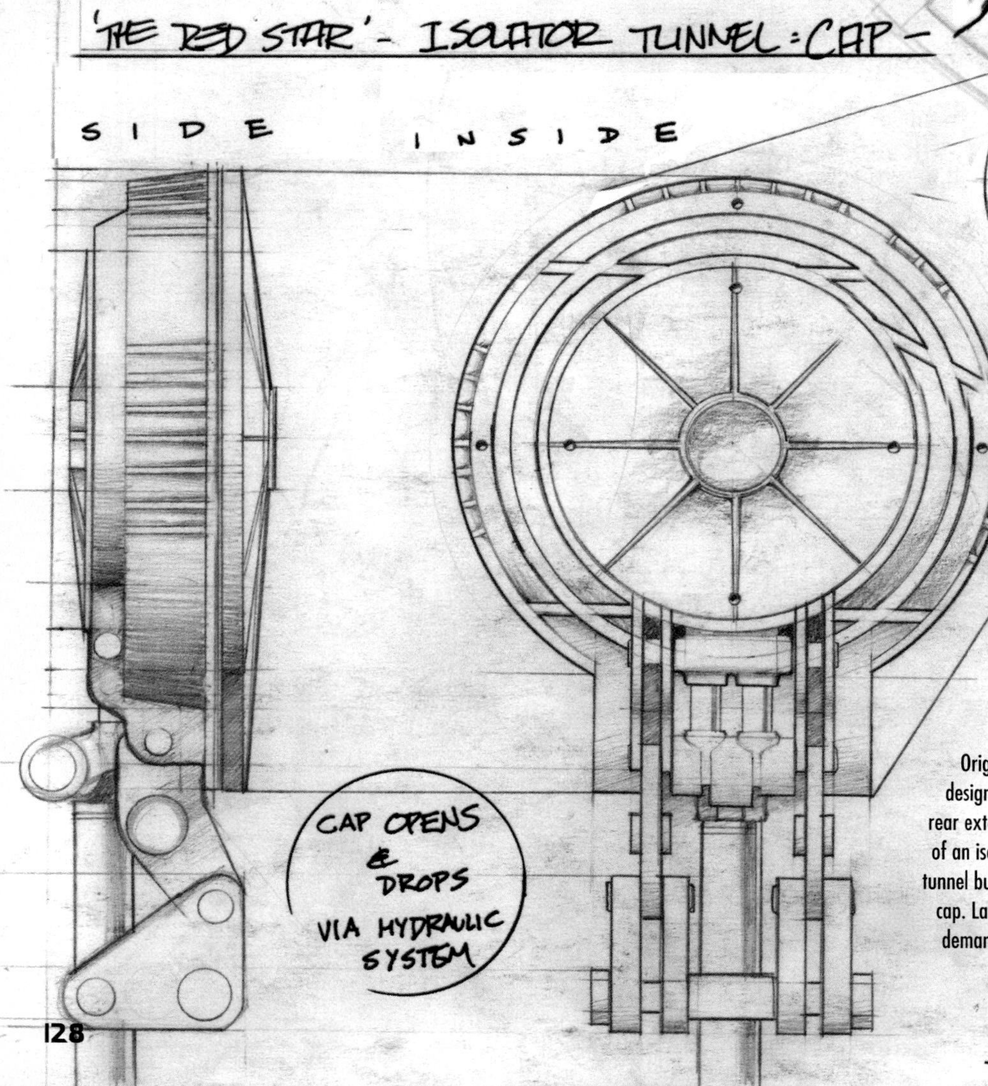

'THE RED STAR' - ISOLATOR TUNNEL: CAP -
SIDE
INSIDE
OUTSIDE
SCALE
CAP OPENS & DROPS VIA HYDRAULIC SYSTEM

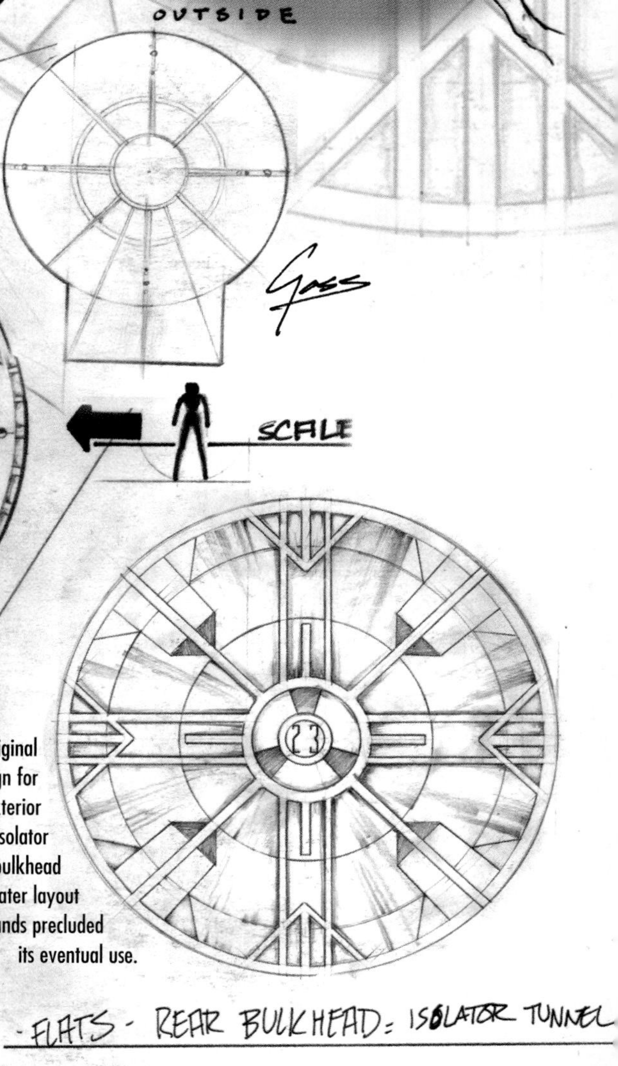

23
-FLATS- REAR BULKHEAD: ISOLATOR TUNNEL

Original design for rear exterior of an isolator tunnel bulkhead cap. Later layout demands precluded its eventual use.

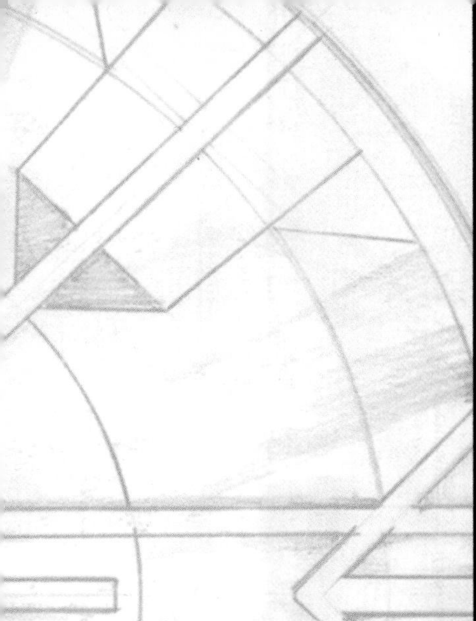

Schematic blueprint of the RSS Konstantinov. These blueprints are the first steps in the process of creating a 3D model.

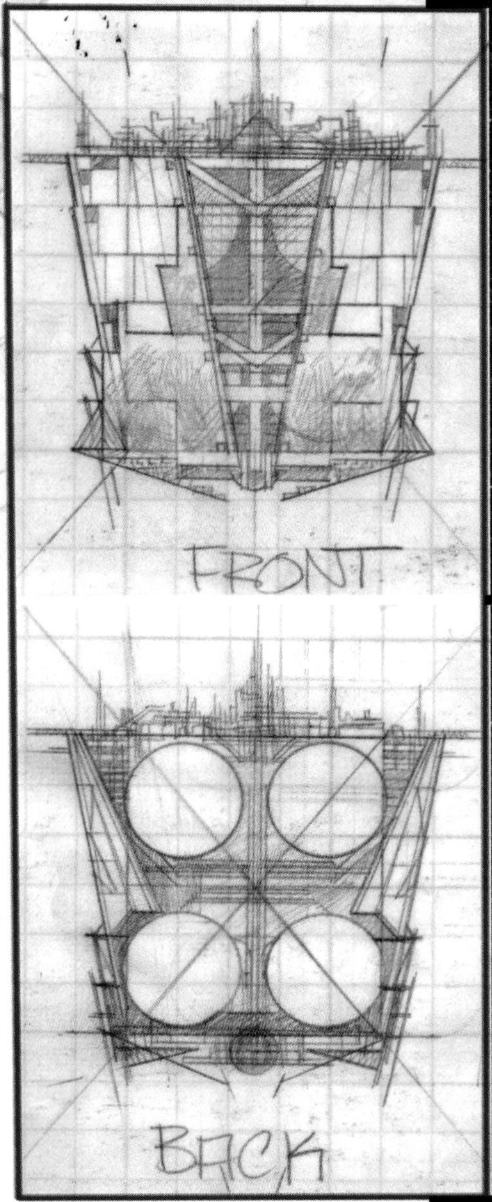
FRONT
BACK

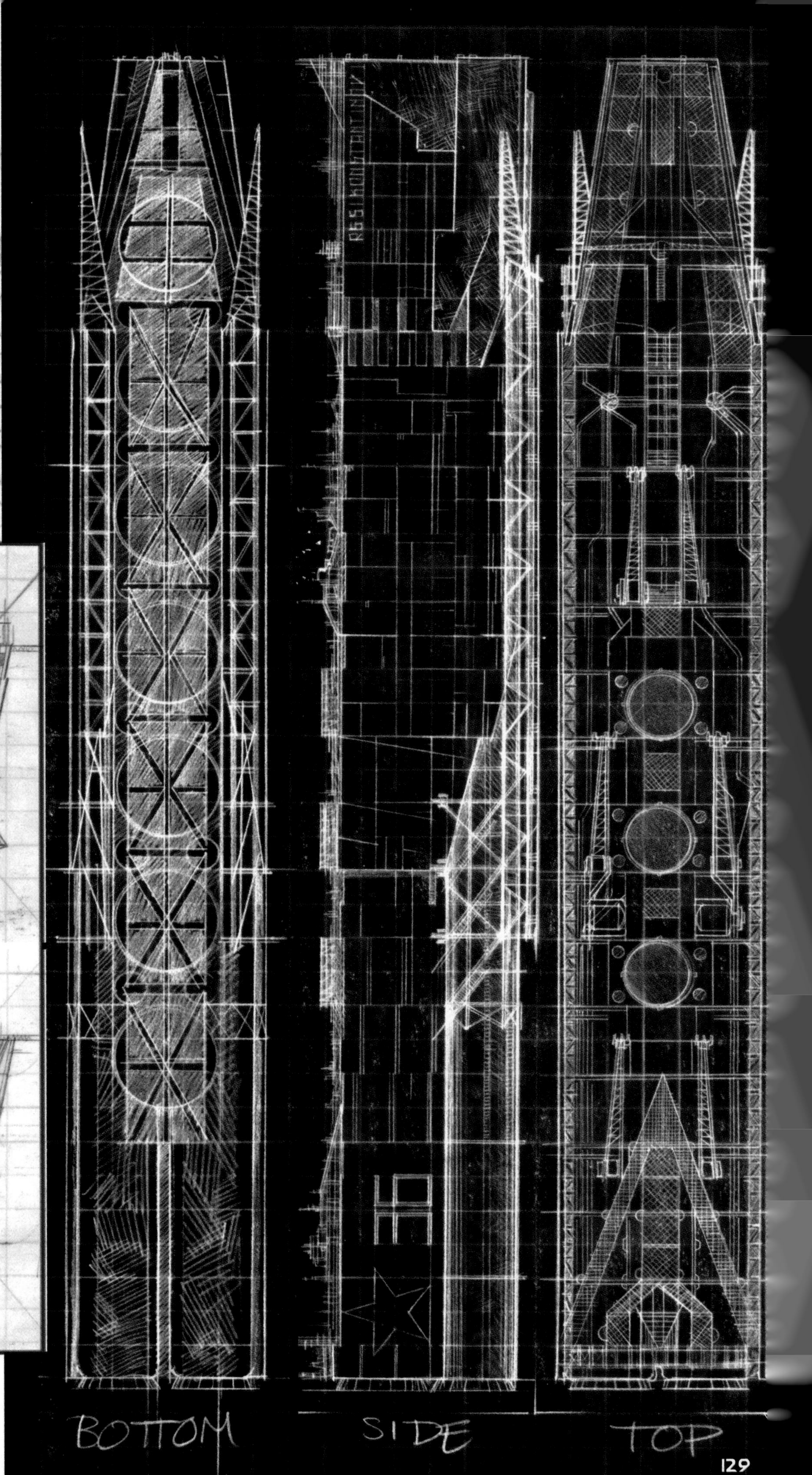
BOTTOM
SIDE
TOP

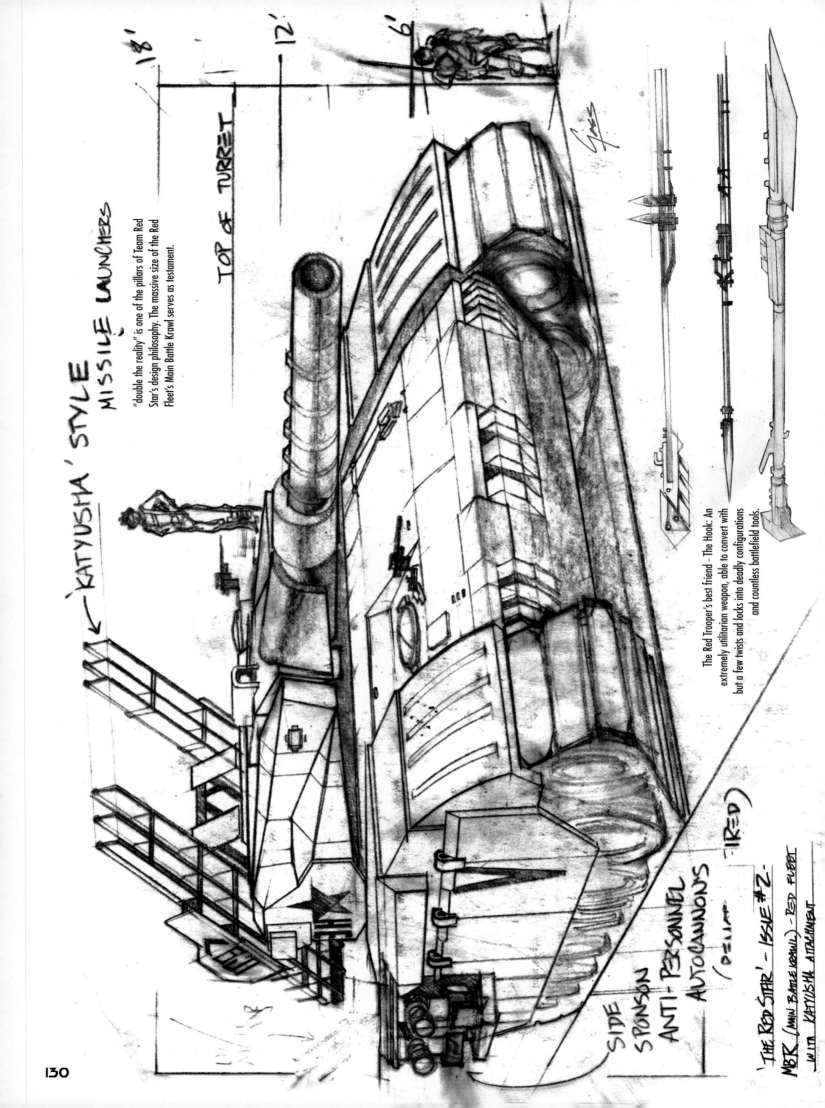

KATYUSHA' STYLE
MISSILE LAUNCHERS

"double the reality" is one of the pillars of Team Red Star's design philosophy. The massive size of the Red Fleet's Main Battle Krawl serves as testament.

TOP OF TURRET

18'

12'

6'

The Red Trooper's best friend - The Hook: An extremely utilitarian weapon, able to convert with but a few twists and locks into deadly configurations and countless battlefield tools.

SIDE SPONSON ANTI-PERSONNEL AUTOCANNONS

'THE RED STAR' - ISSUE #2-
MBK (MAIN BATTLE KRAWL) - RED FLEET
WITH KATYUSHA ATTACHMENT

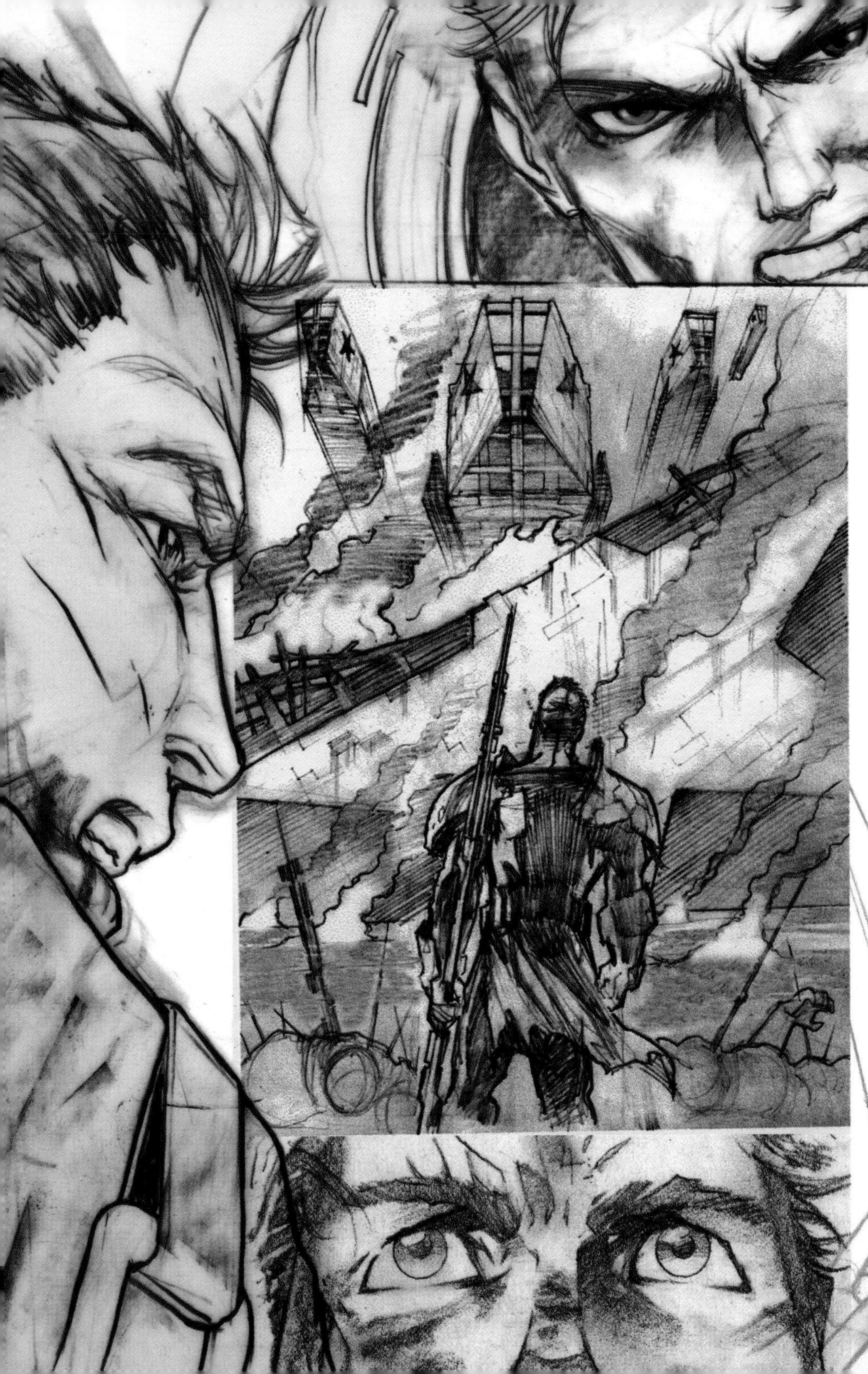

The trials of Marcus Antares at the battle of Kar Dathra's Gate.

After witnessing the fall of the Red Fleet, the Red Woman assures him before taking him into the spiritrealm, "...It was not our people that were defeated here, but our past-- and the path to our future begins with you."

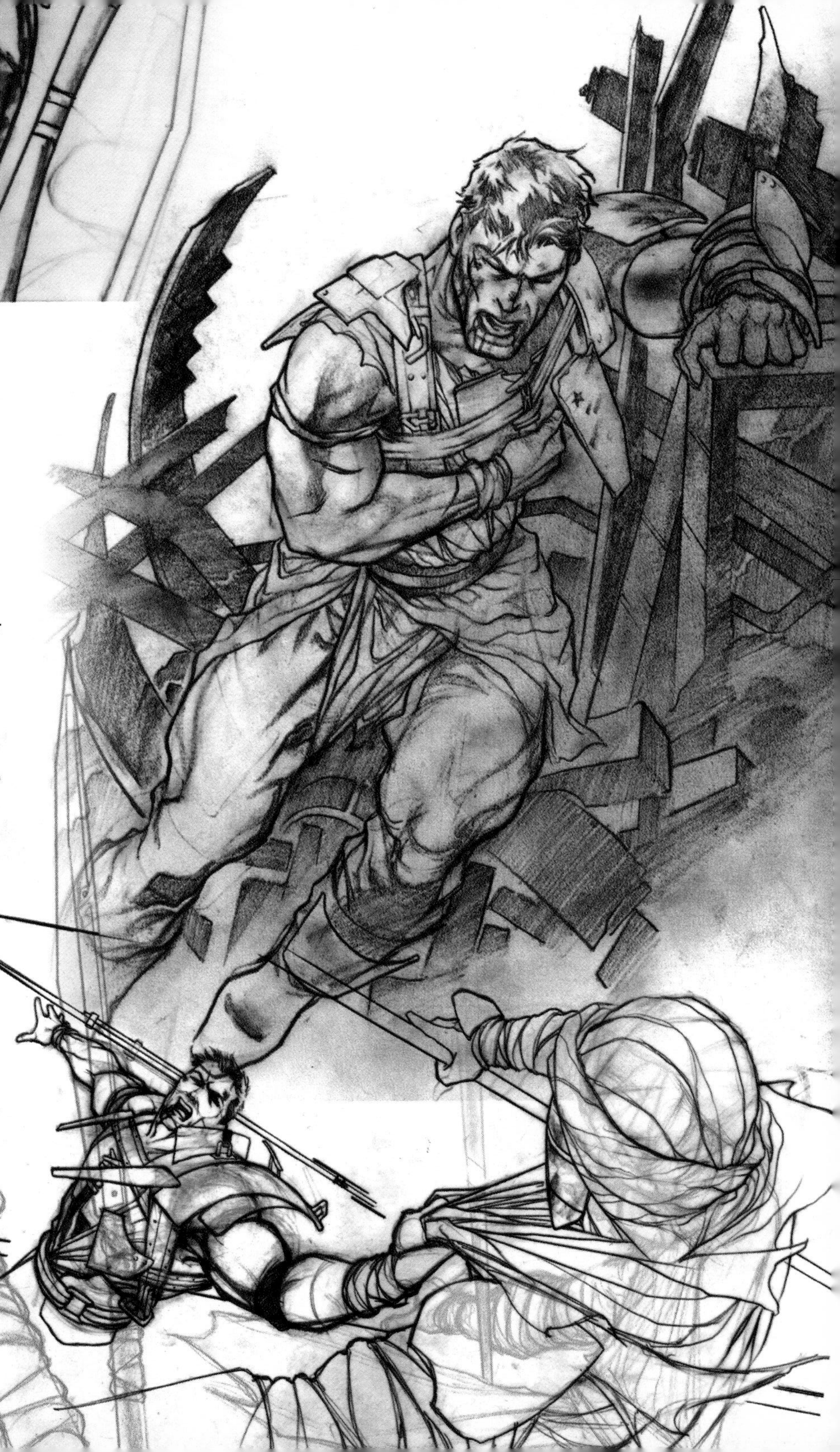

Marcus as he prepares to impale a Nistaani Warrior - note how his hook hovers just above his hand.

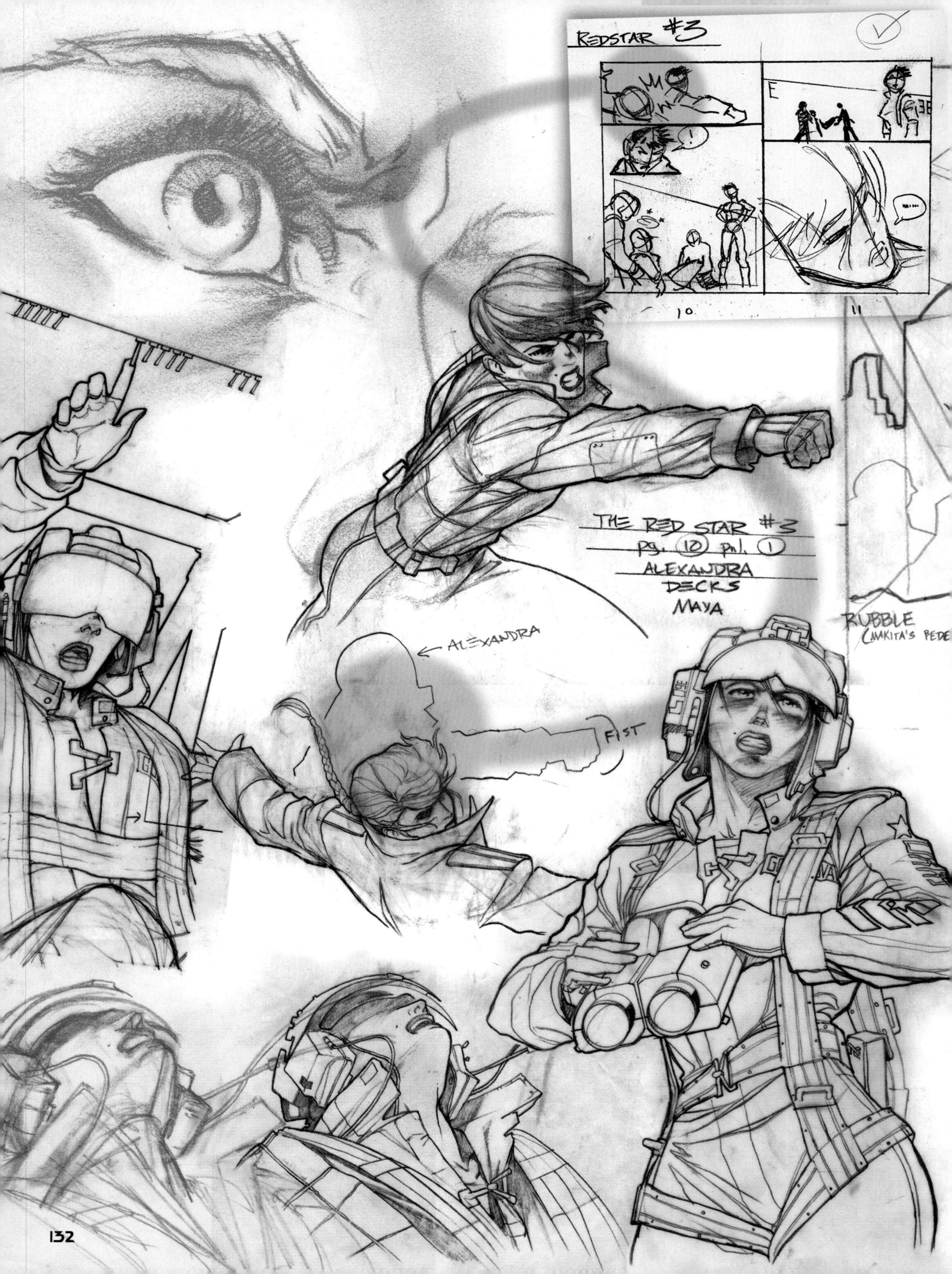

REDSTAR #3
10
11
THE RED STAR #3
pg. 10 pnl. 1
ALEXANDRA
DECKS
MAYA
RUBBLE
ALEXANDRA
FIST

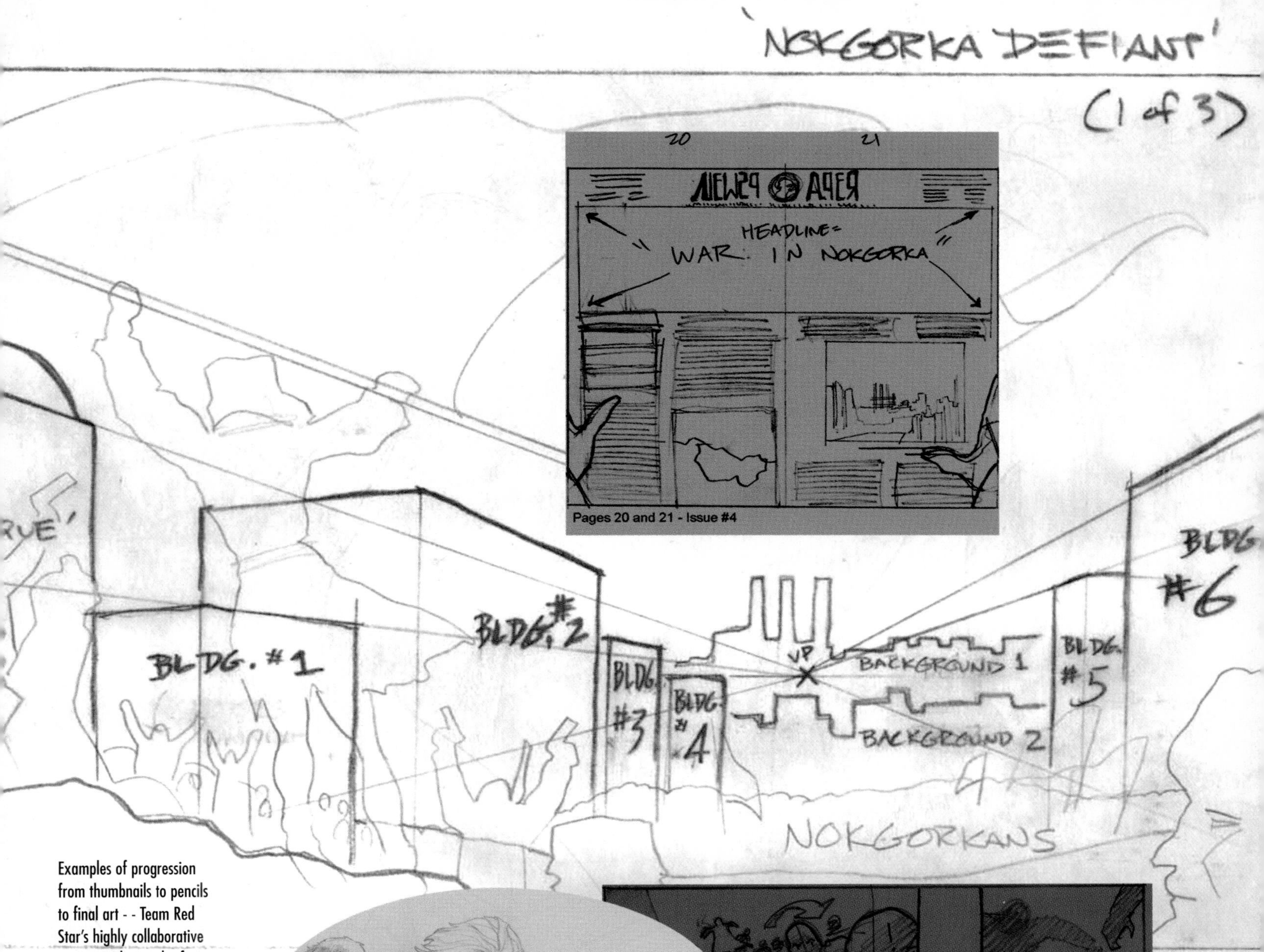
'NOKGORKA DEFIANT'
(1 of 3)
BLDG. #1
BLDG. #2
BLDG. #3
BLDG. #4
BLDG. #5
BLDG #6
VP
BACKGROUND 1
BACKGROUND 2
NOKGORKANS
20
21
HEADLINE=
"WAR IN NOKGORKA"
Pages 20 and 21 - Issue #4

Examples of progression from thumbnails to pencils to final art - - Team Red Star's highly collaborative process is the result of a combined fifty years of professional experience between Goss, Coulter and Snakebite.

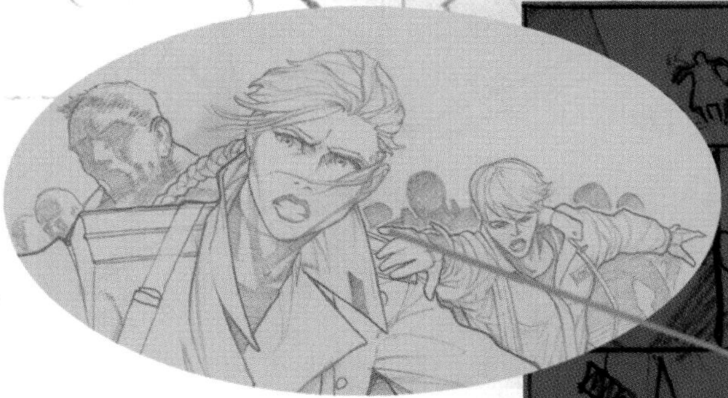

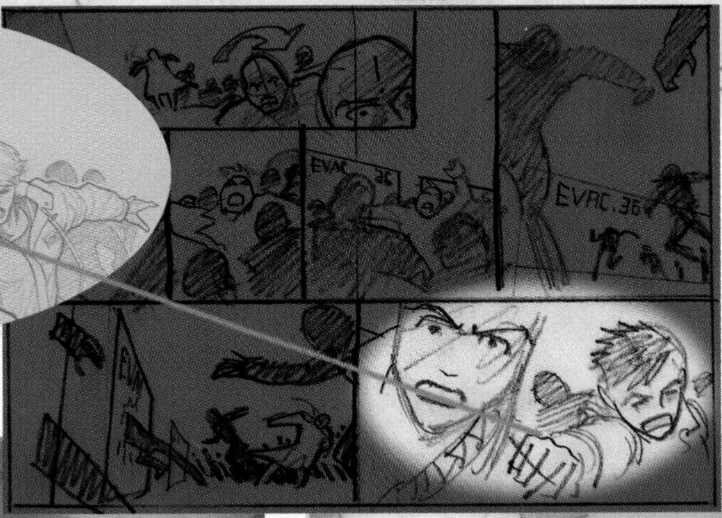
EVAC. 35
EVAC. 35

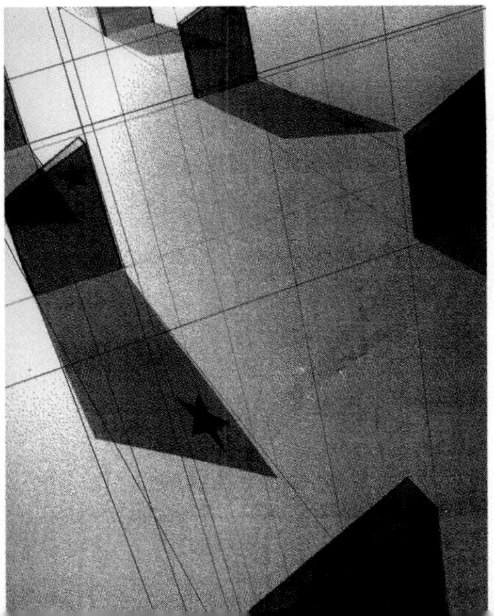

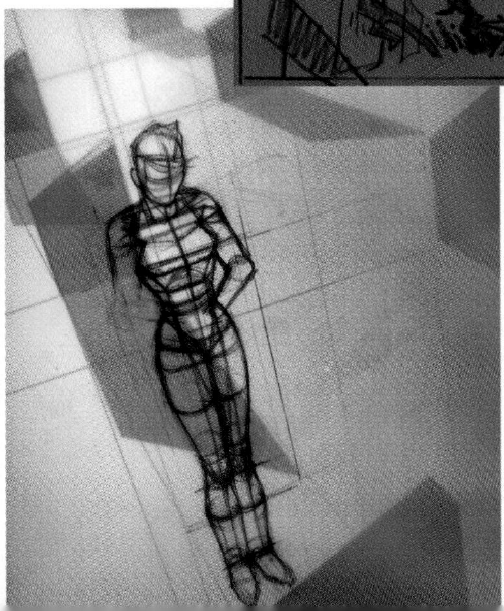

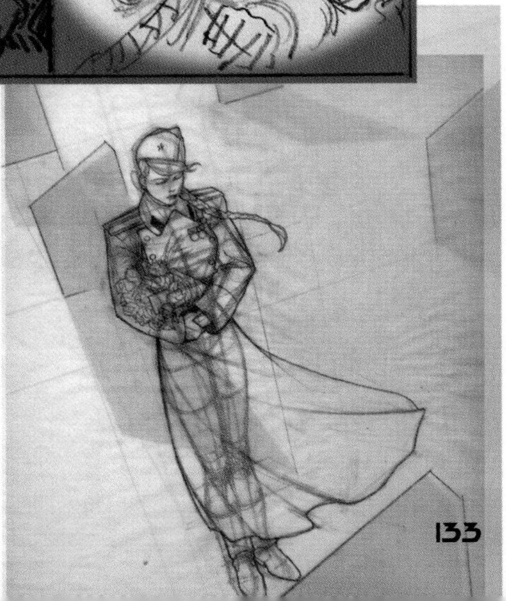

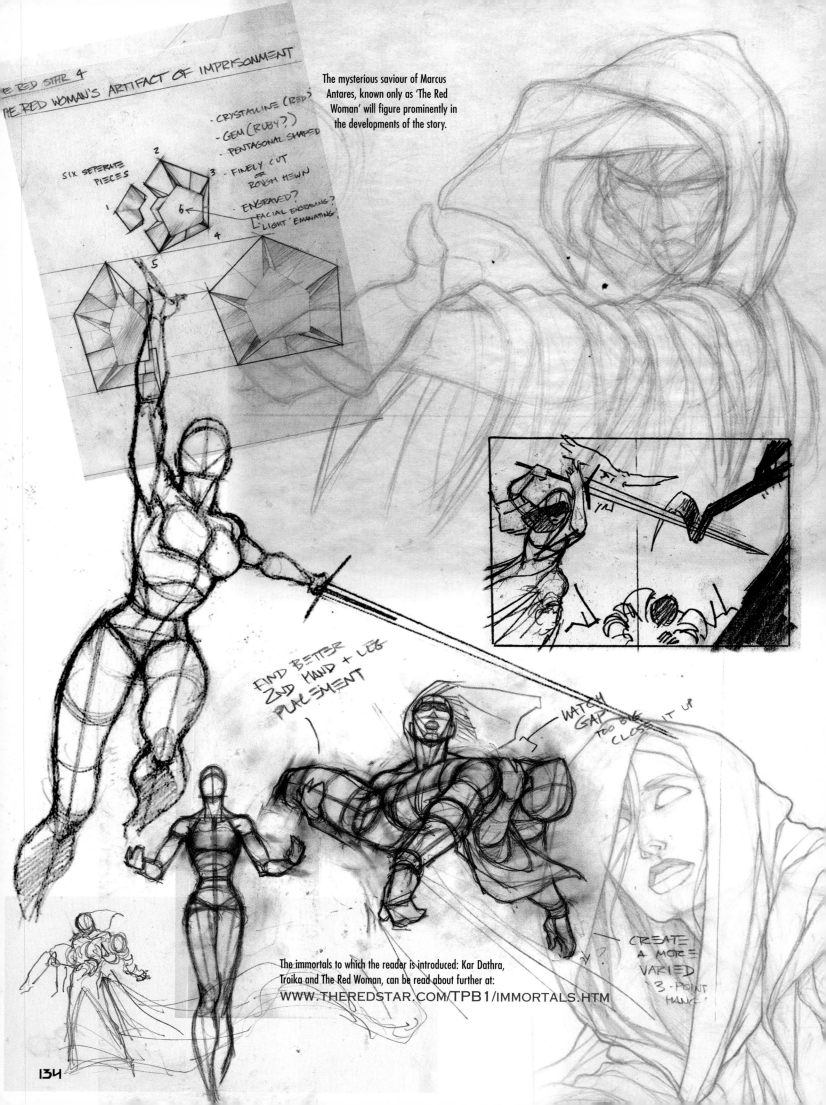

E RED STAR 4
THE RED WOMAN'S ARTIFACT OF IMPRISONMENT

- CRYSTALLINE (RED?)
- GEM (RUBY?)
- PENTAGONAL SHAPED
- FINELY CUT
  OR
  ROUGH HEWN

SIX SEPERATE
PIECES

- ENGRAVED?
  FACIAL ENGRAVING?
  'LIGHT' EMANATING

The mysterious saviour of Marcus Antares, known only as 'The Red Woman' will figure prominently in the developments of the story.

FIND BETTER
2ND HAND + LEG
PLACEMENT

WATCH
GAP
TOO BIG
CLOSE IT UP

CREATE
A MORE
VARIED
3-POINT
HANG

The immortals to which the reader is introduced: Kar Dathra, Troika and The Red Woman, can be read about further at:
WWW.THEREDSTAR.COM/TPB1/IMMORTALS.HTM

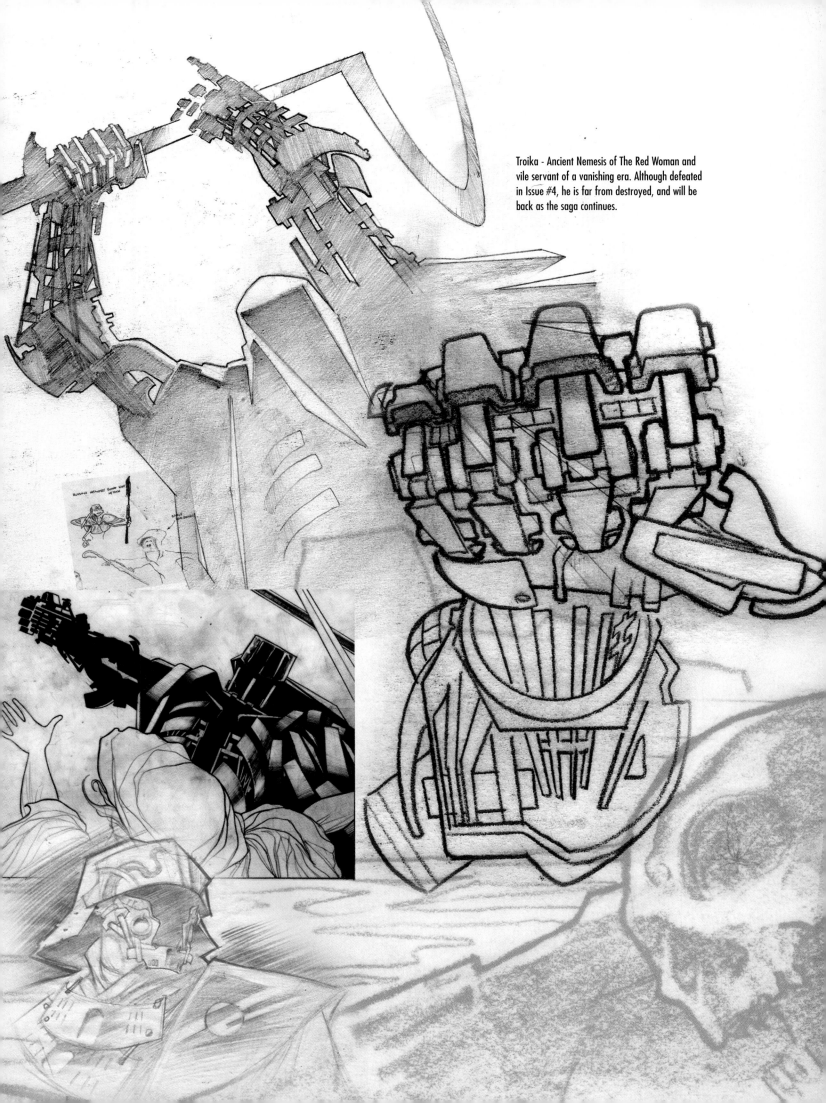

Troika - Ancient Nemesis of The Red Woman and vile servant of a vanishing era. Although defeated in Issue #4, he is far from destroyed, and will be back as the saga continues.

COMMENTARY

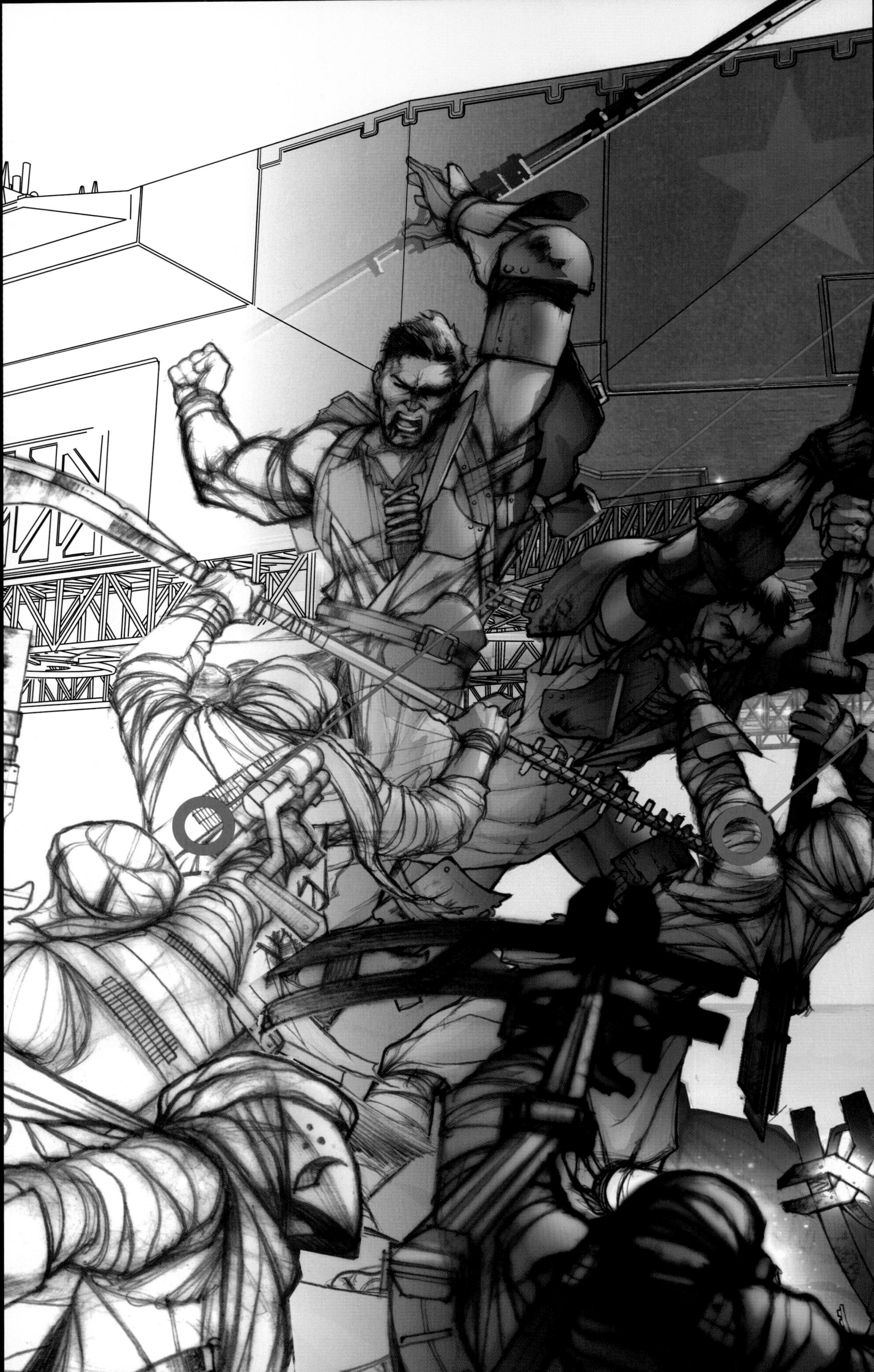

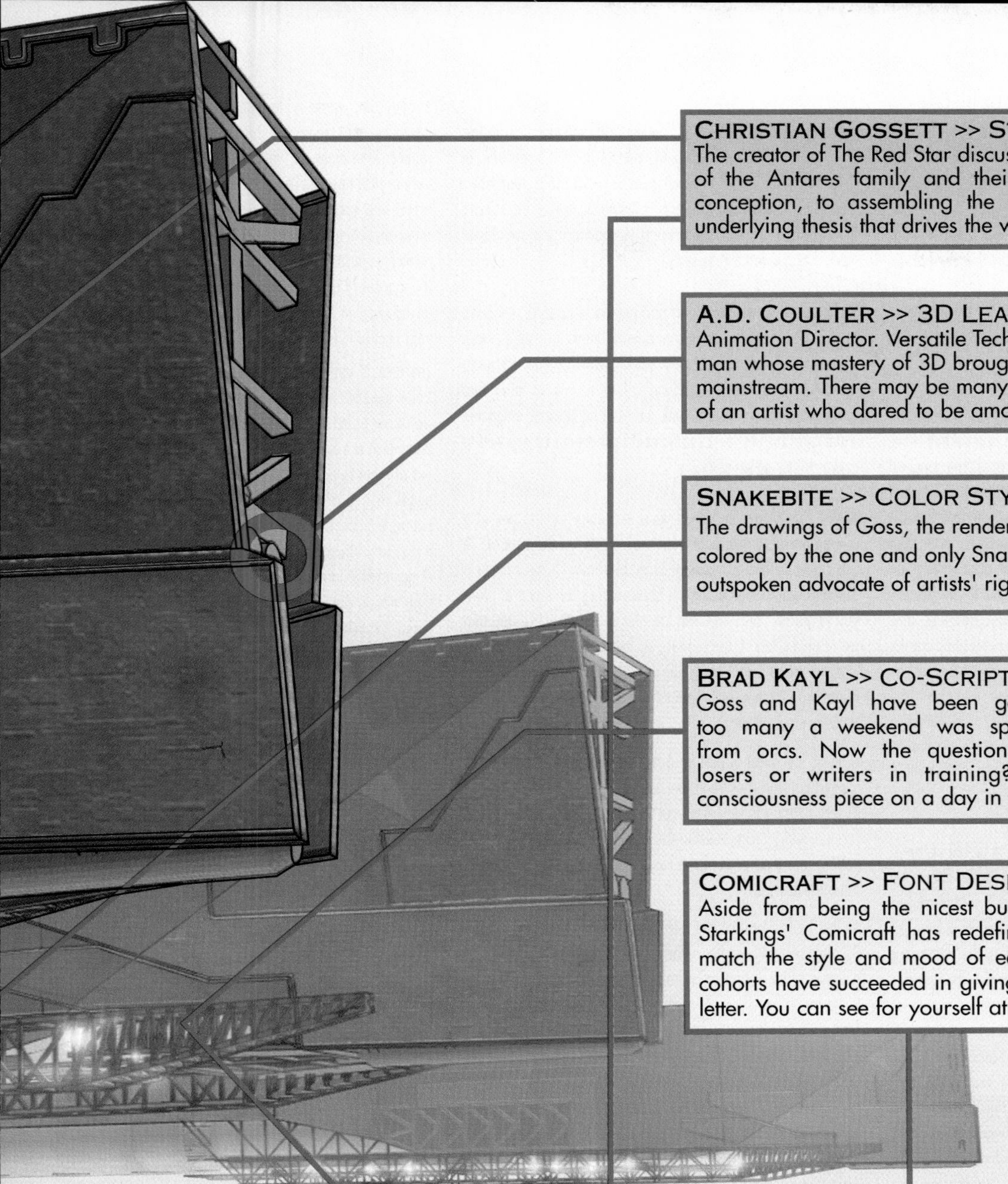

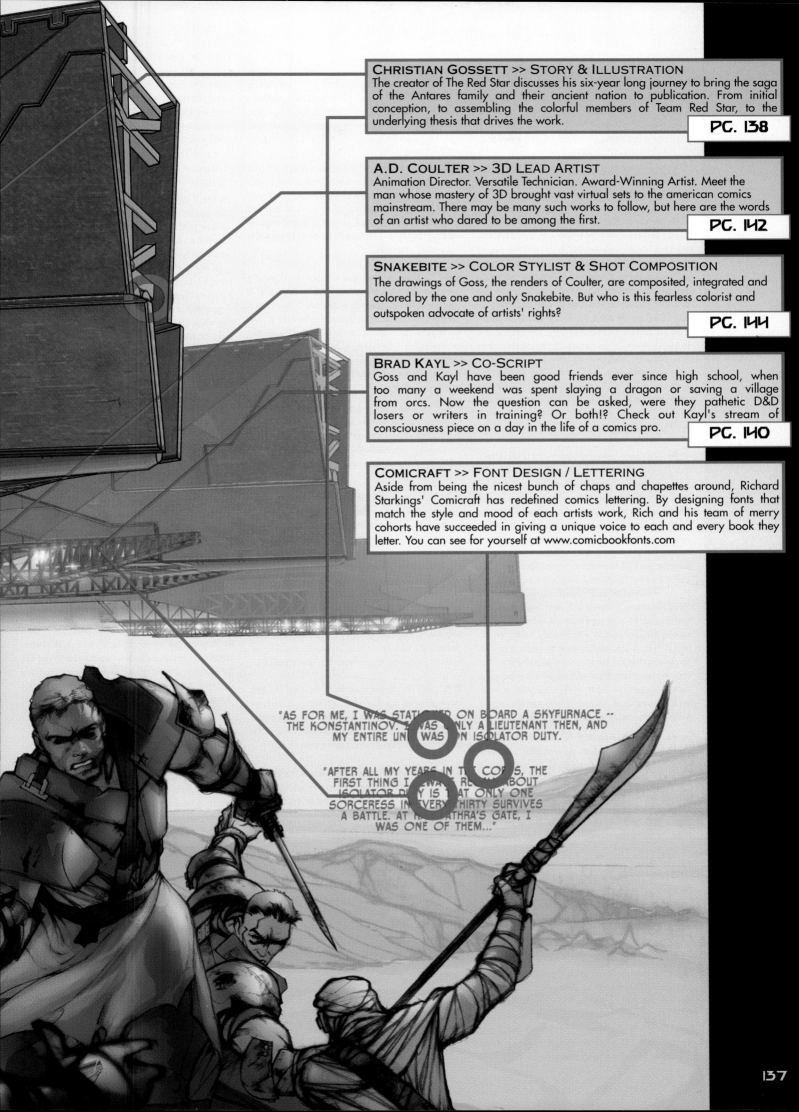

CHRISTIAN GOSSETT >> STORY & ILLUSTRATION

The creator of The Red Star discusses his six-year long journey to bring the saga of the Antares family and their ancient nation to publication. From initial conception, to assembling the colorful members of Team Red Star, to the underlying thesis that drives the work.

PG. 138

A.D. COULTER >> 3D LEAD ARTIST

Animation Director. Versatile Technician. Award-Winning Artist. Meet the man whose mastery of 3D brought vast virtual sets to the american comics mainstream. There may be many such works to follow, but here are the words of an artist who dared to be among the first.

PG. 142

SNAKEBITE >> COLOR STYLIST & SHOT COMPOSITION

The drawings of Goss, the renders of Coulter, are composited, integrated and colored by the one and only Snakebite. But who is this fearless colorist and outspoken advocate of artists' rights?

PG. 144

BRAD KAYL >> CO-SCRIPT

Goss and Kayl have been good friends ever since high school, when too many a weekend was spent slaying a dragon or saving a village from orcs. Now the question can be asked, were they pathetic D&D losers or writers in training? Or both!? Check out Kayl's stream of consciousness piece on a day in the life of a comics pro.

PG. 140

COMICRAFT >> FONT DESIGN / LETTERING

Aside from being the nicest bunch of chaps and chapettes around, Richard Starkings' Comicraft has redefined comics lettering. By designing fonts that match the style and mood of each artists work, Rich and his team of merry cohorts have succeeded in giving a unique voice to each and every book they letter. You can see for yourself at www.comicbookfonts.com

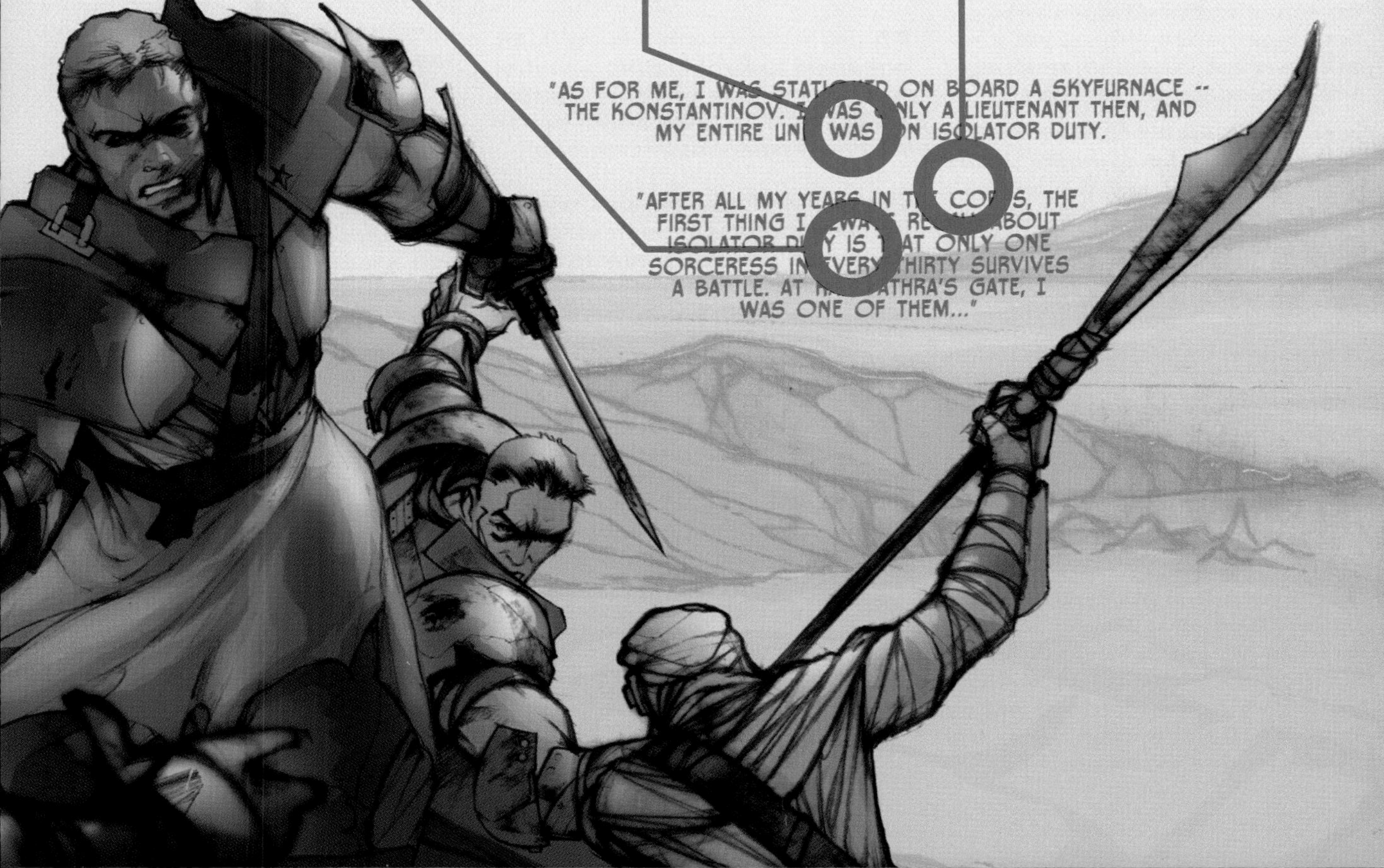
"AS FOR ME, I WAS [...] ON BOARD A SKYFURNACE -- THE KONSTANTINOV. [...] ONLY A LIEUTENANT THEN, AND MY ENTIRE [...] WAS [...] ISOLATOR DUTY.
"AFTER ALL MY YEARS IN [...], THE FIRST THING I [...] ISOLATOR [...] ONLY ONE SORCERESS IN [...] THIRTY SURVIVES A BATTLE. AT [...] GATE, I WAS ONE OF THEM..."

GOSS

The following is an excerpt from an online interview conducted by Dave Thomer of NotNews.Org, a thought-provoking website that is a must for students of American political science and general culture. For sake of page-space, this is an edited version. If you actually want to hear more of Gossett's hot air, you can check the internet at www.notnews.org/2000-12/comics.html to get the whole story.

DT: For those who might not be familiar with comics, could you describe the creative process of The Red Star and how it differs from most conventional comics today?

CG: Actually, even for most people that are die-hard comics fans our process is a complete mystery. I am approached more and more about people wanting to purchase the original 'pages' from The Red Star, when there aren't any. Each page of The Red Star is a composite of many different visual elements. The elements are created separately, and then composited together in Photoshop for final publication. The only 'pages' are the digital files that we send to the printer. There are very few comics that do it this way. However, now that we've proven that the marriage of computers and comics does offer many viable publishing alternatives, there will be many more as time goes on.

DT: What impact does the use of the CGI have on your storytelling style – what does it let you do that you don't think you'd be able to do otherwise?

CG: CGI (computer generated imagery) is a highly versatile tool. To give an example of its possibilities, think about the many ways in which you may have seen it used already. From way back to the lightcycles in the underappreciated Tron, all the way up to Pixar's Toy Story series, back to the photo-real universe of George Lucas, etc. etc. You can do flat, graphic styles, photo-real styles, strange surreal styles, there is no end. For Team Red Star, it was a matter of finding a way to use CG (computer graphics) to emphasize the vast scope and mythic scale of the story. The 3D Artist, Allen Coulter, was a rare find. We met while working on a Playstation game for Activision (Pitfall 3D) and really enjoyed each other's work. We decided to embark on this crazy experiment and test results were so stunning that they drove us enthusiastically forward into the process. Using CG has definitely given me license to open up the pages in a way that I've always wanted to. During my Star Wars work, I was constantly at odds with my writers over panel count on a page. I wanted to redefine 'epic scale' as far as comics were concerned. I wanted to have a greater sense of drama and emotional impact throughout the story.

For me, this meant taking shots that would traditionally be quite small and blowing them up to gigantic proportion. In issue one for example, pages 10-11 begin with a bandit-shot of Maya's eyes spread across both pages. In any other comic, such a shot is a throwaway, sacrificed by the urge to do yet another clenched-teeth, fists-balled, leaping at the camera fight scene. Where most comics choose plot-based action, we choose character-based drama. Also, we arrive at this extreme close-up from having been out in the desert with miles and miles of distance between us and the horizon, with massive ships looming overhead. So not only are the sizes of the panels extreme, but the range of 'motion' between panels (or 'cuts' as we like to say) is also extreme.

Another aspect of our process that is just as 'CG' as '3D' is Photoshop. Our colorist, the infamous Snakebite, came on to the project to color the figures and most non-3D aspects of each page, not to mention the nuts and bolts compositing work that takes Allen's 3D plates and my 2D drawings and integrates them into what have become the final composites. There are not many colorists in the industry that could pull off such a trick. To be able to color figures with the subtlety necessary to integrate them into a 3D environment is by no means automatic and demands a highly experienced sensibility.

At this point in my career, I am a big fan of the big panel and two-page spread. Such panels have a bad rap in comics but this is, in my mind, ignorance. Many people have this old idea in their head that comics is about a lot of panels on a page and I think such a prejudice is hilarious. Using 3D would be a waste if the panels weren't big enough to showcase the wonderful work that our team is doing.

DT: Speaking of big panels and two panel spreads – I have read or heard several people comment that as a result of those spreads, each issue reads very quickly. How do you use a big spread to maximize storytelling value? Is this an issue that concerns you? And do you think the traditional comic magazine is the right format for a character-driven drama as opposed to a plot-driven action story?

CG: I'm always surprised when someone says to me at a convention "Hey, this book reads too quick – I want more!" It was really bothering me until Snakebite said, "It ain't never a problem when your audience is screaming for more of what you're puttin' out." He was absolutely right – it's not that we're giving less to the readers, in fact every issue of The Red Star has more pages in its story than almost every comic out there. We average 24-26 pages of story an issue as compared to the typical 22 pages.

Now, if my team is putting out 26 page stories that are so captivating that they read like 12 page stories, and if the rest of the industry is stretching out 22 pages that seem to go on forever, which team is achieving drama? Which team is really getting into the heads of the readers and not letting them put the book down?

As for the last part of the question, I definitely think that the 32-page format is limited. When I read Shirow's Appleseed and a single conversation scene can be 12 pages long, or a fight scene go on for 40, I get very jealous. Jealous of the lengthy format, in which true exploration of dramatic theme can occur, and very jealous of Shirow's culture and market. In Japan, comics are not demonized – comics readers are not made to feel ashamed of supporting this form of entertainment. This being said, the standard American pamphlet of 32 pages per story is only as good as the creators working within such limitations. Length is not necessary for greatness, nor does it guarantee it. Haiku, for example, is incredibly evocative, and has never needed any more syllables than the form calls for.

DT: Since the allegorical nature of the story has been heavily promoted, how do you balance fidelity to history (since people might be reading the book expecting to learn some 'truth' about the USSR) with the needs of the story you want to tell (since you do want to do more than a mere retelling)?

CG: Good question. There was a time when I thought that I would not emphasize the allegorical aspect for just that reason. I did have a choice, and my writing partner Bradley Kayl and I gave it a lot of thought. Should we not mention the source material, in this case Russian History, but simply let the work go forward as yet another action tale in the comics world? Should we let people figure it out for themselves? Will they? However, as the writing process continued, I realized that this story owed so much to its source, and that I simply couldn't bring myself to silence the voices that had inspired it: The photographs of the baby-faced soldiers that gave their lives to defeating Hitler on the Eastern front, the letters of the artists pleading to Stalin to let them live, or at least allow their work to be seen by the public, the testament of Alexander Solzhenitsyn as he spoke of the millions of his people that were sacrificed on the pyre of Bolshevik modernization; the list is so vast that it is for all intents and purposes infinite. I was too eager to bring these lives to light in any way possible. This choice has turned out to be incredibly satisfying for us and, thankfully so far, for our readers. I suppose a lot of writers would consider this a shackle, but for us it's been pure joy. Just as our visuals integrate 2D and 3D elements into a working image, our words have integrated fact and fiction into a narrative that continues to surprise us with its expansive nature. One example, yet to be published by us, takes us to a very crucial moment in the history of 20th Century Russia, the arrest and murder of Tsar Nicholas II and his family. At first mention, this sounds like something that would make very dry comics material. Yet, through our established style of allegory, the murder of the Tsar, and many other such historic events will be adapted to the pages of The Red Star in a very exciting, very dramatic fashion.

The trick is making the story captivating for both those who know the history and those who don't. There's the rub, since we're not pointing out which aspects of the story are metaphor and which are historic. That's up to the reader, and represents our attempt to engage the audience. What is portrayed on the pages as metaphor is an expression of a historic event. An example is Maya's transformation in Issue #1. On the surface, it's a very attractive woman transforming herself into a pillar of destructive energy, but in metaphor, all soldiers that kill for their nation are in fact pulling off such a trick. Her dialogue, "Then, thankfully, the mind is silenced . . . I am the heat of my nation's anger . . . the burning will of the state." We all are very comfortable in the West with our notion that 'those poor Russians had to suffer under the despotic Communists' but what we don't realize is how such self-righteous pity blinds us to our own patriotic shackles. Maya's loyalty at the cost of her individuality is something that all humans are prone to. After the fall of the Soviet Union, it is now our jingoistic ignorance that should be pitied. We hope that through exploration of these themes, that we stir in the readers a need to question the story in such a way that the historic lesson is made clear. It's ambitious, but it's where our head trip as artists happens to be right now. So far, thankfully, we have found an expanding readership that appreciates the enigmatic nature of the stories. Hopefully this continues.

DT: You're telling a story about very noble people who are saddled with leaders who are obviously not worthy of them. What is it about the people of the URRS (and by allegory, the former USSR) that you think accounts for this?

CG: As Maya says in issue 3, "All the leaders of the world . . . they are all liars. Petty lords with petty schemes . . ." I believe this. I believe that not only in Russia, which is an extreme example, but most statesmen of the world are self-serving liars that represent the worst possible strata of human experience from which to draw leadership. Not only in our current time but throughout history. There is a lot of nobility in our country, and yet we've elected more than our share of buffoonish figureheads into the seats of power.

The Red Star, in this case, does also gain its inspiration from the internationalist mindset of the early Russian Revolutionaries. No story about the Soviet Era could be complete without giving due time to agitation. How the theme of populist agitation is handled by the author in question has much to say about the stance of said author. As far as I am concerned, and I know Bradley feels the same way, our voices stand for radical political upheaval. This political stance is one of the most subtle inspirations for choosing the material we've chosen. Within this facet of our work lies the core of the story: What is to be learned from the Cold War? Why did this institution of paranoia exist? Why is our nation's hegemony over the world failing to offer the majority of its citizenry the utopian lifestyle we were promised if ever we were able to 'overcome the threat of communism'? We feel very strongly about these questions, and these beliefs expose what might be called our thesis: The greatest irony of the 20th Century is that in outlasting the Soviet Union, the U.S. is not liberated from any struggle against it, but is only revealing its own tyrannical nature. Further, that with every corporate merger, with every sweeping deregulation made possible by the fall of its greatest economic rival, our country continues along a path of reckless economic centralization heretofore comparable in the modern era only with Lenin's Russia.

DT: From the story so far and hints from other interviews and message boards, it seems you're setting up the Antares family to challenge some of the institutions and traditions that have led the URRS to its current state. Is that something you think our own society needs to do?

CG: Indeed. The Antares family is our symbol of hope against all odds. Their courage represents the best chance their nation has to overcome the tragic legacy that imprisons them. They are the heroic face in a cycle of renewal that civilization has engaged in since it was born. In the eternal struggle of humanity vs. society, they are the hands of freedom that tear down the walls of any nation that has forgotten the basic truth of law. Law must serve humanity to build their civilizations. When humanity becomes a blinded slave to their civilization's laws, that society must renew itself somehow, if it is to survive.

I think it's clear that, given my answer to the previous question, I feel our nation is on the brink of a very difficult transition. The transition from an industrial to an information society is something that is going to cause major international flux. It is a time in which the resources of the world, and the structures of power that profit from their distribution, are going to be challenged. New players on the world scene have become powerful, others have become weak. The aftermath of the Cold War has left us in a calm before what I feel will be a very destructive storm. In the analogous world of my fiction, the Antares family represents the common people, whose lives will somehow have to find a way to survive as the scheming manipulators that rule the world throw it into a chaos of their own greed.

To get back to the last part of your question, how can common folk not only survive, but challenge the institutions that are leading us? Well, history has the answers listed quite clearly. The catch is, such actions represent a subset of human endeavors that are incredibly costly, selfless and bloody. To write a comic about revolution, this is simplicity itself-- but inspiring large hordes of humanity to take their destiny into their hands for better or worse? This is history at its most vital, and most complex.

DT: Chris, you said that we can effect positive change, but that the actions required to do so are "incredibly costly, selfless and bloody." Upon one reading, that comment seems pretty pessimistic . . . do you really think that's the only way to make things better?

CG: Actually, yes. As you say, the pessimistic reading is only one take on this comment. My own sentiment when I expressed this thought was more objective than emotional. When in human history has positive change not been incredibly costly, selfless and bloody? Martin Luther King's quest to bring civil rights to the black community wasn't a Disneyland ride. Nor was Abraham Lincoln's fight to preserve the Union from the southern hordes of racist farmers. The Russian people pushing back the Nazis in the 1940's was a journey of utter horror, but without the sacrifice of the Red Army, Hitler could not have been defeated before millions more were killed on all fronts.

Nothing truly worth achieving is simple. The easier something is to achieve, the less likely it is to effect any kind of far-reaching change. We'd all like to think that making a charity music video can end world hunger, and such notions are pleasant sentimentalist fiction, but I think one of the reasons history is such an unpopular subject is because its main lesson is that if you want to change the world, you are lining yourself up for excruciating agony.

DT: You also seem to dismiss writing about revolution when you call it "simplicity itself" – what, exactly, do you think is necessary to transform ideas into action? In your wildest dreams, what do you see people learning, thinking, and doing as a result of reading The Red Star? What else do you feel that you, personally, need to do to put the ideals you express into practice?

CG: Again, I was being objective. To write about revolution is easy – any marketing drone can splash 'REVOLUTION' on an advertisement for a luxury car and feel gratified by their own alleged genius – an actor can put on a costume and portray Che Guevarra or George Washington and perceive what it is to be a 'revolutionary' in some internal fashion; but to place ones self at the forefront of human conflict, to attempt to have your life and work alter the course of events, this is a very advanced set of human skills. To study the history of the Russian Revolution is to absorb a sober truth in regards to how difficult it is to really have a positive effect on the world. The Socialist Revolutionaries wanted to build Utopia, instead they became victims of a monstrous totalitarian experiment. Americans have many lessons to learn from this utopia gone wrong, and I wonder if we'll heed even one of them.

In my wildest dreams . . . well, I'm a writer, so my dreams get pretty wild… I'd feel more comfortable talking about my hopes and goals regarding the project. I'd like a continuation of what's happening right now. Most days I get messages from people around the world or even in my own neighborhood talking about how The Red Star is touching them, affecting them, making them curious about what happened in Russia in the 20th Century, and how it affected their lives wherever they happened to live. Hungarians, Poles, Mexicans, Germans, and of course, Russians and Americans – our lives took place in an extraordinary period in human civilization. The Red Star is, at its best, a primer to remind us of that. It is also a valentine to the industrial age – a time quickly giving way to the era of computerization. The great thing is that these themes are working. People are getting it. My hope and goal is that more and more people out there continue to 'get it.' What they do with it once they get it, that's in the lap of providence. All I can do is stay true to the enthusiasm and vision that inspired me and try my best to make it all worthwhile to the phenomenal group of friends that decided to join me in this humble cause.

DT: You both spend a fair amount of time on the redstar.com message boards - what do you get from that interaction with readers?

CG: Fun! Concerning the message boards, publishing The Red Star is like beginning a conversation with as many strangers as possible, and the boards are the means by which that communication occurs. Obviously, our entire creative team is very invested in our work emotionally and artistically. We're a tight group. We see each other socially, we work very close, and we are telling a story that, according to your typical marketing report, shouldn't be as commercially or critically successful as it has proved to be. Therefore, communicating on our boards directly with the people who appreciate this work is very special for us.

DT: What do you think the rest of the comics industry can learn from the success of The Red Star thus far?

CG: This is a question that I am asking myself. Will we influence the industry at all? In what way? Superficially? Will double-page spreads and big panels take hold? Technically? We've at least given 3D a long-awaited beachhead in the comics wars, but will other waves of soldiers support us as we continue the invasion? Artistically? Will our 'no-ink' style make obvious the fact that inking is no longer a necessity of production but a traditional, stylistic preference? Lyrically? Will our writing be of any impact? Will the story continue to gain respect? Will we keep getting offers from other companies to do what it is we do?

Since we can't foresee what might happen, we are remaining thankful for the success we have. A comic book allegory about Russia? Boy, the looks I got the first few times I shared that idea with my friends in the industry! They thought it was some kind of sad bankruptcy scheme. It's really quite remarkable that we're doing as well as we are and we're thankful to everyone whose picked up a copy. Or ten (laughter).

DT: You have made wisecracks and comments about more cheesecake-oriented books, and there definitely appears to be a commitment to a different portrayal of women in Red Star – the sorceresses are women, you have women tank commanders, one of the major supernatural forces takes the form of a woman. Were you making a deliberate attempt to put women at the center of this story? If so, was that at least in part motivated by the traditional or stereotypical treatment of women in mainstream comics? How much of it was a deliberate decision to try to show the industry a different way of telling stories?

CG: When it comes to the Women of The Red Star, and the romantic nature of the story, my parents are the true source of that. They loved each other in a way that is rare and incredible. Their respect was born of adoration and my brother and I basked in the glow of it. My respect for women starts right there with the great example that my father gave me to live by.

Going from there, 'Love' as an element in fiction is one of the qualifiers that separates heroic fiction from meaningless tales of commercial exploitation. Joseph Campbell talks about all Drama being concerned with human origin, with all feats of greatness supplying a metaphor for birth, death and rebirth of the soul.

The Women of The Red Star, Maya, The Red Woman, Alexandra, Makita (who we'll meet in issue 6) were never intended as some kind of artificial quota -- they are the characters whose motivations and presence supply the best thrust and counterthrust for the motion of the story. This strong female presence is also accounted for historically. In Russia during World War II, there were husband and wife teams that operated tanks together, a celebrated wing of female fighter pilots, and the great Roza Shanina was a sniper who recorded over a hundred kills. When you're in a war that will cost 30 million lives, you don't have sexism to use as a cheap excuse against the abilities of women. You need every able body you've got. The women of Russia were up to the task.

DT: Looking ahead -- what are your hopes and plans for 2001, now that Red Star is off the ground?

CG: 2001 is all about continuing to put out work, and in so doing thanking the retailers and readers for putting us in the 'genuine hit' category. 2001 is kind of a reward for 2000. I'm constantly boring the team with my World War II analogies, but here I go again…it's like we made it off of the beach at D-Day, we didn't get shot to pieces right out of the boat, we're tired and thankful to have survived-- but at the same time-- it's still a helluva long way to take Berlin. There is a lot to be thankful for. Our numbers are steadily rising, our publisher believes in us, and no one could possibly foresee the kinds of stuff we have planned.

Gass

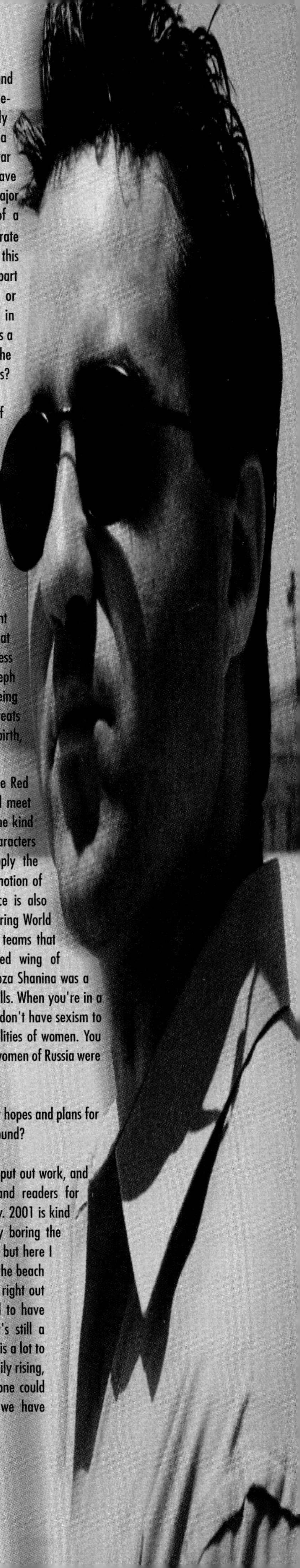

A day in the life of a comic(s) writer...

When's our next issue due again? Check calendar--What?! Omigod. Okay, don't panic. What about the CSN ad? Damn! Tomorrow?! Panic. Coffee. Coffee. Where's the coffee? Ah yes. Swig. French roast!--blech! Panic some more. Issue due. Ad due. TPB stuff due. Okay, steadee, steadee. No time--NO TIME. When does the script have to be finished then -- TOMORROW!!! JESUS! Drink more of the exceedingly bitter, yet masochistically flavorable, French roast. Beer. Beer is exceedingly bitter and masochistically flavorable--screw coffee, desperate times call for desperate measures. Open fridge. WHO DRANK ALL THE BEER?!? Fine. Pout. Buckle down. Begin typing.

<TAP TAP TAPTAP TAP>
PAGES SIX AND SEVEN - DOUBLE PAGE SPREAD (FOUR PANELS)
PANEL 1 - MAYA BEGINS CASTING
THE RE-ENACT PR...

<RRRRRRIIIIIINNNNNGGGGG!!!!!>
Damn it! Hello? Who? Yes, speaking. No, I'm sorry, I don't read the Times. Why? Well, to start with it's poignantly misinformed, amazingly biased, and run by a bunch of corporate lick boo...Coupons?!? Are you listening to me? No, I don't use coupons! I was just tell...uh huh. Uh huh. I understand that. Listen, I really just don't want the paper. Do you underst...What? That's none of your godamn business! No, I said DON'T send the pap...hello? Hello? Damn telemarketers; there's gotta be a special place in Hell for 'em. Where was I? Maya kasting. Right.

<TAPTAP TAP TAPTAP TAP TAP>
PANEL 1 - MAYA BEGINS CASTING THE RE-ENACT PROTOCOL. THE FIRST CANISTER SHE THROWS BEGINS TO SPEW FORTH A REDDISH SMO...

<RRRRRRRRRIIIIINNNNNNGGGG!!!>
DAMMITT!! Hello? Who? Jack Stephan? No, no one by that name lives here. Yes I'm sure; I think you have the wrong numb...What? No, I didn't order a Lucy Lawless blow up doll! Why the hell would...Yes, I'm sure. Huh? No, I don't want it for half price! I'm sure it's very lifelike...Look man I'm busy. Can't you bug someone else toda...? Hello? HELLO!? *SIGH* Dial phone. Hey. Listen, I can't seem to get anything done over here. What? But the script...uh huh. Uh huh. A week? Be right there. Yes I'm tired. Ha ha, very funny--you can

sleep when you're dead too. Sure. I'm waaay ahead of ya'. Hey, do you have any beer over there?

So, you still want to write comics Brad?

Sure, what the hell.

G: Why don't we tell them about that first weekend in the Desert?

B: That'll be fun.

G: So basically, we had talked at Denny's in North Hollywood, I ran the stuff by you, and we decided to give working together a shot, right? Go from there:

B: Right.

G: No, really, I want you to talk now.

B: We started that Denny's Noho session at like, 11:30 at night, right?

G: That late?

B: Yeah. It ran to, what, four?

G: Jeez.

B: So then, we went out to Ridgecrest, California-- to write out in the beauty and peace of the High Desert, and we end up working at Denny's again! For hours!

G: I know, Damn! What can I say, it was familiar!

B: We sure became familiar with all the waitresses, that's for sure.

G: Yeah, they got sick of us, buying nothing but coffee and sitting there for days.

B: Eventually we had a kind of Kerouac & Ginsberg moment out at the rocks.

G: It sure was strange with that natural landscape and those waitresses still in their Denny's uniforms...It was like a Video. Anyway, this is supposed to be a commentary about the work, dude. I'll ask you a question. Why did I pick you to help me write this you think?

B: I don't know. (laughter) I guess because we have a similar vision about when things sound right, when things flow and don't flow. Similar sensibilities regarding character design and motivation. What narrative moments work and don't work. We've known each other a very long time, but that is because we're the Corsican brothers. We were finishing each other's thoughts since we first met at early D&D sessions. Only as time went on did we realize that we liked the

When does the script have to be finished then -- TOMORROW!!!

same directors, writers, had the same tastes as far as culture and media are concerned. Once we were at a rave, and we were both wasted and completely lost in the throngs of people. So I decide to try and find you, and after, god, I don't know how long-- I figure, 'fuck it-- why am I wasting time looking for him? I should just be having a good time! I'll find him eventually…' at that moment, there you were!

G: And we tripped out laughing for like ten minutes because I had, just a split-second before, given up on my quest to find you, and there you were! Hilarious.

B: That's the kind of dynamic that works in collaborative expression. It's not very scientific, but it's very visceral and anyway, Art isn't always Science. The whole experience has been liberating for me. I've never been, I don't see myself as a nine to fiver, I can't live in a cubicle. So that's why I enjoy being able to work the way we work. The Red Star is not a typical comic book in the way that we're used to in America. We're trying in our own small way to elevate the art form. I want to try and change the perception of comics as a whole. It doesn't have to be men in tights or scantily clad women. We can do historical fiction, we can do Epic Poetry, our boundaries are not limited. As a matter of fact, they are limitless. Words and Pictures together should not be a liability. I work toward those ideals. The railcar sequences, for example: They are cinematic in scope and very mundane. No explosions, no intrigues. What makes it poignant is that these are believable characters that we identify with because they are multi-faceted.

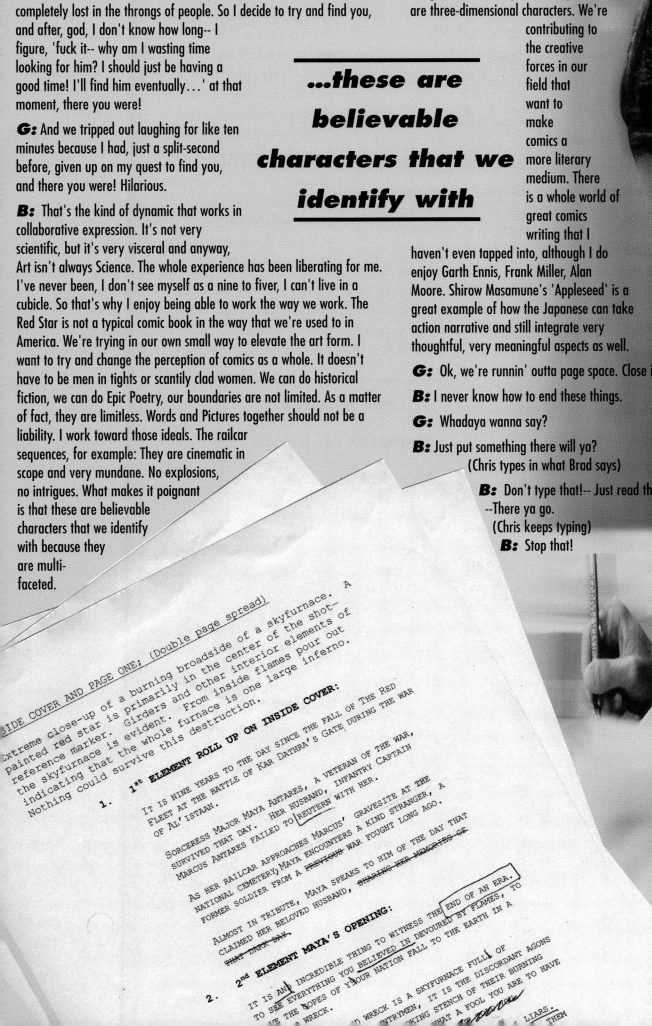

...these are believable characters that we identify with

Loss, loneliness, anxiety, we've all felt these things and so do Maya and Vanya. These are three-dimensional characters. We're contributing to the creative forces in our field that want to make comics a more literary medium. There is a whole world of great comics writing that I haven't even tapped into, although I do enjoy Garth Ennis, Frank Miller, Alan Moore. Shirow Masamune's 'Appleseed' is a great example of how the Japanese can take action narrative and still integrate very thoughtful, very meaningful aspects as well.

G: Ok, we're runnin' outta page space. Close it up.

B: I never know how to end these things.

G: Whadaya wanna say?

B: Just put something there will ya?

(Chris types in what Brad says)

B: Don't type that!-- Just read the book --There ya go.

(Chris keeps typing)

B: Stop that!

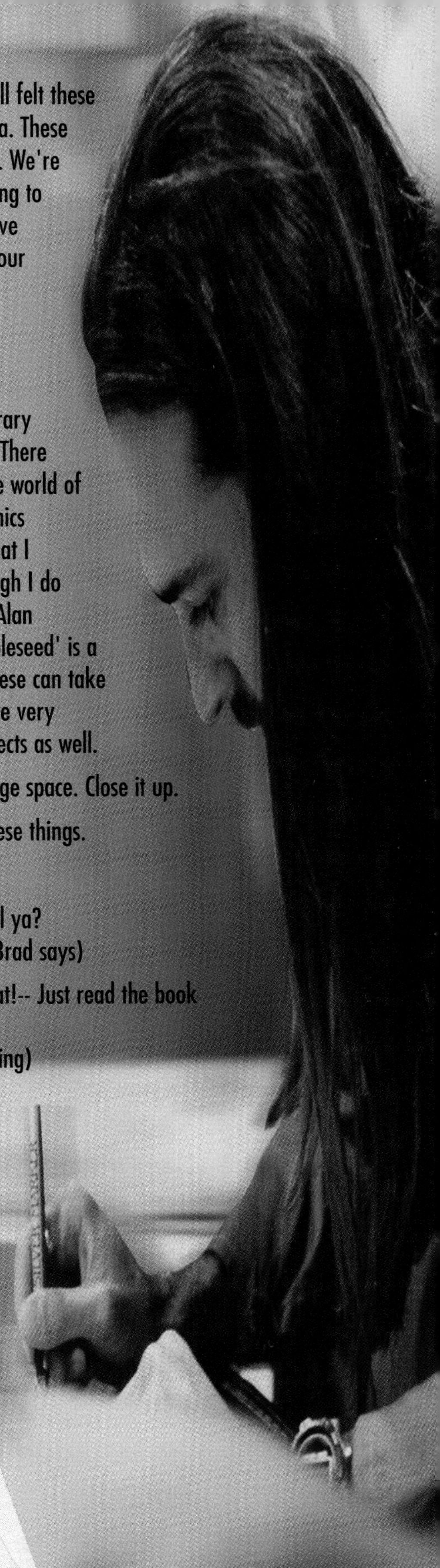

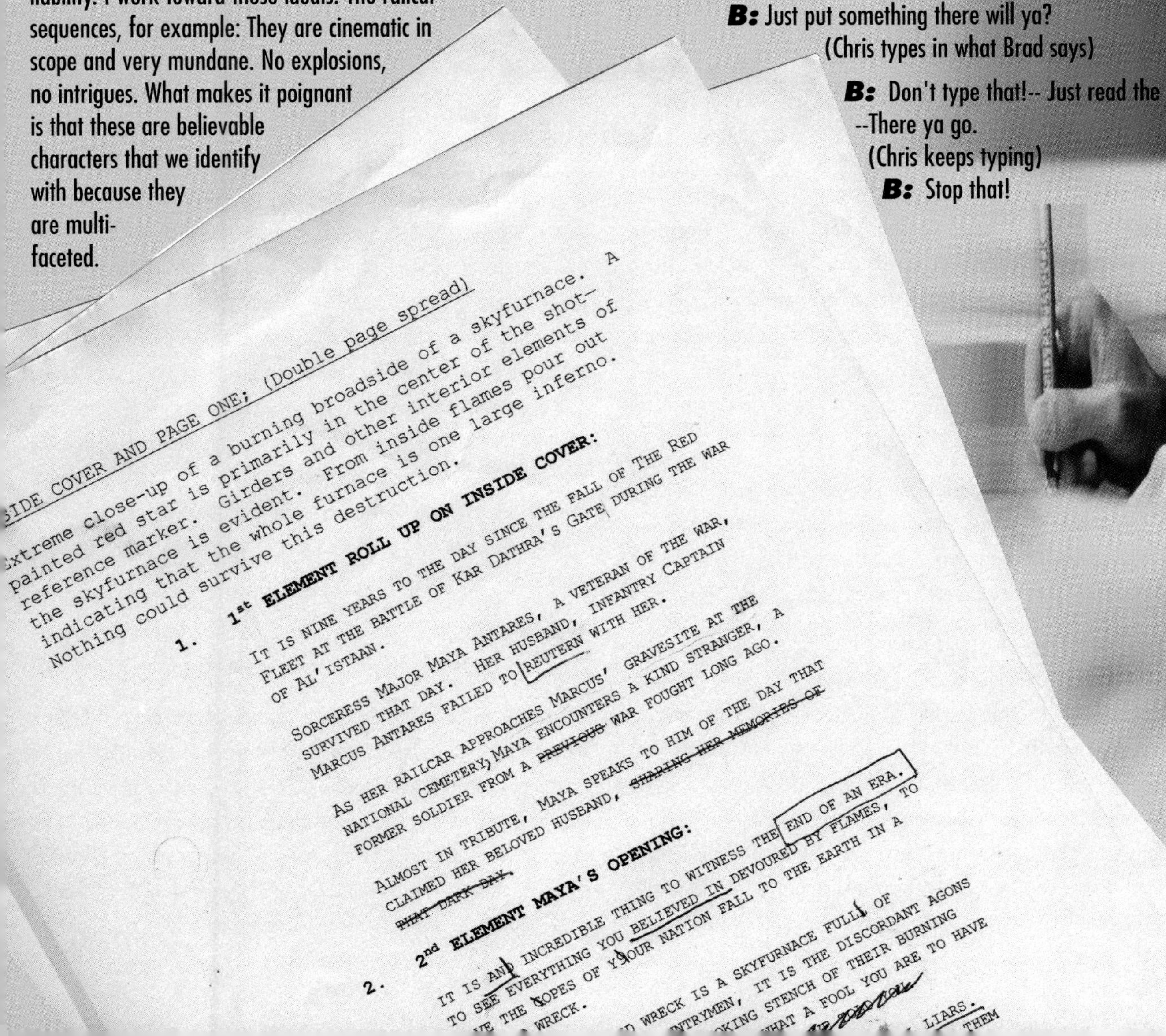

SIDE COVER AND PAGE ONE; (Double page spread)

Extreme close-up of a burning broadside of a skyfurnace. A painted red star is primarily in the center of the shot-- reference marker. Girders and other interior elements of the skyfurnace is evident. From inside flames pour out indicating that the whole furnace is one large inferno. Nothing could survive this destruction.

1. 1st ELEMENT ROLL UP ON INSIDE COVER:

IT IS NINE YEARS TO THE DAY SINCE THE FALL OF THE RED FLEET AT THE BATTLE OF KAR DATHRA'S GATE DURING THE WAR OF AL'ISTAAN.

SORCERESS MAJOR MAYA ANTARES, A VETERAN OF THE WAR, SURVIVED THAT DAY. HER HUSBAND, INFANTRY CAPTAIN MARCUS ANTARES FAILED TO REUTERN WITH HER.

AS HER RAILCAR APPROACHES MARCUS' GRAVESITE AT THE NATIONAL CEMETERY, MAYA ENCOUNTERS A KIND STRANGER, A FORMER SOLDIER FROM A ~~PREVIOUS~~ WAR FOUGHT LONG AGO.

ALMOST IN TRIBUTE, MAYA SPEAKS TO HIM OF THE DAY THAT CLAIMED HER BELOVED HUSBAND, ~~SHARING HER MEMORIES OF THAT DARK DAY.~~ END OF AN ERA.

2. 2nd ELEMENT MAYA'S OPENING:

IT IS AND INCREDIBLE THING TO WITNESS THE END OF AN ERA. TO SEE EVERYTHING YOU BELIEVED IN DEVOURED BY FLAMES, TO ... THE HOPES OF YOUR NATION FALL TO THE EARTH IN A WRECK.

... WRECK IS A SKYFURNACE FULL OF ... COUNTRYMEN, IT IS THE DISCORDANT AGONS ... CHOKING STENCH OF THEIR BURNING ... WHAT A FOOL YOU ARE TO HAVE ... LIARS. ... THEM

'Digital Imaging' '3D', 'CGI', ... Having revolutionized filmmaking and videogames, this new visual medium was introduced into the American comics mainstream by Team Red Star. The man whose unique talents made this possible is the unassuming Allen Coulter. Having been essential to the genesis of a truly unique aesthetic in the industry, Allen sat down with Goss and recorded some reflections on how it all came together.

Goss- First and foremost, give us a look into some of the projects you've been involved with.

Coulter- Some of my favorite projects I've worked on are top secret study models of nuclear submarines, a 200 square foot model of Boston's "Big Dig" highway project, an 18 foot tall fire breathing mechanical dragon, an 8' tall bigfoot, an 18" tall homicidal doll, a house, and more model WWI airplanes than I can find space for. As one of the handful of artists and technicians who introduced 'high tech' to the Makeup Effects end of the film industry, I designed one of the first radio control creature masks for Rick Baker on the movie "Harry and the Hendersons" (we got an Academy Award for that one). As a mechanical animator and puppeteer, I lead the building and performing of characters including Chucky in the first "Childsplay", a talking robot called Decks, Ronald McDonald's "Fan club" and at ILM I got to lead the team that created the insanely mechanized version of Slimer and some of his friends for Ghostbusters II. Computer animation was starting to come into it's own around that time, promising to make even more fantastic creatures possible, so I headed off to the game business to learn how to use the tools of the new media. It really did open up whole new horizons. I've done previsualization set models for movies like The Cable Guy, design models, magazine and game cover art and - my favorite - computer art and animated characters for games like "Spot Goes to Hollywood" and "Hercules". Next came Full Motion Videos for games like "Pitfall 3d" and "Muppet Monster Adventure". From there it's been concept art, level design, and now, The Red Star.

Goss- I'd like you to speak a bit more about how many influences you have outside of comics. For the aspiring artists out there, I'd like you to give them a sense of how, in order to reach their desired level of professionalism, they need to open up to as many interests as possible.

Coulter- Everything's sort of interwoven. For example, one of my greatest pleasures is in making music. I've been in a couple of bands, written and recorded songs, some of which have been the musical backing for animated pieces I've done, which is where I've developed the 3d skills used in The Red Star. See how it sort of loops back around? Here's another example — I've always been fascinated by space exploration. When I was a kid I never missed a minute of the moon walks. I even built a low-tech version of a lunar gravity simulator with some friends. We used ropes and wood and nails to build this harness

It was always a priority to keep the art ahead of the technology.

that you'd hang sideways in. You'd 'stand' on a sloped board and you could walk and jump as if you weighed as little as you would on the moon. Naturally, being built of sticks and nails, it was a rickety affair and of course, after a few rides, the whole thing came crashing down, moonwalker and all. The frustration of not being able to build a proper version of that wonderful toy led to learning to weld and machine, which led to building military prototypes, which led to working with the people who design missile launchers and tanks, which is where a lot of the believability of the machinery in The Red Star comes from. The line between work and play is almost not there at all.

Goss- Any creator trying to assemble a team of cohorts knows how difficult it can be to find other creators of like-mind. I can't tell you how excited I was when I first mentioned the project to you only to find that we had both been studying a lot of the same material. What was it about the history of Russia that gained your respect?

Coulter- Well, when you first let on that you had this Soviet styled epic in mind, it really found a place deep down for me. The whole time I was growing up the Russians were the perfect foil, sort of like the Nazi's were for the generation before us. No matter how you felt about them, you couldn't keep from watching what they were up to. They sent the first man into space. They paraded huge missiles down the streets of Moscow every May 1st. People were convinced that they were monsters that wanted to eat our babies! And they were so secretive about everything that it was hard to say what was true and what wasn't. Once the cold war ended, all sorts of things started crossing those once-closed borders. About a year before we started kicking this idea around, I came across a fantastic model manufactured in Ukraine, of a huge 4-engine passenger plane built in Russia by a fellow named Igor Sikorsky way back in 1911. It carried 5 people and flew to altitudes of thousands of feet — only 7 years after the Wright brothers first flew their motorized kite at Kitty Hawk. In the heat of the cold war, we never spent much time thinking of Russians as anything but 'the enemy' so this, this pioneering, this innovation really blew me away. So along comes you, possibly the only person I've ever met interested (and then some) in taking a different view on this nation — the people, not the country...I was so up for the idea. Timing is everything...you know?

Goss- What are some of the inherent problems we had to overcome in order to create the aesthetic we achieved in integrating 2D and 3D?

Coulter- I'd be more protective of the 'secrets' of the Red Star's style, except that it doesn't boil down to a set of tricks that can be canned or ripped off. Any ass can rip a style — I mean, take a look at half the comics on the racks. What makes TRS look like TRS took years to get to. It really started before you and I had even talked about the book. When we started doing the first of the hundreds of panels for the Pitfall 3d FMV, the first thing we had to do was strike a balance between ink and color – where you would shade with ink and where we'd leave blank so I could color the fill lighting. Having to produce as many panels in the time we had, we started looking for shortcuts. I remember noticing that scans of heavier pencil roughs looked a lot like the inked panels, but we'd started with ink, so we had to see it through. When we were done with Pitfall and started talking TRS, one of the first things we did was drop the ink. Next was the search for the line weight that would work with the 3d cell shading lines. That actually took a while because we only wanted to change the line weight, not the line quality. It was always a priority to keep the art ahead of the technology. Painting the 3d models so they'd blend with the 2d was done by combining the 2d coloring as we'd done on Pitfall with techniques I'd picked up doing movie props and miniatures. After over a year of tests and trials, the balance of 2d and 3d, the palette and the composition all came together on the first poster. Next, we had to scale up to full-scale production. As I remember, we figured that Goss and I could put out the art for maybe 4 books a year. Enter Snakebite on color and Jon Moberly building our models. Jon brought his enthusiasm for the details that make the hardware so intense, and Snake, well he hit the floor running from book one, merging his own distinctive palette right into the pipeline. Total time to put the look and team together – about a year and a half. Nothing to it!

Goss- What are some specific pieces from the first four issues that you are particularly proud of?

Coulter- Hmmmm. That's hard. There are a few pages and sequences I really enjoy. I think Page 22 from book 1, where the sky furnaces first fire up and we see 4 panels across the bottom of the impact – I've always felt should be a poster. Book 2 is my favorite as of this writing (5 hasn't come out yet) – especially the tank battle. Really enjoyed getting to throw in designs on the tank drop pods and sky furnace interiors, but mostly I liked that we took the time to play the scene out. The one casualty of our complex production is that sometimes we have to do whole scenes in just a few pages, but I think we make up for it by packing a lot into those pages!

Goss- On many occasions, professional modelers/animators look at the book and don't know that we are using 3D models. This 'invisibility' of your work is a double-edged sword however. On the one hand, one wants the immense scale and depth that 3D offers, and at the same time one must avoid the classic blunder that one is vulnerable to when using 3D: letting the 'special-effects' overtake the sense of drama. Very rarely has another comic used 3D and not been a victim of this mistake. How did you avoid this trap and tame the 3D for sake of integration?

Coulter- As a 3d Artist, most of the projects I work on are animated pieces – a few independent shorts, some commercials, and a series of concept/promo pieces for video games. Some hits, some misses. All learning experiences. Two of the hardest things for me have been keeping the storytelling clear and flowing, and making the camera disappear. By this I mean outgrowing the overly clever, or swimmy camera moves that make CG look, well, like CG. The best camera moves, it turns out, are the ones you don't even notice.
One of the things that got me excited about TRS was your appreciation for the idea that comics are fundamentally cinematic. We'd be able to combine your composition and my visual storytelling skills, your flare for characters and my understanding of lighting and scenery. In with all that was the idea of creating a look that was neither 2d nor 3d, but something that was just art. Also, I was excited about getting free passes to Comicon.
When the team first started going around to promote the book they called me the 3d modeler, or the computer modeler. I objected. First of all, Jon's the modeler. Secondly...well, there is no second... Anyway, I put out the phrase '3d artist'. It took a while for it to catch on, and longer still for them to see why I felt it mattered. As much as anything, it was about staying away from the whole computer technologist mindset and getting into the idea of the look being the work of artists. The idea has been to stay focused on the characters and the story and to take the idea of making the camera disappear a step further – to making the artwork disappear! To make the 3d blend with the pencil and color to the point where the 3 parts get lost in each other. Personally, I think it worked out pretty well.

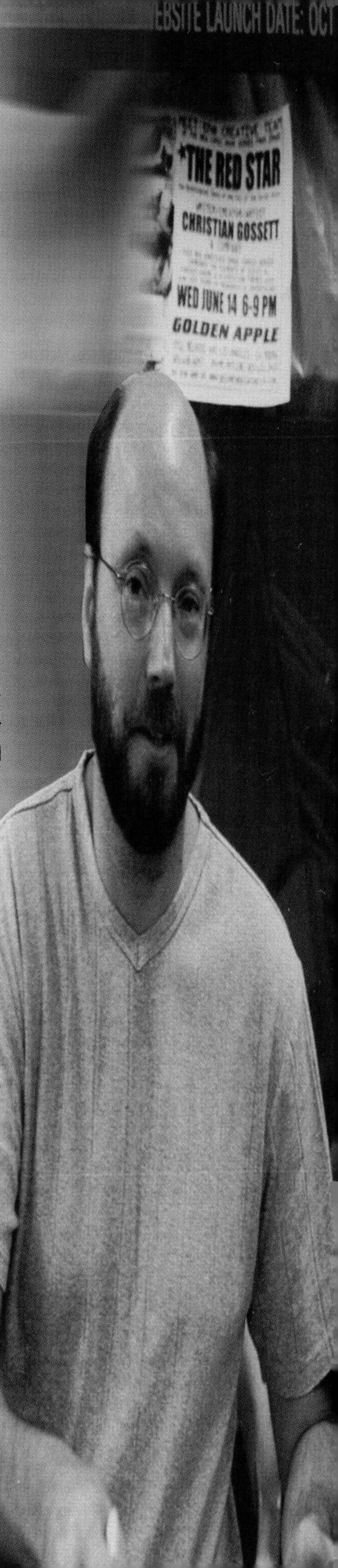
EBSITE LAUNCH DATE: OCT
THE RED STAR
CHRISTIAN GOSSETT
WED JUNE 14 6-9 PM
GOLDEN APPLE

The infamous Snakebite, his past shrouded in mystery, has shown the entire comics industry that 'colorist' should be synonymous with 'fearless innovator'. His painterly commitment to subtlety has caused his peers at all levels of the industry to take notice. Here is an excerpt from a conversation between Snake and Goss about a milestone image in the development of the visual style so unique to The Red Star: Pages 8-9 of Issue #1. The same image that begins this commentary section.

(De La Soul in the background)

G- So, Snakebite, to the best of your recollection, how did 8 and 9 begin? Go back to the farthest point you can remember.

SB- Well, it began with you bringing a thumbnail layout to the academy, (The Animation Academy in Burbank) and we went to Bob's (Big Boy) to go over them. That meeting was actually one of the first we had about process; about what roles we were going to be playing. This double page spread became the focal point for that meeting as we were talking about process and flipping through the thumbnails. Talking about separating everything into planes, and treating each plane as its own asset.

G- Each plane, as a subject, or a set of subjects.

SB- Yea, a set of subjects. From then, I started getting a bunch of assets from you, hehe, assets.

G- ...and I had taken the concept a bit far...

SB- Yea, which is cool, its better to pull back on a brutha than to have to push him along, so that's all good.

G- Right on. I had called you from my place 'cause I had drawn a lot of elements and had to explain that...

SB- ...and I was like, don't tell me, show me! You were getting all meticulous and I was getting excited and wanted to see the stuff. Then when I saw it I said "you drew every element on a separate piece of paper??? Different sizes, not to scale? And they were supposed to be fighting each other?" Every character was drawn separately, except for the two dudes who were making contact with each other, and I had to fix it in post.

G -The red trooper with the impaled Nistaani...

SB- Everything was drawn separately, and the 3 ships were rendered together. I got them as their own assets... The background was drawn separately..... Actually there were two assets for the background. There was the background background and there was that mound of dirt in the foreground...that you don't even see!

G- I think I got rid of that didn't I?

SB- No it's still there.

G- There was even a mound of dead guys I had drawn...

SB- That's right! We ditched some things because-- since nothing was drawn to scale, we slapped everything on the page in PhotoShop. We had twenty to thirty layers at one point and we were doing this little dance, transforming this, transforming that.

G- We really sacrifice ourselves to the story.

SB- We use our egos more constructively than destructively.

G- What was it like to develop a process which was defined by me being late, and throwing stuff at you and Allen... with no time at all? (Laugh)

SB- We had a verbal concept developed as to how we were going to approach this project, but at the same time, the best laid plans don't necessarily get you laid the way you planned. There are always solutions. Solutions to problems come constantly throughout this journey. Even things that you've worked out in your head, written down and you thought were gonna be fine, don't always work out. Communication is a big thing. Can't really get caught up in the fact that you don't get it the first time, because you gotta communicate. You can talk about Superman having a cool red cape, but everyone has a different idea about what that red is, or what makes that cape cool. I really learned a lot about that in animation. I worked with bigger teams, all different types of animals, and animal instincts. Especially when we had a group of businessmen mixed in with artists, it didn't always work. The problems we're running into are painless. They're nothing. They may have been tedious or time consuming, but they are nothing. Again, it's about working with a team of people that you're down with. They understand, it's not a group of egos. Egos saying "do it my way, make it work because I say so, not because I've presented you with a bunch of good points", we are more open to the drama of the page. Pages 8 and 9 were so early in the process, it is no mystery why we were making so many mistakes on it.

G- There's a major improvisational aspect of the way we were all working. Allen would look at issue 2, the tank sequence, for example, and he would suggest changes in movement, and recommend adding pages...

> ## My Lady says my palette is always yellows and blues, but that's how I see life, in yellows and blues.

SB- That's part of what makes our process effective.

G- We were still figuring it out, on the fly. It really is a proof of concept.

SB- We were trying to figure out how best we could integrate the 3d. What were the things that other people were missing?

G- Let's talk about, what you call the view master effect. Where did you come about that? Why do you use it when describing this process?

SB- When I was 3 or four years old, picking up a viewmaster, the way it captured 3D like depth with 2D objects, it always stuck in my head. I could say a million things about working on this, but what it comes down to is application of the fundamentals. A series of problems, with a series of solutions. But separating things into layers, into planes of existence, like viewmaster, you get the ultimate control of depth, you can constantly tweak it, until it's where you want it. There's no excuse in PhotoShop for getting a color you don't want, 'cause you can easily change it. Not like when I use to do it with paint. Paint commits you for the most part. But in PhotoShop, there is no reason not to explore how far you can push things. The way I look at a page is not "how would I color it?", but more like how would a DP (Director of Photography) look at it? What lens would he pick for his camera, and how does that lens effect that shot? Or, how would your eye look at that shot? What illusion does life play? What's the emotional content of the piece?

G- What we're really talking about is integration. That's where we had to work as a team. Because in order to get that effect, there is no way our egos would have served, we had to surrender all that stuff.

SB- ...and we're all into it.

G- There's a lot of line art changes in this book. (A 'Line Art Change' is when the pencil line is changed via Photoshop to a colored line.)

SB- If you had inked your work, it would have looked like drawn, inked artwork pasted on top of 3D, the usual complaint of this type of medium integration.

G- the 'colorforms' (an ancient and insidious toy that poisoned our generation) look that is the bane of creators everywhere.

SB- I think that the answer to integrating 3d and 2d is in the things you are integrating themselves. Let the organic be organic, and let the technology be the technology. Don't overcompensate to make the organic more constructive because you are putting it on top of 3d. It doesn't work.

G- It's the cinema look we were after, live action cinema, intense production storyboard comp thing, anime feature.

SB- Iron Giant was brilliant. With projects like Futurama and Iron Giant you're talking about old school animation tactics, with flat 3D to help the integration. But with Blue Submarine #6 they were pushing it all the way. As much as I love Blue #6 the integration wasn't quite there.

G- Personally, I wish they had pulled back to flat.

SB- I hear ya, would've helped the integration, but you gotta commend them for pushin' it.

G- What other influences do you have?

SB- Well, all praises go to Moebius. Huge influence on me. His color, art, keeping it pure. I love his style, even though my style doesn't always go that way; it starts with that foundation. Gotta give it up to Linda Medley who was the reason I picked up color in the first place and Steve Oliff who influenced all us color bitches. I collaborate with some really amazing artists at The Animation Academy as well, students influence me the most. Not into a lot of 2d 3d. If someone were to have told me two years ago that I'd be working on a 2d 3d book for Image, I'd have to ask them what they where smokin', and why they weren't sharin'. First of all, I didn't start off as a digital colorist, but as a PhotoShop User. I was as pure as pure gets. I even had a hard time photographing stuff and using it in the artwork for myself. It was still considered like a cheat. But Allen has really shown me that beauty can come from 3d when it is done right. If I saw this work in a feature, I'd be blown away, let alone in a comic book. So it puts fire in me. You guys all put fire in me. I can go on with a list of people who have fired me, hehe, but the team has to inspire me. If the team doesn't inspire me, I don't learn from the experience and if I don't learn, what's the point? I've always been the guy that fights for the underdog, cheering for the guy with all the talent, but who doesn't fit the profile.

G- In The Red Star, we move right into pages 10 and 11, in which Maya is in the isolator tunnel. How did you make that work?

SB- Synchronicity is a niche, Brutha. That's why we all work well together. Allen and I have an affinity for color. It is not hard to work him, I mean work with him, hehe. Even though he has no problem with me making color adjustments, to work in the atmosphere that we are establishing 'cause you always have to tweak stuff, his art is really on point. But I think mostly in color choices, and color theme; it is not hard to work with each other, because we go to the same place. He goes to the same values of blue as well as the same orange and yellow choices. My Lady says my palette is always yellows and blues, but that's how I see life, in yellows and blues. My mom recently told me that when I was young, my room was painted a specific yellow and blue. So I think Allen must have had that same yellow and blue room....Allen, is that you my brother?

G- I was amazed how on page ten and eleven, even though we were now inside, Maya carried the color theme of the desert, she was the sand value, but the tube value she's in is the panel value of the ship, the green of the steel, all around her. She became the earth values. Allen supplied a consistent tech value, and you matched with a consistent organic value.

SB- When I color, I always think about the moment, like acting. Painting teaches you composition that way. Color tells a story. To dictate emotion, and tie things together. That's why I always want to paint the skies, rather than 3D render them, on key scenes. I think it helps tell the story better.

G- Here's a place where you painted a sky, using gradients. (pg8-9)

SB- I kept it simple here. It is hot; these guys are getting cooked! It's a killing stove! I felt like anything in the sky would take away from the beautiful graphic the furnaces are making. Sometimes it's not what you do, but what you don't do. When I first started doing this, I was workin' for individuals finding new ways to put as much detail on a page to over-compensate for their lack of creativity....Photoshop will allow a person to do this, but again, most of the time its what you don't do that can make a page.

G- This double page spread page was a make or break thing; it really showed the emotional investment in this book.

SB- (pointing at pg.8-9 and making direct reference to the composition of figures) It represents the struggle, you on top, Brad by your side, me down here, fighting off some enemies. GI Jo up in the Konstantinov worrying about us, ready to fix our broken asses. That's our allegory. That's why I like this spread so much. And the Nistaani are the monkey boys trying to take us down.

G- That's the revolution!

SB- There's Allen, kicking as much ass as the rest of us, if not more. There's Nedro, drivin' the ship.

G- What a steel curtain those four guys in the front are, I never really noticed it until this moment. That's what post-production brings. I mean, a comic that does post-production?

SB- I know, it's crazy. But it's really post-production while producing, because it's done during the coloring. It's a beautiful thing. You do a little dance, and if you don't bust out the moves like you planned last night in front of the mirror, there's always next issue.

G- It takes some daring, but look what you get. Where do you want to take this project?

SB- I think if I put a prerequisite on it, it may fuck up the journey were on.

G- That's very Zen of you, dude.

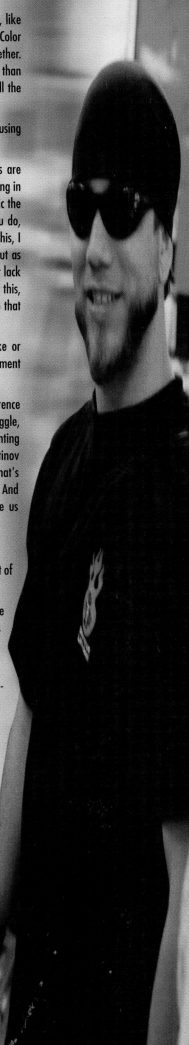

THE REVOLUTION IN CONTENT...

IS UNTHINKABLE WITHOUT A REVOLUTION IN FORM.
NOBODY KNOWS WHAT GIANT SUNS WILL LIGHT UP
THE LIFE THAT IS TO COME. PERHAPS ARTISTS CLAD IN
HUNDRED COLORED RAINBOWS WILL TRANSFORM THE GRAY
DUST OF THE CITIES. PERHAPS THE THUNDEROUS VOLCANOES
TURNED INTO FLUTES WILL SOUND CEASELESSLY FROM THE
MOUNTAIN TOPS, PERHAPS WE WILL MAKE THE OCEAN WAVES
PLUCK AT STRINGS STRETCHED FROM EUROPE TO AMERICA.
ONE THING WE KNOW CLEARLY - WE HAVE OPENED THE
FIRST PAGE OF THE HISTORY OF THE ART OF OUR DAY.

-MAYAKOVSKII
OPEN LETTER TO THE WORKERS
1918

bibliography

Sources Consulted

Books

Alexievich, Svetlana, *Zinky Boys; Soviet Voices from a Forgotten War*, Chatto and Windus Ltd., London,c.1992

Davis, Patricia, *201 Russian Verbs*, Barron's Educational Series, Hauppoage, New York, c. 1968

Doyle, Hilary, *Stug III, Assault Gun 1940- 1942*, Osprey Publishing, Oxford, UK, c. 1996

Dunstan, Simon, *Challenger, Main Battle Tank 1982 - 1987*, Osprey Publishing, Oxford, UK, c. 1998

Gessen, Masha, *Dead Again; Russian Intellegencia after Communism*, Verso, New York, NY. c.1997

Gogol, Nikolai, *Dead Souls*, Penguin Books, Ltd., New York, NY, c. 1961

Gregory, Paul R., *Soviet Economic Structure and Performance*, Harper Collins Publishers, New York, NY c. 1990

Guggenheim Museum, *The Great Utopia*, The Guggenheim Foundation, New York, NY, c. 1992

Gulland Milner, Robin, *Atlas of Russia and The Soviet Union*, Phaden Press, Ltd., Oxford, England c. 1989

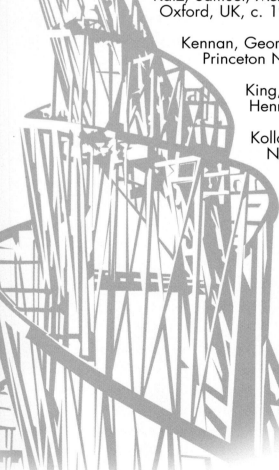

Hutchings, Jane, Russia, *Belarus and the Ukraine*, APA Publications, Verlag, Singapore, c. 1999

Jukes, Geoffrey, *Kursk; The Clash of Armor*, Ballantine Books, New York, NY, c. 1969

Katz, Samuel, *Merkava Main Battle Tank*, Osprey Publishing, Oxford, UK, c. 1997

Kennan, George, *Russia Leaves the War*, Princeton University Press, Princeton NJ, c. 1956

King, David, *The Commissar Vanishes*, Metropolitan Books, Henry Holt and Co. , New York, NY c. 1997

Kollontai, Alexandra, *Selected Writings*, WW Norton and Co., New York, NY c. 1977

Leonidov, Andrei, *Ivan Leonidov*, Rizzoli International Publications, Inc., New York, NY, c. 1988

Moynahan, Brian, *The Russian Century*, Barnes and Noble, Inc. Colville Mews, London c. 1994

Nicolle, David, *Lake Peipus 1242, Battle of The Ice*, Reed International Books, Great Britain, c. 1996

Pack, Susan, *Film Posters of the Russian Avant-Garde*, Benedikt Taschen Berlag GmbH, Hohenzollernring 53, Koln Germany, c. 1995

Platinov, S.F., *The Time of Troubles; A Historical Study of the Internal Crisis and Social Struggle in Sixteenth and Seventeenth Century Muscovi*, University Press of Kansas, Lawrence, Kansas c. 1970

Rabinowitch, Alexander, *The Bolsheviks Come to Power; The Revolution of 1917 in Petrograd,* WW Norton and Co., New York, NY c. 1978

Remnick, David, *Ressurection; The Struggle for a New Russia,* Random House, Inc., New York, NY c. 1997

Rowell, Margarite, *Art of the Avant-Garde in Russia,* Solomon R. Guggenheim Foundation, New York, NY c. 1981

Stanley, Peter, *What Did You do in the War, Daddy,* Oxford University Press, Oxford, NY c. 1983

Steiner, Evgeny, *Stories for Little Comrades,* University of Washington Press, Seattle, Washington. C. 1999

Tucker, Robert, *Stalinism; Essays in Historical Interpretation,* Transaction Publishers, New Brunswick, NJ, c. 1999

Volkogonov, Dmitri, *Lenin ; A New Biography,* The Free Press, New York, NY c. 1994

White, Steven, *The Bolshevik Poster,* Yale University, Boston, Massachusetts, c. 1988

Yergen, Daniel, *Russia 2010,* Vintage Books, New York, NY, c. 1993

Zaloga, Steven, *Inside the Soviet Army Today,* Osprey Publishing, Oxford, UK, c. 1987

Zaloga, Steven, *IS-2 Heavy Tank 1944 -1973,* Osprey Publishing, Oxford, UK, c. 1994

Zaloga, Steven, *KV- 1 & 2 Heavy Tanks, 1941 - 1945,* Osprey Publishing, Oxford, UK, c. 1995

Zaloga, Steven, *The Eastern Front, Armor Camouflage and Markings, 1941- 1945,* Arms and Armor, London, c. 1983

VIDEOS

Liberation, Arnold Schwartzman Film, Simon Weisenthal Center, 1997

Red Files, Episodes I and II, Directed and Written by Elizabeth Dobson, 1997

Saving Private Ryan, Directed by Steven Spielberg, Paramount Pictures, 1998

Seven Samurai, Directed by Akira Kurosawa, Toho Studios, 1954

Star Wars, Directed by George Lucas, Twentieth Century Fox, 1977

The Adventures of Buckaroo Banzai, Directed by W. D. Richter, Twentieth Century Fox, 1984

WWII Through Russian Eyes, Historical Achievements Museum, LLC, 1999

MUSIC SUPPORT

New Radicals, "Maybe You've Been Brainwashed, Too"

Run Lola Run, Original Motion Picture Soundtrack

Sacred Songs of Russia

Ghost in the Shell Original Soundtrack

MealTicket, "Misconceptions"

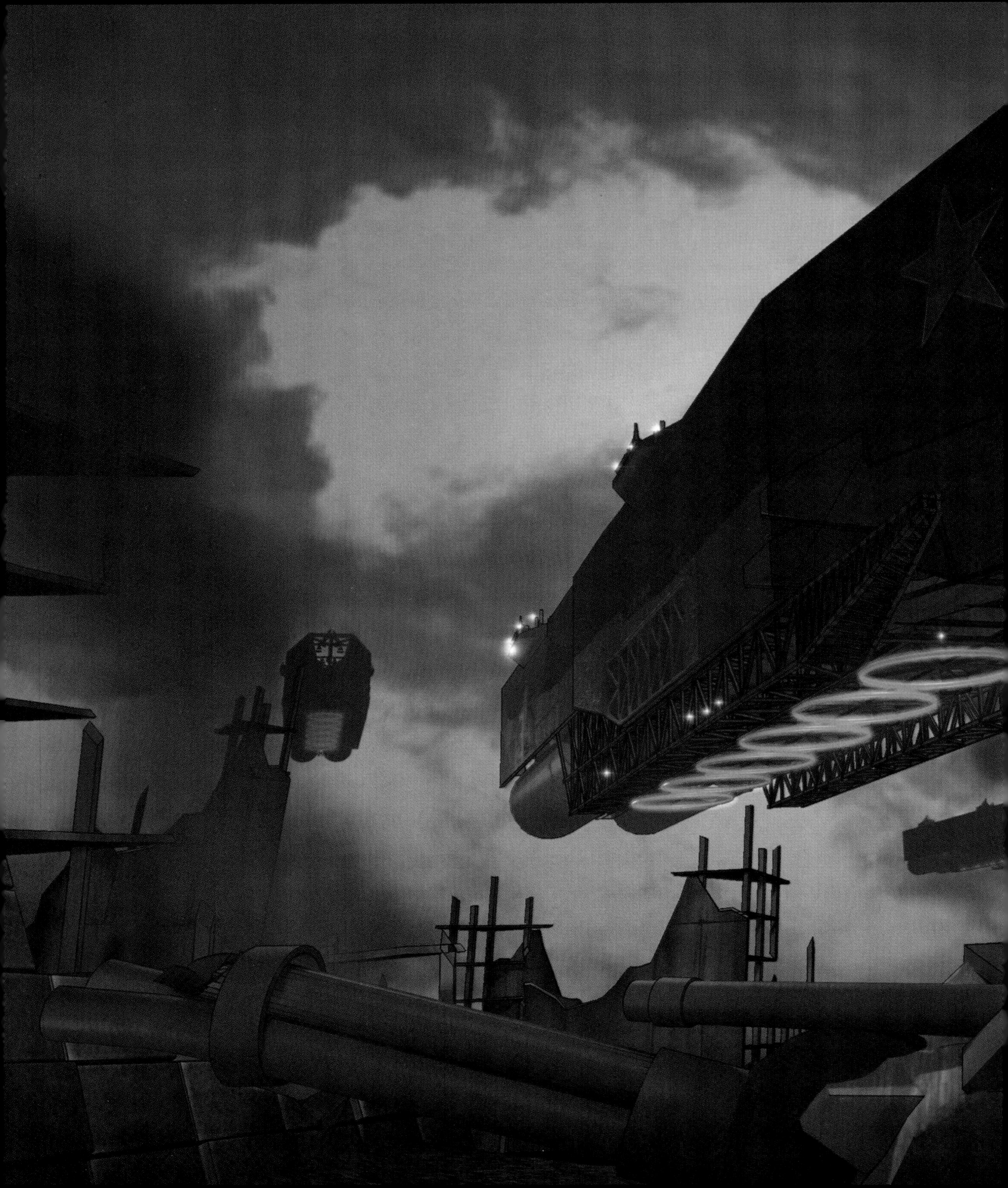

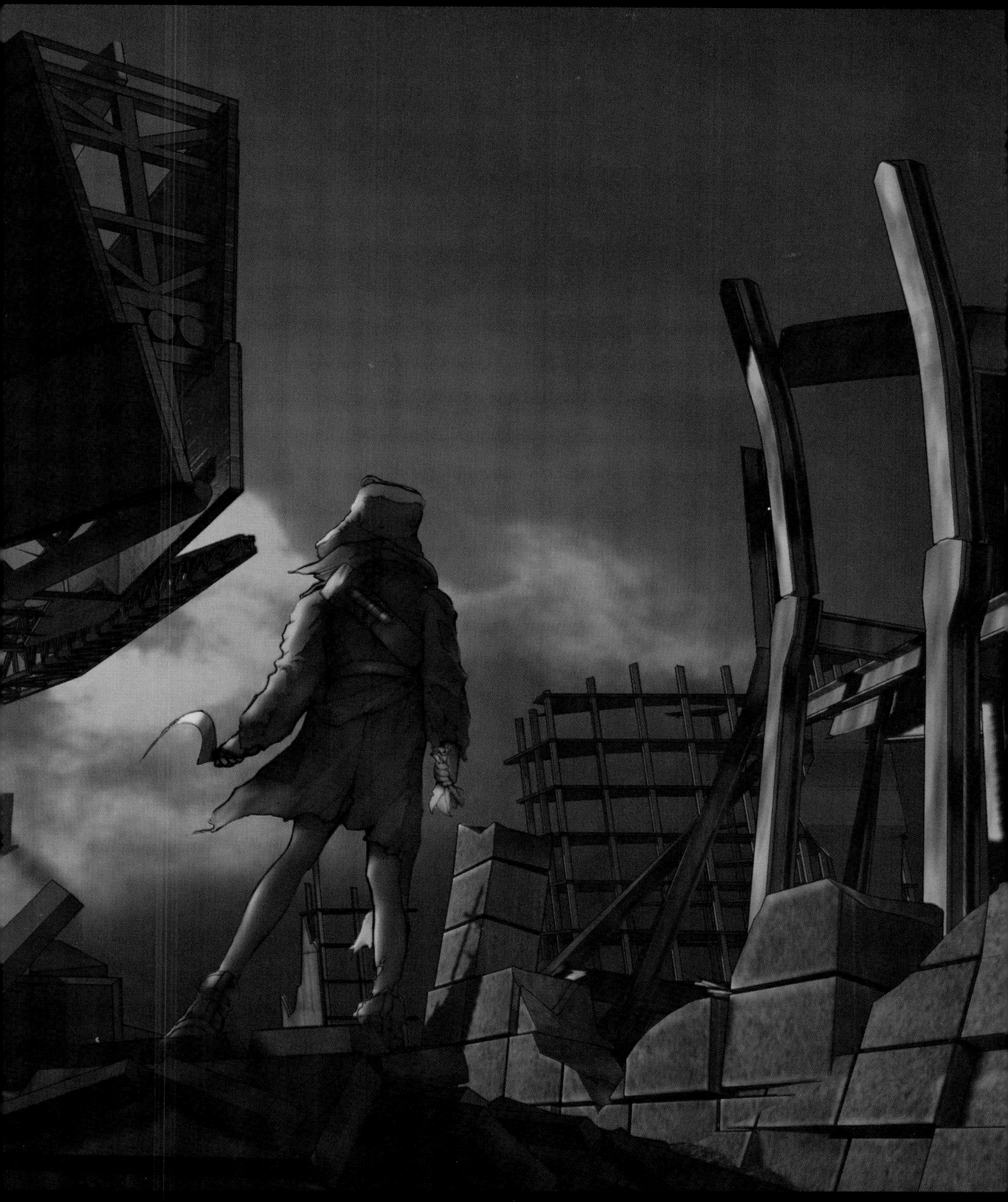